Real Americans

I0109898

CONSTITUTIONAL THINKING

Sandord Levinson
Jeffrey K. Tulis
Emily Zackin
Mariah Zeisberg

Series Editors

Real Americans

National Identity, Violence, and the Constitution

Jared A. Goldstein

University Press of Kansas

© 2022 by the University Press of Kansas

All rights reserved

Published by the University Press of Kansas (Lawrence, Kansas 66045), which was organized by the Kansas Board of Regents and is operated and funded by Emporia State University, Fort Hays State University, Kansas State University, Pittsburg State University, the University of Kansas, and Wichita State University.

Library of Congress Cataloging-in-Publication Data

Names: Goldstein, Jared A., author.
Title: Real Americans : national identity, violence, and the constitution / Jared A. Goldstein.
Description: Lawrence : University Press of Kansas, 2021. | Series: Constitutional thinking | Includes index.
Identifiers: LCCN 2021018746
  ISBN 9780700632831 (cloth)
  ISBN 9780700632848 (paperback)
  ISBN 9780700632855 (ebook)
Subjects: LCSH: Constitutional law—Political aspects—United States. | Constitutional history—United States. | United States—Politics and government.
Classification: LCC KF4552 .G65 2021 | DDC 342.7302/9—dc23
LC record available at https://lccn.loc.gov/2021018746.

British Library Cataloguing-in-Publication Data is available.

Printed in the United States of America

10 9 8 7 6 5 4 3 2 1

The paper used in this publication is acid free and meets the minimum requirements of the American National Standard for Permanence of Paper for Printed Library Materials Z39.48-1992.

To my father, David Goldstein, who despite everything always believed in e pluribus unum; to Leonard Zeskind, who has fought tirelessly to expose the reality of hate movements; and to Louis Pollak, whose love for the Constitution inspired and baffled me.

Contents

Series Editor's Preface

One of President Barack Obama's favorite declarations, particularly when something truly amiss, such as racist violence, had happened within the United States, was that the action did not truly represent the United States. "This is not who we are," he often said. He was certainly not alone in his use of that meme. Indeed, President Joe Biden, responding to the horrific massacre of six Asians in Atlanta (as well as at least two of their non-Asian customers), described the attack as "un-American." The point of the assertion is to suggest that "we," that is, both the speakers and the presumably appreciative audience, represent the "real" America, who would never behave so badly as the individuals or groups being criticized.

The Supreme Court often engages in similar rhetoric. For example, in *Bolling v. Sharpe*—the 1954 case arising from Washington, DC, that was a companion case to the far better known *Brown v. Board of Education*—Chief Justice Earl Warren wrote, "Classifications based solely upon race must be scrutinized with particular care, since they are contrary to our traditions." Objectionable they may be, but it requires a willful ignorance of American history to believe that they are necessarily "contrary to" the more lamentable aspects of "our traditions." What joins Obama, Biden, and Warren is the suggestion that the miscreants committing the ostensibly aberrant behavior are in some profound sense not really American themselves, not part of the American family that generates the complex mosaic of American political traditions (plural). Part of American exceptionalism may in fact be an anxious concern about what it means to be an American and to identify a singular American political tradition. This in turn carries with it the concomitant desire to identify those who are "un-American," not really one of "us."

How does this relate to the extraordinary—and, alas, all too timely—book by Jared Goldstein, with its evocative title, *Real Americans: National Identity, Violence, and the Constitution*? The answer is simple, though not at all simplistic. Goldstein identifies an important strand of American political thought that he labels "constitutional nationalism." That is, to be an American is to stand with, and by, the Constitution. Whatever may be our differences in an

America that has always, from its beginning, contained what Walt Whitman identified as "multitudes" of quite different peoples, we are united, it is often claimed, by our belief—indeed, our faith in and veneration for—the centerpiece of the American civil religion, our Constitution. Consider only the oath taken by anyone becoming a member of the United States military, which begins by the oath taker's "solemnly swear[ing or affirming] that I will support and defend the Constitution of the United States against all enemies, foreign and domestic; that I will bear true faith and allegiance to the same." In fact, Article VI of the 1787 Constitution requires that *all* public officials, at whatever the level of government, take an oath of loyalty to the Constitution. And, of course, the Constitution specifies the very words of the oath to be taken by a president, who solemnly swears "to the best of my Ability, [to] preserve, protect and defend the Constitution of the United States." It would be surprising if many readers of this book have not themselves, at one point or another in their lives, taken such an oath.

The problem is that Americans scarcely agree on what exactly counts as faithful compliance with the solemn oath, sworn by many in the name of God. Indeed, the military oath quoted above continues with the promise "that I will obey the orders of the President of the United States and the orders of the officers appointed over me, according to regulations and the Uniform Code of Military Justice. So help me God." But does this mean that *all* orders, even those that might be regarded as manifestly illegal under the Code of Military Justice itself, are to be obeyed? Consider in this context the statement by the Joint Chiefs of Staff in 2020 that their loyalty was to the Constitution and not to President Trump, which for many carried the implication that they would refuse to obey what they considered to be unlawful orders given by the ostensible chief executive and commander in chief.

Philosophers often refer to "essentially contested concepts," by which they refer to particular notions that carry a positive valence—think of "democracy," "justice," or "nondiscrimination"—but are, nonetheless, subject to multiple, and often conflicting, interpretations. Not surprisingly, people can get especially angry if one suggests that their notion of one of these concepts is fatally flawed. So it is with the term of what might be called "constitutional fidelity." One might agree that it is very important and then discover that there are very different notions of the term. It is well to recall that Southern secessionists in 1860–1861 claimed to be faithful to the "true" Constitution that they argued—wrongly, no doubt, in the eyes of most of us—was being violated by their adversaries, including Abraham Lincoln.

Jefferson Davis and Robert E. Lee, both graduates of West Point who had taken vows of constitutional fidelity, did not view themselves as "traitors" waging war against the Constitution. Abraham Lincoln obviously had a very different view, and 750,000 Americans died in the ensuing dispute over what constitutional fidelity really meant. Perhaps this only underscores the reality that what might be called "intra-family" disputes, including those within the "American family," are often the most acrimonious of all.

Goldstein is not writing a book about abstract jurisprudential issues, however. Instead, he notes several especially virulent forms that "constitutional nationalism" has taken throughout our history and then extends the discussion quite literally into the present moment. He wrote the introduction to his book after January 6, 2021, when an insurrectionist mob stormed the Capitol and invaded the chambers of the United States Senate, acting, they proclaimed, in defense of the Constitution. There is nothing "academic" about such assertions and disputes. Throughout our history, people have died and the survival of the nation has been put at risk by those advocating radically different interpretations of what constitutional fidelity requires. As with certain Thanksgiving dinners, where one desperately wishes to ignore and otherwise deny the reality of cantankerous uncles or cousins—or perhaps even one's siblings and parents—it is important to realize that the "American family" does indeed contain multitudes, and not all of them are attractive in any way.

Goldstein emphasizes those groups that have viewed "true American-ism"—and the Constitution—through the lens of "ascriptive identity." As argued two decades ago by the political theorist Rogers Smith, the idea, much embraced by Obama, that the Constitution—and therefore American identity—consists of a group of abstract and basically universal values, sometimes labeled "the American creed," found in the Preamble, such as "establishing justice," is met by the very different assertion that only *some* members of the populace are truly legitimate members of the national family. Most common have been such ascriptive identities as race, religion, and ethnic background. Chief Justice Roger Taney in the 1857 *Dred Scott* case notoriously asserted, with the support of a majority of the Supreme Court, that Blacks could not be part of the American political community, that they had, in his words, "no rights that" the hegemonic white majority were "bound to respect." To the extent that some Blacks did indeed enjoy some legal rights, which Taney did not deny, they were basically gifts of grace from the white hegemons, and they could be withdrawn at will. Nor, of course, did it matter that many of the so-called Blacks were children of their white masters, the most notorious example being Thomas Jefferson and the children he fathered with Sally Hemings. Identifying the "American family" often required ignoring the reality of biological kinship.

And, of course, immigration has been the subject of political contention since the beginning of the nation, with certain Nordic countries being viewed by many American leaders as more proper candidates for "true Americanism" than their swarthy fellow Europeans from Southern or Eastern Europe. The original immigration acts passed by Congress under its power to create a "uniform" law of naturalization limited such naturalization to whites. That changed after the Civil War, but only in limited ways. Blacks emigrating from Africa or the West Indies could now be naturalized, but immigrants from Asia were not welcome to become part of the American political community until after World War II (save for Chinese, who were made eligible in 1943). The bitter debates about immigration and fitness for "Americanization" (whatever exactly that means) continue to be a part of contemporary political debate, even if couched on occasion in the language of competition for jobs.

Similarly, there have always been those who have been eager to define the United States as a "Christian nation," with the obvious implication that non-Christians (or even non-Protestant Christians such as Roman Catholics) might at best be tolerated but otherwise not truly embraced as fellow Americans. Indeed, one of the many illuminations Goldstein provides is that there were some Christians in the nineteenth century who rejected the Constitution because it did not explicitly recognize the primacy of God and divine commandments; they were succeeded, in effect, by those who asserted that the Constitution, correctly understood, *did* require subordination to Christianity. And Goldstein elaborates vociferous attempts, led at one point by Supreme Court Justice William Strong, to adopt a constitutional amendment specifically establishing the United States as a Christian country. They were, in a sense, vindicated when the Supreme Court in 1892 described the United States as a "Christian nation," a designation rejected by most contemporary scholars—and not repeated by any modern justices—but still cited by Christian nationalists.

Race, religion, and ethnicity have been by far the most important ascriptive identities that have challenged more universalistic and inclusive notions of constitutional nationalism. But Goldstein also writes incisively of the degree to which the Constitution was viewed as strongly protecting the business community and the propertied classes more generally. He presents an illuminating retelling of the presidential campaign of 1936 that focuses on the way Franklin Delano Roosevelt skillfully set up as his primary adversary the Liberty League, financed by millionaires but with FDR's former friend (and predecessor as governor of New York and Democratic candidate, in 1928, for the presidency) Al Smith as one of their principal spokespersons. Such figures as the Koch brothers—or Mitt Romney when he distinguished, in his 2012 campaign, between the productive "makers" of American prosperity and the parasitic "takers" who wanted to tax or regulate them—echo the themes of the Liberty League.

And, of course, there is also what Goldstein calls the "partisan Constitution," which divides the world into those who are faithful to the one true view of the Constitution and those who would, on the contrary, "subvert it." Thus the infamous House Un-American Activities Committee (HUAC) fixated on the threat from "international communism" for over two decades before it was abolished in the 1960s. But it has been race and religion that have been most pervasive and most likely to be the justification of the violence that Goldstein writes about. HUAC might have wrecked lives, but, unlike, say, the Ku Klux Klan, which also claimed to be an ardent defender of the "real" Constitution, it did not lynch its victims.

It is an unfortunate reality that Goldstein's book is so completely timely, altogether relevant to understanding contemporary headlines (and the American psyche). The FBI has pronounced "domestic terrorism" to be perhaps the major threat facing the United States at the present time. It would be a profound error to believe that most such terrorists reject the Constitution. Consider Timothy McVeigh, the perpetrator of the most serious single act of domestic terrorism in our history, the Oklahoma City attack that killed 168 people on April 19, 1995. "We members of the citizen's militias do not bear our arms to overthrow the Constitution," he wrote, "but to overthrow those who PERVERT THE CONSTITUTION." Goldstein also quotes a letter that McVeigh wrote to a childhood friend, defending the prospect that "blood will flow in the streets" as part of the attack on those "who betray or subvert the Constitution." McVeigh, a veteran of the armed forces, noted that he had "sworn an oath to uphold the Constitution against all enemies, foreign and domestic, and I will. And I will because not only did I swear to, but I believe in what it stands for in every bit of my heart, soul, and being."

There is no good reason to question McVeigh's sincerity, or that of the many other truly frightening people Goldstein brings to our attention, including the January 6, 2021, insurrectionists. The real point is that communities organized around central symbols of faith, be they Bibles or Constitutions, will almost inevitably develop bitterly contentious sects, each convinced that they alone have discerned the true meaning of the faith and its organizing documents and that those who disagree must be treated not as friendly adversaries but as outright enemies.

Goldstein's book is not only tremendously illuminating as a traditional academic work but also profoundly troubling in terms of the questions he raises for his fellow citizens who are worried about our contemporary reality. If, in fact, it is facile to believe that a professed collective faith in the Constitution is enough to preserve a united American community, let alone achieve the "liberty and justice for all" promised by the Pledge of Allegiance to the flag, then what *will* relieve the contemporary sense of a divided country and even existential angst about its survival? It would be unfair to expect Jared Goldstein to provide answers to that question. It is enough to praise him for his probing analysis of the complexities attached to the notion of "constitutional nationalism."

Sanford Levinson
April 2021

Acknowledgments

This book would not exist without the incredible work of many research assistants: Katherine "Ronnie" Cooke-Caraway, Ryan Coyne, Michael da Cruz, Andrew Fischer, Amy Greer, Alison Hoffman, Madalyn McGunagle, and Adam Riser. I am also deeply grateful for the help provided by Nicole Dyszlewski, one of Roger Williams University's extraordinary research librarians. I also wish to thank the librarians at the David M. Rubenstein Rare Book and Manuscript Library at Duke University and the Wilson Library at the University of North Carolina for helping me sort through their collections of Ku Klux Klan materials.

Portions of this book have previously appeared in different form in other publications and appear here with the permission of the *Alabama Civil Rights and Civil Liberties Law Review, Arizona Law Review, Denver Law Review, Hastings Law Journal, Northwestern Law Review, Temple Law Review,* and *University of Pennsylvania Journal of Constitutional Law.*

Introduction
The Constitution and the Mirror

On January 6, 2021, just as I was finishing the manuscript for this book, a mob of hundreds of supporters of President Donald Trump stormed the US Capitol in an attempt to overturn the results of the 2020 presidential election. One of the insurrectionists was shot and killed, and more than a hundred officers and protesters were injured. The insurrection was widely denounced as an "attack on America" and an "attack on the Constitution."[1] The subsequent impeachment trial was framed in constitutional terms, as a defense of constitutional government against what Representative Jamie Raskin described as "the most devastating and dangerous assault by a government official on our Constitution . . . in living memory."[2] In the indictments and prosecutions of the perpetrators of the January 6 insurrection, prosecutors and judges likewise described the insurrection as an attack on the Constitution and the nation itself.

What received little attention was that the January 6 insurrectionists themselves justified the violence they perpetrated as a defense of the Constitution, as they understand it. In the days leading up to the attack, Oath Keepers, a right-wing militia group, called on its members to come to Washington: "Patriots must prepare to do whatever must be done to honor our oaths to defend the Constitution against all enemies, foreign and domestic."[3] After marching down Constitution Avenue, the insurrectionists surrounded the Capitol and announced their mission: "To protect the Constitution of the United States."[4] After battling the Capitol police and breaking doors and windows, the mob marched inside, chanting, "Defend your liberty, defend the Constitution."[5]

It should come as no surprise that those who launched the violent assault on the Capitol saw their actions as a defense of the Constitution. Throughout American history, political movements that have sought to defend the power of long-entrenched groups have justified their actions as a defense of the Constitution. In the 1860s and 1870s, when the Ku Klux Klan launched a massive campaign of violence to prevent Black people from exercising the right to vote, they had a name for what they fighting for: they called it the Constitution. In 1882, when nativists in Congress voted to exclude Chinese immigrants, and in the 1920s, when they excluded Catholics and Jews, they too said they were acting to protect the Constitution. In 1995, when Timothy McVeigh exploded a truck bomb that destroyed the Alfred P. Murrah Federal Building in Oklahoma City and killed 168 people, he had a simple explanation for his crime: he was defending the Constitution.

This book seeks to explain how the Constitution, which is widely understood as a central embodiment of American identity, has long been used to justify hatred, violence, and exclusion.

Americans famously love the Constitution. It is "the most wonderful instrument ever drawn by the hand of man," declared Supreme Court Justice William Johnson in 1823.[6] It is "our Ark of the Covenant," Congressman Caleb Cushing professed in 1834. Expressions of devotion to the Constitution can be heard from the left and right, rich and poor, Democrat and Republican. "If there is a single point of consensus in this heated political moment," wrote journalist Jeffrey Toobin in 2013, "it's that everyone loves the Constitution."[7]

The Constitution is frequently described as the central expression of the American Creed, a distillation of the nation's fundamental values and the heart of American national identity. As President Barack Obama put it in his second inaugural address, "What binds this nation together is not the colors of our skin or the tenets of our faith or the origins of our names. What makes us exceptional—what makes us American—is our allegiance to an idea."[8] That essential American idea, Obama explained, was first expressed in the Declaration of Independence and later codified in the Constitution.[9]

Scholars of nationalism have largely agreed that American national identity is defined by commitment to a creed expressed in the Constitution. In 1944, Gunnar Myrdal popularized the notion of an American Creed, a set of shared beliefs that serve as "the cement in the structure of this great and disparate nation."[10] Like others, Myrdal identified the Constitution as the central expression of the Creed.[11] The first book-length examination of the nature of American nationalism, Hans Kohn's *American Nationalism*, published in 1957, agreed: "The American Constitution represents the lifeblood of the American nation, its supreme symbol and manifestation. It is so intimately welded with the national existence itself that the two have become inseparable."[12]

Not surprisingly, those in my line of work—professors of constitutional law—are among the most fervent and devout believers in the centrality of the Constitution to American identity. As many have said, the Constitution is the "sacred text" in America's "civic religion," which makes constitutional law professors among the high priests. Devotion to the constitutional faith transcends politics. Leading liberal constitutional scholar Laurence Tribe has written that the Constitution's "text and invisible structure are part of the nation's beating heart," while leading conservative scholar Steven Calabresi has declared that "the Constitution is the focal point of American exceptionalism: it is our holiest of holies, the ark of the covenant of the New Israel."[13]

Despite frequent claims that devotion to the Constitution is the core of what it means to be American, little academic study has actually examined the role of the Constitution in national identity. The belief that the essence of American identity involves a shared commitment to principles found in the Constitution is so ubiquitous and unquestioned that there is no name for it. In this book, I call that belief *constitutional nationalism*.[14] *Nationalism* refers to the belief that there exists a community that is entitled to self-government as a nation-state.[15] Varieties of nationalism are frequently categorized by how national communities define group membership. Some nations understand themselves in ethnonationalist terms, identifying the national community by membership in a racial or ethnic group; others are religious nationalists, identifying the national community by membership in a particular religion; and others are civic nationalists, defining membership in the national community through commitment to a set of political values.[16] *Constitutional nationalism* is the belief that what binds together the national community is a shared commitment to principles expressed in the Constitution. In the conventional conception, American nationalism is a type of civic nationalism, which identifies the common bond holding the people of the United States together as a shared devotion to principles articulated in the national constitution.

In the academic literature, constitutional nationalism represents the dominant conception of American nationalism, embraced by thinkers as diverse as the European sociologist and philosopher Jurgen Habermas and the American conservative political scientist Samuel Huntington. Habermas asserted that the American experience demonstrates that national identity can be based on "constitutional principles" and "by no means has to be based on all citizens sharing the same language or the same ethnic and cultural origins."[17] Huntington likewise declared that "In the United States . . . ethnic cultural identities coexist with a national identity rooted in a particular set of political ideas and institutions."[18] Similar descriptions of American nationalism can readily be found throughout the academic literature on nationalism.[19]

Constitutional nationalism is also the dominant conception of American nationalism expressed in American political life, exemplified by a 1943 speech given by President Franklin Roosevelt: "The principle on which this country was founded and by which it has always been governed is that Americanism is a matter of the mind and heart; Americanism is not, and never was, a matter of race or ancestry. A good American is one who is loyal to this country and to our creed of liberty and democracy."[20] Every president from Roosevelt to Obama proclaimed similar notions of what it means to be American. In his first inaugural address George W. Bush declared: "We are bound by ideals that move us beyond backgrounds, lift us above our interests and teach us what it means to be citizens."[21] In his second inaugural address, Barack Obama said precisely the same thing in nearly identical language.[22] In this conception, American nationalism is defined by commitment to a creed, a set of principles found in the Constitution, and it is entirely distinct from—and opposed to—all forms of ethnonationalism.[23] This characterization of American nationalism is so commonplace as to be unquestioned and banal.

What this book sets out to show, however, is that the conventional conception of the role of the Constitution in American nationalism is fundamentally mistaken. While Americans frequently invoke the Constitution as the embodiment of American national identity, those invocations serve to express a wide variety of differing and deeply conflicting conceptions of national identity. Instead of serving to unify the nation, constitutional nationalism creates a neutral and patriotic language for making widely varying claims of national inclusion and exclusion.

Although it has been the conventional wisdom since at least the 1940s to assert that American identity has always focused on a shared commitment to constitutional ideals, American history has not been marked by a single consistent conception of American nationalism and American identity. As Rogers Smith has shown, multiple nationalist traditions have competed for dominance throughout American history, including varieties of both civic and ethnic nationalism.[24] Hierarchies based on race, gender, and religion, Smith has argued, "have had great prestige through most of American history," and it has not been a mere "inconsistent afterthought" or an aberration from mainstream thought to believe that power and status properly belong to Americans based on race, religion, ethnicity, and sex.[25]

As Smith has argued, these competing views should be acknowledged as independent and traditional conceptions of American identity, albeit highly contested ones.[26]

Consistent with Smith's work, surveys of Americans have confirmed that Americans do not hold a monolithic conception about what it means to be American and who is authentically American. Many believe that being American involves commitment to a core set of values, while others believe that being authentically American is limited to people with specific social identities, and still others believe that American identity involves a mix of both civic and ethnonationalist elements.[27]

Despite a growing recognition that American nationalism has involved commitment to hierarchies based on race, religion, ethnicity, and gender, as well as commitment to universal ideals, it has gone unnoticed that all of the varied and competing conceptions of American national identity have been expressed in the language of constitutional nationalism. While the prevailing conception of American nationalism teaches that the Constitution "establishes our core values" and "tells us who we are," there are wide variations about what Americans understand those values to be and who Americans think they are.[28] When libertarians read the Constitution, they find confirmation that the United States is a libertarian nation.[29] When progressives read the Constitution, they find proof that the United States is a progressive nation.[30] Democrats and Republicans may have differing values and differing visions for the nation, but they both believe that their values and national vision can be found in the Constitution.[31] This is hardly a new phenomenon. As Supreme Court Justice Joseph Story remarked in 1845, "It is astonishing how easily men satisfy themselves that the Constitution is exactly what they wish it to be."[32]

Throughout American history, movements devoted to racial, ethnic, and religious nationalism have likewise proclaimed that their national visions are grounded in constitutional devotion. From its founding in 1866 until today, the Ku Klux Klan has proclaimed that its mission is to "protect and defend the Constitution of the United States."[33] The Klan has been devoted to the belief that the United States is a white nation, and it has long declared that the Constitution should be understood as the source of white power.[34] At the same time, Christian nationalists have long found in the Constitution proof that at heart the United States is a Christian nation. As Reverend Jerry Falwell put it, "Any diligent student of American history finds that our great nation was founded by godly men upon godly principles to be a Christian nation."[35] Nativist movements have similarly argued that the Constitution was written for people with the ethnic background of the nation's founders and that protecting the Constitution requires excluding immigrants who cannot embrace the Constitution.

This book sets out to show that instead of supplying the essence of what it means to be American, the Constitution has served as a magic mirror onto which Americans have gazed and found projections of themselves and their dreams for the nation. While Americans frequently identify the Constitution as the source of national identity, their understanding of this identity varies dramatically. The nationalist visions that Americans have found in the Constitution range from pure civic nationalism to pure ethnonationalism, with many variations in between. These varieties of constitutional nationalism can be broken down into three broad categories:

1. National identity based solely on commitment to universal principles. In national visions of this type, exemplified by the speeches of Franklin Roosevelt, George W. Bush, and Barack Obama quoted previously, American identity is defined solely by commitment to a set of universal principles found in the Constitution that can be embraced by anyone. As Roosevelt put it, "A good American is one who is loyal to this country and to our creed of liberty and democracy."

This category of American nationalism includes what can be characterized as the thin view that the sole essential principle of American identity is agreement with the Declaration of Independence's proclamation that all men are created equal, a principle later codified in the Fourteenth Amendment. This view may perhaps be exemplified by Justice Oliver Wendell Holmes's assertion that the Constitution does not embody any particular theory of government or identity but instead "is made for people of fundamentally differing views."[36] That is, people may disagree about fundamental values and still be true and authentic Americans.

This category includes thicker conceptions of national identity that identify a broader set of principles that binds together all true Americans. Martin Lipset, for instance, declared that "the nation's ideology," articulated first in the Declaration of Independence and later codified in the Constitution, "can be described in five words: liberty, egalitarianism, individualism, populism, and laissez faire."[37] Others, agreeing with the general point, have identified a different set of core principles that define what it means to be American. In this conception, being American requires commitment to a set of principles but does not depend on social or ascriptive identities, such as race, religion, or ethnicity.

2. National identity based on commitment to universal principles plus social identity. For many Americans, national identity is defined by a commitment to principles that can be found in the Constitution and those principles are associated to some degree with social identities, most prominently race, ethnicity, religion, and sex.

This category too encompasses a continuum of beliefs. At the weak end are those who consider the Constitution's principles to be universal yet seek to emphasize that these principles arise out of a specifically English and Protestant tradition. This view can be seen in the work of Samuel Huntington, who declared that Americans are "a people defined by and united by their commitment to the political principles of liberty, equality, democracy, individualism, human rights, the rule of law, and private property" while also emphasizing that these principles "can only be understood as an expression of 'Anglo-Protestant culture.'"[38] In this conception, it may be appropriate to celebrate the ethnic and religious history out of which the nation arose. As *National Review* editor Rich Lowry put it in his defense of American nationalism, "Our rituals and holidays reflect the dominant culture. Christmas is a national holiday; Yom Kippur is not. And they reflect our national identity. Independence Day is a holiday; Cinco de Mayo is not." In this view, the nation arose out of a white and Protestant tradition, yet American identity remains open to anyone because the nation's constitutional principles are universal and can be embraced by anyone.[39]

A somewhat stronger version of constitutional nationalism that embraces both abstract principles and social identities can be found in various movements that have declared that the nation's constitutional principles arise out of a particular tradition and identity, and people with that identity generally make better citizens because they are more likely to embrace those principles. This ideology can be seen in the immigration restriction movement that led to the passage of the National Origins Act of 1924. In enacting the law, Congress declared that because the nation's constitutional principles arose out of Anglo-Protestant culture, preservation of constitutional government requires preserving the dominance of the nation's Anglo-Protestant population. As the House Committee on Immigration and Naturalization put it: "If, therefore, the principle of individual liberty, guarded by a constitutional government created on this continent nearly a century and a half ago, is to endure, the basic strain of our population must be maintained."[40]

A stronger version of this type of constitutional nationalism declares that the nation's constitutional principles arise out of a particular identity, and *only* people with that identity are capable of embracing these principles. Under this view, some ethnicities are incapable of embracing these principles and must be excluded from the national community. This view can be seen in the ideology that led to the Chinese Exclusion Act of 1882, which declared that Chinese people must not be allowed to immigrate because they could not adapt to the nation's constitutional principles. As one senator of the time declared, "Free institutions are only possible with the favored races."[41] The same ideology can be seen in contemporary movements to ban Muslim immigration on the ground that Islam is simply inconsistent with the American Constitution.[42]

3. National identity based centrally on social identity. Numerous movements in American history have argued that American national identity is limited to those with a particular identity and have argued that the Constitution itself imposes this limit. Proponents of this type of constitutional nationalism do not merely believe that the principles found in the Constitution can be embraced by people with a particular identity; they believe that a central principle of the Constitution itself is that the national community must be limited to those with a particular identity. The Ku Klux Klan of the 1960s espoused this kind of ideology, declaring that "the United States through its white, Protestant citizens holds a Divine commission for the furtherance of white supremacy and the protection of religious freedom; that its Constitution and laws are expressive of the Divine purpose."[43]

To be sure, these three categories of constitutional nationalism should be understood as general types. In practice, individuals and political movements often hold fuzzier views about the connections between constitutional principles, social identities, and what it means to be American. For instance, many Americans declare devotion to the prevailing ideology of universal ideals described in the first category above, but nonetheless believe that in some perhaps undefined way being a real American has something to do with social identity. As Elizabeth Theiss-Morse has shown through empirical research, many Americans identify those who are native-born, white, Christian, and English-speaking to be *prototypical* Americans; they believe that the values of prototypical Americans represent the nation's true values; and they consider Americans who do not share the traits and values of prototypical Americans to be less authentically American.[44] Yet the associations between social identities, national values, and perceptions of who are full members of the national community often occur at a level of unconscious biases, rather than as an explicit element of a nationalist ideology.[45]

In documenting the ways that political and social movements have framed their movements in constitutional terms, I do not attempt to assess whether any of these movements have actually been true to the Constitution and the nation's traditions or whether they have betrayed the Constitution and those traditions. To be sure, some of the claims they make about American history are more farfetched than others. Yet all nationalist movements rely on distorted versions of national history to advance their causes.[46] Because American history is filled with competing traditions, nationalist movements can readily identify proof texts to support a wide range of nationalist visions. Social and political movements espousing universalist national visions can rely on a history that begins with the proclamation in the Declaration of Independence that all men are created equal. At the same time, supporters of the notion that the nation's fundamental constitutional principles are limited to those who have a particular race, religion, or ethnicity can also point to a myriad of sources from *The Federalist Papers* to numerous Supreme Court cases.[47] The claim that racism, sexism, and xenophobia are contrary to American traditions and are therefore *un-American* is just as false as the claim that the United States is a white Christian nation.

Just as it is not my goal to show that some forms of nationalism are more true to the nation's constitutional traditions than others, it is not my goal to show that some varieties of constitutional nationalism are benign while others are dangerous. All varieties of nationalism pose dangers of exclusion, hatred, and violence against those deemed to be alien to the national community. Those dangers are most readily apparent in the many examples of constitutional nationalism that embrace racial, religious, and ethnic hierarchies, which have a long history of violence in the United States. Yet even in its more universalist formulations, constitutional nationalism has served to justify violence and exclusion.

What I seek to show is that the Constitution has played a very different role in American nationalism than is widely believed. While the conventional wisdom teaches that the Constitution is a central expression of American identity, the Constitution has been understood to express many conflicting conceptions of what it means to be American. The belief in the Constitution's centrality in American identity—constitutional nationalism—has created a language that translates conflicts over national identity into constitutional terms. As chapter 1 shows, when white Americans felt threatened by movements for racial equality, they formed the Ku Klux Klan, which justified violence as a defense of the Constitution. As chapter 2 shows, when Protestant Americans felt threatened by the growing population of Catholics and Jews, they organized mass movements to defend their status and power by declaring that the Constitution was made for a Protestant nation. As chapter 3 shows, when native-born Americans felt threatened by the rising population of immigrants, they mobilized to exclude unwanted immigrants by arguing that the newcomers brought alien ideas that threatened the Constitution. As chapter 4 shows, when the New Deal undermined the power of corporations, corporate leaders fought back by arguing that the New Deal was unconstitutional and un-American.

As these chapters show, when dominant groups have found their status and power threatened, they have frequently experienced the threat in nationalist terms, as an attack on the nation as they conceive it, and they have mobilized to defend their position by asserting that the Constitution is threatened. The rhetoric of constitutional nationalism has thus served as a premier language that Americans employ to preserve the power of long-dominant groups, to assert that some people and some values are authentically American while others are dangerously foreign and must be rejected. At the same time, movements challenging established power structures typically articulate their own claims in constitutional terms and argue that the power of entrenched groups betrays the nation's fundamental principles. In this way, intergroup conflicts over power and status have long been carried out as contests between competing national visions expressed in constitutional terms.

In short, the Constitution does not define who Americans are. Instead, constitutional nationalism has provided the language by which Americans have carried out conflicts over national identity.

How the Constitution Became Our Magic Mirror

A Brief History of Constitutional Nationalism

It's a persistent folk belief that each of us has a true self, an inborn essence that remains constant throughout our lives and that represents who, deep down, we truly are. Although the search for the true self is a cliché of memoirs and coming-of-age novels, mountains of psychological research suggest that the true self is a myth. A person's self-conception changes considerably over time. Through an unconscious process we select certain memories, some true and some distorted, to fashion a narrative in which who we are today is the same person we've always been.[48] While conceptions of our true selves are always incomplete or even false, they serve as a useful heuristic for decision making. Instead of asking ourselves difficult questions like, *Should I buy these shoes?* or *Should I take this job?*, it's often easier to frame the questions in terms of personal identity and to ask, *Am I the kind of person who would buy these shoes? Am I the kind of person who would take this job?*

Much the same is true for nations. National ideologies teach that each nation has its own true self, a fixed essence sometimes called a national identity or a national character. Conceptions of national identities are typically conveyed through national histories, legends, and myths. As with personal mythologies, national mythologies are constructed to portray the nation as having a fixed essence. National mythologies not only seek to remind citizens of the nation's past but also send a powerful lesson about the present: we should strive to stay true to what the nation truly is.[49] National mythologies, like the belief that being American has always meant devotion to liberty and democracy and has never been about race or ethnicity, are always based on distorted versions of history. As Ernest Renan wrote, "Getting its history wrong is part of being a nation."[50] Instead of assessing whether mythological history is true or false, national mythologies are best assessed for the function they play in a national community.[51]

Conceptions of national identity provide a way for a nation to reconcile its present with its past. By proclaiming that American identity is based on a commitment to ideals embodied in the Constitution, constitutional nationalism helps make Americans feel better about the shameful parts of their history—slavery and race discrimination, the displacement and genocide of Native Americans, and the denial of equal rights for women, among others. Constitutional nationalism provides a framework for telling ourselves that these episodes are anomalous and do not reflect who we really are.[52] As Justice Antonin Scalia put it, in reviewing the history of Italian Americans: "There have, to be sure, been instances and periods of discrimination against Italian Americans, just as there have been against all other new arrivals. But that was the aberration, the departure from the norm, the failure to live up to the principles on which this Republic was founded."[53]

As with personal conceptions of the true self, beliefs in a national identity provide a way of thinking and talking about national decision making. Instead of simply asking whether the nation-state should take a particular course of action (go to war, restrict immigration, or recognize a new individual right), conceptions of national identity help frame decisions in terms of whether the nation is staying true to itself: Are we the kind of nation who would take this action, or would it be un-American? Could we take this action and stay true to ourselves, or would it betray our traditions?

In the first half of the twentieth century, an army of social scientists devoted their careers to meticulously cataloguing and describing national characters from around the world. Perhaps the most notorious example of this work was the *Dictionary of Races or Peoples*, issued in 1911 by anthropologists working for the United States Senate, which sought to help Congress determine immigration policy by identifying the physical and mental qualities of all of the world's peoples.[54] According to the *Dictionary*, Albanians were said to be "brave, but turbulent in spirit—warriors rather than workers," Serbo-Croatians were said to be "well adapted to hard labor," and Bohemians were "unsurpassed" as musicians and artists.[55]

Today, political science has largely abandoned the idea that nations have distinct and fixed national characters, just as psychology has largely abandoned the idea that individuals have unchanging true selves. Studies have repeatedly revealed that descriptions of national character are little more than unsubstantiated stereotypes.[56] Even the smallest nations are too diverse to have definite personalities.[57] At most, studies show that certain traits are more or less prevalent within a nation.[58] The national mythologies of some nations define the traits of a ruling elite to be national traits, while other nations identify more common traits as national traits. Either way, identifying some traits as the *true* national character serves to privilege certain members of the nation by deeming them to be authentic exemplars of the nation and to marginalize others who don't share these traits.

Although Franklin Roosevelt declared that being American has "always" been defined by loyalty to the nation's creed of liberty and democracy, and has "never" involved race or ancestry, American identity has not always been understood to be centered on devotion to a common creed. In this section, I sketch a brief history of how devotion to the Constitution came to be understood as the core of American national identity. Like the construction of all national narratives, this account is highly selective. I focus on a few episodes to make a simple point: constitutional nationalism is a relatively recent invention that we have come to believe is long-standing and even eternal.[59]

From the time of the nation's founding, if not before, Americans have been obsessed with identifying their true national self, with identifying what, if anything, Americans hold in common and binds them together as a nation. Writing in the 1780s, Hector St. John de Crevecoeur asked a question Americans have been asking ever since: "What then is the American, this new man?"[60] Because the United States was founded by colonial settlers and immigrants from many nations who lacked a common history, it was hard to identify the glue that held the people together. Many have agreed with de Crevecoeur that American identity represents something unique in the history of the world. A vast body of literature on American exceptionalism has declared that the United States and the American people are unique, but exactly what makes them exceptional has long been subject to dispute.[61]

As it prevails today, constitutional nationalism was unknown at the nation's founding—and not just for the obvious reason that the Constitution had not yet been written. In the nation's early years, descriptions of American identity sometimes focused on the people's dedication to liberty and republican government, but this dedication was often understood to reflect the people's ethnic heritage. As historian John Higham explained, Americans had long "proclaimed orderly self-government as the chief glory of Anglo-Saxons—an inherited capacity so unique that the future of human freedom surely rested in their hands."[62] Thomas Jefferson, for instance, claimed that "our Saxon ancestors" had bestowed upon Americans a heritage of democracy, and he proposed that the Great Seal of the United States should depict "Hengist and Horsa, the Saxon chiefs from whom we claim the honor of being descended."[63]

Some members of the founding generation were explicit in connecting the nation's republican and constitutional values with the people's British and Protestant heritage. In *Federalist*, no. 2, John Jay described the Constitution as an expression of the nation's common culture: "Providence has been pleased to give this one connected country to one united people," he declared, "a people descended from the same ancestors, speaking the same language, professing the same religion, [and] attached to the same principles of government."[64] As Sanford Levinson has discussed, Jay's description of a homogeneous people was far from accurate.[65] The nation's residents included Native Americans and persons of African descent, who were not seen by the governing class to be part of the national community. Even within the category recognized by the founders as fellow Americans, the American people exhibited considerable diversity in ancestry, religion, language, and political beliefs. As de Crevecoeur pointed out, Americans were a "mixture of English, Scotch, Irish, French, Dutch, Germans, and Swedes."[66]

Despite its inaccuracies, the belief that Americans shared a common ethnicity and culture helped shape the young nation's policies about who could become American. In 1790, the year after the Constitution was ratified, Congress adopted the first Naturalization Act, which imposed two qualifications for becoming a naturalized citizen: citizenship was limited to those who were both a "free white person" and who swore to "support the Constitution of the United States."[67] These two traits were understood to be connected; only white persons were thought capable of embracing the nation's constitutional values.[68]

Although support for the Constitution was a requirement for naturalized citizenship from the nation's start, it took many decades before the Constitution itself became an object of national veneration and devotion. Substantial segments of American society rejected the Constitution well into the nineteenth century. Anti-Federalists opposed the Constitution on the ground that it would foster a new aristocracy that would betray the values of the American Revolution.[69] A group of evangelical Christians considered the Constitution to be heretical because it declares that its authority comes from "We the People" and not from God.[70] Abolitionists publicly burned the Constitution because of its support for slavery, and William Lloyd Garrison spoke for many in denouncing the Constitution as "a covenant with death and an agreement with hell."[71] Devotion to the Constitution was not universally considered a requirement to be a good and patriotic American, and dissent from the Constitution was not seen as unpatriotic.[72]

In the nation's early decades, American leaders frequently expressed glowing praise for the Constitution as a governing law that bound together the states—in James Madison's words, it served as the "cement of the Union"—but they did not describe it in cultural terms, as a force that unified the American people or defined what it meant to be American.[73] Instead, many questioned whether the new nation had any unifying characteristics. In 1831 Alexis de Tocqueville wrote that he did not believe that Americans could work together toward a common interest because the United States was "a society which comprises all the nations of the worlds," its people "differing from one another in language, in beliefs, in opinions; in a word a society possessing no roots, no memories, no prejudices, no routine, no common ideas, no common character."[74]

It took at least fifty years after ratification of the Constitution before anyone began to speak of a shared devotion to constitutional principles as a force that might unify the American people. Even then, such expressions were aspirational and signaled a hope that the nation might someday become united by devotion to the Constitution. The first stirrings of constitutional nationalism, in the sense of a national ideology based on a common devotion to the Constitution that bound the people together, can be found in two speeches given in the late 1830s by future president Abraham Lincoln and former president John Quincy Adams. Both feared that the nation might fall apart if nothing could be found to unite the people, and they both urged the nation to come together by developing a devotion to the Constitution akin to their devotion to God.

In his first major speech, given in the Springfield, Illinois, Lyceum in 1838 when he was twenty-eight years old, Lincoln pointed to ominous forces of anarchy that he believed threatened to destroy the nation.[75] He pointed to the lynching of a mixed-race freeman in Saint Louis and the massacre in Mississippi of blacks and whites accused of supporting a slave insurrection. Lincoln feared that the country was descending into "mob law." To avoid anarchy, Lincoln urged Americans to unite around the Constitution: "As the patriots of seventy-six did to the support of the Declaration of Independence," Lincoln declared, "so to the support of the Constitution and Laws, let every American pledge his life, his property, and his sacred honor."[76]

Lincoln believed that it would not be enough for Americans merely to support the Constitution and the laws adopted under it. For the nation to survive, he explained, Americans needed to develop a passionate commitment to the Constitution: "In short," Lincoln declared, "let it become the political religion of the nation." To generate this kind of constitutional devotion, Americans would need to make reverence for the Constitution an everyday part of their lives: "Let [it] be breathed by every American mother, to the lisping babe, that prattles on her lap—let it be taught in schools, in seminaries, and in colleges; let it be written in Primers, spelling books, and in Almanacs;—let it be preached from the pulpit, proclaimed in legislative halls, and enforced in courts of justice."[77]

The year after Lincoln's Lyceum speech, former president John Quincy Adams gave a speech to mark the fiftieth anniversary of the ratification of the Constitution, and he too declared that the nation could only be saved if the people united around a common devotion to the Constitution. Like Lincoln, Adams feared that the United States faced disintegration because little held the people together.[78] Where Lincoln saw looming threats of anarchy and violence, Adams feared the political threats of nullification and secession. To address those threats, Adams recommended the same solution as Lincoln: the American people must become passionately, devoutly, and religiously devoted to "the principles of the Declaration of Independence," principles that are "practically interwoven in the Constitution."

As Sanford Levinson has noted, Adams's speech riffed on Deuteronomy

6:5–9. Just as that biblical passage commands the faithful to make devotion to God part of every aspect of their daily lives, Adams preached that Americans must make expressions of constitutional devotion a central part of their daily lives:

> Lay up these principles, then, in your hearts, and in your souls—bind them for signs upon your hands, that they may be as frontlets between your eyes—teach them to your children, speaking of them when sitting in your houses, when walking by the way, when lying down and when rising up—write them upon the doorplates of your houses, and upon your gates—cling to them as to the issues of life—adhere to them as to the cords of your eternal salvation.[79]

Like Lincoln, Adams hoped that devotion to the Constitution could become the glue to bind together a heterogeneous nation and keep the nation from falling apart.

As these speeches make clear, Lincoln and Adams did not believe that the American people were already united by devotion to the Constitution. Instead, they saw Americans as a divided and fragmented people with no strong common bond, and they feared that the nation would dissolve unless they found one.

In the decades that followed these speeches, as the nation moved toward secession and civil war, politicians frequently pointed to the Constitution as the embodiment of the nation's values, but these declarations served principally to emphasize deep-seated divisions, not unity. Republican leaders like Lincoln declared that the North had stayed true to the Constitution while accusing Southern secessionists of threatening to betray the foundational principle of national union.[80] Secessionists, in turn, claimed that the South had remained true to the Constitution while accusing the North of constitutional betrayal through various measures and proposals to limit the spread of slavery.[81] Northern and Southern leaders each claimed the Constitution as their own, just as they each claimed that God and the Bible were on their side.[82]

After the end of the Civil War, the Constitution remained a source of division, and each of the major political parties proclaimed that it alone was loyal to the Constitution and the other party had betrayed it. In 1868, in the first presidential campaign after the war, the Republicans accused the Democrats of betraying the Constitution by supporting secession, while the Democrats campaigned on a platform that equated fidelity to the Constitution with the maintenance of white rule. The Democratic platform warned that if the Republicans won, white rule would come to an end and the Constitution would be lost: "We will meet, as a subjected and conquered people, amid the ruins of liberty and the scattered fragments of the Constitution."[83]

In the wake of the Civil War, many movements arose that used the language of constitutional devotion to advance various conceptions of the national community that focused on race, religion, and nativism. The Ku Klux Klan pledged to support the "sacred prerogatives vouchsafed to us by the Constitution," which they understood to mean white rule.[84] At the same time, a group of evangelical Protestants, alarmed at the rising numbers and power of non-Protestants, mobilized a national movement to add a proclamation of the nation's Christian faith to the Constitution and thereby preserve the nation's Christian identity. Nativist movements sought to exclude unwanted immigrants who they said would undermine the Constitution. These movements invoked devotion to the Constitution to unite some Americans (whites, Protestants, native born) against others (blacks, Jews, Catholics, freethinkers, and Chinese), who they accused of betraying and undermining the Constitution.

By the early twentieth century it had become commonplace to declare that constitutional devotion was a core American trait. When the federal and state governments launched "Americanization" campaigns to transform new immigrants into good Americans, they focused especially on providing lessons about the Constitution and founding fathers. As Secretary of the Interior Franklin Lane declared in 1916: "We know that there are principles enunciated in the Declaration of Independence and in the Constitution of the United States which are necessary to get into one's system before [an immigrant] can thoroughly understand the United States."[85]

While it had become common to identify devotion to constitutional principles as central to American identity, this belief was not perceived to conflict with the belief that American identity also involved race, religion, and ethnicity. President Calvin Coolidge, for instance, declared that "to support the Constitution . . . is to be true to our own higher nature."[86] At the same time, Coolidge asserted that the United States was, at heart, a Christian nation, declaring that "there is something essential in our civilization which gives it a special power. I think we shall be able to agree that this particular element is the Christian religion."[87] When Coolidge signed the National Origins Act of 1924, which restricted immigration from southern and eastern Europe, he declared that keeping out unwanted ethnic and religious groups was necessary to preserve the American character, or, as he succinctly put it, "America must be kept American."[88] Coolidge thus believed that being American meant devotion to the Constitution, it meant

Christian faith, and it meant preserving the nation's dominant ethnic stock. These beliefs were not understood to be contradictory.

The fight against fascism in World War II, however, brought a change to how American leaders began to talk about national identity. US leaders began to declare that devotion to constitutional principles *alone* was—and had had always been—the core of American identity and values. This can be seen in Roosevelt's 1943 declaration that Americanism had always meant dedication "to our creed of liberty and democracy" and "never was a matter of race or ancestry." Of course, Roosevelt's declaration that American identity is and always has been defined by commitment to universal principles and has never involved race or ancestry was neither true to the nation's past nor its present. Roosevelt made the declaration in a speech to commemorate the creation of an all–Japanese-American army unit, whose members were selected for service solely by their race and ancestry, and Roosevelt's administration had put thousands of Japanese Americans in internment camps solely because of their race and ancestry. Roosevelt's invocation of a universalist national vision spoke to the need to create national unity in wartime, when the nation was fighting regimes expressly dedicated to racial and ethnic dominance. Unlike the nation's wartime enemies, Roosevelt declared, American identity was based solely on commitment to universal values of liberty and democracy, and in fact it had always been so.[89]

In 1944 the notion of a unifying American Creed that transcends race, religion, ethnicity, and national origin was further popularized when Swedish sociologist Gunnar Myrdal published *An American Dilemma.* It declared: "Americans of all national origins, classes, regions, creeds, and colors, have something in common, a social ethos, a political creed." As Myrdal concluded, devotion to that creed is "the cement in the structure of this great and disparate nation." Like others, Myrdal identified the Constitution as the central embodiment of the American Creed. For Myrdal, the American Creed represented America at its core; racial hierarchy enforced through the vast system of legalized segregation, he suggested, was simply an aberration from America's true self.[90]

In the following decades, the civil rights movement frequently invoked a universal version of constitutional nationalism to express its aspirations for the nation. Martin Luther King Jr. called on the nation to "rise up and live out the true meaning of its creed."[91] He stated that "the magnificent words of the Constitution and Declaration of Independence" amounted to a promise "that all men—yes, black men as well as white men—would be guaranteed unalienable rights of life, liberty and the pursuit of happiness."[92]

The movement portrayed overcoming racial segregation as a way for the United States at long last to be true to itself. As Langston Hughes put it, "Let America be America again/The land that never has been yet—/And yet must be."[93]

The Cold War further entrenched the belief that American identity was and always had been defined by devotion to constitutional principles. The belief served important foreign policy interests because the United States sought to project that it was the leader of the free world, that it was devoted to universal principles and not merely its own material interests. American leaders depicted their fight against communism as a means of carrying out the nation's constitutional values on the global stage.[94] Racial segregation, in contrast, was an embarrassment, a betrayal of the universalist ideology understood to form the American Creed.

Historians in the post–World War II era helped spread the growing constitutional faith and embraced the belief that American nationalism had always been about a shared creed expressed in the universal principles of the Constitution and had never involved race, religion, or ethnicity.[95] The most prominent historians of the 1940s and 1950s formed what is now described as the consensus school, whose members asserted that, despite superficial conflicts and divisions, American political and cultural life had always reflected an underlying unity that focused on shared constitutional values.[96] Historians of the consensus school included Richard Hofstadter, who explained that American culture reflected "a kind of mute organic consistency" built around a "central faith in American political ideologies."[97] The consensus school also included Hans Kohn, whose book on American nationalism declared what has become the prevailing view, that the United States "was not founded on the common attributes of nationhood—language, cultural tradition, historical territory or common descent—but on an idea which singled out the new nation among the nations of the earth."[98] That idea, Kohn declared, is expressed most centrally in the Constitution.

Thus, by the 1950s constitutional nationalism—and in particular, the version of constitutional nationalism that asserts that American identity is based solely on commitment to universal principles and not on race, religion, or ethnicity—had become the dominant conception of American identity. The consensus declared that this conception was not new—American identity had always been defined by devotion to constitutional principles. That view remains dominant today, and it is widely believed, as Roosevelt declared, that American identity has always been defined this way.

Constitutional Nationalism Everywhere

With a national consensus in place that American identity is defined by commitment to the Constitution, Americans have at last heeded Lincoln and Adams's advice and have made expressions of constitutional devotion pervasive in American life.

No other legal document in the world generates the devotion and passion Americans profess for the Constitution. The National Archives has created a bronze-and-marble shrine to display one of the signed originals. Shielded by layers of protective glass, the sacred document is kept cold and dark to protect the delicate parchment. Photography is strictly prohibited.[99] Hundreds of tourists line up every day for a chance to glimpse it. Perhaps somewhere there are superfans of municipal zoning ordinances, the Uniform Commercial Code, the Endangered Species Act, or the UN Charter, but none of these documents has become a tourist destination that gets four-and-a-half stars and thousands of reviews on TripAdvisor.com.[100]

Constitutional devotees who are not sated after visiting the National Archives may want to go to the Constitution Center in Philadelphia, a museum created by Congress on the bicentennial of the Constitutional Convention. Dedicated as the "Museum of We the People," it seeks to help visitors experience the Constitution not as an old document written centuries ago or a simple charter for a national government but as something personal that all Americans can claim as their own. Visitors are invited to "walk alongside 42 life-size, bronze statues of the FOUNDING FATHERS" and to "relive the moment that launched a government ruled by 'We the People.'"[101] Museum visitors don't just learn about the drafting of the Constitution; they are invited to sign their own names to it, to dedicate themselves to the Constitution, just as we imagine the Founders did.[102]

Expressions of constitutional devotion are not just reserved for museums. They have become a mundane element in presidential addresses. With the possible exception of Donald Trump, every president elected since Franklin Roosevelt has declared that despite differences in their backgrounds, Americans share a common creed founded in the Constitution. As Ronald Reagan put it, Americans "came from different lands but they shared the same values, the same dream."[103] A decade later, Bill Clinton expressed the same idea, that Americans are like "family—white, black, Latino, all of us, no matter how different, who share basic American values and are willing to live by them."[104] In the following decades, George W. Bush and Barack

Obama repeated the same conception of the role of the Constitution in binding together the American people.

But presidential declarations aren't enough. In 2004 Congress decided that Americans need an annual reminder of their duty to revere the Constitution, and it declared that September 17 would henceforth be known as Constitution Day. Senator Robert Byrd, the chief sponsor of the legislation creating the holiday, rhapsodized that the Constitution "is the soul of the Nation. . . . It is our bedrock. . . . This Constitution touches every day, every hour, every minute of your lives. Practically everything you do is made possible or guaranteed or is protected by this Constitution."[105] He declared that Constitution Day should be considered "more important to our everyday lives than Columbus Day, more important to our everyday lives than Thanksgiving, more important to our everyday lives than the Fourth of July."[106]

The importance of constitutional devotion doesn't stop with an annual reminder. For true patriots, Constitution Day comes every day. In countless ways, Americans receive daily reminders that we live in a nation devoted to constitutional ideals. Inculcation of constitutional devotion starts early, with picture books about the Founding Fathers, the Constitutional Framers, and the Miracle in Philadelphia.[107] The Government Printing Office publishes a primer for young readers, *C Is for Constitution*, and also prints thousands of pocket-size Constitutions every year.[108]

American public schools have always been dedicated to transforming children into good patriotic citizens, and teaching reverence for the Constitution is central to that mission. For decades, millions of American children have started each school day by facing the American flag, placing a hand on their hearts, and reciting the official distillation of the nation's constitutional creed—that the United States is "one Nation under God, indivisible, with liberty and justice for all."[109] High school textbooks depict American history as the story of a people striving, generation after generation, to carry out the nation's ideals.[110] In some places, this depiction of American history is mandated by law. Florida, for instance, requires that in its schools American history "shall be defined as the creation of a new nation based largely on the universal principles stated in the Declaration of Independence."[111] Congress too has stepped in to require that public schools teach that "what it means to be an American" and "what unites us as Americans" can be found by studying our founding documents, most especially the Constitution.[112]

Outside of schools, popular culture reinforces the centrality of constitutional ideals in the nation's collective identity. In *The United States*

Constitution in Film, authors Eric T. Kasper and Quentin D. Vieregge discuss hundreds of American movies that focus on constitutional questions, such as *12 Angry Men*, *To Kill a Mockingbird*, and *Lincoln*.[113] Courtroom dramas and crime shows provide weekly lessons about the workings of constitutional government. Comic books are populated with heroes who bear allegiance to the Constitution. Superman, that most all-American superhero, fights for "Truth, Justice, and the American Way" and served during the 1940s and 1950s as the official spokesman for a campaign to "sell the American public a greater appreciation of the American Creed."[114]

On TV, we learned that the Constitution's magic works even in space. In one memorable episode of *Star Trek*, Captain Kirk brought civilization and democracy to a tribe of spear-carrying, fur-wearing extraterrestrials by giving a dramatic recitation of the Constitution's Preamble. The Constitution "wasn't written for the chiefs or the kings or the warriors or the rich or the powerful, but for all the people," Captain Kirk declared. "These words and the words that follow," he went on, "must apply to everyone or they mean nothing." Glimpsing the light of the constitutional faith, the alien chief answered, "The holy words will be obeyed."[115]

Growing up in the 1970s, my generation learned about the Constitution through Saturday-morning cartoons, where *Schoolhouse Rock* explained the process laid out in the Constitution by which a bill became a law ("I'm Just a Bill").[116] It also gave us a catchy tune to learn the words to the Constitution's Preamble, in a song that explained:

> In 1787 I'm told
> Our founding fathers did agree
> To write a list of principles
> For keepin' people free.
> The U.S.A. was just startin' out.
> A whole brand-new country.
> And so our people spelled it out
> The things that we should be.[117]

In these few words, *Schoolhouse Rock* conveyed the central point of constitutional nationalism: from the time it was written, the Constitution has given us our national identity. Not just an old charter of government, the Constitution teaches us "the things that we should be."

Examined individually, each of these messages that Americans receive about the Constitution may seem trivial; taken together, they convey a powerful message, reinforced daily and in many ways, that devotion to the Constitution stands at the center of what it means to be American. We are the Constitution, we're told, and the Constitution is us.

The pervasive reminders of our presumed communal devotion to constitutional principles represent an example of "banal nationalism," a term coined by British sociologist Michael Billig to explain how nationalism is reproduced in established nations. As Billig points out, in the stable and long-established nations of western Europe and North America, the term *nationalism* is usually applied to separatist movements in distant locales that are fighting to establish independence and sovereignty.[118] Nationalism is often understood as something violent, irrational, and exotic.[119] Loyalty to our own nation, in contrast, is a mild, rational, and contained force that goes by the genteel term *patriotism*, not nationalism.[120]

Left unexplored, Billig asserts, are the almost invisible processes by which national loyalty is inculcated in established nations—processes that not only make it seem natural to think of oneself as part of the nation but that convince patriots to be willing to kill and to die for the nation: "In so many little ways, the citizenry are daily reminded of their national place in a world of nations. However, the reminding is so familiar, so continual, that it is not consciously registered as reminding. The metonymic image of banal nationalism is not a flag which is being consciously waved with fervent passion; it is the flag hanging unnoticed on the public building."[121] As Billig explains, the ubiquitous presence of American flags serves to remind us that we are living in the United States and that the nation deserves our loyalty.

The pervasive expressions of constitutional devotion serve a similar function. They remind us of the kind of nation we live in: a nation devoted to the principles said to be expressed in the Constitution.

Constitutional Nationalism and the Maintenance of National Boundaries

In the 1830s Lincoln and Adams imagined that national unity would result if Americans were constantly reminded of their shared faith in the Constitution.[122] Today, many continue to believe this. As the commission that wrote the nation's current citizenship test explained, "American unity depends upon a widely-held belief in the principles and values embodied in the American Constitution."[123]

In American politics, however, assertions of fidelity to the Constitution and accusations of constitutional betrayal serve to maintain boundaries between competing national ideologies, and not to create unity. In *Purity and Danger*, anthropologist Mary Douglas explored how the word *dirt* serves to maintain boundaries by providing a label for things that are out of place and pollute the proper order.[124] Soil in a field is not dirt but it becomes dirt when brought into a home. In this way, the word *dirt* serves to maintain boundaries by differentiating between what is properly in its place and is therefore pure and clean, and what is out of place—what is foreign—and therefore dirty. Declarations of constitutional devotion and accusations of constitutional betrayal perform the same function in American politics. They distinguish between what some declare to be authentically American and rightfully belongs here, and what they condemn as dangerously foreign and demand to be excluded.

Emblematic is the popular "Obama Is Unconstitutional" T-shirt sold at Tea Party rallies. The message is incomprehensible as a statement of legal doctrine because no person can be unconstitutional. Here, *unconstitutional* works as a synonym for *un-American* and *alien*. Tea Party supporters frequently described Barack Obama as *alien* in various ways.[125] Some said that he was alien because supposedly he had been born outside the United States, contrary to his birth certificate and well-established facts.[126] Some said that he subscribed to an alien religion, that he was secretly Muslim living in what they considered a Christian nation.[127] Some considered the United States to be a white nation and therefore considered a Black president to be alien to American traditions.[128] And he was described as ideologically alien because he did not adhere to what the Tea Party considered the true and authentic American values.[129] By declaring Obama *unconstitutional*, the Tea Party forcefully summed up the accusation that Obama was fundamentally an outsider in American life.

A few people have begun to notice that in popular discourse, perceived fidelity to the Constitution is frequently used as the dividing line between what is authentically American and dangerously foreign. Yale law professors Amy Chua and Jed Rubenfeld condemned this kind of constitutional rhetoric, which they claimed is symptomatic of increasing polarization: "Americans on both the left and the right now view their political opponents not as fellow Americans with differing views, but as enemies to be vanquished. And they have come to view the Constitution not as an aspirational statement of shared principles and a bulwark against tribalism, but as a cudgel with which to attack those enemies."[130] Chua and Rubenfeld imagined that the use of the Constitution to attack political enemies is a new and dangerous phenomenon. They pointed to a past when things were different, when the Constitution served "to forge, out of a diverse population, a new national identity, uniting Americans under a banner of ideas."

The history of constitutional nationalism explored in this book reveals that there was no golden age like Chua and Rubenfeld imagined. American history has long involved fundamental conflicts over what it means to be American, and these conflicts have frequently been carried out in the language of constitutional nationalism. Each of the chapters that follow explores different ways that the Constitution has been invoked to emphasize division and to express competing conceptions of American identity.

The first three chapters explore movements devoted to the belief that American identity is based on race, religion, and ethnicity. Within the spectrum of constitutional nationalism categorized earlier in this introduction, each of these movements proclaimed a national vision that embraced both abstract principles and social identities, and each declared that its national vision was true to the Constitution.

Chapter 1: The White Constitution shows that the language of constitutional devotion has long been central to movements for white supremacy. As that chapter examines, the Ku Klux Klan has always considered the Constitution a central expression of the nation's white heritage that serves as the foundation of white rule. In declaring loyalty to the Constitution "as originally adopted by our fathers," the Klan declared it a foundational principle that "our Republic was established by white men, for white men alone."[131] For 150 years, dedication to the Constitution has been central to how the Klan has justified the widespread violence it has perpetrated and how it has recruited thousands of Klansmen willing to kill and die in defense of a Constitution they believe is dedicated to white rule.

Chapter 2: The Christian Constitution explores the central role of the Constitution in Christian nationalism, the belief that the United States is at heart a Christian nation. In the second half of the nineteenth century, a political movement arose among Americans who were alarmed at the declining power and status of Protestants in the United States. Convinced that the Constitution must accurately reflect who the American people are, the movement mobilized to amend the Constitution to declare the nation's Christian devotion. The Christian amendment movement asserted that the Constitution must be made Christian to keep the American people Christian. Although the Christian amendment was not adopted, the notion of Christianizing the Constitution persists today. Contemporary Christian nationalists no longer believe that an amendment is necessary to make the Constitution Christian and insist instead that the Constitution has always expressed the nation's Christian values.

Chapter 3: The Nativist Constitution examines how nativist movements have used the rhetoric of constitutional devotion to advocate for the exclusion of unwanted immigrants. Until 1965, US immigration policy was based on the belief that immigration must be restricted because only people who share the nation's dominant race, ethnicity, and religion are capable of embracing the nation's constitutional principles. Congress repudiated that belief when it adopted the Immigration and Nationality Act of 1965, which for the first time reflected the conviction that immigrants from any nation are equally capable of taking the oath to support and defend the Constitution. Today, anti-immigrant groups have kept alive the belief that only some people are suited to become American citizens and have sought to exclude Muslim, Asian, and Latin American immigrants, who they believe are unable to embrace America's constitutional values.

As these three chapters show, the rhetoric of constitutional devotion has played a central role in movements devoted to preserving the status and power of the nation's dominant racial, religious, and ethnic groups. When members of these groups have perceived that their place in the American order is threatened, they have seen the threat as an attack on the nation itself and mobilized by rallying around the Constitution, which they understand to be the ultimate embodiment of national identity. This pattern—group threat, nationalist framework, and constitutional rhetoric—provides the paradigm by which America's constitutional culture routinely translates social conflicts into constitutional terms.

The same pattern can be seen in other movements in American history. When women demanded suffrage in the nineteenth and early twentieth centuries, and when they sought passage of the Equal Rights Amendment in the second half of the twentieth century, their opponents recognized a threat to their status and power, denounced the women's rights movements as an attack on the nation's foundational principles, and employed the language of constitutional nationalism to defend their status.[132] Opponents of women's suffrage declared that the Constitution was made by men and for men, and only men are capable of governing pursuant to the Constitution. Reflecting on this history, Mary Anne Franks has written that for many Americans, the Constitution is understood to provide the foundation for male supremacy.[133]

Chapter 4: The Businessman's Constitution explores how, outside the context of race, religion, and ethnicity, conflicts over national policies are often understood as fights over national identity, expressed in constitutional terms. That chapter focuses on the American Liberty League of the mid-1930s, which launched a campaign to reverse the New Deal by declaring it unconstitutional and un-American. To corporate leaders of the 1930s, the New Deal was not just bad policy: it was fundamentally alien to America's true self. Just as white Americans, Christian Americans, and native-born Americans saw threats to their power as threats to the Constitution, so businessmen of the 1930s rallied around the Constitution when their power was threatened. President Roosevelt countered that the Liberty League was un-American and its views would undermine the Constitution. In this way, each side in the fight over the New Deal employed the rhetoric of constitutional nationalism to express competing national visions.

Chapter 5: The Partisan Constitution explores a more recent example of how constitutional nationalism has created a neutral and patriotic language for expressing concerns about race, religion, and ethnicity. That chapter focuses on the Tea Party movement, which rose to national prominence in 2009 by declaring that President Obama had launched an attack on the Constitution. To Tea Party supporters, devotion to the true meaning of the Constitution represented the dividing line between American patriots and the nation's enemies. Although the Tea Party movement did not typically make explicit appeals based on race, ethnicity, and religion, the Tea Party frequently conveyed the belief that departures from the Constitution, as Tea Party members understood it, resulted from the increased power of immigrants, persons of color, and others who did not embrace what the movement believed to be the nation's core values. In this way, appeals to constitutional principles often serve as a seemingly neutral way to express deep-seated concerns over national identity.

Chapter 6: The Violent Constitution examines ways that constitutional nationalism has justified antigovernment violence. Like all nationalist ideologies, constitutional nationalism teaches that the nation's values are worth killing and dying for.[134] For decades, groups like the Posse Comitatus and the militia movement have mobilized around the conviction that the federal government has been taken over by the nation's enemies, who seek to destroy the Constitution. These groups have proclaimed that the Constitution gives them a right, even a duty, to use violence in defense of constitutional values. This ideology has supported many of the nation's most notorious act of domestic terrorism. When Timothy McVeigh set off a truck bomb that destroyed the Alfred P. Murrah Building in Oklahoma City in

1995 and killed 168 people, he declared that he was acting to defend the Constitution.[135] Like Timothy McVeigh, the insurrectionists who took over the Capitol on January 6, 2021, believed that the nation's government had been taken over by un-American forces and that true patriots have a duty to launch antigovernment violence in order to protect the Constitution.

Conclusion: Nationalism without the Constitution briefly examines the 2016 election of Donald Trump and the Trump presidency. Trump's campaign connected with many of the groups explored in this book—white nationalists, Christian nationalists, nativists, corporate leaders, Tea Party supporters, and militia members. Like the supporters of many other movements, Trump supporters believed that their status and power in American life were diminishing, and they experienced the loss as an attack on the nation as they imagined it to be. The Trump campaign used many of the same rhetorical themes that other nationalist movements had employed, such as depicting their opponents as fundamentally alien and hostile to the values that make America great. But one thing was different about Trump: he did not talk about the Constitution. In fact, Trump was the first president since Franklin Roosevelt whose inaugural address made no reference to an American Creed expressed in the Constitution.

As I've tried to show in this book, constitutional nationalism has provided a language for those who consider themselves real Americans to express the fear that they are losing status and power. The election of Donald Trump revealed that many Americans would respond to a candidate who addressed these fears bluntly, directly, and without the rhetorical sheen of constitutional language. Yet Trump's election nonetheless demonstrates the enduring power of constitutional nationalism. Predictably, constitutional nationalism became a dominant rhetoric among Trump's opponents, who, like countless movements before them, expressed their national vision in constitutional terms. And while Trump did not typically articulate his brand of "America First" nationalism in constitutional terms, he turned to a constitutional message in the closing days of his presidency, when he sought to hold on to power and called on his supporters to "fight like hell" because, he told them, the survival of the nation and the Constitution was at stake.

1 | The White Constitution

The Ku Klux Klan is America's oldest and most prominent terrorist organization. For over 150 years, groups calling themselves the Ku Klux Klan have committed uncounted murders, bombings, kidnappings, and assaults, as well as innumerable acts of intimidation and threats, including night riding and cross burning, all in the name of white supremacy and preserving white rule.

What may be surprising, and is certainly less well known, is that since its founding in 1866 the Klan has proclaimed that its mission is to "protect and defend the Constitution of the United States."[1] In the 1870s, when Klan members whipped and murdered thousands of African Americans in an effort to sabotage Reconstruction and to maintain white rule, they said they were acting to defend the Constitution.[2] In the 1920s, when Klan members fought to keep Jews and Catholics out of the country and out of positions of influence, they said they were fighting for the Constitution.[3] In the 1960s, when Klan members bombed churches and murdered civil rights workers, they said they were working to defend the Constitution.[4] Klan members today continue to say they are fighting to restore the true meaning of the Constitution, even as they march arm in arm with neo-Nazis to denounce Jewish control of the government and media.[5]

A large body of scholarship has examined the Klan in great detail, but it has not taken seriously the Klan's expressions of devotion to the Constitution. Hundreds of books have documented the Klan's history, violence, and significance—exploring the role of the Klan in different periods, in different states, the role of women in the Klan, the Klan's religious views, resistance to the Klan, and the FBI's fight against the Klan—among many other subjects. Yet no work contains any analysis of what the Constitution has meant to the Klan.[6] To the extent that published histories mention that the Klan has expressed its mission as a defense of the Constitution, these expressions have been dismissed as meaningless rhetoric intended to cover up their true purpose. Typical is *White Terror: The Ku Klux Klan Conspiracy and Southern Reconstruction* by Allen Trelease, the most in-depth examination of the early history of the Klan, which dismisses the Klan's declaration of a constitutional mission by stating that "it would be hard to imagine a greater parody than this on the Ku Klux Klan as it actually operated."[7]

It's easy to see why Klan expressions of devotion to the Constitution have been so readily dismissed. Throughout its history, the Klan has engaged in widespread violence and terrorism outside the constraints of law to deny African Americans and others their right to full participation in American life, despite the adoption of a constitutional right of all citizens to the equal protection of law. The Klan's asserted dedication to the Constitution has not been taken seriously because the Klan has been "the embodiment of lawlessness and outrage," as Trelease put it, "and it set at defiance the Constitution and laws of the United States."[8]

Although Trelease was of course correct that the Klan has long acted to undermine the Constitution as it's conventionally understood, the Klan's expressed dedication to the Constitution is worth examining both for what it says about the Klan and what it reveals about America's constitutional culture. For 150 years, the Constitution has been central to how the Klan has conceived its mission and how it has justified the widespread violence it has perpetrated. Its expressed devotion to the Constitution has served to recruit hundreds of thousands of Klan members who have been willing to kill and die in the name of the Constitution.

This chapter examines the constitutional ideology that has guided the Klan throughout its long and bloody history. As it shows, the Klan has long been devoted to the belief that the United States is a white nation, that the nation's founders were dedicated to white rule, and that the Constitution should be understood as the source of white power. That ideology has long served as a powerful justification for violence. From its inception in 1866 until today, the Klan has described the violence it has perpetrated as patriotic in nature, undertaken not out of racial hatred but as necessary to defend the nation and the true meaning of the Constitution.[9] Declaring that whiteness is a foundational national principle embodied in the Constitution, the Klan has been able to find adherents in every era who consider racist violence to be acts of the highest patriotism.[10]

While the Klan has been nearly eliminated several times, it has arisen anew whenever white Americans have feared that their dominant status and power are threatened.[11] White dominance has been threatened in different ways in the four distinct eras of the Klan, but in every iteration the Klan has remained steadfast in asserting that, in its original and true meaning, the Constitution protects white rule:

- The first Klan era began during Reconstruction when the Klan was established to fight to preserve white power in the face of emancipation. In declaring that its mission was to "uphold and defend the Constitution of the United States as it was handed down by our forefathers in its original purity," the Klan expressed its dedication to the antebellum Constitution and opposition to the Civil War amendments.[12]
- The second Klan era began in 1915 when the Klan was revived to address the new threat to the power of white Protestants posed by the influx of Catholics, Jews, and other immigrants. The revived Klan asserted that only Anglo-Saxons are capable of appreciating the nation's constitutional values and that other people are dangerously ill-suited for self-government under the Constitution.[13]
- The third Klan era began in the 1950s when the Klan experienced another resurgence in response to the civil rights movement's fight against segregation.[14] The Klan argued that the civil rights movement was the pawn of international Communists, who sought to destroy the Constitution.[15]
- A fourth Klan era began in the wake of the defeat of legally imposed segregation when some white supremacists in the 1970s and 1980s—both within the Klan and outside the Klan—lost faith in the Constitution as a source of white power and began to argue that whites should seek to create a separate ethnic state.[16] The white supremacist movement today is composed of two principal factions: reactionary groups that seek to restore white rule within the existing constitutional framework, and revolutionary groups that seek to establish a separate white nation. Dedication to the Constitution represents the dividing line between the two factions.

As the history explored in this chapter reveals, the Klan's constitutional ideology has always drawn on mainstream American constitutional thought. From before the time of the nation's founding, many Americans considered liberty and self-government to be the unique products of a British heritage that other peoples did not and could not appreciate.[17] In the *Dred Scott* case, the Supreme Court endorsed what was then a widely held view that the Constitution was written by and for white people. The belief that the Constitution is dedicated to white rule persisted long after the Civil War, despite the adoption of the Fourteenth Amendment and the elevation of racial equality as a constitutional value.[18] In the 1920s, when the Klan campaigned that Jews and Catholics were unfit for the Constitution, a majority of the members of Congress agreed that the maintenance of constitutional government required maintaining the dominance of the nation's white ethnic stock. In the 1950s and 1960s, many mainstream white organizations agreed that the Constitution protects white rule.

The history of the Klan illustrates how constitutional rhetoric can advance a narrow conception of American identity. In each era, the Klan has sought to recruit and mobilize members by portraying threats to white power in nationalist terms, not merely as threats to their racial group but as attacks on the nation itself.[19] That appeal has succeeded because many whites consider themselves prototypically American and experience threats to their status as threats to the nation.[20] Mobilizing to protect this nationalist vision, Klan members have rallied around the Constitution, which Americans have long considered the supreme national symbol and embodiment of national values.[21] To those who think of the United States as a white nation, defending the Constitution means defending whiteness.

The First Klan and the Constitution: 1866–1877

The end of the Civil War in 1865 brought massive disruptions in the social structures of Southern life.[22] Slavery was abolished and African Americans became citizens.[23] After several states adopted Black Codes to restrict the freedom of African Americans, Congress responded by enacting the Reconstruction Acts of 1867, which imposed military control over the Southern states until they adopted new state constitutions that granted equality to Black citizens.[24] Congress also disbanded state militias made up primarily of former Confederate soldiers and authorized the creation of new state militias to enforce Reconstruction, many of which were composed of Black soldiers.[25] Congress created the Freedmen's Bureau to provide various forms of assistance to African Americans, including the creation of schools for Black children.[26] Under the control of the Republican Party, Southern states gave the vote to African American men, disenfranchised certain classes of former Confederates, and elected Black candidates to office.[27] With the ratification of the Fourteenth Amendment in 1868, legal equality for African Americans became enshrined in the Constitution.

Thus, within a remarkably short time, the structure of Southern society changed from one where white Southern men as a class had complete control over state and local governments as well as absolute control over the bodies and destinies of African Americans, to a society where African American men were granted political and legal equality, patrolled the states in armed militias, had the right to vote, and were elected to office, while some white men were disenfranchised. And all of these changes had been imposed by force against white Southerners as a result of the Confederacy's defeat.

Unwilling to accept their diminished status, white men across the South formed secret societies to resist Reconstruction.[28] Founders of these groups explained that they sought to address the "alarm" and "humiliation" white men experienced at the prospect of racial equality.[29] The first and most famous of these groups, the Ku Klux Klan, was formed in Pulaski, Tennessee, in May 1866 by six former Confederate Army officers.[30] Although originally organized as a social club, by early 1867 the group began to be involved in vigilante activities against African Americans and Republicans.[31] Inspired by the Klan's example, other groups calling themselves the Ku Klux Klan soon formed across the South, as did similar groups bearing other names— Knights of the White Camelia, the Invisible Empire, and the White Brotherhood—all of which should be understood to be part of the Klan movement, regardless of whether they used the Klan name.[32] These groups were widely recognized as the militant wing of the Democratic Party, fighting for political control of the South against the Republicans, the ruling party in Congress and in all the former Confederate states.[33]

Across the South, Klan groups perpetrated a massive wave of violence. The Klan typically employed violence during night-riding, in which small bands of hooded and robed members came unannounced to the houses of Black residents and accused them of various crimes. Klan violence often took the form of whipping and flogging but frequently also often involved branding, mutilating, shooting, hanging, and drowning. Klan-organized lynch mobs carried out vigilante justice. Although the Klan targeted any behavior that conflicted with white supremacy, the Klan principally targeted attempts by African Americans to participate in the political process. The Klan killed Black voters and assassinated elected Black officials, as well as white officials who supported Reconstruction. In addition to overt violence, the Klan sought to intimidate voters through demonstrations of force, such as by surrounding polling places with armed supporters. It targeted teachers at the newly formed Black schools.[34] By one estimate made in 1872, the Klan victimized more than 23,000 people from 1867 to 1872.[35] A later estimate puts the number killed by the Klan at 50,000.[36] Contemporary historians have largely abandoned the attempt to estimate the number of victims and simply say that there were many thousands.[37]

Klan organizations were largely eliminated before the end of Reconstruction.[38] In April 1871, Congress enacted the Ku Klux Klan Act, which authorized the president to suppress private insurrections and made it a federal crime to conspire to deprive anyone of civil rights.[39] In 1871 and 1872, the United States launched a vigorous campaign of enforcement of the act, which involved the arrest of over fifteen hundred Klansmen.[40] The enforcement effort succeeded in destroying the Klan as an effective organization, although the Klan persisted in a diminished capacity for decades.[41]

Despite the demise of the Klan, violent opposition to Reconstruction increased. Throughout the South, white rifle clubs were established to intimidate Black voters and to show resolve for the return of white rule.[42] In Mississippi and elsewhere, clubs calling themselves the White League were created to get rid of "all bad and leading negroes."[43] Armed groups of white southerners instructed black Mississippians that they would be shot if they attempted to vote. In 1875, a campaign of violence targeted rallies by the ruling Republican Party and shot black school teachers, church leaders, and Republican officials.

Supporters of the Democratic Party became emboldened when the federal government chose not to intervene to stop the violence. By the end of 1874, most states in the former Confederacy had returned to Democratic control, and by the end of 1877, all of the former Confederate states were under Democratic control.[44] That year also marked the end of federal occupation of the South and federal Reconstruction efforts.[45] Under the control of white conservatives, Southern states proceeded to institute a variety of mechanisms for disenfranchising African Americans and removing any semblance of equal treatment.[46] Vigilante violence had succeeded in ensuring white rule across the South.[47]

The Klan's Constitutional Mission

In the years from 1865 to 1877, the secret societies fighting for white rule went by many different names, but they used the same name for what they were fighting for: they called it the Constitution. The 1868 Prescript of the Ku Klux Klan, the organizing document of the Tennessee Klan, proclaimed that the organization was formed to "protect and defend the Constitution of the United States," and it required all new members to swear that they were "in favor of Constitutional liberty."[48] The South Carolina Klan likewise declared that members were "on the side of 'justice, humanity, and constitutional liberty as bequeathed to us in its purity by our forefathers.'"[49] All the groups comprising the Klan movement used similar language.[50]

Exactly what the Constitution meant to the Klan can be seen in the text of the 1868 Prescript; it required new members to declare that they were "in favor of a white man's government in this country" and "opposed to negro equality, both social and political." It also required new members to declare that they were "in favor of maintaining the Constitutional rights of the South," which meant that they were "in favor of the re-enfranchisement and emancipation of the white men of the South, and the restitution of the Southern people to all their rights, alike proprietary, civil, and political."[51] And it required new members to declare their entitlement to use violence if they believed they had been deprived of their constitutional rights.

Klan members declared their dedication to what they understood to be the principles of the Constitution as envisioned by the nation's founders and to reject the Reconstruction amendments that granted legal equality.[52] The Invisible Empire, a Klan group operating in North Carolina, required members to swear to "uphold and defend the Constitution of the United States as it was handed down by our forefathers in its original purity."[53] In testimony before Congress in 1871, Klan members repeatedly confirmed that the Klan's expressed dedication to the Constitution simply meant that "we were opposed to the amendments to the Constitution," as one Klan leader put it.[54] Or as another Klan member testified, the Klan was dedicated to the Constitution "as it was" and to reject the Constitution "as it is," which meant that Klan members were bound to fight for the "overthrow of the Republican party and injure it all they could."[55]

The Klan supported what its members frequently referred to as the "old Constitution," not the Constitution that they believed had been debased through the Reconstruction amendments that guaranteed racial equality and Black male suffrage. This can be seen in a newspaper interview given in 1868 by Nathan Bedford Forrest, the former Confederate general who became the Klan's first "grand wizard."[56] Forrest declared that the Klan was dedicated to protecting the original Constitution: "I loved the old government in 1861; I love the old Constitution yet. I think it the best government in the world if administered as it was before the war. I do not hate it; I am opposing now only the radical revolutionists who are trying to destroy it."[57]

In fighting for the "original" Constitution, the Klan frequently claimed that it remained true to the nation's Founding Fathers whereas its opponents had betrayed that legacy.[58] They considered themselves true patriots who were committed to what one Klan group called the "sacred prerogatives vouchsafed to us by the Constitution."[59] In declaring its dedication to the Constitution "as originally adopted by our fathers," the Klan declared it a foundational principle that "our Republic was established by white men, for white men alone and that it never was in the contemplation of its founders that it should fall into the hands of an inferior and degraded race."[60] Equal rights for African Americans, the Klan declared, betrayed the nation's founding principles.[61]

The Klan asserted that African Americans were incapable of participating in constitutional government. In the official script for initiating new members of one Klan group, the leader declared that only whites had the capacity to create and sustain advanced civilizations; members of other races "have remained in a state of complete barbarity."[62] The attempt to bestow equal citizenship on African Americans violated the nation's foundational principles: it amounted to "an invasion of the sacred prerogatives vouchsafed to us by the Constitution, and a violation of the laws established by God himself."[63]

The Klan's opponents understood exactly what its dedication to the Constitution meant. In 1871 the United States tried numerous Klan members in South Carolina for assaulting and murdering Black militia members.[64] One federal prosecutor pointed to the Klan's expressed dedication to the Constitution as proof that the Klan was dedicated to racist and antigovernment violence:

> Gentlemen, what does that mean—"constitutional liberty as bequeathed to us by our forefathers?" Let us dwell for a moment upon it. Our forefathers framed a Constitution which the Supreme Court of the United States has declared, over and over again, recognized slavery. . . . That Constitution, the Supreme Court of the United States said, meant this, that the black man had no rights that the white man was bound to respect. . . . That is what is meant in this first Section of the Ku Klux Constitution. It meant more; it meant that we stand upon the Constitution in that respect, *as it was*, not as *it is now*—not with the thirteenth, fourteenth and fifteenth amendments in it. . . . We trample upon these amendments of the Constitution, and we intend to destroy and defeat them. That is what this Ku Klux oath meant.[65]

As the prosecutor recognized, the Klan's dedication extended only to what it considered the pure, original Constitution, unsullied by the Civil War amendments.

The Klan was not alone in seeing the fight over Reconstruction as a fight over the Constitution. The Klan's chief rival was the Union League, also known as the Loyal League, which organized clubs throughout the South to promote equal citizenship and to recruit African Americans to the Republican cause.[66] Like the Klan, the Union League articulated its mission in constitutional terms, declaring that its object was "to preserve liberty and the Union of the United States of America; [and] to maintain the Constitution thereof and the supremacy of the laws."[67] Unlike the Klan, the Union League declared loyalty to the new constitutional values incorporated into the Fourteenth Amendment, its members pledging "to secure equal civil and political rights to all men under the Government."[68] Union League members pledged to seek the "complete ascendancy of the true principles of popular government—equal liberty, education and elevation of the workingmen of the nation, and the security of all by means of the elective franchise."[69]

The battle for Reconstruction thus pitted two different visions for the nation against each other, each expressed in constitutional terms. On the one hand, the Union League fought for a nation whose dedication to racial equality had recently been embraced though constitutional amendments. On the other hand, the Klan fought for the maintenance of white rule and the denial of equal rights, which the Klan understood to be supported by the Constitution "as originally adopted by our fathers."[70]

The Roots of the Klan's Constitutional Vision

When the Klan first formed in 1866, the belief that the Constitution protects white rule was far from radical. It had deep roots in American history going back to the nation's founding, and it remained a dominant belief in the South throughout the Reconstruction era.

Although the Constitution as originally adopted makes no mention of race, it contained several protections for the institution of slavery, including the Three-Fifths Clause, the Fugitive Slave Clause, and the Insurrection Clause.[71] From the time of the nation's founding, many Americans identified the values enshrined in the Constitution as the product of an English heritage that other peoples did not and could not appreciate.[72] Thomas Jefferson, for instance, appealed to Americans' "Saxon" heritage, which he declared established in Britain "that system of laws which has so long been the glory and protection of that country."[73] In *Federalist*, no. 2,

John Jay emphasized that the nation's foundational principles arose out of the people's common ethnic and religious heritage: "Providence has been pleased to give this one connected country to one united people—a people descended from the same ancestors, speaking the same language, professing the same religion, attached to the same principles of government, very similar in their manners and customs, and who, by their joint counsels, arms, and efforts, fighting side by side throughout a long and bloody war, have nobly established general liberty and independence."[74] While Jay was wrong in asserting that at the time of ratification the people of the United States shared a homogenous culture, *Federalist*, no. 2 makes clear that at least some of the Constitution's leading supporters connected the nation's foundational constitutional principles and its English and Protestant heritage.[75]

Soon after ratification, Congress directly connected race with the capacity to embrace the nation's constitutional values when it enacted the Naturalization Act of 1795, which provided that naturalized citizenship could only be bestowed upon someone who was both a "free white person" and "attached to the principles of the constitution of the United States."[76] As the Supreme Court later concluded in *Dred Scott v. Sanford*, when Congress limited citizenship to white people it merely "followed out the line of division which the Constitution has drawn between the citizen race, who formed and held the Government, and the African race, which they held in subjection and slavery, and governed at their own pleasure."[77]

To be sure, the connections between whiteness and membership in the American political community was hazy when the Constitution was ratified and for decades thereafter. Representative Charles Pinckney, one of the signers of the Constitution, declared in 1787 on the floor of the House that "there did not then exist such a thing in the Union as a black or colored citizen."[78] Yet citizenship and individual rights were largely determined by state law. Five states gave free Blacks the right to vote at the time the Constitution was adopted.[79] Federal treaties and statutes made some members of Indian tribes American citizens, thus allowing some nonwhites to become US citizens.[80] At the same time, many states imposed severe restrictions on nonwhite persons, and no state granted considered free Blacks to be entitled to the full panoply of rights of white persons. For instance, New Hampshire allowed only white persons to be part of the citizen's militia because Black persons were thought to play no part in state sovereignty and therefore could not be called up to defend the state.[81]

The Court's 1857 decision in the *Dred Scott* case represents the most emphatic endorsement of the view that the Constitution was made to protect white rule.[82] In *Dred Scott*, the Court addressed whether persons of African descent could be considered part of the American people under the Constitution: "The question is simply this," the Court asked. "Can a negro, whose ancestors were imported into this country, and sold as slaves, become a member of the political community formed and brought into existence by the Constitution of the United States, and as such become entitled to all the rights, and privileges, and immunities, guaranteed by that instrument to the citizen?"[83] The Court declared that the answer was definitively no.

The Supreme Court reviewed the nation's history and said that the statement in the Declaration of Independence that "all men are created equal" could only be read to refer to white men. It then catalogued various race-based laws existing at the time of the nation's founding and concluded that, for the generation that adopted the Constitution, "a perpetual and impassable barrier was intended to be erected between the white race and the one which they had reduced to slavery, and governed as subjects with absolute and despotic power." Because the Constitution had been adopted based on the view that enslaved Africans were not members of the national community, the Court declared that those of African descent could make no claims under the Constitution. The Constitution, the Court concluded, was made for white people alone.[84]

Dred Scott's rejection of citizenship and constitutional rights for African Americans represented a view that was widely shared by American leaders from all regions and across political parties.[85] Although *Dred Scott* provoked considerable controversy by limiting Congress's power to restrict slavery in federal territories, Democrats and Republicans, Northerners and Southerners, overwhelmingly agreed with its conclusions that the United States is a white nation and that the Constitution protects white rule. In his debates with Abraham Lincoln in the 1856 campaign for the Senate, Stephen Douglas, a Democratic leader, defended *Dred Scott* by saying that "this government was made by our fathers on the white basis. It was made by white men for the benefit of white men and their posterity forever, and was intended to be administered by white men in all time to come."[86] Lincoln disagreed with the Court on congressional power to restrict slavery in federal territories, but he explained he "never ha[d] complained *especially* of the Dred Scott decision because it held that a negro could not be a citizen." Asserting support for sending Africans back to Africa, Lincoln agreed with Douglas that persons of African descent were incapable of participating in American democracy and should not be made citizens or voters.[87]

The belief that the Constitution itself protects white rule became central to secessionist ideology, from which the Klan later emerged. Secessionists claimed that the South had remained true to the original meaning of the Constitution, while the North had betrayed the nation's founding principles.[88] Secessionists pointed to a variety of alleged constitutional offenses committed by the Northern states and the federal government—such as obstacles imposed to the enforcement of the Fugitive Slave Act and attempts to exclude slavery from federal territories—and asserted that these actions betrayed the Constitution.[89] Secessionists frequently compared themselves to the nation's Founding Fathers, casting the free states, abolitionists, Republicans, and the federal government as latter-day King Georges.[90] In the South's view, the North's betrayals of the Constitution amounted to tyranny that justified secession and, ultimately, violence against the federal government.

Supported by *Dred Scott* and the nation's history of denying political rights to persons of color, whether free or enslaved, secessionists asserted that the Constitution established white rule as a foundational principle. This principle most centrally protected the power of whites to rule over Africans held in bondage.[91] Southern states charged that Northern states had betrayed the core meaning of the Constitution by allowing the formation of abolition societies, which, in the words of Texas's declaration of secession, advocated "the debasing doctrine of equality of all men, irrespective of race or color—a doctrine at war with nature, in opposition to the experience of mankind, and in violation of the plainest revelations of Divine Law."[92] The seceding states charged that free states had further sought to subvert the Constitution by bestowing citizenship and voting rights on African Americans, persons who, in the words of South Carolina's declaration, "are incapable of becoming citizens" under the Constitution.[93]

The debates over secession show that Southerners overwhelmingly considered whiteness and white power to be central to national identity. In its statement of secession, Texas declared that the states and the national government were "established exclusively by the white race, for themselves and their posterity; that the African race had no agency in their establishment; that they were rightfully held and regarded as an inferior and dependent race, and in that condition only could their existence in this country be rendered beneficial or tolerable."[94] Thomas Cobb, in his speech before the Georgia convention on secession (a speech that was called "probably the most powerful speech made in favor of Georgia's withdrawal from the Union"), made the same point in constitutional terms: "This Constitution was made for white men—citizens of the United

States; this Union was formed by white men, and for the protection and happiness of their race."[95]

The Mainstream Nature of the Klan's Constitutional Ideology

The Klan's constitutional ideology, which placed whiteness at the core of American identity, was nothing more than the continuation of the ideology that had prevailed in the South before the Civil War. Like secessionists, the Klan argued that the principle of white rule lay at the heart of the constitutional order, that the Union had betrayed that principle, and that the betrayal justified violence in defense of the true meaning of the Constitution.[96]

The belief that white rule was a foundational constitutional value represented mainstream thought in the postwar South. Testifying before Congress, David Schenck, leader of the North Carolina Klan, declared that the Klan's mission was simply a restatement of "the democratic platform of 1868, the platform upon which Seymour and Blair were running."[97] Schenck apparently intended to convey the message that the Klan should not be seen as a radical organization because its views were identical to the Democratic Party's. In this, Schenck was undoubtedly correct.

The constitutional ideology articulated by the Democratic Party in the 1868 campaign was the same as the Klan's. The Democratic candidates for president and vice president, Horatio Seymour and Francis Blair, relied heavily on constitutional rhetoric in making explicit appeals to white supremacy. Declaring that Republican rule was imposing "unparalleled oppression and tyranny" upon the South, the platform denounced Reconstruction as an effort to disenfranchise whites and establish "negro supremacy" and declared Reconstruction a "usurpation, and unconstitutional, revolutionary, and void." If Republicans prevailed in the election, the platform warned, the Constitution would be lost: "we will meet, as a subjected and conquered people, amid the ruins of liberty and the scattered fragments of the Constitution."[98]

The Democratic campaign of 1868 explicitly connected white supremacy with fidelity to the Constitution. The campaign employed the slogan, "This Is a White Man's Country; Let White Men Rule."[99] It issued a campaign coin, a common campaign item in those days, with the face of presidential candidate Horatio Seymour on one side and on the other a summary of the campaign platform: "The Restoration of Constitutional Liberty: White Men to Govern."[100] The campaign also adopted a campaign song, "The White

Campaign coin for 1868 Democratic Party presidential candidate Horatio Seymour. ©Amos Media Company/Coin World; used with permission.

Man's Banner," which asked voters to stay true to the Founding Fathers by preserving white rule: "Let, then, all free-born patriots/Join, with a brave intent/To vindicate our Father's choice: 'A white man's Government.'"[101] During the campaign, vice presidential candidate Francis Blair argued that Reconstruction denied whites their right to rule, which he said was "to strip the white race of their birthright."[102]

The results of the 1868 election reveal that the ideology advocated by the Democratic Party and the Klan continued to have widespread appeal among Southern white voters: although Republican Ulysses Grant handily won the Electoral College vote 214 to 80, Seymour received over 47 percent of the national popular vote, including more than 70 percent of the votes in Kentucky and Louisiana and over 60 percent in Georgia and Maryland.[103] Seymour probably won the majority of the white vote nationally and might well have won the election if many former Confederates had not been disfranchised and if the states of Virginia and Texas had been allowed to participate in the election.[104]

"Forced by Force to Use Force": The Constitution as Justification for the Klan's Violence

Through violence, the Klan put its mission of restoring white rule into action.[105] The Klan's official documents make clear that the organization

Sheet music for "The White Man's Banner," Horatio
Seymour and Francis Blair's 1868 presidential campaign
song. Library of Congress, Prints & Photographs
Division, LC-USZ62-89310.

drew a direct connection between the Constitution and violence. The North
Carolina Klan declared its constitutional mission and told its members
exactly how to carry out that mission: "each member shall provide himself
with a pistol, Ku-Klux gown, and signal instruments."[106] A South Carolina
Klan group, which described its mission as "the restoration of constitutional

liberty, as taught by our forefathers," similarly declared that it would pursue that mission both through political methods and through methods that were "physical, according to the recognized principles of the law of self-defense."[107]

Although it is impossible to assess what role defending the Constitution played in Klan members' subjective motivations to use violence, what can be shown is that Klan members frequently pointed to the Constitution to explain and justify their actions. In the trial of South Carolina Klan members charged with anti-Black violence, one Klan member was directed to the Klan's oath to defend "constitutional liberty, as bequeathed to us in its purity by our forefathers," and was asked how this purpose was to be carried out.[108] He answered simply: "Well sir, generally, whipping those men who belonged to the [Union] League," the club that recruited African Americans to vote for Republican candidates.[109] Another witness testified that the Klan's method of protecting the Constitution, as he understood it, was carried out by preventing African Americans from voting.[110] In testimony before Congress in 1871, Klan members were asked what the goals of the organization were, and Klan members consistently answered that the Klan's mission was to defend the original meaning of the Constitution and preserve white rule; when asked how the Klan pursued its goals, Klan members pointed to beatings, whippings, and murders.[111]

In some instances, Klan members identified the Constitution as the reason for their actions during the acts of violence themselves. A white Republican state legislator in North Carolina testified that when Klansmen kidnapped him and threatened to kill him, they asked "if I did not know that the Constitution, as they had it before the negroes were free, was better."[112] Klan members told him, "We are going to break up that damned, infamous thing [the amended Constitution], and we are going to kill all men like you who advocate and support any such Government or Constitution."[113] The Klan spared his life only after he promised to support the "Southern cause" and to oppose Black suffrage.[114]

Consistent with its view that it was defending the Constitution, the Klan justified violence against African Americans and Republicans as acts of self-defense.[115] The Klan's 1868 Prescript, for instance, required that all new members affirm their belief in "the inalienable right of self-preservation of the people against the exercise of arbitrary and unlicensed power."[116] Klan members frequently declared that violence to support white rule amounted to self-defense. For instance, in 1871, after Klan members killed several Black militiamen, they posted a public notice that declared: "Once again have we been forced by force to use Force."[117]

Like many others, Klan members considered Reconstruction to be an attack on the constitutional rights of white Southerners. Throughout the South, one witness testified before Congress in 1871, Reconstruction "was denounced as a tyrannical usurpation, the government as a usurped negro government, and every officer as a mean, tyrannical usurper."[118] In the face of such supposed tyranny, Klan members asserted not only a right but a duty to defend themselves. As one Klan group asserted: "It . . . becomes our solemn duty, as white men, to resist strenuously and persistently those attempts against our natural and constitutional rights, and to do everything in our power in order to maintain, in this republic, the supremacy of the Caucasian race and restrain the black or African race to that condition of social and political inferiority for which God has destined it."[119]

Although the Klan committed widespread violence to prevent the enforcement of the Constitution and the Reconstruction Acts, Klan groups uniformly described themselves as a force for law and order, dedicated to defending the Constitution and federal law.[120] Klan members saw no contradiction between the rhetoric of law and order and the use of extra-legal violence because they believed that the federal government was acting to oppress the white people of the South, in violation of the nation's founding principles.[121] In the Klan's conception, violence to restore white rule was not contrary to law but was necessary to defend it.

The Demise of the Klan and the Birth of the Klan Legend

Vigilante activity to protect white rule became unnecessary with the end of Reconstruction and the restoration of Southern state governments committed to white rule.[122] Although the Klan and similar groups largely disappeared by 1877, in the ensuing decades the story of the Ku Klux Klan developed into a legend that continues to inspire new Klan recruits. The legend involves heroic white Southerners who banded together to protect American civilization against Radical Republican oppression, government corruption, and rule by buffoonish freedmen. The Constitution features prominently in the legend: the Klan saved it.

The legend began to take shape in 1884, when John C. Lester and Daniel L. Wilson published *Ku Klux Klan: Its Origin, Growth, and Disbandment,* the first account of the Klan written by one of the group's founders.[123] Lester and Wilson declared that the Klan had performed "immense service" to the South by overthrowing political control by African Americans, who not only were unfit to rule over whites but were "not fitted for the cares of self-control." Without the Klan, Lester and Wilson declared, "in many sections of the South, life to decent people would not have been tolerable." Lester and Wilson offered particularly strong praise for the Klan's dedication to the Constitution, which they said demonstrated the group's patriotism.[124]

Within a generation, a consensus developed among historians that Klan violence had been necessary for Southern "redemption."[125] The legend that the Klan had saved the South from tyranny by blacks and carpetbaggers entered popular culture in the novels of Thomas F. Dixon, including *The Clansman: An Historical Romance of the Ku Klux Klan*, published in 1905.[126] "The truth of history," Dixon declared, "is, that, as originally organized and led, the Ku Klux Klan was the guardian of civilization in the South."[127] Dixon's novels depict the Klan's fight for white supremacy as a fight for the Constitution and American ideals. The protagonist in one novel articulates what Dixon understood to be the Klan's ideology: "We believe that God has raised up our race, as he ordained Israel of old, in this world-crisis to establish and maintain for weaker races, as a trust for civilisation, the principles of civil and religious Liberty and the forms of Constitutional Government."[128] In contrast, the novels depict the Klan's opponents to be dedicated to destroying the Constitution. "The Constitution be damned!," thunders August Stoneman, a thinly veiled fictionalization of Republican Congressman Thaddeus Stevens, who works to empower freedmen and disenfranchise whites without any concern that he was betraying the nation's fundamental principles.[129]

In 1915, D. W. Griffith made *The Clansman* into a movie, *The Birth of a Nation*.[130] The film depicts Reconstruction as a time when the South was ruled by incompetent and corrupt Black politicians, when Black troops humiliated white Southerners, and Black men threatened to rape white women.[131] Restoring order, the Klan is described on one of the film's cue cards as "the organization that saved the South from the anarchy of black rule."[132] *The Birth of a Nation* became one of the most successful and notorious films of all time.[133] After President Woodrow Wilson arranged for a screening of the film at the White House, he reportedly said that it is "like writing history with lighting. My only regret is that it is all so terribly true."[134]

Although it is unclear if Wilson uttered these precise words, the legend had taken hold in the American imagination that through terrorism and violence the Klan had preserved white rule and thereby preserved constitutional government.[135]

The Second Klan and the Constitution: 1915–1944

With the legend of the Ku Klux Klan established in American popular imagination through historical accounts, Dixon's novels, and Griffith's film, it was perhaps inevitable that the Klan name would be revived when a new call was made to protect white power. That is just what happened on the evening of Thanksgiving, November 25, 1915, when William Joseph Simmons and fifteen other men in white robes and hoods climbed to the top of Stone Mountain outside Atlanta, Georgia, burned a giant wooden cross that was visible for miles around, and proclaimed the rebirth of the Ku Klux Klan.[136] Simmons declared himself the Klan's new "imperial wizard." Although he claimed that the new Klan would carry on the traditions of the original Klan, in fact, the costumes and rituals of the new Klan were largely modeled on Griffith's film.[137] Cross-burning, for instance, had played no part in the original Klan, but Dixon had put it in *The Clansman* and Griffith used it in *The Birth of a Nation*, and, life imitating art, it became the central ritual of the new Klan.[138]

It was not merely the success of *The Birth of a Nation* that made it an auspicious time to restart the Klan. The new Klan arose at a time of rapid social and demographic changes in the United States. From 1880 to 1920, more than twenty million immigrants came to the United States, and the percentage of US residents who were foreign-born rose to nearly 15 percent.[139] While most previous immigrants had been Protestants from England, Ireland, and Germany, most of the new immigrants were Catholics and Jews from southern and eastern Europe.[140] During this period, the United States was also experiencing rapid urbanization, and by 1920, for the first time, a majority of Americans lived in cities, which became more ethnically diverse through both immigration and the migration of African Americans from the South.[141] At the same time, numerous social movements divided the nation, including the labor movement, the suffrage movement, and the temperance movement.[142]

Many native-born white Americans viewed these developments with alarm. They believed that the new immigrants brought crime, disease, and poverty, and spread dangerously foreign ideas.[143] They saw cities as hotbeds of sin, corruption, and drunkenness.[144] They considered the labor movement to be dangerous and radical.[145] They saw women's suffrage as a danger to traditional morality.[146] All of these changes—the increasing power of new ethnic groups, the shifting center of power to cities, the increasing power of women—threatened the role of white Protestant men as the dominant force in American culture and politics.

The second Klan emerged to give voice to the fears of white Protestants who felt their status threatened.[147] Hiram Evans, who took over the national operations of the Klan in 1922, declared that the Klan spoke for them: "It gives expression, direction, and purpose to the most vital instincts, hopes and resentments of the old stock Americans, provides them with leadership, and is enlisting and preparing them for militant, constructive action toward fulfilling their racial and national destiny."[148] According to Evans, white Protestants needed to organize because they had become strangers in the land of their fathers, even "a most unwelcome stranger, one much spit upon."[149] The Klan appealed to Americans who felt disdain for immigrants, Jews, Catholics, and African Americans—groups that Klan members considered below them.[150] At the same time, the Klan expressed resentment for political and social elites, who they accused of profiting from immigrant labor and who they believed looked down on regular Americans as "'hicks' and 'rubes' and 'drivers of second hand Fords.'"[151] The Klan spoke for "the plain people," Evans said, the "everyday people," the "salt of the earth," who demanded "a return of power into the hands of the everyday, not highly cultured, not overly intellectualized, but entirely unspoiled and not de-Americanized, average citizen of the old stock."[152]

Within a decade, the new Klan became one of the nation's largest organizations. By 1925 it had between three and five million members, roughly the same number of members as the American Federation of Labor. Unlike the original Klan, the second Klan was a national organization, with strong support in the Midwest and Northwest as well as the South. Klan chapters could be found in Los Angeles, New York City, and Washington, DC, as well as at Harvard, Princeton, and Yale.[153]

Whereas the original Klan had sought to operate in secret, the second Klan sought to participate in national and local politics. It threw its support behind candidates for office that it deemed "100 percent American."[154] In 1922, Atlanta elected a Klansman to be mayor, and Texas elected a Klansman to be senator. Klan support was crucial in the selection of the governor of Oregon and the impeachment of the governor of Oklahoma. In addition to helping elect "100% Americans," the Klan campaigned both nationally and locally for issues that it considered important to white Protestant Americans, most importantly immigration restrictions and opposition to Catholic schools.[155]

Although Klan leaders consistently denied that the organization was involved in crime, the second Klan left behind a substantial record of violence and intimidation. Klansmen were involved in lynchings, floggings, beatings, and murder.[156] The Klan held cross burnings and parades of hooded members that sought to intimidate and terrorize their opponents.[157] They targeted Blacks who they alleged to have harassed, flirted with, or merely looked at white women.[158] They targeted Jews, Catholics, and labor organizers, as well as white Protestants who failed to live up to the Klan's notions of Christian morality.[159] Few of these crimes were ever punished.[160]

The Second Klan's Constitutional Mission

Like the first Klan, the second Klan considered threats to white supremacy to be tantamount to attacks on the nation itself, and it expressed its defense of white power in patriotic terms, declaring that it was dedicated to the "sublime principles of a pure Americanism."[161] And like the first Klan, the second Klan articulated its patriotic mission as a defense of the true meaning of the Constitution. The Klan initiation ritual continued to require new members to swear to protect and defend the Constitution, and the Klan's organizational documents identified the preservation of the Constitution as a central mission.[162] Called to testify before Congress to defend the Klan against the charge that it was a subversive organization, William Simmons, the founder of the second Klan, declared that the Klan was a patriotic organization "founded on the bedrock principles of the Constitution of the United States."[163]

The Klan's constitutional devotion was commemorated in the 1923 song "We Are All Loyal Klansmen," in which Klan members sang of their commitment to the Constitution:

> We are all loyal klansmen,
> And klanish as can be.
> We love our home, this country,
> And its flag of liberty.
> Its constitution handed down,
> Approved by Uncle Sam,
> Will always be defended
> By the Ku Klux Klan.[164]

Unlike the first Klan, which focused solely on white rule, the second Klan focused on preserving what it understood to be the Protestant nature

Sheet music for "We Are All Loyal Klansmen," by William Davis, William M. Hart, Charles E. Downey, and E. M. McMahon, 1923.

of the United States. For the second Klan, the dual pillars of Americanism were the Constitution and the Bible. The Klan frequently declared that Christian values and constitutional values were one and the same.[165] As Imperial Wizard Simmons put it, "our patriotic principles and Christianity are inseparable and indivisible," and therefore Klan members "hold steadfastly to the Constitution and the Sermon on the Mount."[166] The Bible, the Klan asserted, was "the basis of our Constitution, the foundation of our government, the source of our laws, [and] the sheet-anchor of our liberties."[167]

The second Klan expressed an understanding of the Constitution that in many ways was conventional at the time and remains conventional today. The Klan pointed to a number of constitutional principles that it said expressed foundational American values.[168] In a Fourth of July 1923 address entitled "Back to the Constitution" and delivered before thousands of supporters, Grand Dragon D. C. Stephenson explained that the nation's central constitutional principle is self-government, which he said was also the principle that the Klan was fighting to protect.[169] Hiram Evans, the national Klan leader, identified a longer list of core constitutional principles, which included "democracy, fairdealing, impartial justice, equal opportunity, religious liberty, independence, self-reliance, courage, endurance, [and] acceptance of individual responsibility."[170] Similar lists of the nation's core principles continue to be identified today as defining the American Creed.[171]

What made the second Klan's constitutional ideology distinctive was the assertion that the nation's constitutional principles were uniquely the product of white culture and could only truly be embraced by white Protestants. As one Klan pamphlet put it:

The Declaration of Independence, the Constitution, and the Gettysburg Address are descendants of the Magna Charta—supreme symbols of Anglo-Saxon souls striving for freedom, justice, and humanity. Anglo-Saxons established this Nation, wrote its code, and sent their sons into the wilderness to gather fresh stars for the flag. . . . The making of America is fundamentally an Anglo-Saxon achievement. Anglo-Saxons brains have guided the course of the Republic. Our ideals are Anglo-Saxon, our social traditions, our standards of honor, our quality of imagination, and our indomitability.[172]

According to second Klan founder Simmons, white people—or more specifically, whites referred to as "Anglo-Saxons" or "Nordics"—had evolved over thousands of years to embrace the values that they placed in the

Constitution, and they alone had developed the capacity for constitutional self-government.[173]

The science of eugenics (discussed in greater length in chapter 3) provided support for the Klan's claims. Eugenics taught that not only were criminality and laziness inherited traits, so was the ability to embrace America's constitutional principles.[174] In 1916, Madison Grant published the enormously influential *The Passing of the Great Race*, which argued that race was the single explanation for the development of European and American civilization.[175] Grant asserted that America's constitutional principles were the products of what he called the Nordic race.[176] Clinton Stoddard Burr, one of Grant's disciples, wrote: "Americanism is actually the racial thought of the Nordic race, evolved after a thousand years of experience, which includes such epoch-making documents as the Magna Charta and the Declaration of Independence."[177]

In the Klan's ideology, only "pure Americans" could ever truly embrace "the sublime principles of a pure Americanism."[178] Not all men were capable of reaching "the true value of American citizenship."[179] In particular, African Americans could never "attain the Anglo-Saxon level."[180] For Jews, Evans explained, "patriotism, as the Anglo-Saxon feels it, is impossible. . . . Not in a thousand years of continuous residence would he form basic attachments comparable to those the older type of immigrant would form within year."[181]

The second Klan was especially focused on fighting Catholic influence. The Klan argued that Congress should restrict Catholic immigration because Catholics could not embrace the nation's constitutional values. Simmons wrote that the Constitution could be saved only if immigration by non–Anglo Saxons was stopped and the nation returned to being "a homogeneous English-speaking nation. . . . Such a nation will develop according to our Anglo-Saxon methods of free speech, free press, democratic methods and popular respect for the law."[182] In addition to fighting to stop new Catholic immigration, the Klan sought to prevent Catholics who had already immigrated from participating in American democracy because assertedly they would always remain loyal to the Catholic Church and not the nation.[183] Simmons and other Klan leaders accused the Catholic Church of directing Catholic citizens to engage in bloc voting, which they claimed violated the constitutional separation of church and state.[184] The Klan fought to close Catholic schools, which it accused of undermining American values by teaching students to be loyal to the church rather than the nation.[185]

The role of the Constitution in the second Klan's ideology is nicely captured in Branford Clarke's cartoon "Ringing the Liberty Bell," published in 1926. The cartoon depicts an endless sea of hooded and robed Klan members who watch as one Klansman rings the Liberty Bell. To get leverage, the Klansman steps on the Pope's tiara, symbolizing the need to stomp out the evil influence of Catholicism. Patriotic symbols abound. One Klansman holds a giant American flag. George Washington watches approvingly from the sky. The upper corners of the image contain the dual pillars of Klan ideology—on the right, a burning cross, and on the left, the Constitution, together embodying the principles of Americanism.[186] As the cartoon illustrates, the Klan understood its fight against Catholics and other supposedly alien peoples as a patriotic fight for American traditions, for Christianity, and for the Constitution.

Leading Jews, Catholics, and African Americans spoke out against the Klan and offered a more pluralist constitutional vision. Rabbi Joseph Silverman disputed the Klan's claim that the Constitution's invocation of "We the People" referred solely to white, native-born Protestants: "Catholic, Jewish, Negro and atheistic or non-religious citizens are also true Americans—as genuine Americans as the Klansmen claim to be."[187] Silverman charged that the Klan was engaged in nothing less than "guerrilla warfare against the Constitution."[188] James Weldon Johnson, the executive director of the National Association for the Advancement of Colored People (NAACP), argued that American culture, including its political culture, was "the product of fertilization of different races and bloods, different kinds of civilization, brought together through commerce, race mixture, the arts." [189] And Catholic Bishop Joseph Schrembs articulated what in a later generation would become the mainstream view: "We are the blend of all the peoples of the world, and I think we are much the better for that. Americanism is not a matter of birth, Americanism is a matter of faith, of consecration to the ideals of America."[190]

Despite this opposition, the Klan achieved considerable success in its anti-Catholic campaigns. In Oregon, the Klan spearheaded a state referendum that made it a crime to send children to Catholic schools. Supporters of the law asserted that Catholic schools were undermining Americanism and indoctrinating children in communism. As the state later argued in support of the law, if Catholic schools were allowed to proliferate, "it is not only a possibility but almost a certainty that within a few years the great centers of population in our country will be dotted with elementary schools which instead of being red on the outside will be red on the inside."[191] Closing

Catholic schools was necessary, the Klan asserted, to protect the nation's constitutional values. As supporters of the law asserted, "We must now halt those coming to our country from forming groups, establishing schools, and thereby bringing up their children in an environment often antagonistic to the principles of our government."[192] Although the Klan hoped that the Oregon law would be the model for closing Catholic schools in other states, the Supreme Court found Oregon's law unconstitutional, ruling in *Pierce v. Society of Sisters* that the Constitution protects the right of parents to decide how to educate their children, a right that includes the choice to send their children to religious schools.[193]

The campaign to limit Catholic immigration showed greater success. As discussed in chapter 3, in 1924 Congress enacted the National Origins Act, which greatly limited immigration from southern and eastern Europe. In doing so, members of Congress made no secret that the act was intended to maintain white rule—specifically, control by what the law's supporters referred to as the "Nordic" and Anglo-Saxon subcategories of the white race.[194] Members of Congress openly claimed that Asian, Jewish, Italian, and other immigrants must be excluded from immigration precisely because they could never embrace the nation's constitutional values.[195] To protect the Constitution, Congress declared, the nation must stay white.

Although it is not entirely clear how much influence Klan support made in the passage of the National Origins Act, the Klan immediately took credit for it. As a Klan newspaper declared:

> If the flow of foreigners in this country had not been checked, it would have been but a short time until they would have made of America a country far different from the ideals on which it was founded. The Klan has taken the lead in teaching and expounding the ideals of true Americanism, and to it is due most of the credit for warning and protecting the country from the alien hordes that have threatened to overrun it.[196]

By keeping out unwanted foreigners, the Klan declared, it had saved the nation's founding ideals.

The Constitution as Justification for the Second Klan's Violence

Although the Klan has always used violence to put its ideology into action, the second Klan period presents a challenge in examining the Klan's justifications for violence because its official publications of the period uniformly denounce violence. Unlike other Klan periods, Klan members of the 1920s offered few full-throated justifications for violence. In fact, Imperial Wizard Simmons declared that he "vigorously denied that a single crime had ever been committed by the authority of the Knights of the Ku Klux Klan."[197]

Nonetheless it is apparent that the Constitution continued to play a central role in the Klan's justification for violence. Klan literature of the period strongly suggests that violence is justified to protect white rule and thereby preserve American values. For instance, one Klan publication declared that because white supremacy is a "sacred constitutional prerogative," any effort to undermine it "must be resisted": "Every effort to wrest from the White Race the management of its affairs in order to transfer it to the control of blacks or any other color, or to permit them to share in its control, is an invasion of our sacred constitutional prerogatives and a violation of divinely established laws. Every effort to wrest from the White People the control of this country must be resisted."[198] Although the statement does not expressly call for violence as a form of resistance, the Klan clearly believed that militant action was needed to protect the "sacred constitutional" right for whites to rule.[199]

Without publicly calling on white Americans to use violence, Imperial Wizard Simmons asked white Americans to heed the "imperative call of higher justice" and to act to "keep Anglo-Saxon American civilization, institutions, politics and society pure."[200] As this suggests, the Klan's claim that white supremacy is of constitutional status—that it had a claim of "higher justice" than ordinary law—powerfully served to justify violence. Articulating white supremacy in constitutional terms, the Klan presented its mission as a patriotic defense of the nation, a cause for which killing and dying are understood to be justified.[201]

During the second Klan period, the Klan acknowledged only one instance in which it was involved in violence—the notorious massacre of African Americans in Ocoee, Florida, on election day, November 2, 1920—and the Klan's justification sheds light on how the movement understood extralegal violence to be a heroic force for law and order.[202] As detailed by contemporary historian Paul Ortiz, the violence in Ocoee arose in response to a statewide drive to register Black voters conducted in the spring and summer of 1920 and supported by the NAACP and the Republican Party.[203] Klan chapters throughout Florida organized to stop Blacks from voting. In Miami, the Klan posted signs to warn African Americans that voting could cost their lives: "Beware! The Ku Klux Klan is again alive! And every Negro who approaches a polling place next Tuesday will be a marked man. This is a white man's country, boys, save your own life next Tuesday." The Klan demanded that Republican officials halt efforts to register Black voters: "We shall always enjoy WHITE SUPREMACY in this country and he who interferes must face the consequences." Three weeks before election day, the Klan issued a specific warning to the Black residents of Ocoee, Florida, that "not a single Negro would be permitted to vote." A few days before the election, Klan members marched in full regalia in nearby Orlando.[204]

On Election Day, bands of Klansmen drove between polling places and attacked African Americans waiting to vote. One of those waiting to vote in Ocoee was Mose Norman, who had been turned away even though he was lawfully registered. Norman fled the white mob and took refuge at the house of July Perry, an African American farmer. The Klan mob arrived at Perry's house and broke the door down, and Perry shot and killed one of the white attackers. After news of the shooting reached Orlando, carloads of armed white men rushed to Perry's house. The mob captured Perry and lynched him, then left his body hanging from a telephone pole. Unable to find Norman, the mob descended on the nearby Black neighborhood, indiscriminately shooting residents and burning down their houses.[205] The number of people killed in the massacre is unknown—white officials claimed that there were as few as ten, but an investigation by the NAACP estimated that between thirty and sixty African Americans were killed, as were two Klan members.[206] In the days following the massacre, whites threatened that if the remaining Black population of Ocoee refused to sell their property and leave, they too would be shot and burned. In the aftermath, the entire Black population fled, and no African Americans lived in Ocoee for fifty years.[207]

The Klan told a very different version of these events. Imperial Wizard Simmons conceded that Klan members had been involved in violence in Ocoee, but he claimed that Klan members had been the heroic defenders of law and order. Simmons claimed that the riot arose after "one or more Negroes, disqualified by law from voting, were nevertheless demanding that they be permitted to vote." In Simmons's telling, Blacks began to riot and instigated a fight with a group of whites unaffiliated with the Klan, who proceeded to march on the Black neighborhood.[208] Only then, Simmons claimed, did Klan members become involved, and they acted solely to protect law and order, placing "their services at the disposal of the officers of the law." Simmons described the Klansmen as acting with great heroism, succeeding in driving back the white mob, and two Klansmen "lost their lives in defense of the law and while protecting the Negroes of their town."[209]

In the Klan's story, violence erupted when African Americans transgressed the natural and legal order by demanding to vote in violation of the law, and the Klan served to enforce the law, quelling violence, while also protecting constitutionally mandated racial hierarchy. As this story suggests, the Klan understood its violence—terrorism and murder to preserve white supremacy—to be defensive in nature, done in heroic service to the cause of law and order.

The Demise of the Second Klan

As quickly as the second Klan came to national prominence, the movement collapsed. Reborn in 1915, Klan membership dropped precipitously by 1926, and by the end of the 1920s the Klan movement was all but dead.[210] Much diminished in size, the Klan continued to maintain chapters in several states until 1944, when the federal government filed a lien for back taxes and, with no funds to pay the bill, the Klan officially disbanded.[211]

Historians have attributed the collapse of the Klan to poor organization and to the absence of a positive agenda to sustain the movement.[212] The Klan also lost considerable support after it was beset by scandals involving drunken sexual violence by Klan leaders, including the conviction of D. C. Stephenson, the grand dragon of Indiana, for abduction and murder.[213]

The Klan itself, however, offered a different explanation for its diminished role: it had succeeded in protecting Americanism and maintaining the dominance of white Protestants. Imperial Wizard Hiram Evans declared that the Klan had played a pivotal role in the passage of the National Origins Act, had helped elect "100% Americans" from coast to coast, and had turned back the tide of dangerous alien influences.[214] With the election of officials who supported white Protestant rule and the adoption of a national immigration policy designed to keep out dangerous aliens, Evans declared, the Klan's mission had been accomplished.[215]

Later eras of the Klan have looked back on the 1920s as the Klan's second great triumph, when the Klan succeeded again in protecting white rule. In the 1960s the Klan put out flyers for new members that declared that "the KKK has twice saved this nation from destruction, as history clearly records."[216] The first Klan saved the nation from the threat posed by the emancipation, and the second Klan saved the nation from the threat posed by immigration. Later Klan eras declared that they too would remain forever vigilant to protect America and the Constitution against any new threats to white power.

The Third Klan and the Constitution: 1944 to 1971

After the national Ku Klux Klan organization disbanded in 1944, the Klan became a decentralized organization, with many competing groups calling themselves the Klan.[217] In general, Klan groups shifted focus from fighting Catholics and immigration to fighting communism.[218] The Klan experienced a third burst of life in the 1950s and 1960s, however, when white Southerners faced a new threat to their status and power. This time the threat came from the civil rights movement, which sought to end race discrimination in education, employment, housing, and voting. The Klan declared the civil rights movement an alien force that sought to destroy the nation by destroying the Constitution. While other organizations vowed to defend segregation through lawful means, the Klan proclaimed the duty of white Americans to kill and die in the name of the Constitution.[219]

The Klan geared up to defend segregation long before other Southerners recognized the threat. In 1951, three years before the Supreme Court's decision in *Brown v. Board of Education*, Grand Dragon Thomas Hamilton of the Carolina Klansmen promised during a Klan rally, "No, nigras will never enter a white school as long as the Klan exists. And I don't care what the Supreme Court does about it, blood will flow in the streets of that state before that happens."[220]

After *Brown*, white Southerners rallied to defend segregation, and the Klan was one voice in an essentially unified white coalition. This coalition included nearly the entirety of the Southern congressional delegation, which issued a resolution that condemned the *Brown* decision as a violation of the nation's constitutional heritage and called on state and local governments "to resist forced integration by any lawful means."[221] Taking up the suggestion, Southern governors, legislatures, city councils, and school boards adopted numerous obstacles to school desegregation.[222]

White Citizens' Councils positioned themselves as the leading segregationist voice of the political and business establishment.[223] The first such council was founded in Mississippi less than two months after *Brown*.[224] Within four years, councils across the South claimed to have 500,000 members.[225] The councils deliberately sought to distance themselves from the Klan, explaining that, unlike the Klan, the White Citizens' Councils were comprised of "high-principled community leaders" who were "among America's finest citizens," while the Klan appealed to "ruffian whites who may resort to violence."[226]

Like the White Citizens' Councils, Klan membership swelled after *Brown*, although precise numbers remain uncertain.[227] After 1944 membership had dwindled to perhaps a few thousand, but by 1964 Klan chapters had between 40,000 and 50,000 members, and perhaps many more.[228] The Klan positioned itself as the most militant group fighting to preserve white rule. It declared that other groups were merely talking but it alone was taking action: "We will fight with every means at our disposal—the ballot box, in the swamps, or in the hills if necessary, for we shall never surrender."[229] The Klan was the only group defending segregation that openly advocated violence. "If it takes buckshot to keep the black race down, Klansmen will use it," declared Wild Bill Davidson, head of the US Klans, one of the largest Klan organizations of the civil rights era.[230]

The Klan was true to its word. It engaged in a wave of violence intended to terrorize anyone perceived as supporting civil rights. In the first four years after *Brown*, the Klan was involved in at least 530 cases of overt racial violence, including at least six murders, twenty-nine shootings, forty-four beatings, five stabbings, thirty home bombings, eight home burnings, four school bombings, seven church bombings, and four synagogue bombings.[231] The Klan increased its campaign of terror as the civil rights movement gained ground, perpetrating many of the most notorious acts of violence of the civil rights era. In 1961 the Klan fomented riots against the Freedom Riders in Alabama. In 1963 the Klan bombed the Sixteenth Street Baptist Church in Birmingham, Alabama, killing four African American girls.[232] In June 1964, Mississippi Klan members kidnapped and murdered civil rights workers James Chaney, Andrew Goodman, and Michael Schwerner.[233] In March 1965, Klan members shot and killed Viola Liuzzo, a civil rights worker who was helping with the March on Selma, Alabama.[234]

The Centrality of the Constitution in the Klan's Defense of Segregation

White Southerners, from members of Congress to the White Citizens Councils to the Klan, framed the fight for segregation in nationalist terms, as a fight to save America. They described the civil rights movement as a threat to the American way of life.[235] All the groups defending segregation rallied around the Constitution as the central symbol of the nation's principles that they claimed were under attack. While the Klan also focused on the Constitution, it presented a more radical constitutional ideology than other segregationist organizations, an ideology that justified violence.

The Southern Manifesto, signed by nineteen Southern US senators and seventy-seven representatives, typifies the mainstream defense of segregation. It condemned *Brown* as a "clear abuse of power."[236] It relies on the originalist argument that the Fourteenth Amendment's Equal Protection Clause should not be read to address segregation because the same Congress that adopted the Fourteenth Amendment also authorized segregated schools in the District of Columbia. It argues that the Constitution does not address education and therefore leaves control of education to the states.[237] White Citizens Councils similarly pointed to principles that had long been used to defend white rule, including states' rights associated with the Tenth Amendment.[238] Segregationists also argued that the Fourteenth Amendment had not validly been ratified and therefore was void.[239] In 1957 the state of Georgia adopted a resolution urging Congress to declare both the Fourteenth and Fifteenth Amendments void.[240]

In addition to disputing many of the specific legal points supporting the *Brown* decision, mainstream segregationists frequently invoked the Constitution as the embodiment of the nation's core values that they believed were threatened by integration. Mississippi Senator James Eastland, one of the signers of the Southern Manifesto and a frequent speaker at White Citizens' Councils meetings, declared that the fight to preserve segregation was "a fight not only to maintain and perpetuate the laws, customs, traditions and the culture of our Southern way of life, but to restore and revitalize the Republican form of government which is the greatest of our heritages from the past."[241]

Like other segregationist groups, the Klan articulated its mission in nationalist and constitutional terms. "Our fight is for racial integrity and Constitutional Government," the Klan declared.[242] As in earlier periods, Klan bylaws declared that it was committed "to protect and defend the Constitution of the United States of America."[243] While other groups argued that the Constitution protected the right of a state to choose segregation, the Klan asserted that white rule itself was essential to carrying out the Constitution. As one Klan newspaper put it: "We must keep this a White Man's country. Only by doing this can we be faithful to the foundation laid down by our forefathers."[244]

The Klan distinguished itself among segregationists by articulating an ideology that placed white rule at the center of American and constitutional history. The mission statement of the Confederate Knights of the Ku Klux Klan—the "Kreed"—declared: "I believe that God created races and nation, committing to each a special destiny and service; that the United States through its white, Protestant citizens holds a Divine commission for the furtherance of white supremacy and the protection of religious freedom; that its Constitution and laws are expressive of the Divine purpose."[245] The Klan thus articulated a belief that God had helped create the United States and gave its white Protestant citizens the mission of preserving white supremacy, a mission expressed in the Constitution. Similar statements can be found throughout Klan materials from the civil rights era.[246] For the Klan, segregation and white rule were not merely legitimate policy choices left to the states and to be decided by the people. They were ordained by God and enshrined the Constitution.

Not only was the constitutional ideology developed by the Klan in the 1950s and 1960s more radical than the ideology of other segregationists, it was more radical than the ideology asserted by the Klan in earlier eras. The Klan of the 1920s understood the Constitution to protect conventional principles like self-determination, liberty, and equality. It asserted that these principles arose out of white Protestant culture and that other peoples lacked the ability to embrace these values. In contrast, the Klan of the civil rights era came to believe that white supremacy itself was the nation's central constitutional principle. While earlier Klan eras had claimed that the Constitution was the product of white Protestant culture and was best understood by white Protestants, the Klan of the civil rights era declared that the Constitution was centrally devoted to white rule.

In the ideology developed by the Klan during the civil rights era, America simply had no place for those who were not white Protestants. They were wholly outside of the American tradition. As one Klan newspaper put it, to a person of African descent, "The Pilgrim father can never be his fathers," and "the signers of the Declaration can never be his ancestors." The Klan thus declared that an African American could never be a true American because "no man can bestow upon him an inheritance that is not his."[247]

Segregationist organizations routinely described the civil rights movement as an alien force that sought to undermine American values, but the Klan was especially emphatic in identifying supporters of civil rights as enemies of the nation.[248] Mainstream segregationists frequently charged that the civil rights movement was connected to communism or played into the hands of Communists, but the Klan believed that international Communists literally directed the civil rights movement.[249] Frequently using the terms "Jews" and "Communists" interchangeably, the Klan believed that Jews were directing a Communist conspiracy that controlled the civil rights movement.[250] Klan members believed that African Americans were incapable of organizing and managing the civil rights movement on their own, and instead the Klan considered Black civil rights leaders to be dupes of Communist Jews, who were the nation's true enemies. They had orchestrated the civil rights movement as a means of attacking the United States.[251] As one Klan flyer put it, Jews are "trying to destroy everything our forefathers fought for and they hope to some day soon fly the red flag over our land."[252]

Because it considered white rule a foundational national principle, the Klan saw the civil rights movement as even more threatening than other segregationists saw it. While mainstream defenders of segregation asserted that the conflict over segregation would dramatically affect the nation's future, the Klan asserted that the nation's very existence was at stake.[253] As James Venable, leader of the National Knights of the Ku Klux Klan, proclaimed: "We of the Klan and the peoples of the west face the crisis of the ages—the very survival of that which we hold so dear, the basic elements of what we so rightly call civilization."[254]

Depicting the civil rights movement as an alien force devoted to the nation's destruction, the Klan portrayed its own mission as a patriotic crusade to carry on the work of the Founding Fathers. As one Klan group put it, "Let no man forget that the White Knights of the Ku Klux Klan are the Physical and Spiritual heirs of the American Revolution, that Anglo-Saxon triumph of Justice and Equity."[255] The Klan believed that it alone recognized the true threat posed by the civil rights movement and that it alone was willing to do what was necessary to protect the Constitution.[256]

The Constitution and Klan Violence

What most distinguished the Klan from other groups defending segregation was its open embrace of extra-legal violence.[257] The Southern Manifesto, signed by the South's congressional delegation, called for resistance "by any lawful means."[258] White Citizens Councils routinely disavowed Klan violence as the work of "ruffians."[259] In contrast, the Klan openly called for violence against supporters of the civil rights movement. As one Klan newsletter declared, "All those who attempt to destroy the Foundations of American Liberty and Justice must themselves be destroyed by the Americans."[260]

The Constitution played a central role in the Klan's justifications for violence. Depicting the civil rights movement as a hostile foreign force devoted to the destruction of the Constitution, the Klan justified violence as patriotic acts of national defense. The Klan claimed that it was "the incumbent duty of every American to defend the Spiritual Ideals and Principles upon which this Nation was founded, even at the cost of his life."[261] As the civil rights movement succeeded in toppling legal segregation, the Klan grew more emphatic in declaring that whites owed a duty to kill and die to defend the Constitution. "The issue is clearly one of personal, physical SELF-DEFENSE or DEATH for the American Anglo-Saxons," declared the White Knights of the Ku Klux Klan of Mississippi, "The Anglo Saxons have no choice but to defend our Constitutional Republic by every means at their command, because it is, LITERALLY, their Life. They will die without it."[262]

Over the course of the 1960s, the Klan grew more vehement in declaring that the Constitution was under attack and therefore violence was justified. Klan members believed that they were "bound by oath to preserve, protect and defend the Constitution of the United States of America by reason and by force, if necessary."[263] With the growing success of the civil rights movement, the Klan declared that the time for half-measures was over; in the words of Robert Shelton, imperial wizard of the United Klans of America, the fight to save America was now a "total war."[264]

Although the Klan bombed churches, killed children, and attacked numerous unarmed victims, Klan members considered the civil rights movement to be the aggressor, while Klan violence was *defensive* in nature.[265] The Klan adopted an expansive notion of self-defense under which violence was justified for the "self-defense for our homes, our families, our nation and Christian Civilization."[266] In 1964, when the White Knights of the Ku Klux Klan of Mississippi kidnapped and murdered civil rights workers James Chaney, Andrew Goodman, and Michael Schwerner, the group's newsletter insisted that the victims were "Communist revolutionaries . . . actively working to undermine and destroy Christian Civilization" and declared that the murders were justifiably performed by "American Patriots who are determined to resist Communism by every available means."[267]

Although it perpetrated many crimes, the Klan considered itself a force for law and order.[268] It believed that violence served the higher duty of defending the Constitution in the face of tyranny. As the federal government increasingly supported civil rights—by sending in troops to enforce desegregation orders, and by enacting and enforcing federal civil rights laws—the Klan increasingly considered the federal government to be a tyrannical force controlled by Communists, which justified antigovernment violence.[269]

The Klan justified its violence with what has more recently become known as the insurrectionist theory, the claim that the Constitution protects a right to use violence when the government acts tyrannically.[270] As the White Knights of the Ku Klux Klan asserted: "If the minions of material governmental authority threaten, attempt to, or use physical force and violence to enforce compliance with some letter of law which is in clear conflict with the Constitution . . . Private Citizens of America have a right to oppose them with physical force, using the Constitution and the Supremacy of the Will of Almighty God as their Authority."[271] Believing that it was enforcing the true meaning of the Constitution in the face of federal tyranny, the Klan declared that private violence was justified against federal officials, churches, synagogues, and anyone else perceived as supporting the civil rights movement, which was a tyrannical force that sought to impose Communist rule and deprive the people of their constitutional rights.

Although mainstream defenders of segregation like the White Citizens' Councils disavowed the extra-legal violence perpetrated by the Klan, the differences between the groups in their support of violence should not be exaggerated. Many white Southerners were members of both organizations, including Byron De La Beckwith, who was convicted of the assassination of Medgar Evers.[272] White Citizens' Councils condemned Klan violence, but they put the blame for the violence on the civil rights movement. As the director of the South Carolina Citizens' Council declared, if white segregationists committed violence, "every home that is destroyed, every drop of blood that is spilled will be on the hands of racial agitators and those who encourage them."[273] Mainstream segregationists often described violence as an understandable yet regrettable response to the provocation by the civil rights movement. "Violence is caused by frustration," declared Robert Patterson, the founder of the White Citizens' Council, and white Southerners were understandably frustrated because segregation and the American way of life were under attack. The Citizens' Councils aimed to alleviate white frustration and thereby prevent the necessity of violence by showing that they could "protect [their] interests by lawful means."[274] The unspoken implication was that violence would indeed be justified if lawful efforts were ineffective.[275]

The difference between the Klan and mainstream segregationists over the use of violence shrinks further when one recognizes that establishment groups like the White Citizens' Councils only rejected *private* violence while strongly supporting *state-sponsored* violence against supporters of civil rights. Mainstream segregationists routinely voiced support for the brutal tactics used by city police departments, such as the use of fire hoses and dogs employed in 1963 by the Birmingham Police Department under the direction of Bull Connor.[276] The line between public and private violence was often blurred because state officials sometimes worked directly with the Klan to support violence, such as when the Birmingham police allowed a white mob to descend on Freedom Riders in 1961, or when the Philadelphia, Mississippi, police gave the Klan custody of civil rights workers James Chaney, Andrew Goodman, and Michael Schwerner.[277] Even when they were not personally involved in Klan violence, state and local officials were complicit in Klan violence by their decision not to investigate or prosecute Klan members for their crimes.[278]

More generally, the Klan and more mainstream segregationists shared the conviction that they had a right to defy federal law when it conflicted with their personal understanding of the Constitution. In resisting school desegregation, state and local leaders developed theories supposedly grounded in the Constitution for their refusal to follow federal orders. Chief among them was the theory of interposition, which invokes a supposed state right to resist laws deemed unconstitutional.[279] Eight states adopted interposition resolutions that declared that *Brown* had no effect within the state.[280] Virginia's interposition resolution, for instance, vowed to "use all 'honorable, legal and constitutional' means . . . to 'resist this illegal encroachment on our sovereign powers.'"[281]

The Klan's defense of violence merely took interposition one step further. Just as the states asserted a right to defend their citizens against unconstitutional federal actions, the Klan asserted the right of citizens to defend themselves if states were unable to protect them. White moderates argued that state and local officials could defy federal law when federal law was oppressive, and the Klan added that private citizens had the same right to defend themselves against oppression—even if oppression took the form of peaceful protesters demanding equal rights.

The Demise of the Third Klan

Over the course of the 1960s, it slowly became apparent to white Southerners that the civil rights movement was winning. Protests across the South and the often brutal responses by Southern officials galvanized public opinion outside the South.[282] Congress responded by enacting a series of laws that prohibited race discrimination in employment, public accommodations, voting, and housing, and it denied federal funds to schools and other institutions that maintained discriminatory practices.[283] White resistance to formal equality slowly waned. White Citizens' Councils faded from the scene.[284] White political and business leaders came to accept the defeat of segregation and were working, often grudgingly, within a legal system that now included express prohibitions against race discrimination.[285] A social norm was emerging that rejected open expressions of white supremacy.[286]

The Klan too was fading from the scene. By the end of the 1960s, it had become clear that the Klan's campaign of violence to defend a white nation governed by a white Constitution had failed. The demise of the Klan was hastened by an FBI operation to infiltrate and weaken Klan groups, an operation that led to the imprisonment of many Klan leaders.[287] By 1971, when the FBI ended the COINTELPRO operation, total membership in the Klan had fallen to less than five thousand members.[288] Although the Klan had started the civil rights era as part of a unified coalition of white organizations fighting to preserve white rule, by the end of the 1960s it was much diminished in size and was one of the last voices left fighting for segregation and white supremacy.[289]

The Fourth Klan and the Constitution: 1970s to Today

In the early 1970s, when the Klan was declared dead for the third time, white supremacists began to look for new solutions.[290] For some, this meant rejecting the Klan's traditional embrace of patriotism and the Constitution.

During the 1970s and 1980s, the Klan underwent what is sometimes referred to as a "Nazification," a process that, in the words of historian John Drabble, "transformed a reactionary counter-movement that had failed to preserve white supremacy by terrorizing civil rights organizers and black citizens, into a revolutionary white power movement that inculpated Jews and the federal government."[291]

The Nazification of the Klan began in 1973 when David Duke formed the Knights of the Ku Klux Klan.[292] Handsome, well-dressed, and young, Duke appeared frequently on TV talk shows, where he surprised the hosts with his intelligence and articulateness, qualities that were unexpected in a Klan leader.[293] Duke set out to change the Klan's message as well as its image. In college, Duke had called himself a Nazi and was strongly influenced by William Pierce, the founder of the National Alliance, a white supremacist organization that incorporated Nazi principles.[294] Duke agreed with Pierce that the Klan had been too supportive of the existing social and political order: "Traditionally, the Ku Klux Klan has been conservative, parochial, and Christian. It wanted to keep non-Whites 'in their place,' not separate them geographically from Whites, and it was as suspicious of White 'foreigners'—Germans, Poles, Irishmen, Yankees, and just about everyone else—as it was of uppity Blacks. It supported the established social order and parroted the same platitudes as the Jaycees and Lions Clubbers."[295] Inspired by Pierce, Duke argued that Klansmen should stop being "reactionaries longing to return to a previous era of White racial history."[296]

Duke broke with long-standing Klan ideology that framed white supremacy in patriotic terms and that equated the preservation of white power with the preservation of American values. Duke argued that whites should hold no loyalty to the existing governmental system: "We are not fighting to preserve the systems of weakness and degeneration that have led us to this precipice."[297] Loyalty to the white race, Duke argued, should be the preeminent concern of white people, not loyalty to the nation.[298] Duke believed that whites would work to form a white nation once they recognized that race was preeminent. "We are warriors," Duke proclaimed. "We will be the iron fist that strikes down the alien plague around us, and we will be the creative hands that will mold a new society, one that is populated by beings truly in the image of God."[299]

Central to Duke's thinking was his belief that Jewish power, not racial integration, formed the core problem facing white people. Although antisemitism had been prevalent in earlier Klan eras, Duke made concerns about Jewish power central to the Klan, asserting that it was "the most important issue of our time." Duke believed that Jewish influence made it impossible to restore white power within the existing political system.[300] In this view, Duke relied on Wilmot Robertson, the pseudonymous author of *The Dispossessed Majority,* a work of modern scientific racism that Duke praised as "brilliant" and "the most important book since the Second World War."[301] *The Dispossessed Majority* asserts that the nation's white majority had been ousted from power by Jews who used their supposed control of the media and levers of public opinion to discourage whites from gaining racial consciousness.[302] Robertson believed that Jews had brainwashed whites to betray their race by voluntarily agreeing to relinquish power.[303]

Duke recruited other leaders to the Klan who were steeped in Nazi

Members of the Ku Klux Klan burning a cross and a swastika at a rally near Cedartown, Georgia, April 23, 2016. Photo courtesy of Mike Stewart/AP Images. Used by permission.

THE WHITE CONSTITUTION | 69

ideology and who believed in the doctrine of white dispossession. Under Duke's leadership, the Klan fused long-standing Klan rituals with the symbols of National Socialism.[304] Duke's newspaper, *The Crusader*, advertised copies of Hitler's *Mein Kampf* and made Holocaust denial a central element of its message.[305] Under Duke's leadership, Klan and neo-Nazi groups found considerable common cause. Klan leaders like Louis Beam, who for a time was one of Duke's lieutenants, attended the annual Aryan Nations conference, which included the Klan ritual of a cross burning before a gathering of both Klansmen in white robes and neo-Nazis dressed in jack boots and leather.[306] Other Klan groups soon followed Duke in forming hybrid Nazi-Klan organizations.[307]

Nazi ideology and white separatism made further inroads into white supremacist culture with the publication of *The Turner Diaries*. Written by National Alliance founder William Pierce and promoted by Klan newspapers, the novel depicts an American government run by liberals, Jews, and African Americans, in which an "Equality Police" seeks to enslave white people and deprive them of their guns and freedoms. The heroes of the novel are members of a cadre of white resistance fighters called the Organization, who launch a campaign of terrorism that succeeds in gaining control of Southern California. Once victorious, the white patriots drive out Black and Latino residents and kill the Jews. To maintain order, the Organization makes a public spectacle by hanging race traitors—white men and women who slept with nonwhites.[308]

The Turner Diaries inspired the formation of the revolutionary Aryan organization known as the Order, also known as the Brüder Schweigen or Silent Brotherhood, which was based directly on the Organization from the novel.[309] Founded in 1983 by Robert Mathews, the Order called on neo-Nazis and Klansmen to unite to create a separate Aryan nation: "We hereby declare ourselves a free and sovereign people. We claim a territorial imperative that will consist of the entire North American continent north of Mexico."[310] Like other white supremacists, the Order described the United States as the Zionist Occupational Government, or ZOG, which it asserted was dedicated to the extinction of the white race.[311] Members of the Order signed a declaration of war against the United States: "In a land once ours," they declared, "we have become a people dispossessed. Our heroes and culture have been insulted and degraded. The mongrel hordes clamor to sever us from our inheritance. Yet our people do not care."[312]

In 1983 and 1984, members of the Order, drawn from Aryan Nations, the National Alliance, and the Klan, embarked on a crime spree, in which they stole over $4 million from banks and armored cars, bombed a synagogue, and murdered radio talk show host Alan Berg.[313] They distributed the stolen money to other white separatists groups, including Klan groups.[314] Unlike the Organization of *The Turner Diaries*, the Order did not succeed in fomenting revolution. Mathews was killed in a gunfight with a federal SWAT team in December 1984, and dozens of other members of the Order were indicted for a variety of crimes.[315]

While some Klan groups followed Duke's lead and incorporated white separatist and neo-Nazi ideology and symbols, other Klan groups rejected Nazi infiltration. Most prominently, Robert Shelton's United Klans of America (UKA), which had become the largest Klan organization during the 1960s, continued to assert that the Klan's core ideology was "Christian Americanism," under which its goal was to restore what the Klan considered the nation's foundational principles.[316] Shelton rejected Duke as a legitimate part of the Klan, saying that his "entire movement is nothin' in the world but the National Socialist White People's Party, or the Nazi Party."[317] Jim Blair, imperial wizard of the Invisible Empire, agreed with Shelton that the Klan should reject Nazis because they supported totalitarian government, while the "True Klan" supported Christian Democracy.[318]

By the early 1980s, however, membership in hybrid Nazi-Klan groups began to exceed membership in more traditional Klan groups. As one commentator has described, by 1980, "almost every leader of the nation's Klans was a veteran of at least one neo-Nazi organization. . . . It was becoming more and more difficult to know where the Klan ended and the neo-Nazi movement began."[319]

Despite their success in transforming the Klan, many of the Nazi-influenced Klan leaders who rose to power with David Duke chose to leave the Klan to launch new organizations that did not bear the Klan name. Duke himself left the Klan in 1980 and formed the National Association for the Advancement of White People.[320] Tom Metzger, who worked with Duke during his time with the Klan and became a grand dragon in the California Klan, formed the White Aryan Resistance.[321] Frazier Glenn Miller changed the name of his group, the Carolina Knights of the Ku Klux Klan, to the White Patriot Party.[322] These white separatists concluded that the Klan brand had too many historical associations—including the Klan's conception of its patriotic mission—to support organizations that reject loyalty to the United States government and that declare war on the United States itself.[323]

Today, some groups that use the Klan name employ Nazi symbols and advocate white separatism while others employ patriotic symbols and advocate the restoration of white rule in the United States. A 2016 study concluded that the Klan has approximately three thousand members, far fewer than earlier Klan eras, but estimating the number of Klan members has become more difficult because of the significant overlap of groups that employ the white hoods, Confederate flags, and cross-burning rituals traditionally associated with the Klan, and groups that incorporate neo-Nazi ideologies and use Nazi symbols.[324] Today, an organization's use of the Klan name does not necessarily indicate its precise ideology, other than its commitment to white supremacy.

The white supremacist movement of the early twenty-first century is composed of two factions: reactionary groups that seek to restore whites to power within the United States, and revolutionary groups that seek to establish a separate white nation. Dennis Mahon, a former Klan leader who joined the White Aryan Resistance, explained how white separatists see these two factions: "By the 'Movement' we mean the activities and ideology of most Judeo-Christian, Right-Wing, Anti-Communist, Patriotic groups (C.R.A.P.). The CRAP usually consists of most Klan groups, patriotic Christian churches, patriotic veterans groups, and so on. By Aryan or White Resistance we mean groups like White Aryan Resistance, National Alliance, Church of the Creator, skinhead groups, and some radical white survivalist groups."[325] To Mahon, the key distinction between white supremacists who are part of the conservative movement and those who are part of the Aryan Resistance lies in their different attitudes toward the government: white supremacists who are part of the conservative movement "believe that the United States' Federal government is basically historically benevolent, that evil or deceived politicians have temporarily taken control of power, and if we can just awaken the masses, we can get our country back." Members of the "Resistance," in contrast, believe the federal government has "declared total war against the white race" and for more than a century has "continued its planned genocide of our European homeland."[326]

White Separatism and the Constitution

Loyalty to the United States, and in particular dedication to the Constitution, represents a primary dividing line between the reactionary and revolutionary factions of the white supremacist movement. White separatists assert that racial solidarity must take precedence over loyalty to the United States.[327] They believe that white people belong to an Aryan nation and should abandon loyalty to the United States, which betrayed white people by embracing multiculturalism.[328] In his highly influential "Essays of a Klansman," Louis Beam argued that the Klan should no longer work for regaining control of the United States, but should instead adopt a new goal: "Our goal—a Racial Nation of and by ourselves—nothing less." Beam declared that Aryans "must now separate ourselves from the mongrel nation that envelops us."[329]

To white supremacists who believe that the United States is devoted to the destruction of white power, patriotism of the sort long espoused by the Klan has little appeal. White separatists call for a revolutionary movement that would wage war on the United States, not try to restore it. Louis Beam argued that the Klan could never generate a mass political movement capable of achieving peaceful political change because the majority of white Americans are brainwashed by the Jewish-controlled media and would oppose the Klan. Instead, Beam argued, the Klan should recruit a small cadre of militant members who would be prepared to take revolutionary action and establish a white nation "by whatever means necessary."[330]

In rejecting loyalty to the United States, white separatists reject dedication to the Constitution as a guiding principle and touchstone for their movement. This shift can be seen in *The Turner Diaries*.[331] After the novel's heroes oust the Jewish-run federal government and create a white ethnic state, they mock conservatives who issue "idiotic proclamations about 'restoring the Constitution,' . . . and holding new elections to 're-establish the republican form of government intended by the Founding Fathers,' whatever that means."[332] As the novel's narrator explains, it was the Constitution that allowed Jews and Blacks to gain power in the first place. Constitutional democracy is impossible in a multiethnic state, the narrator says, especially one in which Jewish control of the media prevents whites from recognizing that their true loyalty lies in racial solidarity and not devotion to a government controlled by their enemies.[333]

Rather than seeking to take back the United States and return to the true meaning of the Constitution, white separatists envision the creation of a new white nation that would be guided by purely racial principles. In 1996 Aryan Nations issued a "Platform for the Aryan National State," which envisions a white ethnic state devoted to the principles of national socialism, which would nationalize industry, exile all Jews and nonwhite persons, and seize control of the press.[334] Other white separatists agree that the white ethnic state should be based exclusively on racial considerations and should reject the universal principles expressed in the United States

Constitution.[335] A draft constitution developed by members of the Order and other white nationalists for a future Aryan Republic, envisioned to be created in the Pacific Northwest, declares that white racial sovereignty alone should be the state's primary purpose: "The Northwest American Republic shall be a Homeland solely for the use and habitation of White people of all nationalities, cultures and creeds worldwide, in order that Western civilization may be preserved and White children may be raised to responsible adulthood in safety, prosperity and tranquility. We must secure the existence of our people and a future for White children. Such is the overriding principle of this Constitution."[336]

The differing attitudes toward the US Constitution among white supremacists can readily be seen by comparing two contemporary white supremacist organizations, the Nationalist Front and the Knights of the Ku Klux Klan.[337] The Nationalist Front is dedicated to white separatism— "The creation of an ethno-state for White people in North America."[338] It declares that the US government is the enemy of white people, and it urges whites to abandon all loyalty to the United States.[339] In declaring war on the United States, the Nationalist Front rejects not only the specific principles underlying the Constitution but more crucially the notion that any set of universal principles could bind together a nation. Whereas Abraham Lincoln had declared at Gettysburg that the United States was "dedicated to the proposition that all men are created equal," the Nationalist Front rejects civic nationalism altogether: "We reject the notion of a 'proposition nation.' Nations are built on blood, culture, language and traditions; they are organic expressions of a people. The nation must be an embodiment of the will of the people and stand for their best racial, moral and economic interests."[340] Other white separatist groups likewise have rejected devotion to the Constitution in similar terms.[341]

In contrast, the Knights of the Ku Klux Klan continues to employ the constitutional rhetoric long used by the Klan in espousing white supremacy. The Knights declare that whites must rededicate themselves to what the Klan considers traditional American principles, most centrally the belief that the United States was founded as a white Christian nation.[342] Unlike white separatists, the Knights valorize the nation's founders and the principles they stood for, and they emphasize their whiteness: "Those who formed the very ideals that we cherish such as freedom of speech, trial by jury, innocent until proven guilty, free enterprise, etc. were of White European heritage."[343] Like past generations of Klansmen, members of the Knights proudly proclaim their dedication to the Constitution, which they understand to be the product of the nation's white heritage and which expresses specifically white values.[344]

The differing goals of these two white supremacist factions—the creation of a white ethnic state independent of the United States and the restoration of white rule within the United States—have each proven powerful in mobilizing members ready to use violence to achieve their goals. Despite their differences, the two factions share core ideological commitments. Both agree that the federal government has become dedicated to the destruction of white people.[345] Both identify the supposed Jewish control of the government and media as the central force oppressing white people.[346]

Recognizing their common cause, reactionary groups like the Knights frequently work with revolutionary groups like the Nationalist Front. The "Unite the Right" rally held in August 2017 in Charlottesville, Virginia, was expressly called to bring together the "movement" and "resistance" wings of the white power movement, along with fellow traveler groups.[347] Members of both the Nationalist Front and the Knights attended, as did white supremacist luminaries such as David Duke and Richard Spencer.[348] Whether they are for the Constitution or against it, they recognized fellow white supremacists as allies facing a common enemy. Whether wearing Klan robes, bearing swastikas, or both, they marched together in Charlottesville, holding tiki torches and chanting "white lives matter," "blood and soil," and "Jews will not replace us."[349]

Conclusion

What does it say about the United States that for over 150 years the nation's most prominent hate group has considered its campaign of violence and terrorism to be a defense of the Constitution?

The Klan's declaration of a constitutional mission resonates with the long-standing American belief that the Constitution is the defining text of American national identity. Like many Americans, Klan members believe that whiteness is an essential part of what it means to be American. The Klan translated that belief into constitutional terms, declaring that the Constitution itself embodies the nation's white identity.[350] As the next chapters show, other political and social movements have asserted that different aspects of identity—such as being Christian or native-born—are an essential part of American identity and have mobilized to convince their fellow Americans to understand the Constitution as an expression of that identity.

The history of the Klan also shows the ways that constitutional nation-alism has provided a ready justification for violence. If commitment to the Constitution defines what it means to be American, those who are seen as outsiders to the Constitution can be seen as enemies of the nation, as aliens who must be excluded and defeated to protect the nation—by force, if necessary. As the history of the Klan shows, the ideology that equates national identity and constitutional devotion can make it a patriotic duty to kill those who are declared to be enemies of the Constitution.

2 | The Christian Constitution

Just as many Americans have believed the United States is a white nation and have mobilized to protect white rule, many Americans have believed that the United States is at heart a Christian nation. Christian nationalist movements have been a recurrent feature in American politics since before the Civil War. These movements are borne of the conviction that being Christian is an essential part of American identity, that American culture and institutions arise out of Christian traditions, and that American public life should incorporate Christian practices.

Although Christian nationalism has been a persistent feature of American life, the relationship between Christian nationalism and the Constitution has undergone a dramatic change. Nineteenth-century Christian nationalists denounced the Constitution as a godless document unworthy of a Christian nation and fought to amend the Constitution to declare the nation's Christian faith. Today, Christian nationalists laud the Constitution as the highest expression of the nation's Christian identity.

How did this change happen? How did the Constitution become—for many Americans, at least—*Christian?* The answer lies in America's constitutional culture, which channels conflicts over national identity into constitutional disputes. This chapter illustrates the dynamics that transform conflicts over national identity into constitutional conflicts by examining three movements in the long-standing debate over whether the United States should be understood to be a Christian nation: the nineteenth-century Christian Amendment movement, mid-twentieth-century Judeo-Christian nationalism, and the New Christian Right that began in the 1970s and 1980s and continues today.

These movements follow a similar pattern. In each case, members of the dominant religious group mobilized in response to perceived threats to their status. In each episode, members of the mobilized movement considered Christian devotion to be part of the nation's essence and therefore considered threats to Christian dominance as attacks on the United States itself. And in each case, the movement attempted to preserve the nation's supposed Christian identity by demanding that the Constitution be made

Christian. In each of these episodes, Christian nationalists expressed the view that the Constitution must mirror national identity: Since the American people are Christian, they argued, the Constitution must be made Christian. At the same time, they feared that if the Constitution were not made Christian, the American people would lose their Christian identity. Over time, however, the form of their constitutional demands has changed. Nineteenth-century Americans sought to amend the Constitution when it did not express their identity, but today constitutional change is sought more often by advocating a change in the interpretation of the Constitution.

As explored in chapter 1, a similar pattern can be seen in the history of white nationalism, in which threats to the status and power of white Americans were perceived as threats to the nation and helped fuel the rise of the Ku Klux Klan, which expressed in constitutional terms the demand to maintain white rule. Through this recurring pattern, fights about group dominance become fights over national identity, carried out in the language of the Constitution. Rather than embodying what it means to be American, the Constitution provides a seemingly neutral and patriotic language for making claims of national inclusion and exclusion, for asserting that some people and some values are authentically American while others are dangerously foreign and must be rejected.

The Christian Amendment Movement

The US Constitution contains no indication that the American people share a common religion. The Constitution prohibits the imposition of any "religious test" for federal office, which allows people from any religion to serve in government.[1] The First Amendment protects the right to the free exercise of any religion and prohibits the government from establishing a national religion. The only arguably religious reference in the Constitution is the nomenclature used for denoting the date of the signing of the Constitution—"the Seventeenth Day of September in the Year of our Lord one thousand seven hundred and Eighty seven"—but that language was not part of the text of the Constitution voted on by the delegates in Philadelphia or the ratifying conventions in the states.[2]

The absence of any expression of religious devotion in the Constitution was somewhat anomalous at the time of its drafting. The Declaration of Independence contains explicitly religious language, appealing to "the

Supreme Judge of the world for the rectitude of our intentions," invoking the "Laws of Nature and of Nature's God," and declaring that men are "endowed by their Creator with certain unalienable Rights."[3] The nation's first constitution, the Articles of Confederation, also invoked religious faith by declaring that it sought the guidance of "the Great Governor of the World."[4] At the time of the Constitution's adoption, every state constitution except Virginia's contained some kind of religious expression.[5]

Some evangelical Christians opposed ratification specifically because the Constitution gave no special status to Christianity.[6] Luther Martin, a dissenting delegate to the Constitutional Convention, objected to the Religious Test Clause because of his belief that "in a Christian country it would be at least decent to hold out some distinction between the professors of Christianity and downright infidelity or paganism."[7] North Carolina anti-Federalists argued that under the Constitution, "Jews, Mahometans, pagans, &c., may be elected" to federal offices, and therefore the Constitution would serve as "an invitation for Jews and pagans of every kind to come among us."[8] During the ratification debates, it was repeatedly urged that the Religious Test Clause be amended and that an expression of Christian devotion be added.

Long after ratification, many evangelicals continued to oppose the Constitution because of the absence of an expression of religious devotion. In 1793, Reverend John M. Mason of New York preached that "from the Constitution of the United States, it is impossible to ascertain what God we worship, or whether we own a God at all."[9] He predicted that the nation would not long survive if the American people proved to be as irreligious as its Constitution. He was not alone. "Be astonished, O earth!," Reverend Chauncey Lee intoned in an 1813 sermon, the Constitution "has not the impress of *religion* upon it, not the smallest recognition of the government, or the being of God, . . . I leave it with this single reflection, whether, *if God be not in the camp, we have not reason to tremble for the ark.*"[10]

To these ministers, the absence of any reference to God in the Constitution was inconsistent with the nation's Christian identity. As Reverend Ezra Stiles Ely preached in 1827: "We are a Christian nation: we have the right to demand that all our rulers in their conduct shall conform to Christian morality."[11] In 1844 former president John Quincy Adams, while serving in Congress, submitted a petition to amend the Constitution "so that it shall contain a clear and explicit acknowledgment of the Sovereign of the universe as the God of this nation; an entire and avowed submission to the Lord

Jesus Christ as the ruler of this nation."[12] The petition was tabled without recorded debate.

The Reformed Presbytery Church, a sect of Scotch-Irish Presbyterians commonly referred to as "Covenanters," was among the groups that continued long after ratification to reject the Constitution as a blasphemous document.[13] Covenanters believed that legitimate governmental power could derive only from God and that the Constitution sinfully asserts that the government's power comes from "We the People."[14] As one Covenanter explained, the Constitution amounted to a "manifest dethroning of the Lord and his Anointed from the government."[15] Because the Constitution omitted a divine basis for government, Covenanters refused to profess allegiance to the United States, and the church condemned voting or participating in any aspect of national politics.

While opposition to the godless Constitution dates back to the time of its framing, it took the Civil War to give rise to an organized movement to put God into the Constitution.[16] That movement should be understood in light of the religious framework through which that many in both the North and South viewed the war.[17] The issue of slavery was debated as a question of Christian morality, and ministers and laypeople offered conflicting positions on whether the Bible supported or condemned slavery.[18] In the North, the war was frequently described as punishment for the national sin of slavery.[19] In the South, some ministers argued that the absence of an expression of religious devotion in the US Constitution had been a national sin.[20] In one of the few ways it differed from the US Constitution, the preamble to the Confederate Constitution adopted in March 1861 expressly invokes "the favor and guidance of Almighty God."[21] With that change, supporters of the Confederacy could say that it had God on its side because its constitution said so, unlike the US Constitution.

In 1863 a movement began in the North to put God in the US Constitution as well. Members of eleven Protestant denominations met in Xenia, Ohio, on February 3 and 4, 1863, to discuss the spiritual implications of the war. The group was dominated by Covenanters who had long rejected the Constitution due to its absence of any expression of faith.[22] While the movement's founders believed slavery was a national sin, they considered the omission of God from the Constitution to be "the crowning, original sin of the nation, and slavery as one of its natural outgrowth." As the group's first chairman wrote, the Civil War arose because "God is displeased with us as a nation, and has been provoked to bring upon us a terrible calamity."

Americans had provoked God by adopting a Constitution that spoke for "We, the people, without acknowledging God's authority."[23]

Participants in the Xenia meeting soon created a national association dedicated to pursuing a constitutional amendment to express the nation's Christian devotion. First called the National Association to Secure the Religious Amendment to the Constitution of the United States, the organization was later renamed the National Reform Association (NRA). In January 1864 the organization declared its mission: "We deem it a matter of paramount interest to the life, and prosperity, and permanency of our nation, that its Constitution be so amended as fully to express the Christian national character."

The NRA proposed amending the Constitution's Preamble to read:

> We, the people of the United States, *humbly acknowledging Almighty God as the source of all authority and power in civil government, the Lord Jesus Christ as the Ruler among the nations, his revealed will as the supreme law of the land, in order to constitute a Christian government,* and in order to form a more perfect union, establish justice, insure domestic tranquility, provide for the common defense, promote the general welfare, and secure the inalienable rights and the blessings of life, liberty, and the pursuit of happiness to ourselves and our posterity and all the people, do ordain and establish this Constitution for the United States of America.[24]

The proposed Christian amendment did not attempt to give additional powers to any branch of government or to protect any new rights but instead simply sought to add Christian devotion to the underlying purposes of the Constitution. In doing so, supporters of the Christian amendment wanted to make it clear that "We the People" are Christian; that the United States has a "Christian national character."

The proposed amendment quickly received several key endorsements, including Senators Charles Sumner, B. Gratz Brown, and John Sherman, as well as the *Independent*, the nation's leading religious journal, and the faculty of the Princeton Theological Seminary, the nation's leading seminary.[25] In February 1864, a month after the association's formation, a delegation met with President Lincoln to press him to support the amendment. They told Lincoln that the amendment was necessary to bring the Constitution and the people into harmony. "We deem it a matter of paramount interest to the life, and prosperity, and permanency of our nation," the delegation told Lincoln, "that its Constitution be so amended as fully to express the Christian national character."[26] They argued that a declaration of the nation's Christian's devotion would help create national unity, foster national morality, and help the Union win the war. Lincoln was noncommittal and reportedly declared that "the general aspect of your movement I cordially approve," but asked time to consider the particulars of the proposal because "the work of amending the Constitution should not be done hastily."[27]

As it became clear that the Union would win the war, support for the proposed amendment receded. Senator Sumner withdrew his support, telling a Jewish constituent that, while he had no objection to formally recognizing God in the Constitution, he objected to amending the Constitution to declare that the nation was Christian. The *Independent* also rescinded its support, describing the proposal's supporters as "fanatics" for seeking to "engraft the Christian religion into the Constitution."[28] In late 1864 the proposal was nonetheless introduced in Congress, but in March 1865 the Senate Judiciary Committee issued a short report declaring that it was "unnecessary and injudicious, at this time, to make such an amendment." Senator Lyman Trumbull, speaking for the committee, sought to rebut the suggestion that the committee opposed "the recognition of God in the Constitution." On the contrary, Trumbull explained, a constitutional amendment was unnecessary because "the Constitution of the United States does recognize the existence of a Supreme Being." The Constitution implicitly expresses faith by requiring that federal officers take an oath before assuming office, "and what is an oath," Trumbull asked, "but a promise corroborated or confirmed by an appeal to the Supreme Being?"[29]

The Threat to Protestant Dominance and the Growth of the Christian Amendment Movement

The end of the Civil War and the 1865 Senate rejection of the Christian amendment ended the first chapter in the story of the campaign for the Christian amendment, but it was only after the war that the National Reform Association became a true national movement and established itself as a fixture on the national political scene that lasted through the end of the century. By 1872 the NRA had thirty local chapters and thousands of members, concentrated primarily in New England and the Midwest.[30] Its journal, the *Christian Statesman*, claimed to have at least ten thousand readers.[31] In 1874 the NRA submitted a petition to Congress with over fifty thousand signatures on behalf of the proposed Christian amendment.[32] Many prominent political and legal leaders supported the NRA, including Justice William Strong of the US Supreme Court, who served as the NRA president from 1867 to

1873.[33] In 1874 the NRA's vice presidents included senators, governors, and federal and state judges, in addition to leading religious leaders.

The postwar growth of the NRA was propelled by a series of conflicts over the role of religion in public life. Religious minorities began to challenge laws and practices that had long given Protestantism a privileged place in American public life, including state and local laws that required Sabbath observance, that mandated religious oaths to serve on juries or in state governments, and that prohibited blasphemy.[34] The most contentious political disputes over religion addressed the role of Christianity in public schools. Public education in the nineteenth century was generally nonsectarian in the sense that it inculcated generic Protestantism rather than providing education associated with any particular Protestant sect.[35] Public schools typically used the King James Bible to teach moral lessons, and daily Bible readings were common.[36] During the second half of the nineteenth century, however, demands grew louder to take the Bible out of the public schools and make them less Protestant.[37] Catholics, Seventh-Day Adventists, Jews, and freethinkers considered the teaching of Protestant morality and scripture in the public schools to conflict with principles of equality and the separation of church and state. Protestant defenders of the public schools responded by insisting that the Bible was essential to teaching morality and American values.[38]

These disputes over the role of religion in public life reflected the nation's growing religious diversity. At the turn of the nineteenth century, the population of Catholics in the United States had been less than fifty thousand, but by 1850 Catholics numbered approximately 1.5 million and represented the nation's single largest religious denomination. By the end of the nineteenth century, over twelve million Catholics resided in the United States.[39] Catholics were becoming politically organized and vocal. Followers of other religions were also increasing, including Jews, Seventh-Day Adventists, and Mormons, and they too demanded religious liberty.

Conflicts over Protestant preeminence that gave rise of the Christian amendment movement illustrate group threat theory. Developed in the sociology literature, group threat theory posits that members of culturally and politically dominant groups develop hostility to subordinate groups in response to perceived threats posed to the dominant group's interests.[40] Substantial research into American race relations supports the theory and has shown that white racism increases in areas where the population or perceived power of African Americans has increased.[41] Similarly, studies show that native-born Americans develop increased hostility toward immigrants when the population and perceived power of immigrants increases.[42] In the case of the Christian amendment movement, the perceived threat arose from the increased population and power of Catholics, Jews, Seventh-Day Adventists, and freethinkers, which together were understood to challenge the dominant status of Protestants.

As the Catholic population rose, anti-Catholic sentiments grew increasingly prevalent. Denunciations of Catholics could be heard from uneducated nativist rabble-rousers to President Ulysses Grant, who in 1875 predicted that the next civil war would pit Protestants against Catholics, or as he indelicately put it, "patriotism and intelligence on the one side and superstition and ignorance on the other."[43] Many Protestants described the demands for religious equality made by Catholics and other minorities to be tantamount to demands to subjugate the Protestant majority.[44] Religious minorities had no right, they argued, to tell the majority to stop expressing their faith in the public schools and through law.

The Christian amendment movement appealed to Americans who thought opposition to Protestantism in public life was nothing less than a war on Christianity. Reverend David McAllister, general secretary of the NRA, characterized the reason why so many joined the movement: "It was the attack of enemies of our common Christianity upon the Christian features of our national life that struck the alarm, and sounded the rallying cry which has drawn together many of the best citizens of our land, and banded them in this Association."[45] By challenging Bible reading in schools, Sunday observance laws, and prohibitions on blasphemy, McAllister declared, opponents of the Christian amendment were "waging relentless war upon every vestige of national religion yet left us."[46] As leaders of the Christian amendment movement saw it, their opponents were winning: "Step by step the enemy gains," warned one Presbyterian pastor, "and the Christian sentiment is overbalanced by a contemptible minority of the people."[47]

And who were these people who were attacking Protestants? NRA supporters pointed to "atheists and infidels, communists and papists."[48] Others pointed to "the 'secular' party"[49] and those who were "thoroughly determined to sever American society from all religious influence."[50] Still others pointed to "Deists, Jews, and Seventh-Day Baptists."[51] Regardless of the religious or political identity NRA supporters attributed to those who assertedly were attacking Christianity, one fact was clear: they were *foreign*. Supporters of the Christian amendment were often quite explicit that the threat to Christianity came from immigrants, who posed an alien threat.

Speaker after speaker at the NRA conventions declared that the United States must take action to preserve its long-standing Christian identity, which was under siege due to "the character of the immigration which has poured upon us."[52]

The Nationalist Framework: A War on Christianity Is a War on America

Many Protestants understood the threat to their status through a nationalist framework and saw the nation's growing religious diversity as a threat to the United States itself. The response illustrates how group dominance and national identity are deeply connected. As Elizabeth Theiss-Morse has shown, a cohort of Americans consider themselves to be not just American but *prototypically* American, predominately those who are native-born, white, and Christian.[53] Much more so than other Americans, those who consider themselves prototypically American consider their own traits and values to be *national* traits and values, and they consider those who do not share these traits and values to be less authentically American.[54] As Theiss-Morse has also shown, those who consider themselves prototypically American react sharply to criticism from people they consider to be marginal Americans, perceiving their criticisms as attacks on America.[55]

Consistent with these findings, Protestant Americans of the nineteenth century, who had long held a dominant position in America, considered their faith and their values to be defining national features. Speakers at the National Reform Association's annual conventions repeatedly declared that Christianity was central to American identity, and for them Christianity was synonymous with Protestantism.[56] Reverend A. D. Mayo declared at the 1872 convention: "The people understand that this is a Christian country. The mass of the people are Christian in belief. Our whole order of society and government is such as could only have grown up in a land where the people had reached a very advanced and practical form of Christian faith."[57] As proponents of the Christian amendment declared, Christian beliefs are "interwoven in the warp and woof of our national existence."[58]

Convinced that Protestant devotion was a core aspect of American identity, proponents of the Christian amendment considered it un-American to challenge Bible reading in schools, Sunday observance laws, and blasphemy laws. "Secular critics," proclaimed Reverend Mayo, were "born and educated abroad, and ignorant of the first principles of

American life."[59] To supporters of the Christian amendment, immigrants adhering to different faiths could not share in American values because "they did not share in the first settlement of this country; they did not brave the hardships, they did not profess the principles which have made that settlement memorable. They never, anywhere, developed, or even dreamed of such a nationality as ours."[60]

Supporters of the amendment were often explicit in asserting that non-Protestants had no rightful place in America: "If the opponents of the Bible do not like our government and its Christian features," Reverend E. B. Graham told an NRA convention in 1885, "let them go to some wild, desolate land, and in the name of the devil, and for the sake of the devil, subdue it, and set up a government of their own, on infidel and atheistic ideas, and then if they can stand it, stay there till they die."[61]

Before the growth of the US population of Catholics, Jews, and other non-Protestants, many Americans may have assumed, without giving it much thought, that being Protestant was an essential part of being American, but once that status was challenged it became imperative to develop an explanation for *why* the United States was Protestant and should stay that way. Proponents of the Christian amendment responded by developing a comprehensive belief that Christian devotion had always been at the core of US history.[62] As one advocate for the Christian amendment put it: "The principles which we here present are not new in American politics. We are able to plead many precedents, which must have the weight of authority with the American people. Our country was originally settled by men of high religious character, whose only motive in seeking a home in the wilderness was the freedom and safety of religion and the glory of God."[63] Supporters of the Christian amendment pointed to the Mayflower Compact and colonial charters to show that the first European immigrants came on a Christian mission.[64] They pointed to religious language in early state constitutions, in the Declaration of Independence, and the Articles of Confederation.[65] They pointed to state court decisions that declared that Christianity is part of the common law.[66] They pointed to the long-standing practices of appointing legislative chaplains and issuing official declarations of days of thanksgiving and prayer.[67] They compiled anthologies of founding-era quotations that purported to show that the nation had been founded by devout Christians who sought to create a Christian nation.[68]

The Christian history of the United States developed by proponents of the Christian amendment contains the familiar features of a Golden Age narrative.[69] In the movement's explanation, the Founding Fathers created a nation with pure ideals devoted to God. The nation's devotion to Christian values ushered in an era of unprecedented prosperity. Yet now a rising tide of immigrants and secularism was destroying this purity and called into question the nation's Christian values. The American people were losing their way and had stopped following the pure Christian values upon which the nation was founded. As a result, a series of challenges arose, in which foreign-influenced residents tried to remove the Bible and prayer from the schools, overturn blasphemy laws, and repeal Sabbath observance laws. The narrative pointed to a dire future: if they continued to deny their true Christian nature, the American people would lose their Christian soul and face complete destruction.[70] The narrative also offered a solution—a return to the pure ideals upon which the nation had been founded.

For supporters of the Christian amendment, the story of America's Christian history contained a crucial lesson: the nation must rededicate itself to its Christian faith by permanently placing an expression of that faith in the document that embodies the nation's identity.

The Constitution and the Mirror

Group threat theory helps explain why some Protestants in the nineteenth century felt compelled to mobilize in response to the threat to their status posed by the nation's increasing religious diversity, and the social theory of national identity helps explain why they perceived the threat in nationalist terms. One crucial question remains: Why did the mobilization focus on *constitutional* demands?

The answer lies in the role that the Constitution plays in America's nationalist consciousness. Americans have long understood the Constitution to be an expression of national values and character. Supporters of the Christian amendment believed that the best way to preserve the Christian nature of the United States was to place an expression of that identity in the Constitution itself.[71]

Supporters of the Christian amendment frequently proclaimed that it was crucial that the Constitution come into harmony with the nation's true identity. In his address to the movement's 1872 convention, David McAllister declared: "It is a principle clearly stated by the best writers on political science, that in a nation where there is a written Constitution, that instrument should take its character from the nation for which it is framed. A written Constitution is simply a translation into legal language . . . of the facts actually evolved by the social forces of the nation."[72] As amendment supporters understood it, a godless Constitution was inconsistent with the Christian nature of the American people—it did not translate into legal language the true nature of the American people and therefore required correction.[73] As another speaker at the 1872 convention put it, the Constitution was false because it did not accurately mirror the American people: the Constitution, he said, is "without a single word from which it could be determined that this is a Christian nation,—we believe [it] to have been false to the true character of the nation, when it was framed; we believe it to be false to the national character to-day."[74] Amendment supporters explained that they did not so much want to put God into the Constitution as to make the Constitution an accurate reflection of the nation, to "*put the people into it*, trying to make our Constitution . . . a fair and true, and not a libellous [*sic*] exponent of the nation."[75]

Proponents of the Christian amendment believed that putting Christian devotion in the Constitution would not only make the Constitution accurately reflect the nation's Christian identity but also protect that identity. As they saw it, national identity would inevitably mirror whatever the Constitution said. As the NRA's McAllister put it: "The written Constitution must be amended to conform to the facts as they have actually been evolved . . . [or] the Constitution will in time conform everything to itself. The facts, the usages, the legislative and judicial actions, everything, in a word, that is out of harmony with the written instrument, will give way before its moulding and controlling influence, and disappear."[76] In this conception, the Constitution both reflects and shapes national identity. If the Constitution were Christian, the nation would stay Christian, but if the Constitution stayed godless, the people would become godless.[77] McAllister warned that failure to make the Constitution Christian would allow anti-Christian forces to "wipe out everything of a Christian or even moral character, until our whole political page should become a pure, unbelieving, irreligious, Christless, Godless blank."[78]

Opponents of the amendment presented a very different conception of American identity.[79] "We do not believe that this is a Christian nation," declared the Seventh-Day Adventist paper, the *American Sentinel*, "and no amendment to our National Constitution will make it such."[80] Although a majority of Americans may have been Christian, the *Sentinel* explained, that fact did not make the United States a Christian nation.[81] And if the nation were not truly Christian, a constitutional declaration of national faith would therefore be false.[82] Opponents further argued that the proposed amendment conflicted with what they called "the American idea," which they understood in civic republican terms as equality among diversity.[83] "If as a nation we stand for any thing," freethinker John Chadwick wrote in 1875, "it is for 'equal rights for all'; not for 'all white men,' not for all Christians, not for all theists even, but for all."[84] Opponents feared that the Christian amendment would make non-Christians into second-class citizens.[85] As the *American Sentinel* put it, the amendment would have the effect of asserting that "the Jewish and unbelieving portion of our people are not, of right, part of the people."[86]

Although the competing sides in the fight over the Christian amendment disagreed over the nature of American national identity, they agreed that the Constitution was central in defining national identity.[87] As the first witness testifying in support of the amendment before the House Judiciary Committee in 1896 explained:

> The parties in this debate agree substantially in these two things: First, that the Constitution is a secular document; and, second, that the facts in our life are Christian; but the one party claims that a secular constitution is right and that it ought to remain so, and that all the facts in our national life should be brought down to it, viz, abolish prayers in Congress, chaplains in the Army, Bible from the schools, remove everything Christian, and convert our whole civilization into secularism. The other party contends that every Christian feature shall be maintained, and asks that the Constitution be amended so as to secure all such features.[88]

As this testimony reflects, the dispute over the nation's religious identity became a *constitutional* dispute, rather than simply a social conflict or even a conflict on the validity of laws and practices supporting Protestantism, because of the widespread belief, shared by proponents and opponents of the Christian amendment, that the Constitution must reflect the true nature of the American people.

The Many Defeats and the One Lasting Success of the Christian Amendment Movement

The Christian amendment never came close to ratification. Although it was introduced in Congress again and again, it never made it out of a House or Senate committee.[89] Yet by the end of the nineteenth century it appeared that the movement had succeeded after all.

In 1892 the Supreme Court issued its decision in *Holy Trinity Church v. United States* and gave the National Reform Association what it had been asking for: a declaration that the United States is a "Christian nation." The case addresses what today is an inconsequential question involving a long-repealed provision of federal immigration law, which prohibited employment contracts that encouraged immigration. The case is of lasting significance, however, because in ruling that the statute should not be read to cover ministers, the Supreme Court declared that the statute must be construed in light of the fact that the United States is a Christian nation.

The NRA was not directly involved in the case, but the decision unmistakably reflects its influence. The Court pointed to the same evidence of the nation's Christian history that had been developed by the NRA in support of the Christian amendment. In his opinion for the Court, Justice David Brewer points to religious language in colonial charters to show that the nation began with a religious mission. The opinion points to religious language in the Mayflower Compact, the Declaration of Independence, and state constitutions. It cites declarations in state court opinions that the United States is a Christian nation. As well, it cites various state and federal laws that protect Christian practices, including many of the same laws and practices that the Christian amendment was proposed to protect: blasphemy laws, Sunday closing laws, and legislative prayers. The Court quotes approvingly from a statement by Chancellor James Kent that similar protections need not be given to non-Christians.[90]

Holy Trinity Church placed the Supreme Court's imprimatur behind the central claims of Christian nationalism espoused by the Christian amendment movement: the American people are a Christian people and therefore the United States is a Christian nation; American history demonstrates that the nation is devoted to Christianity and therefore Christian practices have a privileged status protected by law; and Christian values and practices are an intrinsic and unobjectionable part of American public life.

The decision was immediately recognized by both sides in the fight over the Christian amendment as an endorsement of the NRA's central claims. In its first issue after *Holy Trinity Church*, the NRA's official newspaper proclaimed victory, declaring the Court's decision the "Greatest Occasion for Thanksgiving":

> "This is a Christian nation." That means Christian government, Christian laws, Christian institutions, Christian practices, Christian citizenship. And this is not an outburst of popular passion or prejudice. Christ did not lay his guiding

hand there, but upon the calm, dispassionate supreme judicial tribunal of our government. It is the weightiest, the noblest, the most tremendously far-reaching in its consequences of all the utterances of that sovereign tribunal. And that utterance is for Christianity, for Christ. "A Christian nation!" Then this nation is Christ's nation, for nothing can be Christian that does not belong to him. Then his word is its sovereign law. Then the nation is Christ's servant. Then it ought to and must, confess, love and obey Christ. All that the National Reform Association seeks, all that this department of Christian politics works for, is to be found in the development of that royal truth. "This is a Christian nation."[91]

The NRA immediately took credit for the decision, accurately declaring that the Court's description of the role of Christianity in US history "reads as if largely gathered from the National Reform Manual."[92]

The joy felt by supporters of the Christian amendment was matched by opponents' alarm. The *American Sentinel* denounced *Holy Trinity Church* as "another *Dred Scott* decision." Just as *Dred Scott* had declared that persons of African descent "had no rights that the white man was bound to respect," the *Sentinel* said that the Court had now effectively announced "that disbelievers in the Christian religion have no rights which believers are bound to respect."[93] It agreed with the NRA that the Court had endorsed the history and adopted the philosophy behind the Christian amendment, declaring that the decision "culminates in the National Reform shibboleth, and the capsheaf has been put to the theory that the Christian religion is part of the common law of the individual States, by declaring, by fiat of the Supreme Court, the United States to be a Christian Nation."[94]

With the decision in *Holy Trinity Church*, it appeared that the Christian amendment movement had achieved in court what it had failed to achieve through the process for a constitutional amendment.[95] At the same time, *Holy Trinity Church* undercut the campaign to adopt the Christian amendment. Perhaps there was no need to amend the Constitution after all, some argued, because the Supreme Court itself had already agreed that the nation was Christian and that Christianity was, in some sense, the law of the land.[96] Continuing the fight for an amendment after *Holy Trinity Church*, the NRA's chief lobbyist argued that an amendment remained necessary so that "the Constitution shall say what the Supreme Court has already said, as to the Christian status of our government, but in a more authoritative form."[97] Now that the Supreme Court had agreed that the United States is a Christian nation, opponents argued, a constitutional amendment was no longer necessary, if it ever had been.

After *Holy Trinity Church*, supporters of the Christian amendment stopped arguing that the Constitution was godlessly secular and increasingly began to argue that the Constitution already was and had always been Christian. As reported in 1900 in a Seventh-Day Adventist paper, supporters of the NRA

> were wont only a few years ago to assail the Constitution as a "Godless instrument" because it contained no recognition of Deity. But now that a justice of the Supreme Court has shown in an *obeter dictum* how to discover in that document something which is clearly not there at all, these men are not slow to avail themselves of this aid and to loudly proclaim that "this is a Christian nation."[98]

While the Christian amendment movement had not succeeded in amending the Constitution, it had gained official recognition from the Supreme Court of its central claim: Christianity, not godless secularism or religious pluralism, was the law of the land.

The Demise of the Christian Amendment Movement

The movement to adopt the Christian amendment never entirely died. Much diminished in size, the NRA continued to push for an amendment until it finally folded in 1945.[99] A new organization calling itself the Christian Amendment Movement was formed the next year for the purpose of continuing the fight.[100] The amendment was still necessary, one pamphlet declared, because Christian practices in public life continued to be challenged and because of the need to "afford a constitutional basis for Christian legislation and judicial decisions."[101] The newly formed Christian Amendment Movement declared anew that the proposed amendment would save Christian America from the threats of secularism.[102] The proposal was endorsed in 1947 by the National Association of Evangelicals.[103]

In both 1954 and 1964 Congress again held hearings on the proposed amendment, which reiterated and expanded on the same arguments and counterarguments that had developed during the nineteenth century.[104] Representatives of groups that had thrived in the nineteenth century but that had shrunk ever since, including the Women's Christian Temperance Union, once again argued that the Constitution failed to reflect the true Christian nature of the nation and that it must be amended to bring the American people and the Constitution into harmony.[105] Supporters of the amendment relied on the comprehensive history of Christian America developed by the amendment's nineteenth-century supporters, presenting a catalog of religious-laden quotations by leading Americans from the colonial era through modern times.[106] Supporters of the amendment pointed to *Holy Trinity Church* as the definitive declaration that the nation is Christian.[107]

The renewed push to adopt the Christian amendment was opposed by several organizations that had gained prominence in mid-twentieth-century America, including the American Civil Liberties Union, Americans United for the Separation of Church and State, and several leading Jewish organizations. Like their nineteenth-century predecessors, opponents of the amendment articulated an egalitarian national vision, which they found in the Declaration of Independence and the Constitution.[108] By that time, however, the diverse groups that opposed the amendment and supported religious pluralism had become mainstream, while those calling for a Christian Constitution had become decidedly marginal.[109] The amendment once again failed to make it out of committee.

Judeo-Christian Nationalism of the Eisenhower Era

While Christian nationalism of the kind advanced by the Christian amendment movement became increasingly marginal in the first half of the twentieth century, a new more ecumenical movement took its place—a movement that valorized the nation's "Judeo-Christian heritage" rather than its specifically Christian or Protestant heritage. Differences aside, Judeo-Christian nationalism followed much the same pattern as the Christian amendment movement. Like the Christian amendment movement, Judeo-Christian nationalism arose in response to a perceived group threat, in this case the threat that many religious Americans perceived from communism abroad and at home. Just as the rise of religious pluralism was seen by many nineteenth-century Protestants as a threat to national identity, the threat from communism was understood in nationalist terms as an attack on the fundamental values of America. As with the Christian amendment movement, Judeo-Christian nationalists sought official recognition of their understanding of American identity. Unlike the Christian amendment movement, Judeo-Christian nationalists succeeded in adding an expression of faith to the nation's laws—winning adoption of changes to both the Pledge of Allegiance and the national motto ("In God We Trust")—but like the Christian amendment movement failed when they sought a constitutional amendment.

American presidents and other leaders had long heaped praises on the nation's Christian heritage, but during World War II that language began to shift and American political and religious leaders started to praise the nation's "Judeo-Christian" heritage.[110] The phrase came into usage to express opposition to the anti-Semitic policies of the nation's enemies and to convey the notion that in the United States Jews shared in the nation's heritage and should not be thought of as outsiders. During the 1930s some prominent right-wing organizations signaled their support for fascism and anti-Semitism by calling their organizations "Christian," including Father Charles Coughlin's Christian Front and Gerald L. K. Smith's Nazi-allied Christian Nationalist Crusade. "Judeo-Christian" became the term of choice for those opposing fascism who sought to convey a more pluralist national conception.[111]

After the war, political leaders continued to use the term, invoking "Judeo-Christian" in much the same ways that earlier leaders had invoked the nation's Christian heritage. President Dwight D. Eisenhower used the phrase to connote the nation's common religious heritage that he asserted was at the root of American history and culture: "Our form of government has no sense unless it is founded in a deeply felt religious faith, and I don't care what it is. With us of course it is the Judeo-Christian concept but it must be a religion that all men are created equal."[112] In this broadened conception of the nation's religious heritage, adherents of Protestant, Catholic, and Jewish traditions could all claim to share in the nation's creed of equality and justice.[113]

With Eisenhower's election in 1952, religious nationalism of a generically monotheistic kind found an enthusiastic advocate. "One of the reasons I was elected," Eisenhower explained, "was to help lead this country spiritually."[114] Religious leadership was necessary, Eisenhower believed, to reinforce the differences between the United States and the atheistic materialism of communism.[115] As Eisenhower declared in his inaugural address, "We who are free must proclaim anew our faith."[116]

Judeo-Christian Nationalism and the Pledge of Allegiance

Eisenhower and his allies quickly found a way for the nation to express its religious faith: by adding a declaration that the United States is a nation "under God" to the Pledge of Allegiance. Although others had advocated for it earlier, the proposal to add a declaration of faith to the pledge gained sudden momentum in February 1954 when Reverend George M. Docherty, pastor of the New York Avenue Presbyterian Church, delivered a sermon attended by Eisenhower, which was entitled "Under God."[117] Docherty began the sermon by trying to define the "American Way of Life." The American way of life means "going to the ball game and eating popcorn, and drinking Coca Cola, and rooting for the Senators." Docherty concluded, however, that "it is deeper than that."[118] He explained that the United States is fundamentally based upon its "Judeo-Christian" heritage.

The nation is committed, Docherty declared, to "fundamental concepts of life [that] had been given to the world from Sinai, where the moral law was graven upon tablets of stone, symbolizing the universal application to all men; and they came from the New Testament, where they heard in the words of Jesus of Nazareth the living Word of God for the world." Assured that the United States is based upon Christian and Jewish values, Docherty said he was shocked when he first paid attention to the words of the Pledge of Allegiance: "I pledge allegiance to the flag of the United States of America and to the Republic for which it stands; one nation, indivisible, with liberty and justice for all." Docherty concluded that something was missing in the pledge: "That which was missing was the characteristic and definitive factor in the American way of life. Indeed, apart from the mention of the phrase, the United States of America, this could be a pledge of any republic. In fact, I could hear little Muscovites repeat a similar pledge to their hammer-and-sickle flag in Moscow with equal solemnity." What was missing, Docherty preached, was an expression of religious devotion, a declaration that the nation's values and liberties come from God. To omit an expression of religious devotion, Docherty said, was "to omit the definitive character of the American way of life."

Docherty's proposal to add an expression of religious devotion to the Pledge of Allegiance bore some similarity to the proposal to add an expression of Christian devotion to the Constitution. Just as some Christians in the nineteenth century were appalled that the Constitution did not reflect the nation's Christian faith, Docherty was appalled that the pledge contained no expression of faith. While the pledge does not have the same legal or cultural status as the Constitution, it too expresses the nation's essential principles: that the United States is "one nation, under God, indivisible, with liberty and justice for all." Just as nineteenth-century Christian nationalists believed that threats to the Christian nature of America necessitated amending the Constitution, Docherty argued that threats to the nation's identity could be met by revising the pledge.

To be sure, Docherty's understanding of America's religious identity was broader than that of nineteenth-century Christian nationalists and included Protestants, Catholics, and Jews. He chose the words "under God" because he thought they were sufficiently ecumenical to express the full scope of America's religious identity and could be embraced by all true Americans. As a Christian, Docherty stated, he might prefer the words "under Christ," but he accepted that the nation had welcomed people of differing faiths.

Docherty conceded that the revised pledge would not embrace one group: atheists. He was adamant, however, that atheists *should* be excluded because they are not real Americans: "Philosophically speaking, an atheistic American is a contradiction of terms," Docherty insisted. "They really are spiritual parasites." To Docherty, secularism was un-American.

Within days of Docherty's sermon, members of Congress had introduced several bills to add "under God" to the Pledge of Allegiance.[119] The short, successful campaign for the proposal echoed the themes of Docherty's sermon. Like Docherty, many members of Congress reiterated the fear that communism and secularism posed a threat to America's religious traditions.[120] They too saw the threat to religion in nationalist terms. As US Representative Louis C. Rabaut declared, the pledge did not match America's true self because it "ignores a definitive factor in the American way of life *and that factor is belief in God.*"[121] As Representative Charles E. Bennett explained, declaring the nation's faith would serve to protect the nation from foreign attack: "At the base of our freedom is our faith in God and the desire of Americans to live by His will and by His guidance. As long as this country trusts in God, it will prevail."[122]

In signing the bill to amend the pledge, President Eisenhower said that an expression of national dedication to God was necessary to make the pledge an accurate reflection of the nation's "true meaning": "From this day forward, the millions of our school children will daily proclaim in every city and town, every village and rural school house, the dedication of our nation and our people to the Almighty. To anyone who truly loves America, nothing could be more inspiring than to contemplate this rededication of our youth, on each school morning, to our country's true meaning."[123] Members of Congress celebrated the enactment of the bill on the steps of the Capitol.[124] They first turned toward the flag and recited the newly amended Pledge of Allegiance, and, as recounted in the *Congressional Record*, "appropriately, as the flag was raised a bugle rang out with the familiar strains of 'Onward, Christian Soldiers!'"[125]

In the next few years, Congress took additional steps to proclaim the centrality of religious devotion in the nation's identity. In 1955 Congress enacted legislation requiring that the words "In God We Trust" be printed on all bills and coins.[126] In doing so, the House Banking and Commerce Committee explained that the phrase expressed "the spiritual basis of our way of life."[127] The following year, Congress adopted "In God We Trust" as the nation's official motto, replacing the pluralist motto *E Pluribus Unum*.[128]

Judeo-Christian Nationalism and the Proposed Constitutional Prayer Amendment

By the mid-1950s, Judeo-Christian nationalists—those who believe that Christian and Jewish devotion is central to American identity—could feel secure that their conception of American identity had gained official recognition. Not only had the Supreme Court declared in 1892 that the United States is a "Christian nation" but Congress had acted to mandate that school children daily acknowledge that they live in a nation "under God," and it had adopted "In God We Trust" as the national motto, to be displayed on every coin and bill. A constitutional amendment declaring the nation's religious identity might have seemed superfluous. Yet a new drive was soon launched to amend the Constitution to further express and protect the nation's religious heritage. As with the drive to amend the Pledge of Allegiance and the national motto, the attempt to amend the Constitution followed the pattern set by the Christian amendment movement: a perceived threat to the status of religious Americans was understood in nationalist terms and propelled members of the threatened group to try to protect their status by mobilizing in support of constitutional demands.

The issue that propelled the new drive to amend the Constitution addressed the place of religious expressions in public schools, the same issue that had been central to the Christian amendment movement. This time, the push for a constitutional amendment arose as a result of decisions by the US Supreme Court restricting public expressions of faith. In *Engel v. Vitale* the Court struck down a nondenominational prayer adopted by New York for use in the New York public schools.[129] New York had adopted the prayer precisely for religious nationalist reasons, declaring that "belief in and dependence upon Almighty God was the very cornerstone upon which our Founding Fathers builded."[130] Citing *Holy Trinity Church* and the addition of "under God" to the Pledge of Allegiance, the New York Court of Appeals had upheld the prayer as an expression of the nation's core religious identity: "No historical fact is so easy to prove by literally countless illustrations as the fact that belief and trust in a Supreme Being was from the beginning and has been continuously part of the very essence of the American plan of government and society."[131]

Yet, in *Engel* the Supreme Court disagreed, ruling for the first time that prayer in public school was unconstitutional.[132] Although the Court conceded that expressions of religious faith had been a regular part of the nation's public life, the Court ruled that a state cannot conduct religious exercises as part of the public school curriculum.[133] The next year, in *School District of Abington Township v. Schempp*, the Court struck down a Pennsylvania requirement that teachers begin the school day with Bible reading.[134]

The decisions in *Engel* and *Schempp* provoked widespread outrage. Many saw the decisions as an attack on the nation's Judeo-Christian essence.[135] Reverend Billy Graham declared that *Engel* was "another step toward secularism in the United States."[136] Former president Herbert Hoover declared that *Engel* accomplished the "disintegration of a sacred American heritage."[137] For some, *Engel* and *Schempp* were proof of a Communist plot to destroy America's distinctive religious faith.[138] Governor George Wallace of Alabama said that the decisions were "part of a deliberate design to subordinate the American people, their faith, their customs and their religious traditions to a Godless state." He warned that if courts were to rule "that we cannot read the Bible in some school, I'm going to that school and read it myself."[139]

Many Americans who considered religious faith to be a central part of their identity saw the decisions in nationalist terms and denounced the rulings as an attack on the nation. They sought to rally support for a constitutional amendment to protect the nation's religious essence, just as the National Reform Association had sought a constitutional amendment to protect the nation's Christian essence.[140] Supporters of an amendment believed that what was really at stake was not simply the validity of religious practices in schools but the nation's very identity. As the National Governors Conference declared, a constitutional amendment "will make clear and beyond challenge the acknowledgment of our nation and people in their faith in God."[141]

When Congress first held hearings on the proposal in the spring of 1964, an amendment appeared likely to pass.[142] Polls showed that 79 percent of Americans supported it.[143] It was supported by leading national organizations, including the American Legion, the Lions, Kiwanis, and Junior Chamber of Commerce.[144] The amendment also received the endorsement of the Republican Party, which remains committed to it to this day.[145]

Within a short time, however, the proposed school prayer amendment also engendered strong opposition. Like the failed Christian amendment, the fight over the proposed school prayer amendment pitted those who considered the United States a Christian nation (or at least a Judeo-Christian nation) against those who believed that religious pluralism was central to American identity.[146] Like their nineteenth-century predecessors, proponents of the school prayer amendment believed that the nation's religious identity must be expressed in the Constitution and encouraged in public life—and especially in the public schools, where national citizenship was inculcated.[147] Opponents countered by arguing that protecting the nation's religious diversity required that the government avoid public expressions of religion, as the Supreme Court had ruled.[148]

The proposed school prayer amendment failed after the leadership of the nation's most prominent faiths turned against it. The National Council of Churches, representing most mainline Protestant churches, came out against the amendment, as did the national organizations for Baptists, Episcopalians, Quakers, Seventh-Day Adventists, and Jews. These churches said that allowing prayer in school would lead to divisions among religious groups, and that supporting religious pluralism was more important than supporting public expressions of faith. The National Association of Evangelicals disagreed and supported the proposed amendment, just as it had the Christian amendment.[149] Despite the defeat, the demand to protect religion in public schools and in American public life generally has remained a recurrent source of dispute, once again channeling a dispute over the nation's religious identity into a public contest over the Constitution.[150]

The New Christian Right

Beginning in the late 1970s, a new wave of Christian nationalism came to national prominence, a movement often referred to as the New Christian Right.[151] The New Christian Right is a loose term for a cohort of evangelical, fundamentalist, and Pentecostal Christians, associated most prominently with Jerry Falwell, Pat Robertson, and James Dobson, and their organizations the Moral Majority, the Christian Coalition, and Focus on the Family.[152] Although the New Christian Right included members of different Christian sects with different theologies, they constituted a movement because together they helped mobilize conservative Christians as an organized force in American politics, inveighing against abortion, feminism, gay rights, pornography, and rock 'n' roll music.[153]

The New Christian Right is not usually considered a constitutional movement. Unlike the movement to adopt the Christian amendment in the nineteenth century and the movement to adopt a school prayer amendment in the 1960s, the New Christian Right did not make demands for constitutional amendments a centerpiece of its agenda. Yet a review of books and speeches by leaders of the New Christian Right shows that the movement often expressed its agenda in constitutional terms. In contrast to the leaders of the Christian amendment movement, who read the Constitution as a godless document out of sync with the nation's Christian identity, leaders of the New Christian Right understood the Constitution to be a quintessentially Christian document intended to govern a Christian nation.[154] Rather than demanding that the Constitution be amended to protect the nation's Christian identity, the New Christian Right campaigned that the Constitution should be *interpreted* to protect the nation's Christian identity.

Despite this difference, the New Christian Right followed much the same script as the Christian amendment movement of the nineteenth century and the Judeo-Christian nationalism of the 1950s and 1960s: (1) the movement was propelled by a perceived threat to the dominant status of Christians, in this case the threat posed by "secular humanism"; (2) the perceived threat to Christian preeminence was understood in nationalist terms, as an attack on the United States itself; and (3) the movement sought to protect the nation's Christian identity by enshrining that identity in the Constitution, in this case by demanding that the Constitution be understood as Christian. As with earlier episodes of Christian nationalism, the New Christian Right was opposed by a variety of groups that offered a pluralist national vision. Like those earlier episodes, the clash between the New Christian Right and its opponents over these competing conceptions of national identity was carried out in constitutional terms.

Group Threat: Secular Humanism

Since the 1950s, America has been growing less Protestant and more secular. In 1954, the year that "under God" was added to the Pledge of Allegiance, 71 percent of Americans identified as Protestant. By 1979, the year Jerry

Falwell founded the Moral Majority, only 58 percent of Americans said they were Protestant. The percentage of Americans identifying as Protestant has continued to decline, and in 2016 only 38 percent of Americans identified as Protestant. At the same time, the percentage of Americans who describe themselves as having no religion has increased, from less than 1 percent in 1954 to 7 percent in 1979 and to 17 percent in 2016.[155]

The rise of the New Christian Right bears out group threat theory, that majority hostility against minority groups increases as the population and perceived power of a minority increases. In the 1970s and 1980s, many Christians looked on the nation's growing secularism with alarm and saw it as a threat to the nation's Christian heritage.[156] The New Christian Right was their response.

In 1979 Jerry Falwell published *Listen, America!*, a best-selling book that set out an agenda for mobilizing conservative Christians.[157] Falwell was a Southern Baptist minister who in response to the civil rights movement had argued that it was inappropriate for clergy to become politically active. Although fundamentalist and other evangelical Christian organizations had significant involvement in political disputes in the first two decades of the twentieth century—including organizing to prohibit the teaching of evolution in the public schools—they largely retreated from organized participation in politics in the 1920s.[158] In 1965 Falwell had criticized Reverend Martin Luther King Jr. for using Christianity in a political campaign.[159] By 1979, however, Falwell had come to believe that conservative Christians needed to participate in politics to protect America's Christian identity.[160]

Falwell saw evidence all around that Christianity was under attack. He saw it in the Supreme Court's school prayer cases. He saw it in *Roe v. Wade* and the acceptance of abortion, homosexuality, pornography, drugs, and rock music, all of which he saw as attacks on the family, which he considered a "God-ordained institution" that forms the "fundamental building block and the basic unit of our society."[161] He saw an attack on Christianity in the women's movement, as a result of which he asserted that "nearly every occupation has been invaded by women," and "many women have never accepted their God-given roles."[162] He saw an attack on Christianity in public school textbooks, which he believed denigrated faith and promoted socialism. And he heard an attack on Christianity in the music of David Bowie, the Rolling Stones, and the Who, which Falwell said celebrated hedonism and led to satanism.[163]

As Falwell saw it, American elites had become hostile to Christianity and were engaged in widespread persecution of Christians. Falwell accused liberals of attempting to victimize and silence Christians through the courts, popular culture, and academia.[164]

Falwell was not alone in these views. Phyllis Schlaffly, who founded the Eagle Forum in 1972, agreed that anti-Christian forces had launched a "direct attack" on "those who believe that God created us, and that He created a moral law that we should obey."[165] Pat Robertson, a Southern Baptist minister, founded the Christian Coalition in 1989, which expressed agreement that Christians in the United States were under attack. As one Christian Coalition pamphlet warned, "Danger! Christian Americans are under siege. Schoolchildren are being threatened and adults jailed for the peaceful practice of God-given rights. It's time to say, enough. Time to regain a voice in government and raise a righteous standard."[166]

Although the New Christian Right identified various threats to Christianity, it had a name for the force that was attacking Christianity: secular humanism.[167] The term was popularized by Reverend Tim LaHaye in his 1980 book, *The Battle for the Mind*, which declared that "only two lines of reasoning permeate all of literature: biblical revelation (the wisdom of God) and the wisdom of man (a.k.a. humanism)."[168] For LaHaye, secular humanism was "the world's greatest evil" and the cause of most societal problems: "Crime and violence in our streets, promiscuity, divorce, shattered dreams, and broken hearts can be laid right at the door of secular humanism."[169] Other fundamentalists and evangelicals soon began to use the term.[170] For Falwell, humanism amounted to a philosophy of autonomy unrestrained by any moral principles, a philosophy that placed man at the center of existence and focused on "self-realization through reason," rather than salvation through faith. Secularism teaches that man, not God, "is in charge of his own destiny."[171]

There was some disagreement among the leaders of the New Christian Right on the exact nature of secular humanism. For Falwell, secular humanism was a new version of godless communism. As he declared, "Humanism promotes the socialization of all humanity into a world commune."[172] Other leaders of the New Christian Right understood secular humanism to be synonymous with the philosophies of fascism, Nazism, or New Age spiritualism.[173] What they agreed on, however, was that secular humanism threatened Christian dominance.[174]

For many in the New Christian Right, the Supreme Court's decisions in *Engel* and *Schempp* to reject prayer and Bible reading in public schools laid the groundwork for the advance of secular humanism.[175] Once God had been taken out of schools, Falwell and others exclaimed, the schools began teaching the philosophy of humanism instead of the word of God. With a foothold in the schools, humanism began to permeate American popular culture and could be found in movies, television shows, and rock music.[176] In his influential book *A Christian Manifesto*, Francis Schaeffer declared that Carl Sagan's PBS show *Cosmos* "indoctrinated millions of unsuspecting viewers" with secularist philosophy. As Schaeffer declared, the "humanist view has infiltrated every level of society."[177]

The Nationalism of the New Christian Right

One might suppose that a decline in the percentage of Americans identifying as Christian would mean that the belief that the United States is a Christian nation would also decline. In fact, just the opposite occurred: the decline in the percentage of Americans identifying as Christians has corresponded with an *increase* in the percentage of Americans who believe that the United States is a Christian nation.[178] Group threat theory helps explain this seeming paradox. The nation's increasing secularism and religious diversity has made many Christians fear for the loss of their dominant status, making them more likely to rally around the idea of a Christian nation. The more threatened Christians feel about their status, the stronger they believe the nation is Christian.

The New Christian Right became the vehicle for defending a Christian conception of American identity. Like earlier Christian nationalists, the New Christian Right did not merely identify secular humanism as a threat to Christianity but declared it a threat to the nation itself. Supporters of the New Christian Right considered themselves to be prototypically American and therefore identified Christian values and beliefs to be American values.[179] They considered threats to Christian preeminence to be tantamount to attacks on what makes America *America.*

If Christianity represented what was truly American, secular humanism was seen as an *alien* force that must be rooted out for the nation to survive. Members of the New Christian Right routinely depicted secular humanism as foreign to the true values upon which the nation was founded.[180] As LaHaye put it, secular humanism was responsible for the destruction of true American values: its influence "has moved our country from a biblically based society to an amoral 'democratic' society during the past forty years."[181]

Looking at the rise of secular humanism, Falwell asked, "What has happened to the America we knew?"[182] He feared that a loss of America's Christian identity would spell the end of America's very existence.[183] Other leaders of the New Christian Right agreed that secular humanism posed an existential threat to the United States. John Whitehead, founder of the Rutherford Institute, a civil rights organization dedicated to protecting Christian practices, declared that "if Christianity is separated from America then America no longer exists."[184] He believed that the point of no return had already passed and lamented that "we live in a post-American culture."[185] Pat Robertson agreed: "We had in America a Christian nation," but with the rise of religious diversity and secular humanism, "it has been taken away from us."[186]

Christian nationalism was the New Christian Right's central message. As Falwell declared in 1993: "We must never allow our children to forget that this is a Christian nation. We must take back what is rightfully ours." Ralph Reed, director of Robertson's Christian Coalition, expressed the same sentiment: "What Christians have to do is take back the country. . . . I honestly believe that in my lifetime we will see a country once again governed by Christians . . . and Christian values."[187] In his presidential bid, Robertson declared that if he were elected, only those in the Judeo-Christian tradition would serve in his administration.[188] Several years later, he defended this proposal: "When I said during my presidential bid that I would only bring Christians and Jews into the government, I hit a firestorm. . . . the media challenged me. . . . 'How dare you maintain that those who believe the Judeo-Christian values are better qualified to govern America than Hindus and Muslims?' My simple answer is, 'Yes, they are.'"[189]

The Constitutional Agenda of the New Christian Right

Perceiving a threat to Christian faith, leaders of the New Christian Right launched a nationalist campaign to "take back" the country and return it to its true Christian values. Like earlier Christian nationalist movements, the New Christian Right presented its nationalist demands in constitutional terms, equating a return to the nation's true Christian identity with a return to the true meaning of the US Constitution.

Leaders of the New Christian Right understood the Constitution to be a central expression of the nation's Christian heritage. As Falwell put it, "the goal of the framers of our Constitution was to govern the United States of America under God's laws." He preached that the United States had been established on biblical principles: "Any diligent student of American history finds that our great nation was founded by godly men upon godly principles to be a Christian nation." Falwell devoted a chapter of *Listen, America!* to a review of the Christian history of the nation, compiling episodes and quotations from the Founding Fathers much like those put together by the Christian amendment movement and recounted in the *Holy Trinity Church* opinion. Reviewing this history, Falwell expresses pride "that our country was born in the tradition of respect for God and the love of Jesus Christ."[190]

Other leaders of the New Christian Right also declared the Constitution to be an expression of Christian values and described the supposed attack on America's Christian identity in constitutional terms. As Pat Robertson declared, "The Constitution of the United States is a marvelous document for self-government by Christian people. But the minute you turn the document into the hands of non-Christian people and atheist people, they can use it to destroy the very foundation of our society. And that's what's been happening."[191]

Robertson blamed the Supreme Court for rejecting what he believed to be the true meaning of the Constitution, which "rests squarely on the Bible."[192] He declared that the Court's treatment of the Constitution was akin to but even worse than rape:

> Rape is a horrible crime, but my message tonight is not about the brutal rape of a young woman. I want to tell you about a much more insidious rape, a rape that has been repeated over and over, a rape that was not directed against the virtue and self worth of a few individuals. I am talking about a rape of our entire society. A rape of our nation's religious heritage, a rape of our national morality, a rape of time-honored customs and institutions—yes, and, especially, a rape of our governing document, the United States Constitution.

To Robertson, the assault on the Christian nature of the Constitution and America's Christian identity began with the Court's 1962 decision in *Engel* to prohibit prayer in public schools: "Back in 1962, some of us screamed for help as the garments of civic virtue were being ripped from our society. We cried out in anguish as each successive assault tore something precious within the viscera of our nation. But . . . few heeded our cries."[193]

Robertson believed that the Court's rejection of school prayer and Bible reading had led to national decadence:

> After a forty year assault on religious faith in our schools and public institutions, the liberal predators have given our nation the following: America leads the

world in the use of illegal drugs. America leads the world in pregnancies to unwed teenagers. America leads the world in abortion. America leads the world in violent crime. America leads the world in the percentage of the population incarcerated in prisons. America leads the world in divorce.[194]

Many leaders of the New Christian Right agreed with Robertson that the Court's decisions in *Engel* and *Schempp* represented a turning point in the nation's history, when governing elites rejected the nation's Christian heritage and embraced secular humanism.[195] In rejecting public expressions of Christian devotion in schools, the Court had essentially overturned what an earlier generation of Christian nationalists had achieved in *Holy Trinity Church*—a judicial recognition that the United States is a Christian nation and that its laws should be read in light of that identity. To leaders of the New Christian Right, *Engel* and *Schempp* were not merely decisions misconstruing the First Amendment's Establishment Clause. These decisions launched a war on Christianity, an attempt by the alien forces of secularism to destroy the religious foundations of the nation.[196]

As it developed, the New Christian Right developed a comprehensive conception of the Christian nature of the Constitution. That theory has been popularized by David Barton, who devoted the bulk of his book *The Myth of Separation* to proving that *Holy Trinity Church* was correct to declare that the United States is a Christian nation.[197] Barton concludes that history demonstrates that the Constitution "was designed to perpetuate a Christian order" and must be "interpreted within the understanding of Christianity."[198] Although Barton has been criticized by professional historians "as a biased amateur who cherry-picks quotes from history and the Bible," his Christian-dominated history and understanding of the Constitution has been deeply influential in conservative circles.[199] For instance, Kansas governor Sam Brownback declared that Barton's work "provides the philosophical underpinning for a lot of the Republican effort in the country today—bringing God back into the public square."[200] Mike Huckabee, a Fox News host and former Arkansas governor, called Barton "America's greatest historian" and said that American students should be "forced at gunpoint" to hear his national narratives.[201]

Like the Christian amendment movement, the New Christian Right presented its claim that the United States is a Christian nation in constitutional terms. Unlike the earlier movements, the New Christian Right argued that the Constitution has been Christian all along. The different strategies—amendment versus interpretation—corresponds to a shift in how constitutional change has generally been effectuated from the nineteenth century to today. Until the 1930s, major changes in constitutional structure were accomplished through constitutional amendments, and movements for abolition, women's suffrage, and temperance carried out their agendas by working to enact constitutional amendments. Since then, most important changes in our constitutional system—such as the end of de jure racial segregation, the recognition of women's legal equality, the adoption of same-sex marriage, and the expansion of presidential power—have been accomplished through new interpretations of the Constitution, rather than amendments.[202] The Christian amendment movement and the New Christian Right each sought to carry out their agenda of Christian nationalism by making the Constitution Christian, using the mode for constitutional change that prevailed in each era.

Conclusion

Movements to make the Constitution Christian have been a recurrent part of American politics. These movements have reflected conflicts for dominance among different sects and disputes over the content of American identity. To be sure, history is filled with much bloodier ways to settle disputes over ethnic and religious dominance than sustained fights over the content of the Constitution. It may well be preferable for disputes over national identity to be channeled into constitutional contests rather than, say, violence, terrorism, or civil war. Yet when disputes over national identity are carried out as disputes over the Constitution, it has served to obscure the real controversy: whether Christian people, Christian values, and Christian practices are entitled to claim a privileged status in American life, and whether competing values should be rejected as dangerously foreign and un-American.

3 | The Nativist Constitution

This chapter tells the story of an idea. It is an old idea, an ugly idea, a discredited idea. For much of US history, some Americans have asserted a nativist belief that the Constitution was made only for people who share the ethnic identity of the nation's founders, while others should be excluded from entering the country out of suspicion that their race, background, or religion make them likely to harbor hostility to the nation's constitutional principles.

Because it's an old idea, there have been different names for the people who are included and excluded. Sometimes the people for whom the Constitution was said to be written were called white, and sometimes they were called Anglo-Saxon, Nordic, or European. Sometimes they were called "real Americans," or "100% Americans," or just plain old Americans. Sometimes the people who were said to be unfit for the Constitution were called Negro or Irish or Chinese or Italian or Jewish or Hispanic or Muslim. But each time the idea has been pretty much the same: the Constitution was not made for them, and they must be excluded out of suspicion that their presence in the United States will undermine the nation's values.

Nativist movements are frequently but mistakenly described as embracing an aberrant conception of American nationalism. The prevailing conception is that American national identity is defined by commitment to a common creed—embodied most centrally in the Constitution—while nativists are said to consider race, ethnicity, and religion to be the core aspects of American identity rather than commitment to the American Creed.[1] In fact, throughout American history, nativist movements have shared the conventional belief that being American means believing in the American Creed. What makes nativism distinctive is the idea that only those who belong to the nation's predominant race, religion, or ethnicity are capable of embracing that creed.

This chapter shows that for most of American history, US immigration policies have been based on the nativist idea that only people who share the nation's dominant race, background, and religion are capable of constitutional devotion; others must be excluded because of the dangers they are suspected to pose to the nation's values. The nativist idea can be seen in the 1790 Naturalization Act, the Chinese Exclusion Act of 1882, and the National Origins Act of 1924. Although immigration law finally rejected the nativist constitutional idea in 1965, it remains a potent force in American politics today.

Who Is Fit for the Constitution? The Nativist Belief That Unwanted Foreigners Are Hostile to the Constitution

As the historian John Higham has explained, nativism should be understood as "intense opposition to an internal minority on the ground of its foreign (i.e., 'un-American') connections."[2] The basis for nativist opposition to different minority groups has varied over time—some were singled out because of their religion, others for their race, others for their ethnicity, and others for their political views. Higham, however, has noted the commonality of nativist movements: "While drawing on much broader cultural antipathies and ethnocentric judgments, nativism translates them into a zeal to destroy the enemies of a distinctively American way of life."[3]

Traditions of American nativism predate the establishment of the United States. Hostility to certain classes of foreigners was well-established by 1751, when Benjamin Franklin argued that immigration to the American colonies should be limited to "the lovely white" and should exclude "all blacks and tawneys." Franklin conceded that his racial preferences arose because he was "partial to the Complexion of my Country"—an indication that he had a racialized conception of the national community—but Franklin insisted that "such Kind of Partiality is natural to Mankind." Franklin further argued that not just whites but British subjects alone should be allowed to immigrate, while Germans (whom he referred to as "Palatines") should be excluded: "Why should the Palatine Boors be suffered to swarm into our Settlements, and by herding together establish their Language and Manners to the Exclusion of ours? Why should Pennsylvania, founded by the English, become a Colony of *Aliens,* who will shortly be so numerous as to Germanize us instead of us Anglifying them, and will never adopt our Language or Customs, any more than they can acquire our Complexion."[4]

Franklin's call to keep out the Palatines expresses several central nativist themes: immigration should be restricted to those who share the traits of the native-born population—their race, culture, national origin, and language. Foreigners who do not share these traits are naturally suspect; they are

"Boors" who "herd together" instead of assimilating and who maintain their own "Language and Manners" instead of adopting British ones. As with many subsequent nativists, Franklin described unwanted immigrants in animal metaphors, as a "swarm" and as a "herd," and he characterized their arrival in military metaphors, as an "invasion."[5] Admitting these foreigners, Franklin warned, would undermine and ultimately destroy the predominant culture of the American colonies—it would "Germanize" the Americans.

Among those of Franklin's generation, beliefs about the nation's republican values were often linked to beliefs about the nation's ethnic heritage. As discussed in chapter 1, the *Federalist* papers emphasized the connection between the nation's civic values and its ethnic and religious heritage. Soon after the Constitution's ratification, Congress adopted the Naturalization Act of 1790, which provided that naturalized citizenship could only be bestowed upon someone who was both a "free white person" and who swore to "support the constitution of the United States."[6] In *Dred Scott*, the Supreme Court agreed that persons of African descent lacked the capacity to participate in constitutional government.[7]

Around the same time as *Dred Scott*, the Know Nothing movement—the prototypical American nativist movement—sought to exclude Irish Catholic immigrants by invoking the same principle, that the Constitution was intended solely to protect persons of English descent, who had a unique capacity for self-government.[8] In 1856 the American Party (the official name of the Know Nothings) adopted a platform that articulated its opposition to Irish immigration in constitutional terms.[9] Irish Catholics brought disease and stole American jobs, the Know Nothings charged, but, even worse, Catholics would always be loyal to the pope and could never embrace the principles of the US Constitution. As one Know Nothing tract warned: "The strange, cruel monster of Rome can never amalgamate with the beautiful form of America. Liberty and Despotism are two eternal opposites."[10] In order to protect the Constitution and the American way of life, the Know Nothings argued, Catholics must be excluded from immigration and barred from positions of power.[11]

Although the Know Nothings achieved only limited success in stopping Irish immigration, in the following decades nativists succeeded in restricting immigration from China. In 1876 the Democratic Party adopted a platform that denounced all "Mongolian" immigration. As the party's platform declared, immigration from China should be barred because it amounted to "the incursions of a race not sprung from the same great parent stock, and in fact now by law denied citizenship through naturalization." The

Democrats declared that the Chinese were unsuitable immigrants because they could not participate in constitutional self-government: they were "unaccustomed to the traditions of a progressive civilization, one exercised in liberty under equal laws."[12] By 1880 the Republican Party agreed that Chinese immigration raised a "matter of grave concernment."[13]

In enacting the Chinese Exclusion Act in 1882, Congress concluded that the Chinese must be excluded because they were alien to the nation's constitutional traditions.[14] As one senator explained, "No one who framed the Constitution or voted for its adoption ever dreamed of incorporating people of the Mongolian race into our civilization."[15] Many members of Congress believed that the Chinese were incapable of participating in constitutional government. As another senator put it: "Free institutions are only possible with the favored races. It is not because they are a monopoly of the favored races, but because no other race is capable of creating them; no other race is capable of perpetuating them; no other race is capable of treading freedom's heights with firm and unwavering step."[16] Congress concluded that only members of the white race could create and sustain a free government, and the US political system would be destroyed if it allowed immigration of people who were incapable of participating in it. As one congressman put it: "If the Republic endures it must be a homogeneous population"; another declared that "unrestricted Mongolian immigration means ultimate destruction."[17] Excluding the Chinese was necessary, Congress declared, to protect the Constitution.

The National Origins Act: Protecting the Constitution from Dangerous Aliens

Although immigration from China and Japan was barred by law, European immigration to the United States greatly increased during the last quarter of the nineteenth century.[18] Not only did the number of immigrants and the percentage of foreign-born residents increase but the national origins and religion of the immigrants also changed.[19] While most immigrants before 1860 had come from England, Ireland, or Germany, beginning in the 1880s immigration from southern and eastern Europe increased, with millions of Italians, Russians, Greeks, Hungarians, and Poles arriving in the United States.[20] A majority of the new immigrants were Catholics and Jews.[21]

Many native-born Americans feared that the new immigrants brought crime, disease, poverty, and dangerous foreign ideas.[22] As discussed in chapters 1 and 2, the reborn Ku Klux Klan feared that the new immigrants would undermine the nation's white Christian heritage, and supporters of the Christian amendment feared that the immigrants threatened the preeminence of Protestantism. Two other movements arose to address widespread fears over the ability of the new immigrants to assimilate and participate in American public life. On the one hand, a movement arose to "Americanize" the immigrants by teaching them English and inculcating American values. On the other hand, a movement arose to restrict immigration from southern and eastern Europe based on the belief that Catholics and Jews were incapable of becoming good American citizens.

Although the Americanization and immigration restriction movements addressed concerns over immigration in different ways, they shared a similar understanding of what it means to be American. Both movements identified being American with adherence to a set of values they associated with the nation's founding, including commitment to personal autonomy, individual liberty, and democratic self-government. Both movements also identified the US Constitution as the embodiment of the nation's core values. Where they disagreed was over who was capable of embracing these values. Americanizers embraced the "melting pot" model, believing that the new immigrants could learn to love the Constitution if they were given the right kinds of encouragement and education. Immigration restrictionists, in contrast, embraced eugenics and believed that immigrants from southern and eastern Europe lacked the capacity for self-government and that no education could change that.[23] In the end, the eugenicists won.

The Americanization Movement

Until 1921, programs to help immigrants assimilate were the primary public response to increased immigration. The widespread belief that immigrants would soon acculturate to American life was frequently expressed through the metaphor of the "melting pot" that became part of the national vocabulary after the production of Israel Zangwill's play of that name in 1908.[24] The idea it expresses is considerably older. In 1782, Hector St. John de Crevecoeur published his "Letters from an American Farmer," which declared that in the United States various nationalities were "melting" together to create a new nation: "What, then, is the American, this new man? . . . I could point out to you a family whose grandfather was an Englishman, whose wife was Dutch, whose son married a French woman, and whose present four sons have now four wives of different nations. . . . Here individuals of all nations are melted into a new race of men." De Crevecoeur asserted that immigrants from across Europe assimilated into American life by embracing the new nation's republican values.[25]

During the nineteenth century, the public schools were the primary institution that sought to help new immigrants assimilate into American ways.[26] From its beginnings in the first half of the nineteenth century, the public school system was dedicated to teaching children to become good citizens.[27] As Steven Green has explained, public schools were created out of a "widespread belief that instilling moral virtue in children was indispensable for perpetuating the nation and its republican system of government."[28]

At the end of the nineteenth century, in response to increasing concerns that public schools could not reach adult immigrants, patriotic organizations representing the nation's established elites began to provide programs specifically to educate immigrants on American values. In 1898 the Daughters of the American Revolution launched a lecture series on American history and government, given in several foreign languages, to teach immigrants the "spirit of true Americanism."[29] Other patriotic societies soon followed. The Young Men's Christian Association (YMCA) began offering evening classes for immigrants that combined English-language instruction with lessons on American civics.[30] By 1914 the YMCAs' Americanization programs had over thirty thousand students.[31]

Some employers began requiring foreign-born workers to attend Americanization classes at their factories, consisting of language training and civics lessons.[32] Henry Ford's program culminated in an elaborate graduation ceremony called Americanization Day" which was held on the Fourth of July. In the ceremony, immigrants wearing the clothes of their native countries would descend into a large round structure labeled "Melting Pot," which the school's teachers would stir with ten-foot ladles.[33] The immigrants would then emerge from the pot wearing typically American clothes and waving American flags.[34] As the director of the program explained, "Into the pot 52 nationalities with their foreign clothes and baggage go and out of the pot after a vigorous stirring by the teachers comes one nationality, viz, American."[35] The ceremony perfectly captured the widespread notion that through education in the common American culture, immigrants would lose their backward foreign ways and become good patriotic Americans.

After beginning as a response by private groups, Americanization programs soon were offered by local and state governments. In the first decade of the twentieth century, many cities with large immigrant populations began offering night classes for immigrants to learn English and civics.[36] In 1907 New Jersey became the first state to support immigrant education classes, a program followed the next year by New York, which declared that its goal was the "making of new races into Americans."[37] At the same time, states increased their efforts to Americanize immigrant children in public schools and began to mandate civics classes, the display of the American flag, and daily recitation of the newly composed Pledge of Allegiance.[38]

Demand for Americanization programs soon became a national issue. In 1912 the Progressive Party platform condemned "the fatal policy of indifference and neglect which has left our enormous immigrant population to become the prey of chance and cupidity" and proposed action "to promote their assimilation, education and advancement."[39] Conservatives too called for Americanization programs as a way to combat communism and anarchism.[40] The US Senate agreed that a program of Americanization was the best way to avert industrial strikes.[41]

World War I led to a surge of interest in Americanization programs. The military discovered that illiteracy was especially common among foreign-born draftees.[42] Foreigners were also suspected of harboring dangerous ideas. During the war, German Americans were frequently accused of disloyalty, and after the war suspicions of disloyalty spread to other recent immigrants.[43] This can be seen in Teddy Roosevelt's denunciation of the "hyphenated Americanism" of those "who spiritually remain foreigners in whole or in part." He declared that all Americans should adhere to "the simple and loyal motto, AMERICA FOR AMERICANS." As Roosevelt put it, "Unless the immigrant becomes in good faith an American and nothing else, then he is out of place in this country, and the sooner he leaves it the better." Failure by immigrants to assimilate, the president warned, "will spell ruin to this nation."[44]

The federal government responded to demands for increased Americanization efforts through the Bureaus of Naturalization and Education, which encouraged states to adopt Americanization programs and sought to coordinate state programs.[45] Since 1790, US naturalization law had required a finding that immigrants were attached to the Constitution as a prerequisite to citizenship, but during the fervor of the Americanization movement the federal government became involved for the first time in trying to teach immigrants devotion to the Constitution.[46] In 1916 the Bureau of Naturalization began to distribute materials for a course on citizenship, which was widely used in Americanization efforts, and in 1920 the Bureau of Naturalization distributed nearly 100,000 citizenship textbooks designed to help immigrants assimilate as rapidly as possible and to protect American culture from foreign infiltration.[47]

Americanization efforts sought to transform immigrants into Americans by "preaching the gospel of Americanism," as one Americanization enthusiast put it.[48] Yet little consensus developed on what it took to transform immigrants into Americans. In practice, Americanization efforts took many forms. California adopted a program that sought to help new immigrants Americanize their homes by making them more sanitary and tidy, declaring: "Before a man should be asked to become a good American by being worthy of his surroundings, those surroundings should be made worthy of a good American."[49] Other Americanization programs focused on increasing wages and living standards for immigrants in the belief, expressed by one Americanization worker, that unless immigrants were provided a higher standard of living, they would continue to live in the "foreign quarters where the native language only is spoken, where the foreign news is printed in the mother tongue, and where the anarchist is reared."[50]

Franklin Lane, the US secretary of the interior who oversaw much of the federal Americanization effort, believed that Americanization could be accomplished in myriad ways:

> America is the expression of a spirit, an attitude toward men and material things, an outlook and a faith. . . . Now, this cannot be taught out of a book. It is a matter of touch, of feeling, like the growth of friendship. Each man is approachable in a different way, appealed to by very contradictory things. One man reaches America through a baseball game, another through a church, a saloon, a political meeting, a woman, a labor union, a picture gallery, or something to eat.[51]

At a 1916 conference on Americanization organized by the Department of the Interior, advocates asserted that Americanization could occur through contact with anything authentically American. They recommended programs to Americanize immigrants through movies, records, dances, and sports; through infiltration of the foreign press; through improved hygiene and housing; through improved working conditions; through participation in unions; and through programs in lumber camps, factories, and farms.[52]

Although Americanization efforts took many forms, a central focus of all Americanization programs was to educate immigrants on American political ideals.[53] English language instruction was considered a predominant component of Americanization program, but teaching English was often described not as an end in itself but as a means to teach American values. As one speaker at an Americanization conference explained, "The fundamental idea has been very largely the idea of giving the newcomer a working knowledge of the English language in the hope that he would, somehow or other, gradually assimilate the American spirit of freedom and gradually conform to the American ideal."[54]

Efforts to inculcate immigrants in American political ideals focused on the nation's founding documents. As Secretary Lane declared: "We know that there are principles enunciated in the Declaration of Independence and in the Constitution of the United States which are necessary to get into one's system before [an immigrant] can thoroughly understand the United States."[55] The focus on the nation's founding principles can be seen in a widely used handbook on Americanization, which included lengthy chapters on early American history and the founding of the nation.[56] By learning to admire the nation's founders and to become devoted to the nation's republican values, immigrants would join the American "race," as one Americanizer explained:

> We need harbor no hazy notions as to what the original Americans conceived Americanism to be. . . . You find it in the Declaration of 1776; you find it in the preamble of the Constitution—liberty, freedom, equality, abolition of destructions that divide us into castes, fraternity, brotherhood, union, cooperation, public welfare. No perusal of the speeches, papers, or letters of the fathers of the Republic is possible without apprehending their distinct and earnest prophecies of a new and better race arising upon these shores.[57]

Although the Americanization movement sought to welcome immigrants, it had a substantial nativist element in that it sought to eradicate foreign cultures from the midst of the United States.[58] As historian Benjamin Schwarz has written, "'Americanization' was a process of coercive conformity [whereby] various nationalities were made into American as ore is refined into gold. 'Americanization' purified them, eliminating the dross."[59] Americanization efforts tried to teach immigrants to adopt American culture and values by presenting immigrants with an idealized American, an American who was white, Anglo-Saxon, and Protestant. As educational sociologist Michael Olneck has written: "Not only did the content of the Americanizers' rhetoric, texts, and rituals symbolically assign status to those adhering most closely to the culture of native-born Americans. The activity of Americanizing the immigrants also assigned to native-born Americans the roles of tutor, interpreter, and gatekeeper, while rendering immigrants the subjects of tutelage and judgment."[60]Although the Americanization movement sought to persuade immigrants to give up their foreign ways, the movement was nonetheless based on an optimistic view of human nature, that all peoples, regardless of national origin, race, or religion, were capable of adopting American values and embracing the nation's constitutional principles.

The Immigration Restriction Movement

At the same time that the Americanization movement worked to transform immigrants into Constitution-loving Americans, another movement arose to exclude immigrants based on the conviction that they could never learn to love the Constitution. In 1894 three Harvard graduates, Charles Warren, Robert DeCourcy Ward, and Prescott Farnsworth Hall, formed the Immigration Restriction League (IRL) and declared that the group's purpose was to advocate for the "exclusion of elements undesirable for citizenship or injurious to our national character."[61]

The IRL's leaders declared that the "new immigrants" from southern and eastern Europe compared unfavorably with the "old immigrants" from northwestern Europe.[62] The league charged that the new immigrants contributed a disproportionate number of the nation's illiterates, criminals, and the insane.[63] It also argued that foreign governments were intentionally dumping their criminals and paupers on the United States.[64] The league further charged that unlike the old immigrants, the new immigrants did not assimilate into American culture and instead lived in ethnic enclaves, where they spoke in alien tongues and continued their alien ways.[65]

The IRL's primary complaint was that the new immigrants were unfit to participate in American political life. The league claimed that the new immigrants did not make good citizens because, by virtue of their foreign races and cultures, they were not adapted to participate in self-government in a nation committed to individual liberty.[66] As an 1896 IRL pamphlet explained, "The immigration of recent years is largely composed of elements unfitted to absorb democratic ideas of government, or to take part in the duties and responsibilities of citizenship under such a form of government."[67] Not only were the new immigrants unsuited to become good citizens, the IRL warned, but they brought over dangerous foreign ideas, and their growing presence in the United States threatened to undermine the American constitutional system.[68]

Leaders of the IRL believed that Americanization could never succeed, a claim they supported with the new science of eugenics, which asserted the inheritability of many human traits, including intelligence, criminality, and morality.[69] Prescott Hall, one of the founders of the IRL, explained that the American character was defined by "energy, initiative, and self-reliance," and this made Americans "impatient of much government, relying upon self-help rather than the paternalism of the State." These traits, Hall asserted, were inherited racial traits specific to people who were "mainly Teutonic, belonging to what is now called the Baltic race, from northern Europe."[70] Immigrants arriving since 1880, in contrast, were people "of entirely different races—of Alpine, Mediterranean, Asiatic, and African stocks," and "these races have an entirely different mental make-up from the Baltic race; they bring with them an inheritance of widely differing political and social ideals, and a training under social and political institutions very different from ours."[71]

Hall recognized that many Americans believed that the new immigrants could be Americanized, that "we can continue, as we have in the past, to assimilate all this material and turn it into good American citizens." He argued, however, that with the new immigrants Americanization efforts could never "appreciably alter their characters." The new immigrants were simply incapable of becoming American: "You cannot change the leopard's spots," Hall declared, "and you cannot change bad stock to good."[72]

The case for immigration restriction received significant support in 1916, when Madison Grant published the enormously influential *The Passing of the Great Race*.[73] Grant was a long-time vice president of the IRL, as well as a famed conservationist and the founder of the Bronx Zoo. He argued that race was the single explanation for the development of European and American civilization: "The progress of civilization becomes evident only when immense periods are studied and compared, but the lesson is always the same, namely, that race is everything."[74] Grant's taxonomy identified three European races—"Alpines," who were "always and everywhere a race of peasants"; "Mediterraneans," who made superior artists but poor athletes; and "Nordics," "a race of soldiers, sailors, adventurers and explorers, but above all, of rulers, organizers and aristocrats."[75] Grant described Nordics as having blond hair, blue eyes, pale skin, and tall stature, and he attributed to the Nordic race all of the key advances in Western civilization, from the Roman Empire to the Renaissance. Nordics constituted a discrete and distinctly superior subspecies of humanity: "*Homo europæus,* the white man par excellence."[76]

The scientific racism advanced by Grant and others had a great deal to say about who was capable of embracing America's constitutional values and who would forever be hostile to it. As Grant asserted, members of the Nordic race were "jealous of their personal freedom both in political and religious systems."[77] With their extreme devotion to individualism and autonomy, the Nordics developed the concept of individual liberty that forms the basis of the US Constitution and core American values. As one of Grant's disciples wrote: "Americanism is actually the racial thought of the Nordic race, evolved after a thousand years of experience, which includes such epoch-making documents as the Magna Carta and the Declaration of Independence."[78]

The Passing of the Great Race purports to tell a racial history of Europe and the United States. As Grant saw it, almost all of the colonists and founders of the United States were pure-blooded members of the Nordic race, and the American populace was predominately Nordic until the Civil War. Not only did the Civil War lead to the deaths of large numbers of what Grant referred to as the nation's "best breeding stock," what was even worse was that the war led the nation to grant citizenship "to Negroes and to ever increasing numbers of immigrants of plebeian, servile or Oriental races, who throughout history have shown little capacity to create, organize or even to comprehend Republican institutions." By giving citizenship to African Americans and allowing immigration by non-Nordics, Grant asserted, "the whole tone of American life, social, moral and political, has been lowered and vulgarized."[79]

Grant argued for the exclusion of immigrants from southern and eastern Europe because, as a matter of racial genetics, they lacked the fundamental American capacity for self-government: "Instead of retaining political control and making citizenship an honorable and valued privilege, [the American] intrusted the government of his country and the maintenance of his ideals to races who have never yet succeeded in governing themselves, much less any one else." Grant argued that foreign races did not embrace American values but instead brought with them the "diseases" of socialism and Catholicism, two value systems he believed inherently conflicted with individualism, which Grant considered the quintessential American value.[80]

Relying on Grant's book and others influenced by it, immigration restrictionists argued that science had disproven the melting pot ideology of the Americanization movement.[81] Robert DeCourcy Ward, a Harvard climatology professor and one of the founders of the IRL, said that Americanizers

had deceived themselves into believing that "we could change inferior beings into superior ones":

> We thought that sending alien children to school, teaching them English, giving
> them flag drills, and making them read the Declaration of Independence and
> recite the Gettysburg Address, would make them Americans almost overnight.
> Yet the laws of heredity are at work. We cannot make a heavy draft horse into
> a trotter by keeping him in a racing stable. We cannot make a well-bred dog
> out of a mongrel by teaching him tricks. Nor can we make a race true to the
> American type by any process of Americanization.[82]

Backed by the best science of its time, the IRL argued that the problems
associated with the new immigrants—crime, unemployment, immorality,
and the spread of radical ideas—could never be solved through education.[83]
The United States should stop trying to transform bad immigrants into
good Americans, the IRL argued, because it was an impossible task. Instead,
the United States should adopt a much more straightforward solution: keep
unwanted immigrants out.[84]

The Literacy Test and the Dillingham Commission

Initially, the IRL's agenda for restricting immigration focused on the
adoption of a literacy test. The league proposed to bar admission to
immigrants unless they could demonstrate an ability to read and understand
portions of the Constitution.[85] The IRL believed that illiteracy was highest
among undesirable races. By excluding immigrants who could not read
the Constitution, it asserted, a literacy test would exclude immigrants who
could never embrace its principles.[86]

In 1896, Senator Henry Cabot Lodge, a longtime IRL supporter,
introduced the first bill to create a literacy test.[87] Lodge made no effort
to hide the fact that the purpose of the test was to exclude ethnicities and
nationalities deemed too foreign to assimilate into American life:

> The illiteracy test will bear most heavily upon the Italians, Russians, Poles,
> Hungarians, Greeks, and Asiatics, and very lightly, or not at all, upon English-
> speaking emigrants or Germans, Scandinavians, and French. In other words,
> the races most affected by the illiteracy test are those whose emigration to
> this country has begun within the last twenty years and swelled rapidly to

enormous proportions, races with which the English-speaking people have never hitherto assimilated, and who are most alien to the great body of the people of the United States.[88]

Although Lodge claimed that the new immigrants increased crime rates and decreased American wages, he argued that "the danger which this immigration threatens to the quality of our citizenship is far worse." To fully understand the threat to American citizenship posed by the new immigrants, Lodge argued, "we must look into the history of our race."[89] Lodge claimed that the nation's greatness resulted from its racial composition, which gave the American people its distinctive qualities: independence, initiative, and a strong sense of morality. The racial qualities of native-born Americans kept socialism and other forms of radicalism at bay, Lodge believed, but the new immigrants came from races that were disposed to embrace radical, un-American politics.[90]

With the support of progressives and organized labor, the literacy bill passed both houses of Congress. President Grover Cleveland vetoed it, however, dismissing the idea that limiting immigration to those who could read the Constitution would somehow protect the American way of life.[91] Cleveland also rejected the underlying characterization of the recent immigrants as "undesirable." "The time is quite within recent memory," Cleveland's veto message explained, "when the same thing was said of immigrants who, with their descendants, are now numbered among our best citizens."[92]

Although Congress was unable to override Cleveland's veto, in 1907 Congress created a commission to study the immigration situation. Known as the Dillingham Commission after its chairman, Senator William Dillingham of Vermont, the commission included Senator Lodge and several other immigration restrictionists.[93] Its conclusions, issued in forty-two volumes over four years and backed by voluminous data, set the stage for decades of debate over immigration restrictions.[94]

The Dillingham Commission concluded that race should be the central focus of congressional efforts to regulate immigration. To help policy makers sort through the various races comprising the nation's immigrants, the commission issued a 150-page *Dictionary of Races or Peoples*, which meticulously attempted to define and describe what its authors identified as all of the world's races and subracial groups. The dictionary gave detailed descriptions of the physical traits said to characterize each race, as well as the unique personal character said to be typical of each race. Albanians, for instance, were said to be "brave, but turbulent in spirit—warriors rather than workers," while Serbo-Croatians were said to be "well adapted to hard labor."[95]

The commission concluded that due to the racial composition of the new immigrants, immigration from southern and eastern Europe posed a severe threat to the United States. It agreed with the IRL that the "old and the new immigration differ in many essentials."[96] The commission reported that whereas previous waves of immigrants had been settlers who sought to work the land and who easily assimilated into American life, the new immigrants were unskilled laborers who sought industrial jobs and kept to themselves. The commission concluded that "as a class," the new immigrants are "far less intelligent than the old," and "racially they are for the most part essentially unlike the British, German, and other peoples who came during the period prior to 1880."[97]

The Dillingham Commission agreed with Lodge and the IRL that the literacy test was "the most feasible single method of restricting undesirable immigration."[98] It noted that the level of literacy represented one of the most striking differences between immigrants from northwest Europe and immigrants from southern and eastern Europe, making literacy a straightforward way to exclude members of unwanted races.[99] The commission said it could not determine whether differences in literacy rates resulted from environmental factors or "racial tendencies," but it suggested that genetics was the likely cause because "races living under practically the same material and political conditions show widely varying results."[100]

With the backing of the Dillingham Commission, Congress renewed its push for a literacy test, and in 1912 Congress once again passed a literacy test bill.[101] President William Howard Taft vetoed it, as did President Woodrow Wilson when it was reenacted in 1915. Finally, in February 1917 the literacy test was enacted over President Wilson's veto.[102]

To the disappointment of immigration restrictionists, however, the literacy test did little to restrict the flow of large number of immigrants from southern and eastern Europe. Although the IRL and the Dillingham Commission believed that literacy rates were tied to race, in fact, literacy in eastern and southern Europe had significantly increased from 1896, when Senator Lodge first introduced a bill for a literacy test, to 1917, when a literacy test was finally adopted.[103] Requiring immigrants to demonstrate an ability to read the Constitution thus failed to achieve its supporters' goal of keeping out members of undesirable and unassimilable races.

The Demise of the Americanization Movement

Americanization efforts waned dramatically in the years after World War I
when the United States entered a period of increased nativism and hostility
to immigrants. Many Americans grew concerned about the loyalties of
immigrants. The Russian Revolution increased concerns that immigrants
would help spread radical political ideas. The war had convinced many
Americans of the urgency of national unity, which they believed was
threatened by ethnic diversity, a conviction captured by the slogan
"100-Percent American" popularized by the Ku Klux Klan.[104] Immigration
greatly diminished during the war, but once the war ended it began to
increase again, and nativists began to fear that a flood of undesirable
immigrants would soon arrive.[105]

In 1920, with the increased suspicion of foreigners and decreased
support for Americanization as a workable solution to the problems
associated with immigrants, Congress largely stopped appropriating money
for Americanization programs. Some state and private Americanization
programs continued, but as a movement Americanization faded.[106]

Even many supporters deemed Americanization efforts a failure.[107]
Frances Kellor, director of the National Americanization Committee,
believed that Americanization had gone too far in demanding that
immigrants give up their cultures and had pushed "more and more toward
repression and intolerance of differences."[108] Some immigrants who were the
recipients of Americanization efforts also complained that Americanizers
demanded more from them than native-born Americans. As one immigrant
representative said, "There is a mistaken notion among some well-meaning
people that the foreign-born would be better Americans if they understood
the Constitution of the United States. We do not agree with this because the
average American native does not know it either."[109]

Others argued that Americanization programs failed because they
did not go far enough in demanding complete assimilation. Henry Pratt
Fairchild, author of *The Melting Pot Mistake*, argued: "The traits of foreign
nationalities can neither be merged nor interwoven. They must be
abandoned. . . . The whole idea of assimilation is that there should be one
body, bringing other elements into conformity with its own character, and
that body in this particular case of assimilation is and must be America."[110]
In Fairchild's view, Americanization programs had allowed immigrants to
hold onto their cultures and values and did not require immigrants to fully
adopt American ways.

To immigration restrictionists like those in the IRL, however, the failure of Americanization efforts confirmed their belief that the new immigrants could never be transformed into Americans.[111] With the demise of the Americanization movement, demands to severely restrict immigration—rather than trying to make immigrants into Americans—became the dominant answer to the issue of immigration.

The Passage of the National Origins Act and the Triumph of the Nativist Constitutional Idea

Advocates of immigration restriction gained control of Congress in March 1919, following the midterm election of 1918. The chairman of the House Committee on Immigration and Naturalization became Albert Johnson, an enthusiastic nativist and member of the Eugenics Research Association, an association created by the IRL.[112] Johnson was convinced that the nation's immigration laws should be based principally on eugenics and the need to preserve the nation's racial heritage. He consulted frequently with the leadership of the IRL and met often with Madison Grant, author of *The Passing of the Great Race*. With Johnson as chairman, the Immigration Committee relied on leading eugenicists and in 1920 appointed its own "eugenics expert."[113]

By 1921, having seen the failure of a literacy test to keep out unwanted immigrants, Congress was ready to impose severe immigration restrictions to maintain the preeminence of the nation's long-governing ethnic groups. That year, Congress enacted what was termed an emergency measure to restrict immigration. The Emergency Quota Act restricted annual immigration to 3 percent of the number of foreign-born persons of each nationality then present in the nation.[114] The quota operated on a country-by-country basis, which had the effect of greatly limiting immigration from southern and eastern Europe.

Three years later, Congress adopted a long-term approach to immigration. The National Origins Act of 1924, also known as the Johnson-Reed Act, extended and made permanent the national origins system it had begun to construct in 1921.[115] The National Origins Act sought to freeze the nation's racial and ethnic mix as of 1920. It greatly reduced immigration from southern and eastern Europe by setting a cap on the total number of immigrants who could be admitted each year and allocating the available slots based on the national origins of the nation's white population as of

1920.[116] Because it was estimated that 79 percent of the white population was descended from the countries of northern and western Europe, those countries were allocated 79 percent of the annual immigration quotas. In contrast, only 15 percent of the white population was estimated to be descended from countries in southern and eastern Europe, and countries in those areas were therefore allocated 15 percent of the annual immigration quotas.[117] In addition, the act prohibited immigration of any people who were ineligible for naturalization, which continued the policy of barring immigration from Asia.[118]

Proponents of the national origins system made no secret that the law was intended to preserve national control by what supporters referred to as the Nordics and Anglo-Saxons.[119] The law's proponents identified many problems caused by Asian, Jewish, Italian, and other immigrants, but their primary concern was that these immigrants were unfit for the duties of citizenship in a constitutional republic. As Representative Johnson said, "we must pick and choose our future immigrants, and admit only such as show some signs as being the stuff of which good Americans can eventually be made."[120]

In enacting the National Origins Act, Congress found that the nation's constitutional values could be preserved only by maintaining white rule and, more particularly, rule by Americans of northwest European ancestry. Members of Congress repeatedly depicted immigrants from southern and eastern Europe as posing a threat to the Constitution. Congressman Charles Stengle of New York explained:

> Mr. Chairman, we hear much on this floor about our great American Constitution, and those whose names appear beneath that sacred document are held in loving remembrance by every true American. Every statute written for the guidance of this Republic is founded upon the doctrines of that organic instrument. We find therein the hopes and aspirations of a free people, the sacred guaranties of our liberties, as well as the protection of our homes and firesides. And yet right here in this country there are those to-day who would make of our magna charta a mere scrap of paper, notwithstanding the fact that we welcomed them to our shores in their hour of distress and need.[121]

Congressman Samuel McReynolds of Tennessee argued that continued immigration from southern and eastern Europe meant an increase in foreigners hostile to constitutional values, which in turn would lead to "the absolute destruction of our form of government and our institutions."[122]

In recommending passage of the National Origins Act, the House

Committee on Immigration and Naturalization made explicit the connection between the preservation of the nation's constitutional ideals and the preservation of the nation's racial composition. After declaring that a nation's government inevitably reflects the character and composition of the people, the committee report proclaims: "If, therefore, the principle of individual liberty, guarded by a constitutional government created on this continent nearly a century and a half ago, is to endure, the basic strain of our population must be maintained." Preserving the Constitution, the committee declared, required preserving "the basic strain of our population" and excluding members of unwanted races.[123]

President Calvin Coolidge, who signed the National Origins Act into law, also connected race-based immigration restrictions with the preservation of the nation's constitutional values. Coolidge had declared that immigration should be restricted to persons who are "temperamentally keyed for our national background," and in identifying acceptable immigrants, "there are racial considerations too grave to be brushed aside for any sentimental reasons."[124] In his 1923 State of the Union message, Coolidge had called for new immigration restrictions, reminding Congress that the nation had been "created by people who had a background of self-government" and asserting that immigration should be restricted to members of those racial groups that shared that background. Preservation of the nation's constitutional values required that the nation must stay white and Protestant. Or as Coolidge succinctly put it: "America must be kept American."[125]

The National Origins Act's Codification of Racial Hierarchy

The National Origins Act succeeded in greatly reducing immigrants that the act's proponents deemed undesirable. Before the passage of the act, around 200,000 immigrants had arrived from Italy each year, but beginning in 1924 the annual quota for immigrants from Italy was set at less than 4,000 per year.[126] Russia and Poland, which together had sent hundreds of thousands of immigrants to the United States, were allotted slightly less than 10,000 per year.[127] Immigration from Japan and China was effectively eliminated. In contrast, the nations of northwest Europe—England, Germany, and Ireland—were together allotted 100,000 immigrants per year. Immigration from these countries remained much lower than allotted, however, because far fewer people from these countries sought to immigrate.[128]

The National Origins Act carried out the conviction that the United

States is and should remain a white nation, ruled by white people. The act did not use the term *white*, but the focus on protecting the predominance of the nation's white ethnic base—what the House Committee on Immigration and Naturalization referred to as "the basic strain of our population"—is unmistakable from the mechanisms created by the act for allocating available immigration slots. Under the act, the annual number of immigrants was allocated based on the nations from which white Americans could trace their heritage. The Census Bureau, working with other agencies, was given the task of determining the national origins of America's white population— that is, calculating the percentage of the American population who are descended from immigrants from England, Germany, Italy, Russia, and so forth, and allocating available immigrant slots based on that calculation. The act explicitly excludes from this calculation all Americans descended from non-European countries.[129]

In determining who the American people were—and therefore who would be allowed to immigrate—African Americans, Asian Americans, Mexican Americans, and Native Americans simply and literally were not included.[130] In particular, the act excludes (1) Americans descended from immigrants from the Western Hemisphere, thus excluding all Americans whose families came from Latin America, (2) Americans who came from nations from ineligible for naturalized citizenship, thus excluding all American citizens of Asian descent, (3) Americans descended from slaves, thus excluding African Americans, and (4) all American Indians. As Letti Volpp has explained, under the 1924 act "the 'colored races' were erased from the history of national origins of America."[131]

Within the group of European Americans whose national origins were counted in allocating spots for new immigrants, the act established an unmistakable hierarchy. At the bottom were recent immigrants who had managed to get to the United States before the doors began to close in 1921.[132] They received few slots for additional immigration. At the top stood so-called Nordics, descendants of the race credited with founding the nation and establishing its constitutional principles, who received the bulk of the available immigration slots. To protect the Constitution, federal policy now provided that the demographic dominance of this group must be protected while immigration from other groups must be restricted.

The principles established in the National Origins Act provided the basis of American immigration policies for more than forty years.

The 1965 Immigration Act and Rejection of the Nativist Constitutional Idea

Public declarations about what it means to be American began to change in the decades after the enactment of the National Origins Act. During World War II, American leaders began to describe national identity in more universalistic terms, declaring that being American meant dedication to a creed of liberty and equality and had nothing to do with race, ethnicity, or national origin, which was therefore entirely unlike the Nazi blood-and-soil ideology.[133] As Franklin Roosevelt put it in 1943, "Americanism is not, and never was, a matter of race or ancestry. A good American is one who is loyal to this country and to our creed of liberty and democracy."[134]America's long-established hierarchies of race, religion, and national origin were an embarrassment that was best ignored.

The shifting tone in public declarations about American identity may suggest that there was a growing acceptance of a more race-neutral conception of American national identity. By 1952 that shift was not yet powerful enough to succeed in repealing the national origin system that restricted immigration. That year, Congress overrode President Harry S. Truman's veto and enacted the Immigration and Nationality Act. The act represented a modicum of progress toward a pluralist conception of American identity, repealing the requirement imposed in 1790 that limited naturalization to "white" persons.[135] However, the act maintained the national origins system that determined who would be allowed to immigrate and continued to leave the door open to immigrants from northwest Europe and exclude most others.

In vetoing the bill, Truman declared that the national origins system was based on nativist beliefs that conflicted with what he considered the nation's fundamental principles:

> The idea behind this discriminatory policy was, to put it baldly, that Americans with English or Irish names were better people and better citizens than Americans with Italian or Greek or Polish names. It was thought that people of West European origin made better citizens than Rumanians or Yugoslavs or Ukrainians or Hungarians or Baits or Austrians. Such a concept is utterly unworthy of our traditions and our ideals. It violates the great political doctrine of the Declaration of Independence that "all men are created equal."[136]

In contrast, Senator Pat McCarran, the chief sponsor of the 1952 bill, defended the national origins principle, which he said served "to preserve best the sociological and cultural balance in the population of the United States."[137] If the nation did not maintain the ethnic balance in which Anglo-Saxons were predominant, McCarran warned, it would cease to be America.[138]

After Congress overrode his veto, Truman set up a commission to recommend new immigration legislation. Its 1953 report, "Whom We Shall Welcome," argued that the national origin system conflicted with the nation's core values: "America was founded upon the principle that all men are created equal, that differences of race, color, religion, or national origin should not be used to deny equal treatment or equal opportunity."[139] Embracing a pluralist conception of national identity, the commission denounced the idea that white Europeans are best suited for American citizenship and declared that "all peoples are inherently capable of acquiring or adapting to our civilization."[140] The commission further noted that the nation's discriminatory immigration laws harmed its foreign policy interests because those laws had been used by Communists and the nation's foreign enemies to arouse anti-American sentiments.[141]

The shift to a conception of national identity that embraced pluralism was propelled by the civil rights movement of the 1950s and 1960s, which demanded that the United States live up to its commitment to equality.[142] "America is essentially a dream, a dream as yet unfulfilled," Martin Luther King Jr. proclaimed. "It is a dream of a land where men of all races, of all nationalities and of all creeds can live together as brothers."[143] Civil rights activists depicted the fight for Black freedom and equality as a fight to carry out America's unfulfilled ideals—ideals embodied in the Declaration of Independence and the Fourteenth Amendment. Based on their vision of a nation committed to racial equality, a vision they believed was embodied in the Constitution, they fought to overcome competing conceptions of nationalism based on race, ethnicity, and religion.[144]

By 1960 the belief that American identity was defined by commitment to a creed and not by race, ethnicity, or religion had become a consensus position. That year both major political parties campaigned to lift restrictions on immigration and to repeal the national origins system. The Republican Party's 1960 platform called for doubling the annual number of immigrants and insisted that admission should be based on individual merit and not an immigrant's race or national origin.[145] The Democratic Party platform agreed that the national origins system should be scrapped as "a policy of deliberate discrimination" that "contradicts the founding principles of this nation."[146]

In the presidential campaign that year, John Kennedy made immigration reform a priority. After Kennedy's election and assassination, President Lyndon Johnson continued the push for immigration reform. In January 1965 Johnson urged Congress to overturn the national origins system. As Johnson put it, "The fundamental, longtime American attitude has been to ask not where a person comes from but what are his personal qualities." Just as Franklin Roosevelt had claimed that Americanism had never involved race or ancestry, Johnson claimed that Americans had always been focused on personal merit, ignoring the inconvenient fact that US law had limited naturalization to whites from 1790 until 1952. The national origins system conflicted with America's long-standing commitment to equality, Johnson declared, because it deemed some people more fit for citizenship than others.[147]

During the summer of 1965, Congress debated an immigration bill backed by Johnson to overturn the national origins system. As with earlier debates over immigration policy, the 1965 debate centered on competing conceptions about the nation's constitutional values and the place of race, ethnicity, and national origin in American identity. Supporters of the bill argued that the national origins system was "contrary to our basic principles as a nation" and "repugnant to our national traditions."[148] They argued that an immigration system that no longer discriminated based on race or national origin would be the natural extension of the principles of the 1964 Civil Rights Act, which prohibited discrimination in employment and public accommodations. As Representative Laurence Burton argued: "Just as we sought to eliminate discrimination in our land through the Civil Rights Act, today we seek by phasing out the national origins quota system to eliminate discrimination in immigration to this Nation composed of the descendants of immigrants."[149]

Defenders of the national origins system, however, continued to argue that the Constitution would be threatened by admitting immigrants who did not share the background of prototypical Americans. Unsurprisingly, opposition to the bill was concentrated in the South and included many defenders of racial segregation. Senator Robert Byrd, for instance, argued that it was "just and wise" to restrict immigration to maintain the nation's ethnic balance, considering that the peoples of the world differ widely in "their inherited ability and intelligence, their moral traditions, and their capacities for maintaining stable governments."[150] Byrd criticized supporters of the bill as employing "sentimental slogans" and called on his colleagues to "resist the pressures for sharply increased immigration of persons with cultures, customs, and concepts of government altogether at variance with those of the basic American stocks." Byrd believed that an influx of brown-skinned immigrants from "Jamaica, Trinidad, Tobago, Indonesia, India, Nigeria, and so forth" would threaten constitutional government because they could "profoundly affect the character of the American population, and, in the long run, critically influence our concepts of government."[151] Other opponents of the bill agreed with Byrd that the preservation of constitutional government required the continued dominance of "the basic American stocks."[152]

Overturning the principles of the National Origins Act, Congress enacted the Immigration and Nationality Act in October 1965 with large bipartisan majorities in both houses of Congress.[153] For the first time, American law prohibited discrimination in immigration based on race, sex, and national origin.[154] Signing the bill into law at the foot of the Statue of Liberty, President Johnson declared that the act would "repair a very deep and painful flaw in the fabric of American justice" and would "make us truer to ourselves both as a country and as a people."[155]

The 1965 act profoundly changed the scale of immigration to the United States and made the nation more racially, religiously, and ethnically diverse.[156] In the first three decades after the act's enactment, more than eighteen million immigrants came to the United States—more than triple the number that had come in the previous three decades. Under the act, Mexico became the largest country of origin for new immigrants, and more than 30 percent of immigrants admitted came from Asia. These changes in immigration affected the nation's demographics. Whereas 85 percent of the US population was white in 1965, in 2017 that figure had fallen to 76.6 percent, and it is estimated that a majority of the population will be nonwhite by the middle of the twenty-first century.[157]

The Persistence of the Nativist Constitutional Idea

The nativist belief that people of European descent are naturally suited to embrace the Constitution has persisted despite its repudiation in the Immigration and Nationality Act of 1965. A new generation of immigration restrictionists has arisen and has maintained the belief that only certain immigrants will embrace the Constitution. They consider the 1965 act a national betrayal, in which America stopped being America and opened the floodgates to immigration by Asians and Latin Americans, whose presence is destroying the nation's culture and values.

Since 1979, one of the leading nativist voices has been the Federation for American Immigration Reform (FAIR).[158] Although FAIR's official position has been that immigration should not be restricted based on race or ethnicity, it has advanced a nativist agenda, sometimes quietly and sometimes openly.[159] FAIR received much of its initial funding from the Pioneer Fund, a eugenicist organization that has worked since 1937 to demonstrate white supremacy.[160] FAIR has frequently argued that immigrants from Asia and Latin America undermine American culture and destroy the American political system. As FAIR's founder, John Tanton, wrote, American immigration policy should try to preserve a homogeneous society because "too much diversity leads to divisiveness and conflict."[161] Tanton declared his support for the core principle of the National Origins Act: "for European-American society and culture to persist requires a European-American majority, and a clear one at that."[162] Tanton was especially concerned that immigration from Latin America undermines American political culture, telling FAIR employees that Latinos make poor citizens because they come from a culture marked by a "lack of involvement in public affairs."[163]

FAIR's skepticism of the ability of Latin Americans to embrace America's constitutional values has not been limited to private comments by Tanton but has been a significant part of its agenda. In testimony before Congress in 1996, Dan Stein, director of FAIR, testified that immigrants should only be allowed to become naturalized citizens if they can demonstrate that they share America's fundamental values—which he defined to include ambition, hard work, patriotism, "a commitment to understand and support our republican form of government, and a commitment to participate and vote in it," and "a willingness to recognize and support the Constitution and the nation's boundaries." Stein told Congress that he doubted the ability of Mexicans to meet those standards.[164]

Although FAIR has usually kept its nativist agenda coded, it has worked frequently with anti-immigrant advocates who openly espouse a return to race-based immigration policies. FAIR has frequently publicized the work of Peter Brimelow, one of the leading voices of white nationalism and anti-immigrant nativism.[165] Brimelow is the author of *Alien Nation: Common Sense about America's Immigration Disaster.*[166] *Alien Nation* argues that the United States is fundamentally a white nation, and ethnic pluralism is destroying the nation.[167] Brimelow longs for the days when America was whiter and therefore more truly American: "As late as 1950, somewhere up to nine out ten Americans looked like me. That is, they were of European stock.

And in those days, they had another name for this thing dismissed so contemptuously as the 'racial hegemony of white Americans.' They called it America."[168] Brimelow characterizes the 1965 Immigration and Nationality Act as an act of revenge taken by liberals like Ted Kennedy and by America's ethnic minorities, who despise the nation's native core. FAIR's President Dan Stein has agreed with this claim.[169]

Brimelow has praised earlier generations of nativists, including the anti-Catholic Know Nothings of the 1850s, describing them as patriots who were primarily concerned about preserving constitutional liberty.[170] Much like the scientific racists of the Immigration Restriction League, Brimelow has argued that today's immigrants are genetically inferior to white Americans and bring crime and disease, steal jobs, destroy the environment, and drain government resources.[171] What most concerns Brimelow, however, is that today's immigrants are radically undermining America's national character, turning the United States into what he calls an "Alien Nation," unrecognizable from what he considers the real, authentic America. Immigrants from Asia and Latin America, Brimelow argues, "are from completely different, and arguably incompatible, cultural traditions."[172]

Like earlier nativists, Brimelow believes that the Constitution was written to protect the nation's white ethnic core. He cites the Constitution's Preamble, which declares the purpose of forming "a more perfect Union . . . [for] ourselves and our posterity." Brimelow argued that the phrase "our posterity" refers to "the Founders' posterity, not posterity in general." That is, the Constitution was written by the nation's white founders to establish liberty for themselves and their white descendants.[173]

FAIR has also publicized the work of Jared Taylor, founder of the white nationalist journal American Renaissance, which bills itself as a "race-realist" publication that promotes "white identity."[174] Like other white nationalists, Taylor has sought to keep alive the belief that "the Constitution was written for white men, and that its protections were not intended for blacks."[175] In a 2012 essay, "What the Founders Really Thought about Race," Taylor agreed with the notion that Americans should be united by dedication to an American Creed but argued that the United States could become a nation with a shared creed only if it were racially homogeneous.[176]

FAIR also worked with Samuel Francis, who has been described as the "philosopher-general" of the radical right. Francis had been a columnist at the Washington Times until he was fired for making racist comments, and he went on to openly embrace the white supremacist cause. Like other champions of white power, Francis connects the nation's racial identity with the American Creed embodied in the Constitution and argues that only by reasserting white supremacy can the nation protect its constitutional values.[177] Embracing eugenics, Francis stated that nonwhites are incapable of adapting to America's constitutional values.[178] He believed that the "white European character of the United States" is under attack by the nation's growing nonwhite population and by the elite's embrace of multiculturalism.[179] Francis argued that America will cease to be America unless whites gain greater racial consciousness and rally around the long-standing historical conception of the United States as a white nation.[180]

Patrick Buchanan and the Return of Nativism to the Mainstream

The rhetoric of nativism returned to mainstream politics in 1992 when Patrick Buchanan challenged President George H. W. Bush for the Republican presidential nomination. Buchanan had been a speechwriter for President Richard Nixon and became a frequent guest on cable TV. In the 1980s, Buchanan's newspaper columns began to address white nationalist themes, when Buchanan asked how the United States could "remain a white nation." In 1992 Buchanan entered the Republican presidential primaries as a more mainstream version of Ku Klux Klan leader David Duke, who was also running in the primaries. Buchanan argued that rather than denouncing Duke, the GOP should adopt his message: "Take a hard look at Duke's portfolio of winning issues," Buchanan wrote, "and expropriate those not in conflict with GOP principles."[181]

Buchanan made what he described as "economic nationalism" the centerpiece of his campaign, arguing against free trade and in favor of immigration restrictions. He frequently articulated these positions through blunt appeals to white nativism. "Who speaks for the Euro-Americans, who founded the U.S.A.?," Buchanan asked. "Is it not time to take America back?"[182] He argued against the principle behind the 1965 Immigration Act, declaring that a million English immigrants would be better for the United States than "a million Zulus."[183] He called for a complete moratorium on immigration and proposed the construction of a border fence. He depicted the global situation as a battle between "Christian truths" and "Western Civilization," on the one hand, and "barbarians" and multiculturalists, on the other.[184]

Mainstream conservatives denounced Buchanan as a bigot. William F.

Buckley, editor of the *National Review*, rejected Buchanan because of his thinly veiled anti-Semitism.[185] Columnist George Will accused Buchanan of peddling a brand of nativism that conflicted with the prevailing belief that American identity depends solely on a commitment to a creed and is "not a matter of membership in any inherently privileged or especially appropriate group, Caucasian or otherwise."[186] Rejected by establishment conservatives, Buchanan was embraced by the extreme right.[187] Buchanan made clear that he shared the same white nativist worldview as Francis, Brimelow, and Taylor.[188] Francis served as a campaign advisor and urged Buchanan to focus on trade and immigration because these issues directly address the "racial dispossession of the historic American people."[189]

Buchanan articulated this nativist message in constitutional terms, asserting that the Constitution can only be understood as created by and for a white nation.[190] In doing so, he evoked many of the nativist themes of earlier anti-immigrant movements but with a crucial difference. In the early twentieth century, the Immigration Restriction League spoke for American elites. They were Harvard men, senators, and Ivy League scientists who were alarmed at the arrival of immigrants they considered a crass, dirty, and uneducated foreign rabble, which they believed would threaten the constitutional order that placed them at the top.[191] Buchanan, in contrast, sought to speak for white working-class Americans and attacked not only less privileged Americans but also American elites, who he accused of abandoning America's ethnic core.[192]

Buchanan expressed the resentments of what Sam Francis called Middle American Radicals. Francis argued that the nation had been taken over by liberal elites, who used their tax power to steal money from the white middle class to pay for welfare benefits for poor persons of color.[193] Middle American Radicals resent both the elite establishment that governs the nation and the poor, who they see as the undeserving beneficiaries of government largesse. Francis identified Middle American Radicals as the natural constituency for any movement supporting white rule.[194]

Buchanan's campaign proved that anti-immigrant nativism was alive and well. Although George H. W. Bush handily beat Buchanan in the 1992 Republican primaries, Buchanan received nearly three million votes, roughly a quarter of the votes cast.[195] Four years later, Buchanan ran again, won three primaries, and received over three million votes.[196] Although he never came close to winning the Republican nomination, Buchanan tapped into a constituency who saw themselves as prototypical Americans and who believed that American elites and racial minorities had deprived them of their rightful place as the center of American cultural and political life. Identifying their core values with the nation's foundational values, Buchanan's supporters believed that the Constitution itself was under attack. While these beliefs had flourished among extremists for decades, Buchanan succeeded in bringing them back into the mainstream.

Donald Trump and the Return of Nativism to the White House

In 2016 the United States elected the first president in decades who openly espoused nativist views and who made clear he intended to implement a nativist agenda. Donald Trump's election represented a dramatic reversal after the presidency of Barack Obama, who, perhaps more than any other president, articulated a national vision that placed devotion to a shared creed at its center.[197] In his second inaugural address, President Obama articulated what since 1965 has become the orthodox view that American national identity is defined solely by commitment to the American creed: "What binds this nation together is not the colors of our skin or the tenets of our faith or the origins of our names. What makes us exceptional— what makes us American—is our allegiance to an idea."[198] Obama often argued that key moments in American history—the Revolution, the Civil War, Reconstruction, the New Deal, the civil rights movement, the women's rights movement, and the gay rights movement, among others—were "the manifestation of a creed written into our founding documents."[199]

As a leading proponent of *birtherism*, the unfounded allegation that Obama was foreign-born and therefore constitutionally unfit for office, Donald Trump attacked the validity of Obama's presidency.[200] Trump repeatedly claimed that Obama was not born in the United States, that Kenya was his true homeland, that he might be Muslim, that he faked his birth certificate, and that he was not a legitimate president.[201] The birther charge echoes the nativist constitutional idea explored in this chapter, that the Constitution is made only for some people, defined by race and birth. Rather than directing that charge against a group deemed too foreign to become legitimate Americans, Trump and other birthers targeted the particular legitimacy of the nation's first Black president.

Trump's 2016 presidential campaign was built on the same nativist themes that animated the birther movement. His central campaign promises—building a wall on the Mexican border and barring Muslim immigration—invoke nativism by playing off fears of foreign infiltration and the need to exclude dangerous foreigners. Trump argued that undocumented Mexican immigrants were destroying the United States.[202] Like earlier generations of nativists who alleged that unwanted immigrants brought crime, Trump said that Mexican immigrants were rapists and murderers.[203] He faulted them for speaking Spanish and failing to assimilate.[204] He argued that Muslims should be barred from immigrating to the United States because they hate the United States and plot acts of terrorism.[205]

Trump embraced the view that federal immigration policy should distinguish between immigrants who are likely to embrace American values and immigrants who are likely to be hostile to American values: "We want people to come into our country, but we want people that love us. We want people that can cherish us and the traditions of our country. We want people that are going to be great for our country. We don't want people with bad, bad ideas. We don't want that."[206]

Trump's campaign advisors made clear that they believe that immigrants, especially brown-skinned immigrants, are destroying America's constitutional values. Michael Anton, who went on to become White House director of strategic communications at the National Security Council, wrote a widely circulated campaign essay, "The Flight 93 Election," which was described as "as an intellectual statement of Trumpism."[207] It accused Democrats of deliberately "importing" un-American foreigners to destroy the Constitution and pave the way for a leftist takeover:

> The ceaseless importation of Third World foreigners with no tradition of, taste for, or experience in liberty means that the electorate grows more left, more Democratic, less Republican, less republican, and less traditionally American with every cycle. As does, of course, the U.S. population. . . . This is the core reason why the Left [and] the Democrats . . . think they are on the cusp of a permanent victory that will forever obviate the need to pretend to respect democratic and constitutional niceties. Because they are.[208]

In arguing that "Third World foreigners" are making America "less American" and destroying "democratic and constitutional niceties," Anton expressed a sentiment akin to white nationalists, who believe the Immigration Act of 1965 marked the beginning of a "white genocide," a deliberate plot by leftists and Jews to destroy white rule.[209]

The Trump campaign used many of the nativist themes developed by the Buchanan campaigns of the 1990s, as Buchanan himself repeatedly said.[210] Like Buchanan, Trump called his domestic agenda "economic nationalism," which, like Buchanan's agenda, focused on opposition to free trade and immigration. Like Buchanan, Trump sought to tap into the resentments of Middle American Radicals.[211] The Obama years increased the resentments of this cohort, who believed that the nation had been taken over by un-American forces bent on the destruction of fundamental American values.[212] Speaking directly to the concerns of Middle American Radicals, Trump promised to reverse their fortunes and to "Make America Great Again."

Trump's nativist appeals were enthusiastically cheered by the conservative press. Conservative columnist Ann Coulter quickly published a book, *In Trump We Trust*, which praised Trump for recognizing that America's ethnic core was the sources of its core values and foundational documents: "There's a reason the Magna Carta and the Glorious Revolution happened where they happened and that the Declaration of Independence was written in a British colony. It's not in the Anglo-Saxon character either to take orders or to give them. That's why the socialist left finally gave up on traditional Americans and pinned their hopes on immigrants, who bring their socialism with them."[213] In this passage, Coulter repeats the core of the nativist conception of the Constitution: the Constitution was written by white people, and American constitutional culture depends on maintaining a white ethnic base; nonwhite immigrants, in contrast, bring dangerously foreign ideas that threaten to undermine the Constitution and therefore destroy America. These long-standing beliefs, which Coulter identified as the heart of Trump's appeal, display the same nativist orientation as the Know Nothings, the Immigration Restriction League, FAIR, and Pat Buchanan.

The Campaign to Exclude Muslim Immigrants on the Ground That Islam Is Incompatible with the Constitution

Within days of taking office, Trump signaled his intent to put into practice the old nativist constitutional idea that peoples who don't share the ethnic and religious background of America's founding stock should be barred from immigration because they are likely to be hostile to constitutional values. On January 27, 2017, President Trump signed an executive order that barred entry into the country for citizens of seven predominately Muslim countries.[214] The order did not use the word *Muslim*.[215] Instead, it declared that the ban was necessary to prevent entry by dangerous foreigners who are hostile to the Constitution. Section 1 of the order declared that it excluded those who "bear hostile attitudes" toward the United States "and its founding principles" and who "do not support the Constitution."[216]

The travel ban should be understood in light of a decade-long campaign that has targeted Muslims as anti-American. In the week after the attacks of September 11, 2001, President George W. Bush spoke at the Islamic Center of Washington, DC, and tried to make clear to the American public that the United States was not at war with Islam and that Islam was not to blame for the attacks: "The face of terror is not the true faith of Islam. That's not what Islam is all about. Islam is peace."[217] In the years since then, a group of conservative activists billed themselves as experts on Islam and asserted that Bush was wrong and that Islam is dedicated to violence and global domination.[218] They claimed that Islam demands that believers strive to replace Western democracies with Islamic theocratic states. As Robert Spencer of Jihad Watch declared: Islam is "the only religion in the world that has a developed doctrine, theology and legal system that mandates violence against unbelievers and mandates that Muslims must wage war in order to establish the hegemony of the Islamic social order all over the world."[219]

The organized anti-Muslim campaign focused especially on Islamic law, known as sharia, which campaigners describe as a "totalitarian ideology" that is fundamentally inconsistent with the American Constitution.[220] The Center for Security Policy (CSP), a key player in the campaign, claimed that Islam seeks "to supplant our Constitution with its own totalitarian framework."[221] In 2010, CSP issued a 372-page report, *Sharia: The Threat to America*, principally devoted to demonstrating that Islam "rejects fundamental premises of American society and values."[222] As the Center for American Progress explained, characterizations of sharia from anti-Muslim activists are "unrecognizable to the overwhelming majority of Muslims here and abroad. . . . [Sharia] is, for Muslims, the ideal law of God as interpreted by Muslim scholars over centuries to achieve justice, fairness, and mercy through personal religious observance such as prayer and fasting."[223]

The anti-Muslim campaign spread. At first, groups on the fringes of national politics began repeating these claims. By 2011, Tea Party groups began to argue that Muslims seek to infiltrate the United States and replace the Constitution with sharia law.[224] National Tea Party groups began to argue that Islam poses a threat to the Constitution. TeaParty.org, one of the leading national Tea Party groups, asserted that Muslims can never be loyal to the United States because Islam teaches that supreme loyalty is owed to the Quran.[225] Many other conservative groups began to echo these views, including the Family Research Council, which warned that Muslims were infiltrating the United States for the purpose of establishing an Islamic theocracy.[226]

Soon anti-Muslim claims made their way into mainstream politics. Andrew McCarthy of the *National Review* warned of "creeping sharia," the concern that American Muslims were slowly finding ways to subvert American democracy in preparation for a theocratic state.[227] Former Speaker of the House Newt Gingrich warned an audience at the American Enterprise Institute that sharia represents "a mortal threat to the survival of freedom in the United States and in the world as we know it." Gingrich made clear that Islam itself is incompatible with American values: "Sharia in its natural form has principles and punishments totally abhorrent to the Western world."[228] The hysteria launched by anti-Muslim activists that Islam seeks global domination propelled a campaign to ban sharia in several states.[229]

With the election of President Trump, the belief that Islam threatens constitutional values moved from the margins to the White House. Trump's advisors made clear that they agree that Islam threatens constitutional values. In September 2015, Jeff Sessions, then a senator and later appointed attorney general by Trump, gave a speech on the Senate floor in which he denounced Islam (or at least what he termed "theologically-based Sharia") as fundamentally incompatible with American constitutional values: it is "incompatible with the laws and freedoms we see as central to our liberty and prosperity. . . . It just will not merge with and accommodate with the freedom that we believe is essential in the Western world. Theologically-based Sharia law fundamentally conflicts with our magnificent constitutional order."[230] During the 2016 presidential campaign, Republican candidate Ben Carson, later appointed secretary of Housing and Urban Development, agreed that Islam is incompatible with the Constitution and argued that a Muslim must never become president because he or she would be loyal to Islam, not the Constitution.[231] Trump's advisors also included Steve Bannon, who asserted that Islam and Christianity are engaged in a global war and Muslims are temperamentally opposed to democratic values.[232] Bannon said that Western democracies should not accept Syrian refugees because they were not bred for self-government: "These are not Jeffersonian democrats. These are not people with thousands of years of understanding democracy in their DNA."[233]

Anti-Muslim activists immediately understood that Trump's immigration order put the force of law behind their long-standing view that Islam is incompatible with the Constitution. Brian Thomas, a writer for Jihad Watch, was exultant. In his view, the immigration order confirmed that the Trump administration had decided "to treat Islam as a hostile political ideology," Thomas explained. "That is what has been needed for decades."[234]

The president's policies follow a long history of American nativism in which allegations of hostility to the Constitution have served as a justification for exclusion of unwanted immigrants. Like nativists of old, Trump tried to justify policies of exclusion in patriotic terms, claiming that he does not target foreigners because of their race or religion but because they hate our constitutional ideals.

Conclusion

American nativist movements are usually described as simple ethno-nationalists, who believe that national identity in the United States is defined solely by race, religion, or ethnicity.[235] Nativists are often depicted as the opposite of civic nationalists, who believe that American nationality means commitment to civic values and not ascriptive categories. But American nativist movements have long articulated their agendas in the language of constitutional nationalism. They too ascribe to the prevailing ideology that commitment to constitutional values lies at the center of what it means to be American. What distinguishes nativists from others is their conviction that only some people—those who share the racial, ethnic, and religious traits of historically dominant groups in the United States—are capable of embracing America's fundamental values.

Nativist movements have invoked allegations of hostility to the Constitution as the touchstone for identifying dangerous foreigners. To say that some people are hostile to the Constitution is a way of saying that they are hostile to the United States, that they are un-American, and that they don't belong here. This way of speaking about the Constitution comes naturally to Americans as a result of the long tradition of identifying what it means to be American by reference to the Constitution. As the history of nativism shows, devotion to the Constitution has often been invoked to justify excluding unwanted people who, by race, religion, or national origin, do not share the traits of native-born Americans.

4 | The Businessman's Constitution

As the first three chapters have shown, constitutional nationalism has provided a rhetoric for conflicts over racial, religious, and ethnic dominance. Using the language of constitutional nationalism, movements like the Ku Klux Klan, the New Christian Right, and the Immigration Restriction League have sought to preserve the status and power of whites, Christians, and native-born Americans, asserting that the Constitution was written by white people and for white people, that the Constitution arises out the nation's Christian traditions, and that preserving the Constitution requires excluding dangerous foreigners. Opponents of these movements have asserted competing conceptions of American identity, conceptions that embrace the nation's racial, religious, and ethnic diversity. They too articulated their ideologies in constitutional terms. In this way, fights over intergroup status and national identity have routinely been carried on as fights over the Constitution.

Constitutional nationalism has furnished the rhetoric for other disputes over the nation's core commitments. This chapter tells the story of the American Liberty League and its campaign to defeat the New Deal.[1] The Liberty League was founded in 1934 by a group of corporate leaders, who charged that the New Deal was unconstitutional and un-American. It generated massive media coverage by vilifying President Franklin D. Roosevelt as a radical socialist who sought to foist un-American policies of "collectivism" on an unwilling public.[2] The Roosevelt reelection campaign chose to make the league the central focus of the 1936 reelection campaign.[3] It made the perfect villain in the constitutional drama. At a time when big business was widely blamed for causing the Great Depression, the Liberty League was the unabashed voice of corporate America, asserting that above all else, the Constitution protects the right of business owners to do as they please.[4] Roosevelt argued that the Liberty League and its leaders were not merely wrong about the Constitution but also that the league's asserted constitutional philosophy was a ruse to protect its backers' power and wealth.[5]

It is not surprising that in the mid-1930s a group of prominent businessmen tried to organize a movement to oppose substantial new business regulations imposed under the New Deal.[6] It is also not surprising that, in the midst of the Great Depression, the movement failed to convince the American people to give millionaires unrestricted freedom to run their businesses and to reject newly won protections for workers, the elderly, and the unemployed.[7] In fact, the Liberty League not only failed to topple the New Deal but also may have helped generate a consensus *in favor* of the New Deal.

What is remarkable is that the American Liberty League honed a distinctly constitutional and nationalist rhetoric, which depicted the New Deal not just as bad policy but as contrary to core American ideals as expressed in the Constitution. This rhetoric has remained at the core of subsequent movements that have challenged the modern administrative state.[8] Little acknowledged today, the Liberty League was recognized in the generation after its demise as "the root movement of . . . modern conservatism."[9] Its rhetoric and philosophy show it to be the direct antecedent of Barry Goldwater and Ronald Reagan Republicanism, the John Birch Society, and the Tea Party movement.[10] Like these later groups, the Liberty League argued for a return to what the movement identified as the fundamental national values of self-reliance, individualism, hard work, property rights, and freedom from government, values the movement identified with the Constitution.

The American Liberty League's Campaign to Save America

After Franklin Roosevelt was inaugurated in March 1933, he moved quickly to create what he called a New Deal for American workers and the American public to address the nation's devastated economy and to provide relief for the millions of Americans who had lost their jobs. In the first year of his administration, Congress enacted significant reforms to banking and securities, suspended the gold standard, created a multi-billion-dollar public works program, regulated agricultural prices and production, adopted programs to regulate wages and hours in most major economic sectors, and provided billions of dollars in relief to the unemployed and to farmers. Together the new programs greatly enlarged the size of the federal government and expanded its regulatory authority in unprecedented ways.

By 1934 a group of the nation's most prominent business owners had

THE BUSINESSMAN'S CONSTITUTION | 143

come to believe that the New Deal was destroying the foundations of American life.[11] The group included Pierre, Irénée, and Lammot du Pont, leaders of one of the nation's most powerful corporate families; Alfred P. Sloan, president of General Motors; Edward F. Hutton, chairman of General Foods; and J. Howard Pew, president of Sun Oil.[12] The group also included both John W. Davis and Al Smith, the 1924 and 1928 Democratic Party presidential candidates, as well as Jouett Shouse and John Raskob, two former chairmen of the Democratic Party.[13] These men saw the proliferation of New Deal regulatory programs as an assault on core American values, and they believed that Americans would rise up against the New Deal if only they realized that it was a radical, socialist, un-American form of tyranny.[14]

Recent experience gave these men good reason to believe that the American people could be roused to rise up against what they considered federal tyranny. Most of them had played leading roles in the Association Against the Prohibition Amendment (AAPA), which fought to repeal Prohibition.[15] Employing a distinctly constitutional rhetoric, the AAPA declared that its mission was much grander than merely making booze legal: it sought nothing less than "to preserve the spirit of the Constitution of the United States."[16] To the leaders of the AAPA, Prohibition represented an unprecedented expansion of federal power that deprived the people of their liberties, most especially the liberty of business owners and consumers to choose what to buy and sell.[17] Prohibition, the AAPA declared, represented a repudiation of the principles laid out by the Founding Fathers.[18]

In December 1933 the repeal amendment was adopted, and the AAPA quickly disbanded. It declared, however, that its leaders would continue to meet and might form a new group that "would in the event of danger to the Federal Constitution, stand ready to defend the faith of the fathers." Just a few months later, the former leaders of the AAPA decided that the New Deal posed an even greater threat to the "faith of the fathers" than had Prohibition.[19] Like Prohibition, the New Deal deprived business owners of the liberty to operate as they chose, centralized power in Washington, and interfered with states' rights.[20] While Prohibition deprived business owners of the liberty to sell one kind of product, the New Deal imposed federal commands on almost every aspect of business life.[21] Not only did New Deal regulations deprive business owners of their liberty and property rights, New Deal relief programs undermined the incentive to work.[22]

In March 1934, R. R. M. Carpenter, a retired DuPont vice president, expressed the gist of these concerns in a letter to John Raskob, the former chairman of General Motors and also former chairman of the Democratic

Party. Carpenter believed that the New Deal sapped the American work ethic: "Five negroes on my place in South Carolina refused work this Spring . . . saying they had easy jobs with the government. . . . A cook on my houseboat at Fort Myers quit because the government was paying him a dollar an hour as a painter." In light of the difficulties he was having with the "help," Carpenter wondered whether anything could be done to save America.[23]

Raskob wrote back and agreed that the New Deal was undermining the entrepreneurial spirit and said that a new organization was needed to "protect society from the suffering which it is bound to endure if we allow communistic elements to lead the people to believe that all businessmen are crooks." Raskob suggested that perhaps the du Ponts could take the lead because "there is no group, including the Rockefellers, the Morgans, the Mellons, or any one else that begins to control and be responsible for as much industrially, as is the du Pont company." As Raskob put it, the du Ponts were "in a position to talk directly with a group that controls a larger share of industry . . . than any other group in the United States."[24]

GM and DuPont executives soon met at Al Smith's office in the Empire State Building to discuss the formation of a new group modeled on the AAPA and devoted to challenging the legitimacy of the New Deal. Alfred Sloan of GM suggested calling the new group the "Association Asserting the Rights of Property." Jouett Shouse, former Democratic Party chairman, suggested the "National Property League," and E. F. Hutton suggested the "American Federation of Business." John W. Davis, the 1924 Democratic presidential candidate, garnered a consensus with the more patriotic sounding "American Liberty League."[25] Raskob, Sloan, Irénée du Pont, and others immediately donated $40,000 to launch the new organization.[26] Shouse, who had just stepped down as president of the AAPA, was appointed to serve as the new league's president.[27]

It was not merely their success in defeating Prohibition and the vast resources at their disposal that made leaders of the American Liberty League optimistic that they could succeed in defeating the New Deal. When the league was formed, it was widely believed that Roosevelt's prospects for reelection in 1936 were dim.[28] In 1934 there appeared to be definite signs that the American people were turning against Roosevelt. Public opinion polling was in its infancy, but according to the public surveys of the day, Roosevelt's popularity had been falling since February 1934.[29] Unemployment and poverty rates remained stubbornly high— notwithstanding the proliferation of expensive federal programs sold to the public as the solution to the Depression.[30]

On August 22, 1934, Shouse held a press conference to announce the establishment of the American Liberty League.[31] He described the league as nonpartisan and declared that, as its acronym "ALL" suggested, the league spoke for *all* of the American people, whose liberties were under attack by the New Deal.[32] Shouse declared that the Liberty League's central mission was the preservation of the nation's constitutional values:

> [The American Liberty League] is a non-partisan organization formed . . . to defend and uphold the Constitution . . . [to] teach the necessity of respect for the rights of persons and property as fundamental to every successful form of government . . . to encourage and protect individual and group initiative and enterprise, to foster the right to work, earn, save and acquire property, and to preserve the ownership and lawful use of property when acquired.[33]

Liberty League leaders were optimistic that they would quickly gain widespread support.[34] At the opening news conference, Shouse predicted that within a year the league would have two to three million members.[35]

The following day, the *New York Times* reported that business leaders cheered the formation of the new organization: "Talk in Wall Street yesterday indicated that the announcement of the new American Liberty League was little short of an answer to a prayer."[36] Leading stockbrokers told the *Times* that they had been hoping that an organization would arise to protect the property rights of stock holders against government interference. "The financial community sees in the movement a new force for conservatism," the paper reported. E. F. Hutton declared that the league would become "the voice of business" and would ensure that the president give due consideration to corporate interests in determining plans for economic recovery.[37] A *Times* editorial declared that all Americans could stand behind the league's goals of defending the Constitution and protecting property owners from government interference.[38]

President Roosevelt responded with mockery. He told reporters that he "laughed for ten minutes" after reading that the league was the answer to Wall Street's prayers.[39] Roosevelt said he agreed with the league that property rights should be protected, but the league emphasized property rights to the exclusion of all other goals. As Roosevelt put it, the Liberty League was like a church devoted to upholding two of the Ten Commandments while disregarding the other eight.[40] Roosevelt mocked the league's emphasis on individual liberty as a philosophy that only served the interests of the moneyed class while ignoring the needs of the people.[41] With Roosevelt's rejoinder, it was anticipated that the Liberty League's campaign against the

New Deal could, in the words of the *New York Times*, "precipitate the greatest conflict of constitutional and economic philosophy of the times."[42]

The initial publicity was good for the Liberty League. The week after the news conference, Shouse declared that the "response from all parts of the country to formation of the league has been astounding," with thousands of pledges already arriving.[43]

Money from the du Ponts and like-minded businessmen flowed in. In its first year of operations, the American Liberty League raised half a million dollars, giving it unprecedented resources to carry out this campaign.[44] By January 1936 the league was poised to become the leading opposition to the New Deal. It had more resources than the Republican Party.[45] It had more cash than the Republicans and operated from a headquarters in Washington with thirty-one rooms and more than fifty full-time staff members—almost triple the size of the Republican Party's national offices and triple its staff.[46] That year, Shouse was the nation's highest-paid political operative.[47] The Republicans, meanwhile, had largely capitulated to Roosevelt and offered no comprehensive program to compete with the New Deal.[48]

The league's founders declared that, with enormous resources and a mission to waken the nation to the threat to liberty posed by Roosevelt, the American Liberty League was bound to attract widespread attention and public support.[49] They were half right. As the organization's leaders predicted, the league generated enormous media attention, but it never gained much public support and instead remained the pet project of a small group of corporate leaders.[50] At its peak, the league claimed 150,000 members, and that claim is almost certainly highly exaggerated.[51]

The Constitutional Rhetoric and Philosophy of the American Liberty League

The American Liberty League declared that the 1936 election would determine nothing less than whether the Constitution and the American way of life would survive. Asserting that President Roosevelt had betrayed his oath to defend the Constitution, the league declared that the election would resolve whether "we are to continue to enjoy a government of laws and not of men, or shall have foisted upon us an Americanized copy of Old World dictatorship."[52] To save America from dictatorship, the league launched a massive campaign to educate the American public on what it declared were the evils of the New Deal.[53]

The Liberty League's chief weapons were pamphlets, newsletters, speeches, and radio addresses. In 1935 and 1936 the league published 135 pamphlets and a monthly newsletter, which were distributed across the country to millions of homes and thousands of libraries. The league also sponsored dozens of speeches broadcast on the national radio networks, many of which it later reprinted in pamphlet form.[54] Some of the league's pamphlets and speeches addressed specific New Deal legislation, with titles such as *The AAA Amendments: An Analysis of Proposals Illustrating a Trend toward a Fascist Control not only of Agriculture but also of a Major Sector of Manufacturing and Distributing Industries,* and *The Bituminous Coal Bill: An Analysis of a Proposed Step toward Socialization of Industry.*[55] Most of the pamphlets, however, took on the New Deal in broad terms, bearing provocative titles like *Is the Constitution for Sale?, Americanism at the Crossroads,* and *What Is the Constitution between Friends?*[56]

The Liberty League reached the American public not only by distributing millions of pamphlets and sponsoring radio broadcasts but also through extensive news coverage of its activities. The American Liberty League quickly became a media sensation.[57] In the two main years of the league's operation—from Shouse's announcement of the creation of the league on August 22, 1934, to November 3, 1936, the day of the 1936 election—the *New York Times* ran over four hundred stories that mentioned the league, the *Washington Post* published over six hundred articles, and the *Chicago Tribune* published over three hundred and fifty.[58] By the start of the 1936 election campaign, the league had become an unavoidable part of the political landscape. Politicians and commentators of all kinds responded to it. Sinclair Lewis attacked it.[59] John Dewey sought to explain it.[60] The assistant US attorney general debated its leaders.[61] By all accounts, President Roosevelt himself took the American Liberty League seriously.[62]

Scholars, in contrast, have not taken the American Liberty League's ideology seriously and have echoed Roosevelt's claim that the league's constitutional arguments were a ruse to obscure its true purpose of protecting its founders' wealth and power.[63] Writing in 1937 Max Lerner said that Liberty Leaguers made a "fetish" of the Constitution, invoking the "sanctity of the Constitution . . . in a coldly instrumental way for their own purposes."[64] In 1950 historian Frederick Rudolph similarly characterized the league's patriotic and constitutional rhetoric as "the cloak in which the Liberty League dressed itself in order to promote its position and its program."[65] Historian Arthur Schlesinger agreed, declaring that "at no point on record did the American Liberty League construe 'liberty' as meaning anything else but the folding stuff," that is, money.[66] More recently, Jeff Shesol declared that the league used constitutional rhetoric to hide its founders' true goals because "the American people, it could safely be assumed, were unlikely to respond to a call to let the rich get richer."[67]

Without question, the Liberty League made a strategic choice to place its focus on the Constitution. William H. Stayton, founder of the AAPA and one of the league's founders, declared that opposition to the New Deal could attract public support only if it were presented as "a moral or an emotional issue," and no issue "could command more support or evoke more enthusiasm among our people than the simple issue of the 'Constitution.'" Stayton urged the league to make the Constitution central because, as he put it, "there is a mighty—though vague—affection for it. The people, I believe, need merely to be led and instructed, and this affection will become almost worship and can be converted into an irresistible movement."[68]

Although the Liberty League's constitutional rhetoric served the strategic goal of putting a patriotic shine on its pro-business message, it is a mistake to dismiss the league's constitutional message as just empty rhetoric. Understanding the league's message is necessary to understand how constitutional issues were presented to the public in the fight over the New Deal. Many opponents of the New Deal, and not just the American Liberty League, articulated their concerns in the rhetoric of constitutional nationalism.[69] In 1934 Herbert Hoover wrote that the New Deal was "the most stupendous invasion of the whole spirit of Liberty that the nation has witnessed since the days of Colonial America."[70] Like the Liberty League, Hoover believed that the New Deal had created a totalitarian state with "daily dictation by Government in every town and village every day in the week, of how men are to conduct their daily lives."[71] Hoover charged that the New Deal was sapping America of the rugged individualism that he believed defined its national character.[72] Hoover and other conservatives believed that the New Deal threatened the basis of national identity and feared that unless the New Deal were reversed, "America will cease to be American."[73]

Regardless of whether it adopted constitutional rhetoric solely as a matter of marketing, Liberty League pamphlets and speeches reveal a comprehensively articulated philosophy, in which adherence to a set of libertarian principles defines both what the Constitution requires and what it means to be American.[74] In this philosophy, the Constitution functions less as a legal text to read and interpret than as the embodiment and symbol of American values.

The American Liberty League professed itself devoted most centrally to protecting *Americanism,* a broad term encompassing the nation's fundamental values.[75] As discussed in previous chapters, the Ku Klux Klan defined Americanism in racial terms, Christian nationalists defined Americanism in religious terms, and nativist movements defined Americanism by reference to the traits and values of the nation's "native stocks." As the creature of America's corporate leaders, the American Liberty League defined Americanism in business terms.

To the league, Americanism most centrally entailed a commitment to individual liberty, and the most important liberty was the ability to make choices in economic matters. This is the liberty that one league pamphlet called the people's "fundamental right of using their own private property and of running their individual farms and businesses in the manner which seems to them best."[76] Government power must be limited to avoid interfering with the economic liberties that are at the heart of individuals' ability to choose their own paths.[77] The league thus took a strict libertarian position, under which all government regulation portended tyranny.[78]

The league defended its libertarian vision in nationalist terms, its leaders repeatedly declaring that they were "bitterly and aggressively opposed" to any "alien ism."[79] The Liberty League assessed the New Deal to be alien to American traditions because it imposed substantial regulations on business and thereby undermined the core American value of individual freedom.[80] In the league's words, New Deal protections against low wages and relief for the unemployed and elderly were based on a philosophy of "collectivism" that conflicts with the principle that individual merit should determine a person's fate.[81] As one league pamphlet declared, "the weak should not be artificially maintained in wealth and power. . . . Each individual must rise or sink to the level for which he is fitted by the quality of his tissues and of his soul."[82] To the league's leaders, individualism was at the core of the Constitution. By offering protections for "the weak," Roosevelt had "repudiate[d] the Constitution and declare[d] war on the whole system of American freedom."[83]

The American Liberty League proclaimed that in standing up to the New Deal it was standing up for the Founding Fathers. William Stayton sought to rouse Liberty Leaguers by reminding them that "he who takes the 'Constitution' for his battle-cry, has as his allies the Fathers of old."[84] Roosevelt, the league repeatedly claimed, had abandoned the Founding Fathers in favor of the philosophies of European Communists, Socialists, and Fascists.[85] The league said that Roosevelt and his brain trusters "sneered" at the Founding Fathers and that Roosevelt sought to replace a government built upon "the philosophy of Thomas Jefferson" with "a totalitarian government, one which recognizes no sphere of individual or business life as immune from governmental authority and which submerges the welfare of the individual to that of the government."[86]

The Liberty League warned that the New Deal was not just misguided but also threatened to "destroy the essential features of our government" and "substitute Americanism with Totalitarianism."[87] It warned again and again that the New Deal threatened the existence of the United States.[88] If the New Deal continued, one Liberty League pamphlet warned, it would "mean the defeat of the American theory of democracy."[89]

To the Liberty League, the New Deal had replaced American individualism with a "spirit of dependency."[90] "We used to be a virile, self-reliant people," one pamphlet explained. "We were at one time willing to ascribe our misfortunes to our own lack of wisdom and self-control, to tighten the belt, and to repair our own shortcomings."[91] No longer. The American people were now unwilling to take personal responsibility for their misfortunes and deal with the Depression by tightening their belts. Under the New Deal, the league believed, little was left of liberty: "No business man was his own master" because New Deal programs "rigidly enslaved its devotees."[92] Indeed, enslaving the people to an all-powerful government was the very point of the New Deal.[93] Roosevelt must be defeated, the Liberty League warned, or all Americans would soon be enslaved.

Convinced that the New Deal represented a breach of faith with American values, the league believed that the election of 1936 would determine whether the nation would survive.[94] The nation stood at a crossroads, the league warned, in which it could choose to continue down "the old American 'horse and buggy' road of democracy with the Constitution as its foundation" or follow Roosevelt down a "foreign slave trail of arbitrary government built upon the will of man."[95] As one league pamphlet explained, the issue to be decided through the 1936 election was not "whether the Constitution shall be amended, but whether it shall be destroyed."[96]

Once the American people recognized what was happening—in the words of one Liberty League pamphlet, once they "awaken[ed] . . . to find the Roosevelt administration has virtually tricked them, and substituted the Socialist Party platform" for the Democratic Party platform—the people would surely vote to oust Roosevelt and restore Americanism.[97] Showing the American people the truth about the New Deal was precisely what the Liberty League sought to do.

Roosevelt's Campaign against the American Liberty League

In 1935 and 1936 the Supreme Court issued six major rulings that held New Deal laws unconstitutional.[98] The Court ruled that the Constitution did not give Congress power to regulate agriculture and coal production, did not authorize the establishment of industrial regulations, and did not give the government power to set minimum wages and maximum hours. The Court's decisions left in grave doubt the validity of Roosevelt's bold approach to addressing the nation's economic crisis. Leading up the 1936 election, President Roosevelt and his advisors were concerned that doubts on the constitutionality of New Deal programs would become a major campaign issue.[99]

In 1937 the Supreme Court changed course and began to rule in favor of the New Deal. How this change came about has been debated ever since. In the most popular tale, the change arose because Roosevelt responded to the Supreme Court's anti–New Deal rulings by deciding "to run against the Court in the next election and seek to gain a mandate from the People."[100] That account of the 1936 election features prominently in Bruce Ackerman's highly influential book *We the People.* In the conventional account of how the Supreme Court reversed course, in 1936 Roosevelt campaigned against the Supreme Court and won a landslide victory that was tantamount to a public mandate in support of his constitutional philosophy, which helped persuade the Supreme Court to adopt a broader understanding of federal power.[101]

But the tale isn't true. Roosevelt did not campaign against the Supreme Court in the 1936 campaign.[102] He rarely mentioned the Court or its rulings against the New Deal.[103] In fact, Roosevelt considered but rejected a proposal to campaign against the Court. Harold Ickes, Roosevelt's political advisor and secretary of the Interior, urged Roosevelt to make the Court the central campaign issue, but Roosevelt rejected the advice, apparently concluding that disputes over the meaning of the Commerce Clause and General Welfare Clause were too abstract for a national campaign.[104] Roosevelt agreed with Felix Frankfurter that the American people held the Court in too high esteem and that an attack on the Court would let Roosevelt's opponents portray him as radical.[105] This left the Roosevelt campaign in a quandary, wondering how to address doubts over the constitutionality of the New Deal program without challenging the Court's authority.

The American Liberty League was an unexpected gift. Its campaign against the constitutionality of the New Deal gave the Roosevelt campaign just what it needed to make the constitutionality of the New Deal central to the campaign without any need to attack the Supreme Court. Early in 1936 the Roosevelt reelection team came to the realization that the American Liberty League provided Roosevelt the opportunity to make the constitutional case against an opponent that was much easier to discredit than the Supreme Court.[106] Roosevelt's campaign manager, James Farley, concluded that the league was "one of the most vulnerable ever to appear in politics" because it was founded and managed by millionaire businessmen like the du Ponts who were widely blamed for the Depression and who personally stood to gain from defeating the New Deal.[107] Farley declared that the league should be called the "American Cellophane League" because "first, it's a du Pont product, and, second, you can see right through it."[108]

With the recognition that the American Liberty League was just what the campaign needed, the Roosevelt reelection team decided to make the league—not the Court and not the Republicans—the main focus of the 1936 campaign.[109] As Farley later wrote, the "first 'battle-order' was to ignore the Republican Party and to concentrate fire on the Liberty League."[110] Charles Michelson, the director of press operations for the Roosevelt campaign, described the strategy: "It was not difficult for us to get and keep before the public the Liberty League as the symbol of massed plutocracy warring on the common people. Thus the Liberty League was an asset and not a liability to the Roosevelt forces."[111] The Roosevelt campaign did everything it could to keep the Liberty League in the news. As Farley put it, "the more they [the Liberty League] work, the happier we are."[112]

In countless speeches, advertisements, editorials, newspaper interviews, and even a well-publicized Senate investigation, Roosevelt and his supporters mocked the Liberty League as the voice of business tycoons who had long tyrannized the American people and whose power the New Deal was instituted to check. In doing so, Roosevelt presented the voters a choice between competing constitutional philosophies: The league argued that the New Deal conflicted with foundational notions of individual liberty and freedom from excessive government, and Roosevelt presented a constitutional philosophy that emphasized government authority to protect the people from excessive industrial power.

The first major speech of the 1936 campaign was Roosevelt's State of the Union address.[113] It was the first time that a president had delivered the address at night, which allowed it to be heard on the radio by most of the nation's populace.[114] Roosevelt made little attempt to catalog the state of the nation but instead gave a detailed and forceful denunciation of the American Liberty League's constitutional philosophy.[115] He did not mention the league by name, but it was widely understood to be the chief target of the speech.[116]

The central message of Roosevelt's State of the Union address was that New Deal opponents represented the forces of "entrenched greed" who hid their true goals in patriotic and constitutional rhetoric. Roosevelt declared that he had proudly "earned the hatred of entrenched greed" because he recognized that it was "necessary to drive some people from power and strictly to regulate others." His opponents sought to undo the New Deal, Roosevelt warned, solely for their own benefit: "They seek—this minority in business and industry—to control and often do control and use for their own purposes legitimate and highly honored business associations; they engage in vast propaganda to spread fear and discord among the people—they would 'gang up' against the people's liberties." Roosevelt told Americans not to be fooled by the patriotic, constitutional rhetoric employed by his opponents: "They steal the livery of great national constitutional ideals to serve discredited special interests."[117]

A central part of the address consisted of a series of rhetorical questions that amounted to a point-by-point response to the Liberty League's arguments that the New Deal conflicted with the nation's foundational principles:[118]

- In response to the Liberty League's argument that federal relief efforts undermined the nation's commitment to hard work and individual responsibility, Roosevelt asked: "Shall we say to the several millions of unemployed citizens who face the very problem of existence, of getting enough to eat, 'We will withdraw from giving you work. We will turn you back to the charity of your communities and those men of selfish power who tell you that perhaps they will employ you if the Government leaves them strictly alone?'"[119]

- In response to the Liberty League's argument that the federal government lacked power to address unemployment, Roosevelt asked: "Shall we say to the needy unemployed, 'Your problem is a local one except that perhaps the Federal Government, as an act of mere generosity, will be willing to pay to your city or to your county a few grudging dollars to help maintain your soup kitchens?'"[120]

- In response to the Liberty League's argument that child labor was a local issue, Roosevelt asked: "Shall we say to the children who have worked all day in the factories, 'Child labor is a local issue and so are your starvation wages; something to be solved or left unsolved by the jurisdiction of forty-eight States?'"[121]

- In response to the Liberty League's argument that federal protections for workers conflict with individual freedom, Roosevelt asked: "Shall we say to the laborer, 'Your right to organize, your relations with your employer have nothing to do with the public interest; if your employer will not even meet with you to discuss your problems and his, that is none of our affair?'"[122]

- In response to the Liberty League's argument against federal power to protect the elderly through measures like social security, Roosevelt asked: "Shall we say to the . . . aged, 'Social security lies not within the province of the Federal Government; you must seek relief elsewhere?'"[123]

Roosevelt thus used the State of the Union to express the core of his philosophy, that the Constitution empowers the people to protect themselves from economic exploitation at the hands of business leaders like those behind the Liberty League.[124] Through these rhetorical questions, Roosevelt argued that the Liberty League's constitutional philosophy served only to protect the rich and ignored the needs of workers, the elderly, the homeless, and the unemployed.[125] The theme offered by Roosevelt in the speech crystallized the Roosevelt campaign's response to the American Liberty League, and Roosevelt and his supporters repeated these points throughout the campaign.[126]

Liberty Leaguers responded with unrestrained fury, calling it "the most dangerous speech that ever came from a President of the United States." They charged that the speech expressed "contempt for the Constitution"[127] and was "an insult to the Nation and a desecration of its sacred principles."[128] To the great delight of the Roosevelt campaign, the league responded to the attacks on corporate greed by defending the importance of big business. It issued a statement that declared: "Business is the source of the entire living of the people, of the wages of labor, of the very food, clothing, and shelter of the nation. . . . It is high time that men who live soft lives from taxation on business cease their attacks on the institutions that make our civilization possible."[129] Criticized as the embodiment of "entrenched greed," the league defended the beneficence of wealth, declaring that "no country in the history of the world has ever benefitted more than America from the concentration of capital."[130]

The league planned what was certain to be a dramatic response to the

State of the Union address: a nationally broadcast speech by Al Smith, former New York governor and the Democratic Party's 1928 presidential nominee.[131] The league's directors bet that Smith, known as "the greatest apostle of the common people in America," would help the league shake off the perception that it was the mouthpiece of millionaires.[132] Leading up to the speech, newspapers eagerly anticipated the criticism that Smith would level at the president.[133] The *New York Times* reported, "Few events other than national conventions staged by the two major parties have aroused keener political interest—and concern—than the American Liberty League dinner here tonight which Alfred E. Smith will address."[134]

The speech promised great political theater because Smith had once been Roosevelt's political mentor, and Roosevelt had nominated Smith for the presidency in 1928.[135] After Roosevelt edged out Smith for the 1932 Democratic Party nomination, Smith turned against him and the New Deal.[136] Media attention increased with the news that Smith had rejected Eleanor Roosevelt's invitation to stay at the White House the night of the speech, apparently out of concern that the Roosevelts would not feel kindly toward him after they heard what he had to say.[137]

In the days leading up to the speech, Democrats openly feared that Smith would lead a revolt against Roosevelt from within the Democratic Party.[138] Some speculated that Smith would attempt to split the Democratic Party, with Smith as the nominee of a Liberty League faction.[139] Secretary of the Interior Harold Ickes privately professed that Smith's speech gave the administration real reason to worry.[140]

Broadcast nationally in prime time over the CBS radio network, Smith's speech was as fiery a denunciation of the New Deal as the hype had suggested. Smith charged that the New Deal was nothing less than an "attack . . . upon the fundamental institutions of this country." He asserted that the New Deal was incompatible with American values: "This country was organized on the principles of a representative democracy, and you can't mix socialism or communism with that. . . . They are just like oil and water, they refuse to mix." Smith concluded by issuing a "solemn warning" that if the Democrats renominated Roosevelt, the American people would have to choose between the Constitution and communism: "There can be only one capital, Washington or Moscow. There can be only . . . the clear, pure, fresh air of free America, or the foul breath of communistic Russia. There can be only one flag, the Stars and Stripes, or the flag of the godless Union of the Soviets. There can be only one national anthem, 'The Star-Spangled Banner,' or the 'Internationale.'" In the battle between traditional

American values and the New Deal, Smith closed, "There can be only one victor. If the Constitution wins, we win."[141]

Liberty Leaguers were thrilled with the speech. "It was perfect," Pierre du Pont declared.[142] The league issued a statement proclaiming that Smith had succeeded in "dispelling the fog over Washington," leaving no doubt about the fundamental crisis facing the nation.[143] Having long believed that the American people would rise up against the New Deal if only they woke up to its un-American nature, Shouse declared that "the people have awakened."[144]

In the immediate aftermath of Smith's speech, newspaper columnists speculated that the speech might have turned the tide of public opinion against Roosevelt.[145] Republicans and some conservative Democrats expressed strong agreement with Smith. The *New York Times* reported that "the trend away from the New Deal has been easy to see for months," and with Smith's speech it was now "highly possible" that the Democrats would lose their hold on key states.[146] Columnists speculated that Smith might lead mass defection by Democrats against the New Deal.[147]

New Deal Democrats expressed a very different reaction to the speech, and their reaction eventually carried the day. They declared astonishment that Smith delivered his remarks at a black-tie dinner in a resplendent ballroom attended by wealthy businessmen, including twelve members of the du Pont family.[148] The *Washington Post* estimated that the leaders of the Liberty League attending the dinner had wealth exceeding $1 billion.[149] One congressman doubted that any of the attendees at the speech "missed a meal during the depression."[150] Another Democratic leader said, "Al Smith now stands for Millionaires' Row as against 'the sidewalks of New York.'"[151] Senator Joseph Robinson, Smith's running mate in 1928, gave a nationally broadcast response to Smith and declared that Smith had discarded his trademark brown derby for a "high hat."[152]

The attention created by Smith's speech spurred organized labor to increase their support for Roosevelt.[153] John Lewis, president of the United Mine Workers, condemned Smith for speaking to a "billion-dollar audience of predatory financial interests."[154] The union adopted a resolution characterizing the Liberty League as the mouthpiece of millionaires "who have piled up huge fortunes while denying their employees the right to organize" and denounced the league as "wholly selfish in its aims, un-American in its methods and policies and inimical to the interests of the people of the United States."[155] Other unions followed, organizing their efforts to reelect Roosevelt by pointing to the Liberty League.[156] In May

1936 a confederation of unions formed "Labor's Non-Partisan League," the object of which was the reelection of President Roosevelt.[157] Labor leaders said that the organization was necessary to counter the American Liberty League.[158] The new labor league never mentioned opposition by the Republican Party.[159] As one labor leader later declared, the league was the true opponent, and whoever the Republicans nominated would merely be a "spokesman for the American Liberty League, a holding company organized by the big interests and an institution that is a threat to our liberties."[160]

The media attention on Smith's speech gave Democrats new opportunities to mock the Liberty League's constitutional rhetoric.[161] One speaker denounced Liberty Leaguers' penchant for invoking the Founding Fathers, saying that "they apparently think the Revolution was fought to make Long Island safe for polo players."[162] A Democratic senator said that the American people understood that the "liberty" advocated by the Liberty League is "the liberty to exploit and profiteer upon the American people."[163] One congressman succeeded in blocking a bill to prohibit teaching communism in federally funded schools by introducing as a joke an amendment to prohibit schools from teaching the Liberty League's philosophy. Both groups are radicals, the congressman said, and "the only difference between the American Liberty League and the Communists is that Communists seek to divide all and the American Liberty League seeks to take all."[164]

Within a few weeks of Smith's speech, some commentators had cooled in their assessment of its success, declaring that the speech had served to help both Roosevelt and his opponents.[165] That perception did not last long. By April, the *Washington Post* reported that Roosevelt's popularity had steadily increased following Smith's speech.[166] By August, the *Post* stated what had become conventional wisdom: after Smith's speech, the public had turned against the Liberty League because it had become apparent that it was the "spokesman for special and selfish interests."[167]

The negative reaction against the league that started with Smith's speech became so strong that political commentators claimed that it was the turning point in the election and marked the moment when Roosevelt regained popularity, leading to his overwhelming reelection.[168] Although the *New York Times* had reported in August 1934 that the league was the answer to Wall Street's prayers and that all Americans could stand behind it, *Times* columnist Arthur Krock now declared that it had been obvious all along that the league's campaign was bound to backfire: "A political neophyte could have told the founders of the American Liberty League that its concentration of du Pont backing, and its array of disappointed

Democrats, threatened at the outset to turn it into a rich political gift to the President."[169]

The Democrats' coordinated response to the Liberty League went beyond speeches mocking the league. On January 25, 1936, the same day that Al Smith gave his speech at the American Liberty League dinner, Senator Hugo Black announced that he was launching an investigation of the league.[170] By all accounts, Black's investigation was a deliberate attempt to discredit New Deal enemies, and it proved quite effective.[171] It generated a great deal of media attention and has been credited by many as a key part of the Democrats' strategy to undermine the league.[172]

Black was chairman of the Special Committee to Investigate Lobbying Activities, which had been established in July 1935 to investigate unethical corporate lobbying against the Public Utility Holding Company Act.[173] Many leaders of the Liberty League had in fact lobbied against the act.[174] Yet it was quickly apparent that Black's investigation would not focus in any significant respect on lobbying activities.[175] The New York Times picked up on this almost immediately, describing the investigation as "further indication that the administration forces in Congress intend to wage war against the Liberty League and its membership."[176]

Black set out to show that the business interests controlling the league secretly coordinated a variety of groups opposing the New Deal.[177] Echoing the president's State of the Union address, Black alleged that these groups sought to "conceal their sinister activities behind lofty names and sonorous phrases."[178] Black's investigation succeeded in demonstrating that the Liberty League was deeply connected to other groups fighting the New Deal.[179] Liberty League backers had funded the Fascist-leaning Sentinels of the Republic, which declared that "old line Americans . . . want a Hitler" and claimed that a "Jewish threat" was undermining "the fundamental principles of the Constitution."[180]

Black's investigation also showed substantial connections between Liberty League backers and the Southern Committee to Uphold the Constitution, which incorporated race-based appeals to the campaign against the New Deal.[181] Pierre du Pont and John Raskob had each given $5,000 to finance the "Grass Roots" Convention organized by the Southern Committee, which had become notorious after news spread that convention organizers had distributed thousands of copies of a photo showing Eleanor Roosevelt being escorted to her car by two African American men, accompanied by an editorial denouncing Franklin Roosevelt for inviting "Negroes to come to the White House Banquet Table and sleep in the White House beds."[182] As the committee hearings revealed, the du Ponts apparently were untroubled by the distribution of these racist materials and contributed more money after learning of them.[183]

Although support for the Liberty League waned in the months after Smith's speech, Black's investigation kept the league in the news, painting its backers as shadowy figures who pulled the strings on a variety of radical organizations and who used constitutional rhetoric to attack the New Deal.[184] At Roosevelt's campaign headquarters, James Farley no doubt had reason to smile.[185]

At the same time that the Roosevelt campaign was making the Liberty League synonymous with "entrenched greed," the campaign was also making the Republican Party synonymous with the Liberty League.[186] Again and again, Roosevelt and supporters charged that the Republican Party was merely a stand-in for the league.[187] Roosevelt campaign chairman Farley declared that "the Republican National Committee has a little cry-baby brother, called the American Liberty League. The brothers are always together. They pal around together, they think the same thoughts, they echo the same phrases and they seek the same end."[188] As Farley charged, "Whether they like it or not, the Republican leaders represent the same forces of reaction that the Liberty League represents. They would go back to the Old Deal and let those people run the country who presided over its downfall."[189]

In fact, Liberty Leaguers worked hard to elect the Republican nominee Alf Landon. The du Ponts donated $144,000 to the Landon cause, making them by far the largest contributors to the Republican campaign.[190] The *New York Times* described Farley as "jubilant" over revelations that Liberty League supporters had given large contributions to Landon's campaign efforts.[191] Few were surprised when Al Smith endorsed Landon, and no one was surprised when the du Ponts endorsed him, making it clear that Landon had the support of the most well-known Liberty Leaguers.[192]

It was not merely the endorsements and financial backing of Liberty League leaders that made it easy for the Roosevelt campaign to portray the Republicans as puppets of the American Liberty League. The philosophy and rhetoric advanced by the Republicans in 1936 sounded just like the league. In January 1936, Liberty League executives said they would actively support the Republican nominee if the Republicans adopted a platform that advanced the league's policies.[193] Six months later, the party adopted a platform that employed the same kind of constitutional rhetoric familiar from Liberty League pamphlets. Echoing league materials, the Republican platform charged that the New Deal was un-American and unconstitutional. The platform declared that "America is in peril" because the New Deal "dishonored American traditions," and it dedicated the Republican Party to preserving free enterprise and the "American system of Constitutional and local self government."[194]

In his campaign speeches, Alf Landon took up many of the themes advanced by the Liberty League. Before the campaign, Landon was known as a "practical progressive," but his positions during the campaign echoed the rhetoric of the Liberty League.[195] He argued that the "essence of the New Deal" was "that the Constitution 'must go' in order to give men in Washington 'the power to make America over, to destroy the American way of life and establish a foreign way of life in its place.'"[196] In a nationally broadcast speech devoted to contrasting Landon's earlier progressive views with the positions he took during the campaign, Harold Ickes surmised that Landon had shifted to follow "the lead of the American Liberty League, founded by the liberty-loving DuPonts."[197]

Having accepted substantial campaign contributions from Liberty League leaders and adopted the league's constitutional rhetoric, the Republicans were slow to recognize the political harm they were causing by their association with the league.[198] Soon, however, it became obvious, and the *Times* reported that the "political liability of the League was so great by June that . . . Chairman Hamilton of the Republican committee would have walked a mile out of his way rather than be seen in the company of a leaguer."[199] When the Republican National Convention met in June 1936, Republican operatives feared that open support by the league would hurt Landon.[200] Republicans begged the Liberty League not to endorse Landon or to work openly for his election.[201]

To comply with Republican requests to distance the party from the league, the Liberty League issued a press release declaring that its opposition to the New Deal was strictly "nonpartisan" and that the league endorsed no candidate.[202] No one believed it.[203] Secretary of Agriculture Henry Wallace quipped that although Liberty League supporters "pretend that they are in no way identified with the National Republican leadership their money is and so are some of their trained seals."[204] By the end of the campaign, Republicans realized that any association with the American Liberty League was poisonous.[205] By then it was too late. The league had become a liability that Landon and the Republicans could not shed.

The American People's Endorsement of Roosevelt's Constitutional Vision

On November 2, 1936, Franklin Roosevelt won reelection in a historic landslide. He received 60.8 percent of the vote to Landon's 36.5 percent, the largest margin of victory since the uncontested election of 1820.[206] Roosevelt captured the electoral votes of every state except Maine and Vermont, giving him 523 electoral votes to Landon's 8, the largest share of the Electoral College vote since the establishment of the two-party system.[207]

The election results were widely understood as an expression of overwhelming public support for the constitutional philosophy of the New Deal and a repudiation of the Liberty League's contrary views.[208] The Democrats naturally understood the election that way, and many in the press agreed.[209] Republicans, too, apparently saw the election returns as a rejection of the Liberty League's philosophy.[210] After the defeat, the Republicans abandoned the rhetoric of constitutional nationalism they employed in the campaign and did not challenge the foundations of the administrative state again until the Barry Goldwater campaign in 1964.[211]

By effectively throwing in the towel after the election, the founders of the Liberty League also signaled that they understood that the election amounted to a public repudiation of their philosophy. In the days following the election, the Liberty League put a brave face on the defeat, vowing to continue operations.[212] Unprepared for the magnitude of the defeat, however, the league drastically shrank its staff and decided to end its publicity campaign.[213] A month later, the press was already asking: "What has become of the league, anyway?"[214] The election had made the Liberty League name toxic, and public support by the league was now understood to undermine any cause the league would support. The next year, the league's leaders vehemently opposed Roosevelt's Court-packing plan, but other opponents of the plan begged the du Ponts and the Liberty League not to play any public role in the fight against it, declaring that "they are black beasts in the popular imagination and if they rally against the President, they are liable to make him friends instead of enemies." In 1940 the league closed down with little notice.[215]

By themselves, the election results cannot resolve whether the 1936 election amounted to a popular mandate in favor of the New Deal constitutional philosophy. As Barry Cushman has written, "Election returns alone tell us no more than which person or persons won."[216] Nor does the fight between the American Liberty League and President Roosevelt reveal the extent to which voters actually supported the New Deal constitutional philosophy, rejected the league's philosophy, or gave any consideration to constitutional issues. The sources relied on in this chapter—pamphlets, radio addresses, campaign speeches, news articles, and editorials—do not show why the American people actually chose Roosevelt; whether it was because they sought to endorse his constitutional philosophy or merely because they liked the cut of his jib.

Yet the fight between Roosevelt and the American Liberty League shows that the 1936 election was presented to voters as a clash of competing constitutional visions, and questions of constitutional philosophy received an enormous amount of attention in the campaign. All the key participants in the election—Roosevelt, the Democratic Party, the Liberty League, the Republican Party, Alf Landon, the leading newspapers, and countless others—declared that constitutional issues were central to the campaign. The campaigns for each side employed constitutional rhetoric and asked the American people to take a stand on fundamental issues of constitutional philosophy. Participants in the campaign believed that the election would resolve what the Constitution means and what values were at the core of the nation's identity.

Conclusion

In 1937 constitutional doctrine shifted dramatically. After issuing rulings in 1935 and 1936 that Congress lacked power to adopt laws regulating the economy and protect workers' rights, in 1937 the Supreme Court dramatically changed course and began to rule in favor of broad federal power to regulate the economy.[217] Scholars have grappled with the legitimacy of the revolution in constitutional doctrine.[218]

The 1936 election plays a central role in the most influential defense of the New Deal revolution in constitutional doctrine, Bruce Ackerman's *We the People*.[219] Ackerman argues that in the 1930s the American people chose to adopt a new constitutional regime.[220] As Ackerman tells it, in 1936 Franklin Roosevelt ran against the Court and won a landslide victory, which is best understood as a ratification for his expansive philosophy of federal power.[221] The 1936 election is crucial to Ackerman's claim that the New Deal revolution amounted to what he has called a "constitutional moment," a moment in which "We the People" made a fundamental choice about the meaning of the Constitution and effectively created a new "constitutional regime."[222] The "Roosevelt revolution," Ackerman asserted, should "be viewed as a constitutive act of *popular* sovereignty that *legitimately* changed the preceding Republican Constitution."[223]

Many scholars have challenged Ackerman's claims about the role of the American people in endorsing Roosevelt's constitutional vision.[224] Terrance Sandalow wrote that "it is doubtful that the People made, or can be shown to have made, the decisions he attributes to them."[225] A central element of the case put forward by Ackerman's critics is that Roosevelt did not actually campaign against the Supreme Court.[226] "Perhaps the most problematic aspect of this thesis," wrote Michael Klarman, "is that Roosevelt scarcely mentioned the Court during the 1936 campaign."[227]

Both Ackerman and his critics are mistaken about the role of the Constitution in the 1936 election because they both imagine constitutional debates the way that lawyers do, as disputes over the meaning of text rather than disputes over national identity carried out in constitutional terms. In Ackerman's view, the dispute pitted Roosevelt against the Court, and the election asked the American voters to mediate the conflict.[228] Ackerman's critics also characterize the constitutional conflict in Court-centered terms. Historian William Leuchtenburg asserted that the 1936 election cannot be understood as a constitutional referendum because voters did not "conceive of the 1936 election as centering on their attitude toward the Supreme Court."[229] If Roosevelt did not actually ask the American people to choose between his constitutional interpretation and the Court's, Leuchtenburg and others assert, the 1936 election cannot plausibly be read as a public endorsement of Roosevelt's constitutional views.[230]

As this chapter has shown, questions of constitutional philosophy were central to the 1936 election, but it was not presented to the voters as a dispute between Roosevelt and the Supreme Court. Ackerman's critics are correct that the campaign did not focus much attention on the Supreme Court's constitutional rulings. Nor did the campaigns address the construction of particular constitutional clauses. Yet Roosevelt did have a public opponent in 1936 that presented a sharply contrasting constitutional philosophy. It was not the Supreme Court. It was the American Liberty League.

Scholars have failed to recognize the centrality of constitutional issues in the 1936 election because the constitutional rhetoric used in the campaign differs from the language of constitutional doctrine used by lawyers.[231] Lawyers and law professors may believe that the central constitutional issues of the 1930s focused on the issues addressed by the Supreme Court in its New Deal rulings, such as the meaning of the Commerce Clause, the

General Welfare Clause, and the degree of deference owed to Congress over the reasonableness of federal laws.[232] The constitutional rhetoric prevalent throughout the 1936 election campaign did not address these issues but instead focused on issues of national identity expressed in constitutional terms.[233] Both Roosevelt and the American Liberty League understood the Constitution to embody a set of fundamental values that they said form the core of what it means to be American.[234]

For the Liberty League, that meant the ability of Americans, especially business owners, to do what they please. They considered the New Deal to be not just bad policy; it represented an alien philosophy that conflicted with bedrock American values. Roosevelt, in contrast, argued that the Constitution gives the people power to protect themselves from the tyranny of big business represented by the leaders of the American Liberty League.

The fight between the American Liberty League and President Roosevelt illustrates how the belief that the Constitution embodies national identity plays out in national politics. While it may be impossible to know why American voters gave Roosevelt an electoral landslide in 1936, it is certain that the issues upon which they were asked to cast their votes focused on questions of national identity expressed in constitutional terms.

5 | The Partisan Constitution

Popular constitutionalism is a theory developed in the legal academy over the past few decades that asserts that the people, and not the courts, should have the final say in determining the meaning of the Constitution.[1] It offers a liberal critique of control of constitutional interpretation by the elite and undemocratic Supreme Court and asserts that the people should control the understood meaning of the Constitution through ordinary politics.[2] For many popular constitutionalists, the New Deal revolution of the 1930s provides the best example of what can happen when the American people are called on to resolve constitutional issues.[3] They point to Franklin Roosevelt's understanding that "the Constitution of the United States was a layman's document, not a lawyer's contract."[4] By endorsing Roosevelt's broad conception of constitutional power, the people helped unshackle democracy from restrictions imposed by a conservative judiciary.[5]

When the meaning of the Constitution is debated in national politics, however, the debates invariably are conducted in the rhetoric of constitutional nationalism. As discussed in chapter 4, that was true in the 1930s, when the American Liberty League and the Republican Party campaigned against the New Deal as an alien and unconstitutional force that must be defeated to save the Constitution and the nation, and FDR and the Democrats argued that the Constitution empowers the people to protect themselves from the forces of entrenched greed represented by the Liberty League. The debate pitted a narrow conception of who and what was American against a more expansive conception.

Although the American people overwhelmingly chose FDR's more expansive constitutional vision, the story of the American Liberty League nonetheless suggests the dangers of nationalism that can arise when disputes over the Constitution become central to national politics. Fights over the Constitution often serve as proxies for fights over national identity and the relative power and status of different groups of Americans. Fights over the Constitution can harness deep undercurrents of nationalism and become a vehicle for arguing that some people and some ideas must be excluded as un-American.

The dangers of nationalism lurking in popular constitutionalism can be seen again with the Tea Party movement, which emerged in 2009 in opposition to President Obama.[6] Like the American Liberty League, the Tea Party movement used the rhetoric of constitutional nationalism to argue that Obama and his supporters were working to destroy the nation's foundational values. Unlike the Liberty League, however, which did not attract a popular following and was always controlled by a small group of Wall Street executives, the Tea Party attracted hundreds of thousands of activists and millions of supporters. By the time of the 2012 presidential election, the Tea Party had become a major force in the Republican Party, which adopted its constitutional rhetoric. The Tea Party and the Republican Party that it came to control campaigned on a platform that declared that Obama and the people who elected him were not authentic Americans and belonged to the "party of treason."

Although the Tea Party rarely made explicit appeals to ethnonationalism, its constitutional rhetoric conveyed racial, cultural, and ethnic anxieties felt by a group of Americans who considered themselves prototypical Americans—who were overwhelmingly white, Christian, and middle class, and who felt threatened by the nation's increasing racial, religious, and cultural diversity. The Tea Party attacked President Obama for his support of "big government" programs like the Affordable Care Act, foreclosure relief to homeowners, and food stamps. Tea Party members considered the beneficiaries of these federal programs to be undeserving of government aid. They understood the recipients of government largesse to be primarily people of color and recent immigrants, who they believed did not share core American values like individualism and free markets. The Tea Party movement said that Obama's election threatened to destroy the Constitution and fundamentally transform the nation into something unrecognizably foreign. In its attacks on "big government," the Tea Party movement conveyed anxieties about the nation's changing demographics in the patriotic language of constitutional nationalism.

The Rise of the Tea Party Movement

By Tea Party supporters' accounts, the movement began on February 19, 2009, during the CNBC show *Squawk Box* when financial analyst Rick Santelli denounced an Obama administration proposal to provide financial assistance to the home mortgage sector.[7] Santelli screamed, "The government is promoting bad behavior!" To Santelli, the proposal to support homeowners facing foreclosure ran counter to fundamental American principles because it was tantamount to "subsidizing the losers":

> This is America! How many people want to pay for your neighbor's mortgage that have an extra bathroom and can't pay their bills? Raise your hand! President Obama, are you listening? You know Cuba used to have mansions and a relatively decent economy. They moved from the individual to the collective. Now they're driving '54 Chevys. It's time for another Tea Party. What we are doing in this country will make Thomas Jefferson and Benjamin Franklin roll over in their graves. We're thinking of having a Chicago Tea Party in July, all you capitalists. I'm organizing.[8]

Santelli's call to form a new "Tea Party" has been described by Tea Partiers as the "rant heard round the world."[9]

Santelli's rant expressed the key elements of the Tea Party rhetoric and ideology. It made an explicitly nationalist appeal, declaring that "This is America!" and suggesting that the Obama administration's proposal was un-American. It presumed that there is a core set of authentic American principles, including beliefs in limited government and individual liberty. Santelli accused the administration of betraying these principles by supporting "the collective" rather than "the individual." He identified true American principles as coming from the Founding Fathers, who would see the Obama administration's proposal as so abhorrent that they must be rolling over in their graves. To Santelli, the proposal to support homeowners facing foreclosure was un-American and smacked of Cuban-style socialism, because it took money from successful, hard-working Americans and gave it to economic "losers." He declared that the right response to Obama's infidelity to authentic American values was to return to the values and tactics of the Founders, to form, as they did, a "Tea Party."[10]

Within days, Santelli's rant had been watched millions of times on the internet. Several local groups calling themselves Tea Parties formed to protest the administration's proposed stimulus package, excessive taxes, and the growing national debt.[11] The next week, dozens of Tea Party protests occurred across the country.[12] Within weeks, hundreds of local Tea Party groups were formed to protest excessive government. Over the next several years, Tea Party groups brought great energy to conservative politics. They protested, marched, and disrupted town hall meetings. Tea Party groups participated in elections at every level. Tea Party–affiliated candidates won elections in local, state, and federal elections. They created several national organizations, political action committees, and lobbying groups.

The movement's principal agenda was to support limited government and to oppose President Obama's economic program, including the Affordable Care Act, the stimulus package, and the proposed cap-and-trade program to address greenhouse gas emissions. Tea Party supporters often expressed this agenda by attacking the president and his supporters as un-American. As Tea Party activist Laurie Roth declared at a 2011 Tea Party meeting, the election of Obama "was not a shift to the Left like Jimmy Carter or Bill Clinton. This is a worldview clash. . . . A man who is a closet secular-type Muslim, but he's still a Muslim. He's no Christian. We're seeing a man who's a socialist communist in the White House, pretending to be an American. . . . He wasn't even born here."[13] Surveys showed that more than half of Tea Party supporters believed that Obama was Muslim and that he was born outside the United States, while less than a quarter of all Americans believed these things.[14]

In many ways, the demographics and issues that drove Tea Party supporters were indistinguishable from those of conservative Republicans.[15] Tea Party supporters overwhelmingly voted Republican.[16] Like other Republicans, Tea Party supporters were overwhelmingly white, and on average they were better educated and made a higher income than most Americans. Most were at least forty-five years old.[17] Like many other Republicans, Tea Party supporters believed that the government does too much to help poor people and people of color.[18]

What most distinguished Tea Party supporters from other conservatives and Republicans was the constitutional nationalist frame through which they understood their grievances. Joseph Farah, who gave the keynote address at the first national Tea Party convention, explained, "While elements of the conservative movement have emphasized the Constitution, the rule of law, and the will of the people, conservatives have traditionally lacked the fiery commitment to that document that I see among tea partiers."[19]

The Tea Party movement follows the same pattern that gave rise to other constitutional nationalist movements discussed in earlier chapters: it arose in response to a perceived threat to the power and status of a long-dominant group, saw that threat through a nationalist framework, and mobilized a movement around constitutional demands. As numerous public opinion surveys showed, at the time the Tea Party movement began, a significant cohort of white Americans believed that their status and power were threatened. They looked with distress on the election of the nation's first African American president and the rising population and political influence of racial and religious minorities. These concerns about status were heightened by the widespread economic anxiety brought on by the economic crisis of 2008 and the subsequent recession. They saw the proposed policies of President Obama as harbingers of transformative change. These events led to increased levels of white racial resentment that gave rise to the Tea Party movement.[20] As surveys showed, the Tea Party focused opposition on government "handouts" to "undeserving" groups, which were heavily influenced by racial and ethnic stereotypes.[21]

Public opinion surveys uniformly found that, more than other Republicans, Tea Party supporters described themselves as angry.[22] They were angry at governing elites, both Democrats and Republicans, who they believed did not care about their concerns but instead took their tax money to give to people who did not deserve it. Tea Party supporters were resentful of those they considered undeserving—poor people, illegal immigrants, racial minorities—who they believed received vast sums of government money paid for by their taxes.[23] For decades, white nationalists have targeted a demographic sometimes described as Middle American Radicals, who feel squeezed between governing elites who treat them with disdain and those they consider undeserving poor.[24] In fact, Tea Party supporters showed greater degrees of white racial resentment than others, and the longer Tea Party supporters remained affiliated with the movement, the more likely they were to explicitly characterize their worldview in racial terms.[25]

Tea Party supporters experienced their anger through a nationalist framework.[26] To Tea Party supporters, the changes associated with the election of President Obama were not merely unwanted but threatened the very existence of the nation. "Many Americans are indeed dispirited," Joseph Farah explained. "They look around and they no longer recognize their country and what it is rapidly becoming."[27] Former congressman Dick Armey, founder of FreedomWorks and author of *Give Us Liberty: A Tea Party Manifesto*, said that the Tea Party was riding a national wave of fear that the Obama administration is "going to ruin our country."[28] As another Tea Party leader explained, Tea Party supporters feared that the Obama administration "would erode everything we believed was good about the United States."[29]

Surveys confirmed that Tea Party support was driven by a perception of group threat seen through the framework of nationalism. Extensively reviewing hundreds of public opinion surveys, political scientists Christopher Parker and Matt Barreto concluded: "People are driven to support the Tea

Party from the anxiety they feel as they perceive the America they know, the country they love, slipping away, threatened by the rapidly changing face of what they believe is the 'real' America: a heterosexual, Christian, middle-class, (mostly) male, white country."[30] Tea Party supporters understood the forces threatening the nation to be un-American and alien. Tea Party supporters claimed that liberals and the Obama administration were "attacking" America, that the president was "anti-American," and that he was seeking to undermine basic American values.[31] More than 70 percent of Tea Party supporters believed that Obama was trying to destroy the country.[32] A rhetoric of foreign invasion and foreign infiltration dominated Tea Party speeches and literature.[33] Tea Party supporters claimed that foreign forces were succeeding in taking over the United States, transforming the country they love into an unrecognizably alien realm.[34]

Tea Party supporters routinely demonized as "un-American" those who supported policies that conflict with what they perceive to be fundamental American values.[35] The Tea Party routinely characterized the Democratic Party as "the party of treason" and portrayed President Obama and his supporters as foreign and anti-American.[36] Judson Phillips, founder of Tea Party Nation, declared simply, "Obama and his regime are not real Americans."[37]

Born of status anxiety and a fear of cultural change, the Tea Party movement framed its message in the familiar language of constitutional nationalism. Addressing the National Tea Party Convention in 2010, Joseph Farah declared, "The Constitution is the glue that holds us together, that binds us as a people, and as a nation-state. And we abrogate it and abuse it at our great peril. . . . Without it, America ceases to be America."[38] As Tea Party supporters saw it, Obama was destroying the Constitution, and the solution was, as Farah put it, "to reclaim the promise our founders gave us uniquely in the Declaration of Independence and the Constitution." The Tea Party argued that only by embracing the nation's foundational principles could the people save the nation from ruin.[39]

Emblematic was the popular "Obama Is Unconstitutional" T-shirt seen at Tea Party gatherings, a slogan that refers to the discredited "birther" theory that Obama was foreign-born and therefore constitutionally unfit for office. The slogan links the allegation that the president is foreign with the allegation that his presidency is unconstitutional. Tea Party supporters described Obama as foreign in various ways.[40] To birthers, he was foreign *by birth*.[41] He was sometimes described as *religiously* foreign by those who believe he is secretly a Muslim living in what they understand to be a

Christian nation.[42] He was sometimes described as *racially* foreign by those who consider the United States a white nation.[43] And he was also described as *ideologically* foreign because he rejected the Tea Party's understanding of American values.[44] More than 90 percent of Tea Party supporters said that Obama was moving the country away from traditional American values and toward a foreign ideology.[45] These points of view share the core Tea Party message: President Obama and his liberal supporters were foreign usurpers, not real Americans, and all true patriots had a duty to rise up to defeat them before they destroyed the Constitution.[46]

The Tea Party's Constitutional Ideology

Summarizing the Tea Party's constitutional vision is somewhat tricky because the movement was decentralized and lacked agreed-upon doctrines or leaders.[47] Nonetheless, an examination of prominent Tea Party books, websites, and speeches shows the movement was committed to a core set of principles that it attributed to the Founders and believed are embodied in the Constitution.[48] In February 2010 a group representing different Tea Party factions issued a "Tea Party Declaration of Independence," which attempted to identify the movement's central commitments.[49] The Tea Party Declaration crystallizes many of the disparate positions of the members of the Tea Party movement and identifies what most Tea Party groups cited as the eternal and unchanging principles at the core of the American nation: beliefs in American exceptionalism, individual liberty, limited government, and free markets.[50]

Perhaps the most cherished of these principles is a belief in the greatness of America itself.[51] Although beliefs in the exceptional nature of the United States have been common since at least de Crevecoeur, the Tea Party movement espoused an especially emphatic version of American exceptionalism.[52] As the founder of Tea Party Nation declared: "America is the most exceptional country the world has ever known and the American people are the most exceptional people the world has ever seen. America and Americans have done more good during the existence of our country than any other country in the history of the world."[53] To Tea Party supporters, faith in America's greatness is what separates true patriots from liberals and progressives like President Obama, who assertedly do not truly love their country. Tea Party favorite Sarah Palin, for instance, complained that "we have a president, perhaps for the first time since the founding of our republic, who expresses his belief that America is not the greatest earthly force for good the world has ever known."[54]

To Tea Party supporters, what makes the United States exceptional is a "unique set of beliefs and national qualities" established by the Founders, which made it "a model to the world."[55] The core of these beliefs is a commitment to individual liberty, which the Tea Party movement understood to mean an unregulated economy.[56] As Tea Party Patriots, one of the national Tea Party umbrella groups, declared: "A free market is the economic consequence of personal liberty. The founders believed that personal and economic freedom were indivisible, as do we. Our current government's interference distorts the free market and inhibits the pursuit of individual and economic liberty. Therefore, we support a return to the free market principles on which this nation was founded and oppose government intervention into the operations of private business."[57] Linked to individual liberty is the principle of "limited government," which prevents interference with individual liberties and free markets.[58] The Tea Party Declaration of Independence proclaims that the Constitution guarantees each person the ability "to direct our own affairs free of the dictates of an ever expanding federal government which is as voracious in its desire for power as it is incompetent and dangerous in its exercise."[59]

The Tea Party movement articulated all of its positions in terms of this set of principles—individual liberty, limited government, and free markets—the same principles that formed the basis of the Liberty League's philosophy and that has been the bedrock of the modern conservative ever since.[60] Any government action the movement opposed, whether it was health care reform, bailouts, taxes, debt, or cap-and-trade legislation, was said to involve excessive government, which unconstitutionally infringed individual liberty and interfered with the free market.[61]

The Tea Party movement grounded these familiar conservative principles on an interpretation of the Constitution that rejected prevailing interpretations. Supporters rejected judicial precedent regarding the scope of federal powers because they believed that the Supreme Court has departed from the true meaning of the Constitution and succumbed to the lure of socialism.[62] To the Tea Party movement, the meaning of the Constitution is perfectly clear. In his book *The Tea Party Manifesto*, Joseph Farah mocks President Obama for being a "constitutional scholar," declaring that "you don't have to be a scholar to understand the Constitution. It was written to be understood easily by ordinary people."[63] To Tea Party supporters, there can be no basis for differing interpretations of the Constitution because "there can be little mistake about what [the Founders] meant, what they had in mind, what they were thinking and why."[64]

The conviction that the Constitution is clear and should be easily accessible to everyone lies at the heart of the Tea Party's efforts to distribute millions of pocket-size Constitutions.[65] Tea Party leaders exhort their supporters to read the Constitution daily, to memorize its passages, and to carry the Constitution with them at all times.[66]

W. Cleon Skousen's Commie-Fighting Constitution

The Tea Party's mission involved not only restoring the Founders' Constitution but also restoring what they consider the true history of the Founders. The movement asserted that historians have distorted American history to paint the Founders in a negative light and to undermine what they view as American values.[67] In July 2010 Glenn Beck, one of the most trusted figures among Tea Party supporters, hosted an hour-long program of his Fox News show entitled "Restoring History," in which he told his viewers that American history books are full of lies produced with "malicious progressive intent."[68] For the past hundred years, Beck explained, leftists (as he characterized them) have been rewriting history because they knew that they had "to separate us from our history to be able to separate us from our Constitution and our God."[69]

To the extent that Tea Party supporters point to written sources for their understanding of the Founders and the Constitution, they relied on narratives that reject conventional history and assert what can only be described as mythological history.[70] The most popular sources about the Founders and the Constitution among Tea Party supporters were a pair of books by the late W. Cleon Skousen, *The Five Thousand Year Leap* and *The Making of America*.[71] Jeffrey Rosen has called *The Five Thousand Year Leap* the "Bible of the Tea Party movement" and Skousen the movement's "constitutional guru."[72] Hundreds of Tea Party groups used Skousen's books as the basis for seminars devoted to educating their members and the public on the principles of the Constitution and to show that the answers to America's problems can be found in the wisdom of the Founding Fathers.[73] Many leading Tea Party and Republican politicians called themselves enthusiastic Skousen followers, including Senators Mike Lee, Rand Paul, Orrin Hatch, and Mitt Romney, as well as Secretary of Energy Rick Perry and Secretary of Housing and Urban Development Ben Carson.[74]

Skousen's books were published in the early 1980s and are the products of the radical right wing of the Cold War era. In the 1960s and 1970s, Skousen was an ardent supporter of the John Birch Society, and he espoused religiously themed Communist conspiracy theories. *The Five Thousand Year Leap* and *The Making of America* depict the Founding Fathers as devout Christians who discovered ancient principles for national success based on the Anglo-Saxons and the biblical Israelites.[75] The central message of each book is that the Constitution provides divine protection against communism. With the end of the Cold War, one might have expected Skousen's books to lose whatever appeal they once had, but the emergence of the Tea Party movement made the books best-sellers.[76]

Skousen and the Tea Party's understanding of American history has been widely attacked by historians. Legal historian Jack Rakove once described Skousen's work as "a joke that no self-respecting scholar would think is worth a warm pitcher of spit."[77] Harvard's Jill Lepore wrote that Tea Party claims about the Founders are "to history what astrology is to astronomy, what alchemy is to chemistry, what creationism is to evolution."[78] She characterized the Tea Party as espousing a form of "historical fundamentalism," which considers the nation's founding to be "ageless and sacred and to be worshipped," that certain texts—"the founding documents"—are "to be read in the same spirit with which religious fundamentalists read, for instance, the Ten Commandments."[79]

While the Tea Party's understanding of American history does not fare well by the standards of professional historians, as a body of mythological history it is fairly typical of many nationalist movements. As political scientists have long noted, nationalist movements often rely on fantastic versions of national history to advance their cause.[80] To dismiss nationalist narratives as historically inaccurate misses the point. As political scientists Matthew Levinger and Paula Franklin Lytle have explained: "Imagined history so expressed cannot be understood merely as a true or false account, but rather as a narrative articulating the elements of a social movement's agenda."[81] Seen this way, the Tea Party's understanding of United States history is more valuable for what it reveals about the movement's agenda than what it says about the past.[82]

Although Skousen's books were published more than thirty years before the Tea Party movement, it is easy to see why they appealed to the movement. Both shared the view that leftists have manipulated what Americans believe about history, undermining belief in the Founders and the Constitution in order to make it possible to trick the nation into accepting alien communist doctrines.[83] According to Skousen, the false history foisted upon Americans succeeded in creating a "generation of lost Americans" and a nation of "un-Americans," who had lost touch with their national identity.[84]

Skousen articulated a golden age narrative of US history that conveys the essential elements of all nationalist histories: (1) assertions of a glorious past, in which the nation once existed as a pure, unified, and harmonious community; (2) declarations of a degraded present, in which the unity of the nation has been shattered; and (3) hopes for a utopian future, in which the movement asserts that the success of its agenda will reverse the conditions that have caused the present degradation and recover the nation's original harmonious essence.[85]

Skousen sought to reintroduce America to what he understood to be its glorious past, presenting the nation's founders as a unified group of chosen disciples to whom God revealed a divine formula for government.[86] He scoffed at conventional versions of American history that depict the Founders as relatively nonreligious deists, declaring that the Founders "continually petitioned God in fervent prayers, both public and private, and looked upon his divine intervention in their daily lives as a singular blessing."[87] Skousen likewise rejected the conventional understanding that the framers of the Constitution were principally influenced by European philosophers of the Enlightenment era, including Hobbes, Locke, and Rousseau. Far from following what Skousen refers to as the "fads of European philosophy," the Founders took their inspiration from the Bible and the ancient Anglo-Saxons. In fact, Skousen declared, the Founders rejected all "European" theories and "made European theories unconstitutional."[88]

The main thrust of Skousen's books is that the Constitution establishes eternal national principles that can protect the nation against the spread of world communism. Tea Party supporters believed that the same principles could protect the nation against the spread of Obama's alien ideology. The first and most important of these "ancient principles" is the establishment of "natural law" as the only reliable basis for government.[89] For Skousen, natural law means "God's laws" and encompasses the necessity for "limited government," the right to bear arms, protections for the family and the institution of marriage, the sanctity of private property, and the avoidance of debt. Such natural law principles, Skousen claimed, are instituted eternally and are not subject to change by mortal legislators. Legislation contrary to God's laws is a "scourge to humanity" and is therefore unconstitutional.[90]

Skousen's anticommunism provided the Tea Party a framework for arguing against Obama's economic policies. Skousen declared that the natural law principles embodied in the Constitution prohibits government efforts to provide welfare benefits or redistribute wealth.[91] He cites a story that when Davy Crockett served in Congress he voted against a bill to provide financial support to a navy widow because Crockett believed that the government has no authority to take money from some taxpayers and give it to others, no matter how worthy the cause or how needy the recipients.[92] The story about Davy Crockett is not actually true, but for Skousen and the Tea Party it confirms a belief that it is fundamentally misguided for the government to attempt to identify people who need assistance. It is tantamount to stealing to tax some people in order to give money to others. By protecting property, Skousen explained, the Founders sought to refute "European philosophers" who believed "that the role of government was to take from the 'haves' and give to the 'have nots.'" As Skousen explains, the Founders did "everything possible to make these collectivist policies 'unconstitutional.'"[93]

In Skousen's narrative, the adoption of the Constitution and the recognition of the eternal constitutional principles of American exceptionalism, individual liberty, and limited government ushered in a golden age of prosperity and freedom that was nothing short of miraculous. The adoption of the Founders' principles made the United States the most prosperous and freest nation the world has ever known.[94] It allowed humanity to make more progress in a short time than had been made in the six thousand years since God created the Earth, hence the title of Skousen's book, *The Five Thousand Year Leap.*[95]

Sadly, however, the nation strayed from its foundational principles.[96] Beginning in the early twentieth century, Socialists sought to convince the public that the Founders and their principles were out-of-date.[97] As Skousen reported, "By the 1920s, the debunking of the Founding Fathers was in full swing."[98] Once the people abandoned faith in the Founders, the United States began to adopt one policy after another that conflicted with its foundational principles.[99] The primary transgression was the establishment of programs like Social Security and Medicare, which violate the fundamental prohibition against "collectivist" measures that redistribute wealth.[100] Labor, environmental, and consumer protection laws followed, which likewise transgress the principles of individual liberty, limited government, and free markets.[101]

Skousen provided Tea Party supporters a source for arguing that almost everything the federal government does today is unconstitutional.[102] Tea Party supporters took this lesson to heart and declared that the purpose of these unconstitutional programs is clear: to oppress the people, take away their freedoms, and establish rule by elites. As the Tea Party Declaration of Independence explains:

> We reject the endless creation of myriad federal government agencies that drown free enterprise and local control in the swarms of education, energy, ecology, and commerce bureaucrats who style themselves "czars" sent to harass us. . . . We reject a profligate Government that is spending TRILLIONS of dollars on worthless socialist schemes designed to bankrupt us and put the American people in a position of dependence on the State, as peasants begging for their very sustenance from self-styled "educated classes" and so-called "experts."[103]

Tea Party supporters believed that the purpose of these federal programs is to create dependency and to undermine the foundational American value of individual self-reliance.

For Skousen and the Tea Party, the source of the attack on the Constitution was clear: un-American forces have taken over the federal government.[104] For Skousen, international Communists had infiltrated the government and were working to undermine the Constitution. For the Tea Party, the attack came from President Barack Obama.

Identifying the rejection of the Constitution as the cause of the nation's crisis, Skousen offered the apparent solution: the nation must embrace the Constitution again. The Tea Party agreed. As Glenn Beck wrote, the Founders anticipated today's problems: "The questions that we face were foreseen by the greatest group of Americans to ever live: the Founding Fathers. They knew that we would be grappling with issues like the ones we face today at some point, so they designed a ship that could withstand even the mightiest storm."[105]

The Tea Party declared that the hour of reckoning had come. The Virginia Tea Party Patriots opened their 2010 convention by holding a funeral for the Constitution. In this act of political theater, a man dressed as Thomas Jefferson led a solemn procession, slowly ringing a bell through downtown Richmond, followed by supporters carrying a black cardboard coffin labeled "The Constitution." "We the people have gathered here today," the Jefferson impersonator pronounced, "to mourn the destruction of our Constitution."[106] As the faux Jefferson explained, the Constitution died from "decades of overreaching legislation, activist judges, and finally the current Congress and the Obama Administration."[107]

Yet it might not be too late. The Tea Party movement was born of the conviction that the Constitution can rise again, if only we believe in it.[108]

The Tea Party's Takeover of the Republican Party

By 2010 the Tea Party movement had become a dominant faction in Republican politics. That year, nearly one-third of Americans said they supported the movement.[109] It was widely credited with helping elect a Republican majority in the House of Representatives.[110] In 2010 five Tea Party–supported Senate candidates and forty House candidates won election, all of them Republican, and these victories played a major role in the Republican takeover of Congress. By 2012 the Tea Party was recognized as the central faction in the Republican Party, and nearly half of Republican voters said that they supported the Tea Party.[111] As conservative columnist Rich Lowry wrote, "The Tea Party rebaptized the GOP in the faith of limited government and constitutional constraints."[112]

Surveys showed that, much more so than other Americans, Tea Party supporters opposed political compromise. At the urging of the Tea Party bloc, Republicans in Congress adopted a position of refusing to compromise with President Obama.[113] As one Tea Party writer put it, there could be no compromise between "hard working Americans who love their country and freedom" and those who supported the "Marxist" policies of the president and his supporters.[114] From the Tea Party's point of view, Obama was not simply a politician with whom they disagreed; he represented a sinister, alien force that sought to destroy American traditions. Refusal to compromise was a patriotic duty.

The Republican Party also adopted the constitutional nationalist rhetoric favored by the Tea Party. All of the candidates seeking the 2012 Republican nomination for president jockeyed for the crown of most Constitution-loving. In his speech announcing his candidacy, Senator Rick Santorum mentioned the Constitution five times, calling it "the owner's manual for America."[115] Not to be outdone, Representative Michele Bachmann brought it up seven times in her announcement speech, promising to "take back our country" and "restore constitutional conservative values to our federal government."[116] That year's champion constitutionalist was Representative Ron Paul, who mentioned the Constitution sixteen times in his announcement speech and succinctly captured the overall theme of constitutional restoration: "I want to go back to the Constitution."[117]

Eager to be seen as a "constitutional conservative" by skeptical Tea Party supporters, the party's eventual nominee Mitt Romney sought to frame the race against President Obama in constitutional terms: "The big issues in this campaign turn on our understanding of the Constitution and how it was meant to guide the life of our nation."[118] Romney routinely suggested that, one way or another, Obama isn't authentically American: "Our president doesn't have the same feelings about American exceptionalism that we do." Obama's philosophy, Romney warned, is "very strange and in some respects foreign to the American experience type of philosophy."[119] Romney further made clear that he shared the Tea Party's belief that Obama represented the nation's "takers"—people who "pay no taxes" and who "are dependent upon government, who believe that they are victims, who believe the government has a responsibility to care for them, who believe that they are entitled to health care, to food, to housing, to you-name-it."[120]

With Tea Party backing, the Republican Party declared in 2012 that it was dedicated to a return to the true meaning of the Constitution. The party platform, dedicated to "the wisdom of the Founding Fathers," announced that the GOP was the "Party of the Constitution" and declared that it was committed to the "Restoration of Constitutional Government." The Republicans wanted Americans to know that Democrats did not share that creed. The platform was entitled "We Believe in America."[121]

The Republicans lost the 2012 election and failed to unseat President Obama. With the defeat, the Tea Party fell into a slow decline. It continued to hold considerable power in Congress through the House Freedom Caucus, which had three dozen members. But as Matt Kibbe, one of the founders of the movement, declared, the movement's momentum ended with Obama's reelection.[122] The number of active Tea Party groups steadily declined.[123] By 2015 only 17 percent of American adults voiced support for the movement, down from a high of 32 percent.[124] Much diminished, the movement changed its focus from fiscal restraints to immigration restrictions. Although opposition to immigration had been part of the Tea Party agenda the beginning, by 2016 these concerns had become the movement's dominant concern.[125]

Constitutional Nationalism and Partisan Politics

Popular constitutionalists like Larry Kramer and Mark Tushnet have argued that democratic values are advanced when the people determine the meaning of the Constitution through everyday politics, rather than ceding control to judicial elites.[126] As Kramer has argued, a distrust of ordinary people forms a significant part of the justification for empowering courts rather than the electorate to determine the meaning of the Constitution:

The modern Anti-Populist sensibility presumes that ordinary people are emotional, ignorant, fuzzy-headed and simple-minded, in contrast to a thoughtful, informed, and clear-headed elite. Ordinary people tend to be foolish and irresponsible when it comes to politics: self-interested rather than public-spirited, arbitrary rather than principled, impulsive and close-minded rather than deliberate or logical. Ordinary people are like children, really. And being like children, ordinary people are insecure and easily manipulated. The result is that ordinary politics, or perhaps we should say the politics that ordinary people make, "is not just low in quality but dangerous as well."[127]

Popular constitutionalism is thus born of the conviction that the people should be empowered to decide fundamental questions themselves.

Advocates of popular constitutionalism believe that popular control of the meaning of the Constitution will lead to the enlargement of popular democracy. The exemplar is the people's role in ratifying the New Deal Constitution. By reelecting President Roosevelt in a landslide, popular constitutionalists assert, the people voted to empower the federal government to adopt broad economic regulations. With the New Deal in mind, popular constitutionalists assert that giving the people control over the meaning of the Constitution serves to lift restrictions on the choices available through the political process.[128]

The Tea Party movement, however, suggests that popular constitutionalists may be overly optimistic about the benefits of injecting constitutional issues into everyday politics. At a minimum, the Tea Party movement calls into question the claim that popular constitutionalism generally advances democratic values. Although the movement brought constitutional issues into everyday politics, it shared many of the antipopulist concerns that Kramer attributed to supporters of judicial supremacy. The Tea Party movement asserted that the people cannot be trusted with too much democracy because they will choose—and have chosen—dangerous and misguided policies. We need to return to the Founders' Constitution, the Tea Party shouted, because the people have run amok. To the Tea Party, the nation faces a crisis because of an *excess* of popular democracy that judicial elites have failed to rein in.

The Tea Party sought to limit democratic power in several senses. Tea Party supporters believed that the people, acting through their electoral representatives, created a variety of regulatory programs—including minimum wage laws, Social Security, Medicare, environmental laws, and the Affordable Care Act—that exceed their power, restrict individual liberty, and interfere with free markets.[129] The people must be protected from doing what they want, the Tea Party argues, and that is the function of the Constitution.[130]

The Tea Party movement did not hide its disdain for democracy. Tea Party supporters routinely disparaged the term *democracy*. Citing Skousen, they claimed that it was international Socialists who first began to describe the United States as a *democracy* to discredit the Founders and lay the groundwork for the acceptance of socialism. To Tea Party supporters, calling the United States a democracy is a lie perpetrated by progressives.[131] Tea Party supporters often repeat the John Birch Society slogan that America is a republic, not a democracy, to emphasize the ways that the Constitution limits democratic power and prevents democratic excesses.[132]

Rather than seeking to empower the people to control their fates, the Tea Party expressed profound distrust of the ability of ordinary citizens to decide important questions. Joseph Farah, for instance, explained that President Obama was elected due to "mankind's innate desire to collectivize and rebel against God's order."[133] The Tea Party's agenda of restoring the Constitution sought principally to protect the nation against the damage the people would do and have done when they decide important questions themselves.

The Tea Party's nationalist rhetoric served the goal of foreclosing democratic deliberation.[134] By characterizing a great number of ideas and people as un-American, anti-American, or foreign, the Tea Party movement sought to marginalize many proposals in political debate. As Tea Party supporters declared, there can be no compromise or dialogue with those who would destroy America.[135]

The Tea Party movement illustrates that ethnonationalist impulses are likely to be an inevitable part of popular constitutionalism and may undermine democratic values. Although it used constitutional rhetoric, the Tea Party was at heart a nationalist movement. Its supporters did not just disagree with their political adversaries; they did not consider them authentic members of the political community. Theda Skocpol and Vanessa Williamson interviewed hundreds of Tea Party activists and were struck by their demonization of groups that disagreed with them: "Organized African-American and Latino rights groups are dismissed as threats to the nation. And so are Democrats—who are not discussed as legitimate competitors dueling with Republicans. They are castigated as unpatriotic, portrayed as threats to national security, and scorned as detrimental to a healthy American society."[136]

In a well-functioning democratic system, participants recognize each other as legitimate members of the political community even when they sharply disagree. A belief that political adversaries are not authentic Americans, in contrast, undermines democratic values. A losing side in a political fight cannot accept the legitimacy of the outcome when they believe that the winners are not legitimate participants and when they believe that their opponents represent alien forces that are attempting to destroy the nation. What the Tea Party movement shows is that, without making explicitly racial or ethnic appeals, the language of constitutional devotion can also be the language of ethnonationalism, advancing one vision of what it means to be American and dismissing competing visions as dangerously foreign.

6 | The Violent Constitution

It's widely believed that constitutional nationalism is an especially benign form of nationalism. Ethnonationalist movements based on race, religion, and ethnicity are seen as appealing to irrational and primitive bonds that readily lead to violence, while civic nationalism is perceived as based on a rational commitment to universal principles like democracy and popular sovereignty and is less likely to foment violence.[1] As this chapter shows, however, constitutional nationalism has frequently served to justify violence.

Timothy McVeigh killed for the Constitution. On April 19, 1995, McVeigh set off a truck bomb that killed 168 people in the Alfred P. Murrah Building in Oklahoma City. "We members of the citizen's militias do not bear our arms to overthrow the Constitution," McVeigh wrote, "but to overthrow those who PERVERT the Constitution."[2] As McVeigh declared, violence is justified to defend the Constitution against the federal government's tyranny: "All you tyrannical mother fuckers will swing in the wind one day for your treasonous actions against the Constitution of the United States."[3]

In its conventional form, constitutional nationalism—the belief that what binds together the United States is a shared devotion to principles found in the Constitution—provides a comforting, even inspiring ideal of the national community. This is the vision espoused by George W. Bush when he declared: "We are bound by ideals that move us beyond backgrounds, lift us above our interests and teach us what it means to be citizens."[4] It is the same vision embraced by Barack Obama when he declared: "What binds this nation together is not the colors of our skin or the tenets of our faith or the origins of our names. What makes us exceptional—what makes us American—is our allegiance to an idea."[5]

As McVeigh's example illustrates, constitutional nationalism can readily justify violence with the addition of just a few toxic ingredients. Start with the conviction that devotion to the Constitution is what makes America *America*. This might make you feel kindly toward your fellow Americans, who share your values. But suppose that there are some Americans who don't share these values. You might even think that they are hostile to the Constitution, as you understand it. You might feel that it's your patriotic duty to oppose them and to defend American values. It may be possible to defeat these enemies of the Constitution simply by exposing them for what they are or through legal and political processes. But suppose that these domestic enemies of the Constitution have managed to gain control of the government. To take back the government, you might need to work outside the political and legal systems. Now add just one last ingredient. Suppose you also believe that the Constitution itself gives you a right to keep and bear guns specifically for the purpose of resisting a tyrannical government. In these circumstances, you might conclude you have a right, maybe even a patriotic duty, to attack the government, to kill the enemies of the Constitution, and to defend the nation you love.

This chapter examines recent movements that rely on the Constitution as justification for antigovernment violence. Chapter 1 examined the Ku Klux Klan, which has perpetrated waves of violence to maintain white rule, which it has long asserted is a central constitutional principle. Klan violence has primarily targeted supporters of racial equality. Since the 1960s, when the federal government adopted civil rights laws, the Klan has become increasingly antigovernment in its rhetoric and violence. With roots in the Klan, the Posse Comitatus movement of the 1970s and 1980s extended the Klan's antigovernment campaign. It declared that the United States government had been taken over by alien Jewish and Communist forces that seek to destroy the true meaning of the Constitution. The Posse Comitatus pointed to a variety of federal actions that it deemed tyrannical, including federal income taxes, gun control, and civil rights laws. It declared that true patriots have a duty to organize cadres of armed resistance to fight the federal government.[6] In the 1990s the militia movement asserted the necessity to organize private groups to provide the armed resistance to "defend the Constitution" and thereby "take back the country."[7] The militia movement, out of which McVeigh arose, declared that the Constitution was being subverted by a shadowy conspiracy that sought to deprive the people of their rights, most especially their right to own guns.

Today, a variety of groups advocate the necessity of armed resistance against what they consider federal tyranny. Contemporary insurrectionists came out in force in April 2014 when the federal government attempted to seize rancher Cliven Bundy's cattle to pay overdue grazing fees. When Bundy declared, "We're standing up for the Constitution," over a thousand armed protesters assembled to stand with him.[8] Bundy told his supporters, "We're going to take this country back by force."[9] When federal officials backed off, citing the risk of violence, Bundy declared it a victory for "We the People."[10]

On January 6, 2021, a mob of Donald Trump-supporting insurrectionists stormed the US Capitol. They believed that the 2020 election had been fraudulent and that the installation of Joe Biden amounted to treason. Wearing bulletproof vests and gas masks and armed with guns, spears, and pipe bombs, they pushed past barricades and the Capitol police and briefly occupied the nation's legislative seat. They too said they were standing up for the Constitution.[11]

Support for armed resistance against the federal government has been propelled by the gun rights movement, which has embraced the "insurrectionist theory" that the Second Amendment protects a right to bear arms so that citizens can protect themselves against an abusive government. According to the theory, the Constitution ensures that citizens have the means to engage in armed resistance. Initially embraced only by antigovernment zealots like the Posse Comitatus, insurrectionist theory has gained considerable mainstream acceptance and has been embraced by the National Rifle Association and prominent Republicans. While many proponents of insurrectionist theory have argued that armed resistance against federal authority is justified only in extreme circumstances, it has become evident that more and more Americans believe that the time for insurrection has arrived.[12]

As the movements discussed in this chapter demonstrate, constitutional nationalism can inspire hatred and murder. The fact that nationalism can turn violent is not surprising. As Michael Ignatieff has written, "Nationalism is an ethic of heroic sacrifice, justifying the use of violence in the defense of one's nation against enemies, internal or external."[13] Constitutional nationalism is no different. If the Constitution is central to what it means to be American, true patriots must be prepared to protect it, even if that means sacrificing their own lives or taking the lives of those who are attacking it. The movements discussed in this chapter do not contradict the nation's prevailing ideology that teaches Americans to love the Constitution and revere it as the nation's sacred text. It is an ideology that leads logically, perhaps inevitably, to violence and murder. Followers of these movements may be radicals, but they are all-American radicals.

The Posse Comitatus Movement

The Posse Comitatus movement was launched in 1972 by William Potter Gale, a minister in the Christian Identity movement. Christian Identity is an explicitly white supremacist religious sect that preaches that white northern Europeans are the true descendants of the tribes of biblical Israel.[14] During the 1970s, Christian Identity became a leading religious sect among white supremacists. Just as the Klan concluded that the Constitution establishes white rule, the Christian Identity movement asserts that the Bible establishes white supremacy.

In 1971 Gale published a series of articles in his Christian Identity newsletter that called for the formation of armed citizen groups to resist what he believed to be federal tyranny.[15] The articles, later collected as the Posse Comitatus handbook, articulate a radically localist political philosophy, in which legitimate government exists only at the county level.

The Posse Comitatus handbook articulates a white supremacist worldview. Like the Klan, the Posse asserted that the Constitution was written for a white Christian nation and that the nation's white heritage was under attack.[16] While the Klan focused on federal civil rights efforts, the Posse handbook identifies a wide range of federal actions that it deems tyrannical, including the federal income tax system, gun control laws, the Federal Reserve system, submission to the United Nations, and federal education measures, as well as civil rights laws.[17]

The Posse's position on these issues was not very different, or necessarily more extreme, than those espoused by others in the anti-Communist right wing, including the John Birch Society, which also asserted that Communists were committed to the destruction of the American Constitution and American way of life, that the civil rights movement was the work of an international Communist conspiracy, and that Communists had secretly taken over the federal government.[18] The two most prominent voices for the conservative movement, Barry Goldwater and William F. Buckley, had declared the John Birch Society too conspiratorial to be part of the respectable conservative mainstream.[19] In launching the Posse Comitatus movement Gale criticized the Birch Society for being too tame because it did not directly confront what he believed to be the *Jewish* nature of communism and because its program focused on educating people to the Communist takeover, instead of acting to fight it.[20]

Gale used the Latin phrase *posse comitatus* to describe his movement, a phrase that means "power of the county." As used by Gale and his followers, the phrase emphasizes their belief that the federal government lacks police power.[21] As the Posse handbook declares, the "County Sheriff is the only legal law enforcement officer in the United States of America."[22] In the Posse's view, the local sheriff owes a duty to protect the people, most especially a duty to protect them from abuses by the federal government. Central to the Posse philosophy was the assertion that, if the sheriff fails to protect the people from federal tyranny, citizens should form armed Posse Comitatus cadres to protect the people themselves.[23]

Although its advocacy of white supremacy and anti-Semitism placed it in the camp of the radical right, what was most distinctive about the Posse movement was its call for antigovernment violence in the name of the Constitution. Gale declared that officials who violated the Constitution should be executed: "He shall be removed by the Posse to a populated intersection of streets in the township and at high noon be hung there by the neck, the body remaining until sundown, as an example to those who would subvert the law."[24] The Posse movement also encouraged local chapters to "arrest" federal officials for trial by "common law courts" created by the movement and acting outside the state and local judiciary system, which could mete out vigilante justice.[25]

The Constitution played a central role in the Posse's call for armed insurrection. The Posse Handbook begins by declaring that it was instituted "by Authority of the Constitution of the United States." Gale and other founders of the Posse movement construed the Constitution in light of Christian Identity beliefs, asserting that God is the only true source of law, a notion they expressed by their asserted allegiance to "natural law," which they also called the "common law." They rejected all man-made or statutory law and believed that the Constitution embodies biblical precepts created for a Christian nation. The Posse Handbook instructs that anyone who attempts to enforce unconstitutional laws, such as federal income taxes, should be arrested by the local posse and subjected to trial by the posse's vigilante courts.[26]

Posse supporters asserted that the Constitution itself justifies citizen violence. The movement's handbook declares that the right of the people to protect themselves by forming an armed posse—or militia—is a "natural right" protected "by authority of the Constitution of the United States," in particular by the Second Amendment's reference to "well-regulated militias."[27] As the self-appointed "marshal" of the San Joaquin County Posse Comitatus put it, the goal of the movement was to prevent "officials from taking away our only means to resist tyranny in government—our guns."[28] The Constitution thus provided the standard for when the Posse Comitatus deemed violence necessary—when the federal government violates the Constitution—and also provided the authority for using violence, through the insurrectionary theory of the Second Amendment. As another Posse leader put it, "I'm not advocating that we shoot every politician who disagrees with us. But there are certain rights I cannot give away, nor can they be taken away, and there comes a time when force of arms is necessary."[29]

Like other constitutional nationalist movements, the Posse Comitatus rejected elite and judicial control over the Constitution. The Posse Handbook asserts that the Consti-tution requires no interpretation: "The Constitution is a simple document. It says what it means and it means what it says."[30] In the Posse's view, the clarity of the Constitution should make it apparent to everyone that the federal government had abandoned the Constitution and thereby provided justification to citizens to resist the federal government through violence. As Gale bluntly said: "These judges who are tearing this Constitution apart and these officials of government. . . . are gonna return to the law of posse comitatus. . . . The law is your citizens—a posse—will hang an official who violated the law and the Constitution."[31]

Although it began with a focus on white supremacy and resistance to federal taxes, by the early 1980s the Posse Comitatus movement had broadened its message to appeal to opponents of environmental regulations and to Midwestern farmers concerned about farm foreclosures. Gale and his followers succeeded in organizing hundreds of local Posse chapters, composed of thousands of armed members who vowed to resist federal tyranny by force. Christian Identity followers and white supremacists were the dominant forces within the Posse Comitatus movement, but Posse groups also attracted others who opposed federal power, including tax protesters, gun rights advocates, and Americans who believed the United States was in the grasp of a Communist or Jewish dictatorship. Posse groups provided paramilitary training and offered advice and support for tax protesters, who sought to resist enforcement of federal tax laws by burying federal courts in meaningless documents.[32] They also issued self-styled "indictments" of federal officials.[33]

The Posse's talk of antigovernment violence soon turned to action, and Posse groups engaged in numerous armed confrontations with state and federal officials. In 1974 a Wisconsin Posse group kidnapped and assaulted an IRS agent, Fred Chicken, then lectured him on their belief that federal income taxes are tantamount to communism and violate the Constitution. By 1975 the FBI had taken notice and designated local Posse chapters as "white hate groups."[34]

The first Posse Comitatus martyr was Gordon Kahl, who stopped paying federal income taxes out of a belief that the United States had been "conquered and occupied by the Jews" and taxes were "tithes to the synagogue of Satan."[35] In 1977 Kahl was convicted of tax evasion and spent eight months in prison. After prison, Kahl vowed that the government would never arrest him again. In February 1983 federal marshals tried to arrest him in North Dakota for his continued tax evasion, but Kahl opened fire, killing two marshals and injuring three others. Four months later, the FBI tracked him down in Arkansas, and Kahl shot and killed another police officer before being shot and killed himself.[36]

Before his death, Kahl sent a letter to his colleagues in the white supremacist group Aryan Nations, explaining that his actions were intended to defend the Constitution:

> I would have liked nothing other to be left alone, so I could enjoy life, liberty and the pursuit of happiness, which our Forefathers willed to us, this was not to be, after I discovered that our nation had fallen into the hands of an alien people, who are referred to us as a nation within the other nations. . . . These enemies of Christ have taken their Jewish Communist Manifesto, and incorporated it into the Statutory laws of our country, and threw our Constitution and our Christian Common Law (which is nothing other than the Laws of God as set forth in the Scriptures), into the garbage can.[37]

With his death, Kahl became a martyr for the Posse Comitatus cause.

Kahl was not the last Posse member to kill and die for the Constitution. In 1984 Arthur Kirk, a Nebraska farmer whose land was in foreclosure, charged a state patrol SWAT team with an assault rifle. He believed that local law enforcement should not enforce the work of Jewish bankers. Before confronting the police, Kirk told a reporter that defending the Constitution required opposing the government: "There's a big move on to try and subvert the Constitution, change the whole thing. Communism? That isn't communism, it's Judaism." Kirk declared that he was ready to die for the cause; he was killed.[38]

By the late 1980s, however, the Posse Comitatus movement began to wane after state and local law enforcement had infiltrated and cracked down on local Posse groups, keeping them under continuous surveillance, and indicting many Posse leaders for violations of tax and gun laws. After Gordon Kahl's shootout with the police, the Posse had become known as a radical group, and Posse groups began calling themselves Patriot groups instead.[39] Though it dissipated as a distinct movement, the Posse philosophy has been carried forward by many successors, including the sovereign citizen movement, which declares that only white Americans are true citizens and that they do not need to adhere to federal law; the county supremacy movement, which carried on the Posse's philosophy that only the county has law enforcement authority; and white supremacist groups such as the Order and Freemen, which carried on the Posse's philosophy of violent resistance to what they perceived as federal tyranny.[40] With the rise of the militia movement of the 1990s, the Posse's philosophy found an even larger audience.

The Patriot and Militia Movements

In the early 1990s, several related right-wing movements began to coalesce as a single movement known as the Patriot movement. The movement included Posse Comitatus chapters that called themselves Patriot groups, various Christian Identity groups that began calling themselves Christian Patriots, and former Ku Klux Klan chapters that also began calling themselves Patriot groups. It also included sovereign citizen groups, who assert that federal law does not apply to them, as well as various groups of tax protestors, survivalists, and gun rights advocates.[41] Some of the groups in the Patriot movement explicitly advocated white supremacy and anti-Semitism; others did not.

Although the Patriot movement included groups with differing ideologies, they shared a core belief that the federal government had become a malicious and alien force that sought to take away the rights of everyday Americans. They saw the threat from the government in constitutional terms, asserting that a far-reaching government effort was underway to destroy the Constitution and instigate what the movement referred to as a "New World Order."

Patriots had various ideas about the nature of the New World Order conspiracy. Some perceived a more-or-less explicitly anti-Semitic conspiracy involving international bankers, the United Nations, and the Zionist Occupational Government.[42] Others saw a shadowy threat posed by liberals. Regardless of the particular details, however, the conspiracy was understood as a threat to the Constitution. Adherents of the Patriot movement frequently declared that overthrowing the Constitution was the main point of the New World Order conspiracy. As Jon Roland, founder of the Texas Constitutional Militia, put it, the Constitution had been "overthrown a little at a time, over a period of decades, or overthrown in secret, allowing the external trappings of constitutional governance to continue while the real power was exercised behind the scenes by persons no longer accountable to the people." The gradual destruction of the Constitution was no accident, Roland declared: "It is too tightly coordinated not to bear the name of Conspiracy."[43]

Fears of the New World Order tapped into anxieties that many Americans felt about the ways that the United States was changing—fears that national leaders had abandoned core American values and that the federal government was becoming (or had become) a tyrannical force that threatened individual liberties. Above all, the Patriot movement focused on the fear that the government would disarm the people and deprive them of individual rights.[44]

With their shared antigovernment beliefs, Patriot groups began communicating openly with each other and sharing their groups' literature. Gun shows were an important meeting ground among groups associated with the Patriot movement. As one report from the era described, in the 1990s gun shows became "a town square where extremists can gather information, make contacts, and mingle with the like-minded."[45] Patriot groups also began sharing information with each other by sending faxes over the American Patriot Fax Network.[46]

The Patriot movement soon spawned a militant wing, which in the early 1990s began to organize armed paramilitary cadres to protect citizens' rights against federal tyranny. These armed groups comprise what became known as the militia movement. Some Posse Comitatus and Ku Klux Klan groups in the Patriot orbit were already armed and self-trained in paramilitary exercises. Other citizen militias began to form in the early 1990s. In 1990, Larry Pratt, executive director of the Gun Owners of America—a more radical gun rights group than the NRA—called on patriots to form citizen militias to protect citizens' rights.[47]

The militia movement expanded significantly due to two galvanizing events that generated widespread attention and confirmed many people's worst fears about what was happening in the country.[48] In August 1992 federal officials attempted to arrest Randy Weaver at his mountaintop home at Ruby Ridge, Idaho, on a charge of selling an illegal sawed-off shotgun.[49] Weaver, a Christian Identity believer, refused to surrender, and federal agents bungled the raid, leaving three dead—a federal agent, the Weavers' fourteen-year old son, and Weaver's wife Vicki, who was shot in the face by an FBI sharpshooter.[50] The following spring, federal agents attempted to serve an arrest warrant related to gun charges at the Branch Davidian compound in Waco, Texas. Like Weaver, the Branch Davidians resisted with force, leaving four federal agents dead and twenty wounded. On April 19,

1993, after a fifty-one day standoff, the FBI stormed the compound, which erupted up in flames, leaving seventy-six Davidians dead.[51]

Ruby Ridge and Waco became rallying points for many constituencies, who saw them as the work of an oppressive federal government that used excessive force to deprive the people of their liberties, most especially the right to bear arms.[52] Jim McKinzey, founder of the Missouri 51st Militia, explained that "Ruby Ridge was a wake-up call for a lot of people in the country, including myself. Until Ruby Ridge came down the pike, I could care less about politics. . . . And then, they're starting to shoot children, and shooting unarmed women in the head. . . . Then, what, less than a year later, these same people are now down in Texas, taking on women and children, and that is really what did it."[53] Jon Roland agreed that the federal raid on the Branch Davidian compound "has been the wakeup call for our generation. . . . The whole world saw agents of the U.S. Government, supposed to be the standard for liberty, get away with murder."[54]

Many who joined militias understood Ruby Ridge and Waco not as tragedies but as an expression of the government's "standard policy" of depriving citizens of their rights.[55] They saw their fears confirmed when Congress passed the Brady Handgun Violence Prevention Act in November 1993, suggesting, in the words of one militia leader, "a more sinister preparation for depriving [the people] of their other constitutional rights after they have been disarmed."[56]

Leaders of Ku Klux Klan and neo-Nazi groups also recognized that Ruby Ridge and Waco could serve as rallying points to advance their missions. Two months after Ruby Ridge, Christian Identity minister Pete Peters organized a three-day retreat in Estes Park, Colorado, to formulate a response to the shootout, a meeting attended by Christian Identity pastors, Aryan Nations members, Klansmen, and other right-wing militants including Gun Owners of America leader Larry Pratt.[57] Louis Beam, who had worked for David Duke and was the author of *Essays of a Klansman*, told the assembled gathering that Ruby Ridge served to unify disparate antigovernment groups: "The federals have by their murder of Samuel and Vicki Weaver brought all of us here together under the same roof for the same reason. For the first time in the twenty-two years that I have been in the movement, we are all marching to the beat of the same drum."[58]

In his speech in Estes Park, Larry Pratt argued that the best response to Ruby Ridge and the so-called Brady Bill was for citizens to form armed militias to resist government overreaching. "The Second Amendment is not about duck hunting," Pratt declared. "It's about guaranteeing protection against government abuse." Pratt argued, "When a government no longer fears the people, atrocities become possible." He ended his speech with a rousing call: "Long live the militia! Long live freedom! Long live a government that fears the people!"[59]

In the first two years after Ruby Ridge and Waco, more than eight hundred militia groups formed around the nation.[60] These groups offered gun training and drilled in formation. Some operated openly while others trained in secret. Through shows of force, they sought to prevent recurrences of Ruby Ridge and Waco. By the spring of 1995, hundreds of militia groups had been organized around the country, with perhaps as many as 100,000 active participants.[61] New militia groups arose in every region, although they were concentrated in the South, the Midwest, and the Far West.[62] Like the Posse Comitatus movement, the militia movement was overwhelmingly white and male.[63]

The militia movement grew out a shared goal of resisting federal tyranny in the wake of Ruby Ridge and Waco, but the movement reflected the same diverse agenda and ideology as the Patriot movement out of which it had grown. It had no national hierarchy or agreed leaders.[64] It attracted white supremacists and neo-Nazis but also had wide appeal to gun rights supporters, libertarians, survivalists, those who feared the loss of United States sovereignty, and people generally concerned about abuses of federal power.[65]

Notwithstanding differences in philosophy and emphasis, the movement was united by its declared devotion to restore the Constitution as the movement's supporters understood it. Jon Roland explained that "there is general agreement within the militia movement that its unifying ideology is *constitutionalism*."[66] John Trochmann, white supremacist founder of the Militia of Montana, agreed that the movement had "one singular mandate which is public and overt: The return to the Constitution of the United States."[67]

To militia members, reclaiming the Constitution meant nothing less than reclaiming everything they considered truly American. They did not agree, however, on what that meant. For white supremacists, returning to the true meaning of the Constitution meant preserving and protecting white rule. The Ohio Unorganized Militia declared that it was open only to "sovereign nationals," code for white Americans.[68] For libertarian-minded militias like the Texas Constitutional Militia, restoring constitutional rule meant overturning the New Deal and the administrative state.[69] Militia members also used constitutional language to express generalized concerns about a decline of America, such as concerns over the perceived liberal bias of the national media, the rejection of family values in Hollywood movies and on television, the rise of "secular humanism," and permissiveness in schools.[70]

Constitutional rhetoric gave the militias a neutral language to express a wide range of views. For some, constitutional rhetoric provided a way to discuss white rule without mentioning race. John Trochmann, for example, had been an early supporter of Aryan Nations and believer in "sovereign citizenship," and had declared that he was a "Freeman," a theory under which only whites are protected by the Constitution.[71] For others, constitutional language provided a way to express a rejection of popular culture, the role of the media, and the validity of the administrative state and the income tax system.[72]

Militia supporters hoped that expressing their views in constitutional terms would make them more acceptable to the American people. When called by Congress to explain the movement, Trochmann and other militia leaders sought to show that the movement was not radical by declaring that the movement was about the Constitution. Norm Olson, one of the founders of the Michigan Militia, used the language of constitutional devotion to defend militias against the allegation that they were racist: "We are not what you think we are. We are not what the press wants to feed to the American people. We are people who love our Government and love the Constitution. . . . We stand against oppression and tyranny in government."[73] Militia members insisted that they were not radicals or racists because they loved the Constitution, and everyone knows that the Constitution is neither radical nor racist.

Even the choice to call their activities "militias" served to highlight patriotism and to connect these groups with the nation's founders. Pointing to the militias that fought in the Revolutionary War, militia leaders of the 1990s described their actions as *reviving* the tradition of citizen militias rather than starting a new movement to offer armed resistance to the federal government.[74] Militia leaders described their movement as responding to the same forces that had motivated the colonial-era militias to fight for revolution. Testifying before the Senate, John Trochmann explained that people joined militias for the same reason that the American Revolutionaries did, because "flagrant injustice continued out of control by oppressive public servants."[75] Militia members expressed a personal connection with the Founders, as one militia supporter explained: "The blood of our ancestors is in *our* veins. The men who fought the American Revolution are *our* forefathers and *we* are their children."[76]

Some militia leaders were explicit in recognizing that constitutional language would serve to obscure the radical beliefs many of them espoused. Jon Roland of the Texas Constitutional Militia advised militia leaders to emphasize the movement's constitutional mission and to avoid language that might sound extreme: "Look like respectable businessmen. Emphasize our primary purpose: to enforce the law, especially the Constitution, and that means to expose criminal wrongdoing in government and abuses of power. Forget all the rhetoric about foreign troops, New World Order, and all the rest of the stuff that sounds bizarre to ordinary Americans."[77] Although Roland urged militia supporters to avoid public discussion of conspiracy theories, he was an avid conspiracy enthusiast himself, firmly believing that the United States was controlled by a "secret government" that manipulated the weather, covered up the reality of UFOs, and may have created HIV as part of its plot to enslave the people.[78] He recognized, however, that explaining the militia's mission in constitutional terms would help the militias be seen as mainstream.

Popular Constitutionalists with Guns

The militia movement espoused a form of popular constitutionalism, the theory that ultimate authority over the meaning of the Constitution belongs not to the judiciary but to the people at large.[79] Militia writings routinely directed invective against the courts, accusing judges of being controlled by anti-American forces and undermining the Constitution.[80] Yet the militia movement did not assert that the people should engage in an interpretive enterprise and insisted instead that the Constitution had a simple, clear meaning embodying the nation's essential values.[81] Members insisted that they were advancing the Founders' own constitutional vision and asserted that the people should simply force the courts to adopt the true meaning of the Constitution. Although they acknowledged that courts and federal officials had adopted contrary constitutional interpretations, militia leaders did not recognize that there might be reasonable grounds for debate over the meaning of the Constitution; they asserted that the only possible explanation for the courts' rulings was that judges were traitors who sought to destroy America.[82]

Critics of popular constitutionalism have asked how the theory could be put into practice—that is, what mechanisms the American people can use to enforce their constitutional understandings.[83] In the leading book on popular constitutionalism, *The People Themselves: Popular Constitutionalism and Judicial Review,* law professor Larry Kramer gives a robust defense for the right of the people to determine for themselves the meaning of the Constitution. In a review of the book, law professors Larry Alexander and Lawrence Solum state, "The obvious question for robust popular constitutionalism is 'How?' How can the people themselves interpret and enforce the Constitution through direct action?"[84]

Although perhaps not the answer that Kramer would offer, the militia movement offered a ready answer: through violence. The movement was based on the philosophy that the people could force the government to accept its constitutional views through violence and threats of violence. The thrust of the movement was to declare that the tyrannical federal government should be confronted and resisted by force.[85] As one militia writer put it, "The militias will be the main defense against tyranny. At this present time, the people are warning the federal government; let us alone or face the consequences."[86] Militias threatened violence with the avowed goal of returning the country to its true constitutional nature. Because they perceived the nation and its Constitution to be under attack, the threatened violence was understood to be purely defensive, threatened solely to restore constitutional government.[87]

As one militia writer put it: "Now, with sworn enemies, both foreign and domestic, making their final moves to replace our Constitution and force us to join a one world government, are we to humbly submit to a New World Order?"[88] A writer for the *Kentucky Rifleman News* put it similarly: "What can we do, in the face of this Government, at once both tyrannical and lawless?" The movement answered that question with the single word *resist*: "We must resist, if we are to stay loyal to the spirit of the Founding Fathers of this Nation and to the Declaration of Independence and the Constitution which they created to guarantee to us our God given natural rights, which no man or Government may deny us."[89] Militia members insisted that all true patriots have a duty to defend the Constitution and resist tyranny. As the Militia of Montana explained: "If the militia is independent and viable, then only laws which are right and just will come forth from the government."[90]

Like members of the Posse Comitatus movement, militia activists asserted that the call for armed resistance was justified by the Constitution itself— in particular, the Second Amendment, which they construed to create a constitutional right to create armed citizen militias to resist government tyranny.[91] Larry Platt's declaration that the Second Amendment "isn't about ducking hunting" found great resonance in the militia movement. The Militia of Montana and others put the slogan on T-shirts.[92]

Responding to the growing militia movement, President Bill Clinton declared that the militias' threats of vigilante violence were the very definition of lawlessness: "How dare you call yourself patriots and heroes? If you appropriate our sacred symbols for paranoid purposes and compare yourselves to Colonial militias who fought for democracy you now rail against, you are wrong."[93] Directly responding to the militias' insurrectionist theory, Clinton said, there is "no right to resort to violence when you don't get your way." Militia leaders countered that they had a constitutional right to use force to resist government tyranny.

A chief difficulty with insurrectionist theory is that it provides no basis for deciding when tyranny is present or who has authority to decide when violence is justified.[94] In the 1990s, some members of the militia movement declared that the time for armed resistance had arrived. Militias asserted that Clinton-era America was the apotheosis of despotism, for which armed resistance was the only appropriate response.[95] They pointed to Ruby Ridge, Waco, and gun control laws; they pointed to the federal income tax, the Federal Reserve, environmental regulations, and civil rights laws.[96] To militia supporters, these measures marked the end of freedom and were the actions of a foreign entity waging war on the American people.[97] To militia supporters, such actions were treasonous.[98]

In threatening violence to enforce the Constitution, the militias claimed that they acted on behalf of the entire American people, even if militias themselves only involved a small fraction of the American people.[99] Militia leaders said that their members were representatives of the entire American population. As Jon Roland suggested in the title of his influential essay, the militia activists were "reviving the ready militia," which consisted "of the whole people" and therefore were entitled to speak for everyone.[100]

Timothy McVeigh's Constitution

The bombing of the Murrah Building in Oklahoma City, which killed 168 people on April 19, 1995, the anniversary of the siege on Waco, represents the culmination of the constitutional ideology of the militia movement. Timothy McVeigh considered himself part of the movement. He traveled to dozens of gun shows, where he bought and sold antigovernment literature. He feared the New World Order and believed that the United States and the United Nations were plotting to establish a single world government. McVeigh talked about forming a militia to fight the New World Order but decided instead to take on the federal government as a lone wolf, aided by a small group of friends.[101] When he sought to justify the bombing of the federal building in Oklahoma City, he asserted that he acted as a member of the people's militia to defend the Constitution.[102]

McVeigh had strong connections to the white supremacist elements in the militia movement. He had once belonged to a KKK chapter. While in the army, McVeigh was known to wear a "White Power" T-shirt on base at Fort Riley, Kansas.[103] He was deeply inspired by *The Turner Diaries*, the novel that depicts an American government run by liberals, Jews, and African Americans, and dedicated to depriving white people of their guns and other freedoms.[104] It is the same book that inspired Robert Mathews to form the Order and launch a violent crime spree. In the chapter McVeigh found most significant, the novel's hero blows up the FBI headquarters using a truck filled with fertilizer and fuel.[105] McVeigh gave away copies of *The Turner Diaries* to any friend who would take it, sold the book at gun shows, and left an excerpt from the book in his getaway car for the police to find.[106] His ties to white nationalism can also be seen in the fact that, weeks before the bombing, when McVeigh was looking to arrange a safe hideout, he placed two calls, one to a representative of the National Alliance, a prominent neo-Nazi organization, and one to an acquaintance in Elohim City, Oklahoma, a Christian Identity and Aryan Nations enclave.[107]

Like others in the militia movement, McVeigh believed that the federal raids on Ruby Ridge and Waco demanded a forceful response. In March 1993, McVeigh went to Waco to observe the standoff and while there sold bumper stickers bearing such slogans as "Fear the Government That Fears Your Gun" and "When Guns Are Outlawed, I Will Become an Outlaw."[108] He gave an interview to a university newspaper, in which he expressed his belief that "we are slowly turning into a socialist government" and "the people need to prepare to defend themselves against government control."[109] McVeigh believed that the raids on Ruby Ridge and Waco were just the first steps in a government plan to seize the people's guns and enslave them.[110] Like others in the militia movement, he believed that today's federal government was equivalent to the colonial-era British government.[111] And like others in the militia movement, McVeigh believed that antigovernment violence was the appropriate response: "Where non-violent checks and balances fail to remedy government abuse or tyranny," he wrote, "the common people reserve the right to rebellion."[112]

Where McVeigh differed from others in the movement was not in his support for violence to defend the Constitution but in his conclusion that, after Waco, the time for violence had arrived. After Waco, he told his sister that he was through handing out pamphlets and selling bumper stickers; it was time to move to the "action stage."[113] Around the same time, McVeigh wrote to a childhood friend that "blood will flow in the streets" as a result of the government's violations of the Constitution:

> Those who betray or subvert the Constitution are guilty of sedition and/or treason, are domestic enemies and should and will be punished accordingly. It also stands to reason that anyone who sympathizes with the enemy or gives aid or comfort to said enemy is likewise guilty. I have sworn to uphold and defend the Constitution against all enemies, foreign and domestic and I will. And I will because not only did I swear to, but I believe in what it stands for in every bit of my heart, soul and being.[114]

Violence, McVeigh believed, would "put a check on government abuse of power where others have failed in stopping the federal juggernaut run amok."[115] And McVeigh had a message to the government about how it could avoid future violence. On a copy of the Declaration of Independence that he left in the getaway car, he wrote: "Obey the Constitution, and we won't shoot you."[116]

After the Oklahoma City bombing, militia leaders did not back away from defending armed insurrection in the name of the Constitution. Instead, the predominant reaction among the movement was to claim that McVeigh was not really part of the movement or that the bombing had actually been perpetrated by the federal government to discredit the movement.[117]

While the Oklahoma City bombing was undoubtedly the most destructive act of violence associated with the militia movement, it was not the only crime to come out of the movement. In March 1996 leaders of the Freemen of Montana—a Christian Identity sect that espoused a Posse-like ideology and declared themselves to be sovereign citizens outside federal authority—were charged with attempting to buy guns with a million dollars in fake checks, as well as other firearms violations, and harassing federal officials with phony liens. When they refused to comply with arrest warrants, a long standoff with the FBI ensued. This time, the government had learned some lessons from Ruby Ridge and Waco and did not force a violent confrontation. In December 1996 the FBI arrested members of the Oklahoma Constitutional Militia after they had assembled a fertilizer-and-fuel bomb like the one used by McVeigh, which they planned to use as part of a bombing spree aimed at gay bars and civil rights offices.[118] In April 1997 members of a militia calling itself the Republic of Texas took hostages and demanded that a referendum be held to make Texas an independent nation.[119] The murderous crime spree by members of the Order, discussed in chapter 1, also arose out of the militia movement.

Membership in militias surged with the enormous media exposure the movement received after the Oklahoma City bombing, but within a couple years the movement began to shrink, apparently as the result of a broad federal crackdown on criminal elements within the movement, as well as continuing negative publicity and the backlash from the bombing.[120] After the Al Qaeda attacks of September 11, 2001, the movement was declared all but dead because their supporters came to believe that foreign terrorists, not the national government, represented the most important threat to the nation.[121] The ideology of insurrectionary constitutional nationalism that the militia movement advanced, however, has become a mainstream philosophy.

Insurrectionist Theory Goes Mainstream

The Posse Comitatus movement, the Patriot and militia movements, and Timothy McVeigh were all adherents of the insurrectionist theory of the Second Amendment, the belief that the Constitution protects a right to bear arms so that the people can employ violent resistance against an oppressive government. For decades, insurrectionist theory was widely dismissed as a crackpot theory espoused only by extremists.[122] Today, it has become a mainstream position advocated by the National Rifle Association (NRA) and leading Republicans.

The first group known to adopt insurrectionist theory was the White Knights of the Ku Klux Klan, one of the most violent and extreme Klan groups of the 1960s. It declared: "If the minions of material governmental authority threaten, attempt to, or use physical force and violence to enforce compliance with some letter of law which is in clear conflict with the Constitution . . . Private Citizens of America have a right to oppose them with physical force."[123] Insurrectionist theory was central to the Posse Comitatus, which asserted that the Second Amendment gives the people the right to organize private militias to resist unconstitutional federal actions and to kill federal officials who attempt to enforce unconstitutional laws.[124]

At the time the Klan and the Posse asserted the belief that the Constitution protects a right to use force against government tyranny, that view was embraced by no mainstream figures. In 1939 the Supreme Court had ruled that the Second Amendment protects the right to bear arms for service in the organized militias and does not limit Congress's authority to restrict the right to possess guns for other purposes.[125] In the 1960s and 1970s, the Second Amendment did not feature prominently in the NRA's advocacy, and the NRA supported some gun control measures.[126] In the mid-1970s, however, libertarians began to argue that the Second Amendment protects an individual right to bear arms. Ronald Reagan was among the early prominent supporters of this view. In 1975, while governor of California, Reagan argued that the people have a right to own guns for self-defense. He added that the Second Amendment also protects the right to bear arms in order to give the people the means to resist government tyranny.[127]

In 1977 a libertarian faction took control of the National Rifle Association and began to argue that the Second Amendment protects an individual's right to bear arms. Although the NRA occasionally mentioned the need for guns to resist government abuses, it primarily emphasized that the right to bear arms served the needs of self-defense and hunting. Gun Owners of America, founded in 1975 as a gun rights organization more hardline than the NRA, also emphasized crime and self-defense, not insurrection, as the primary reason to protect the right to bear arms.[128]

Until the 1980s the insurrectionist theory was still practically unknown outside extremist circles. In 1982, however, at the direction of Senator Orrin Hatch, the Senate Subcommittee on the Constitution published a report on the history of the Second Amendment that gave some support to insurrectionist theory. Relying on historians working for the NRA, the Senate report declared that it had uncovered "clear—and long lost—proof that the second amendment to our Constitution was intended as an individual right of the American citizen."[129] Like the NRA, the Senate report emphasized that an individual right to bear arms served the interests of self-defense and hunting, but it also obliquely mentioned insurrectionist theory, declaring that the Second Amendment protects a citizen's right "to keep and carry arms in a peaceful manner, for protection of himself, his family, and his *freedoms*."[130]

In the 1990s, however, the National Rifle Association adopted insurrectionist theory as its official position.[131] Wayne LaPierre, the head of the NRA, wrote in 1994, "The people have the right to take whatever measures necessary, including force, to abolish oppressive government."[132] Charlton Heston, then-president of the NRA, declared, "The Second Amendment is, in order of importance, the first amendment. It is America's First Freedom, the one right that protects all the others." As he described it, the right to bear arms is the right of last resort; it is "the right we turn to when all else fails."[133] Or as LaPierre said more recently, the right to firearms is "the purest and most precious form of freedom because it is the one freedom that gives common men and women uncommon power to defend all freedoms."[134] Advanced by the NRA, insurrectionist theory began to be embraced by many prominent Republicans. In 1995, Speaker of the House Newt Gingrich declared, "The Second Amendment is a political right written into our Constitution for the purpose of protecting individual citizens from their own government."[135] Senator Ted Cruz of Texas has similarly declared that the Second Amendment is the "ultimate check on government tyranny."[136]

To some extent, insurrectionist theory became the law of the land in 2008, when the Supreme Court adopted an individual rights interpretation of the Second Amendment.[137] The Court concluded that the core of the Second Amendment is a right to keep and bear arms for self-defense, but the Court seemed to speak approvingly of insurrectionist theory and suggested that self-defense includes resistance to government tyranny.[138] As the Court put it, the Framers understood the Second Amendment "to be an individual right protecting against both public and private violence."[139]

While opponents of insurrectionist theory have raised numerous objections based on both the text and history of the Second Amendment, perhaps the main objection to insurrectionist theory is that it empowers anyone who believes the government has abused its powers to take up arms against the government.[140] As Carl Bogus has written, once it is accepted that there is a constitutional right to violent resistance against government tyranny, "Who is to decide whether the government has fallen into the hands of traitors or tyrants? Obviously, that decision cannot be made through the carefully constructed procedures of representative democracy because, by definition, those mechanisms may be controlled by the traitors themselves. Insurrectionists believe the people must decide for themselves. But who are 'the people'? Any group that decides for itself that the government is controlled by traitors?"[141]

As the Klan, the Posse Comitatus movement, the militia movement, and Timothy McVeigh demonstrate, the danger that insurrectionist theory can lead to antigovernment violence is very real. That danger is greatly magnified when insurrectionist theory is combined with constitutional nationalism, which teaches that devotion to the Constitution is the defining element of American national identity. Those who are perceived as not sufficiently devoted to the Constitution can readily be identified as un-American, as traitors, as enemies of the people. When a movement or even a lone wolf concludes that the government has fallen into the hands of the Constitution's enemies, insurrectionist theory provides a patriotic justification for violence rooted in the Constitution itself.

With the mainstream acceptance of insurrectionist theory, movements that tap into antigovernment sentiments have created a new generation of insurrectionists, who have decided to take on the federal government with all the firepower the Second Amendment is now understood to protect.

The New Insurrectionists

The April 2014 confrontation at the Bundy ranch in Nevada marked the coming-out party of a new insurrectionist movement ready to take up arms against the government to carry out its constitutional vision.[142] Like their predecessors, the new insurrectionists declare that the Constitution embodies the nation's core values, that those in power are dedicated to undermining those values, and that the people must take the country back and restore the Constitution, by force if necessary.[143] What is different this time is that the insurrectionists have found a welcoming home within the conservative movement and can spread their message through regular appearances on national television and radio broadcasts, as well as thousands of websites.

The confrontation arose because rancher Cliven Bundy refused to pay the federal government over $1 million in grazing fees for using public lands in Bunkerville, Nevada.[144] The government had also imposed limits on grazing in Bunkerville to protect an endangered tortoise.[145] Federal officials planned to seize Bundy's cattle as partial payment for the unpaid fees, but news of the confrontation went viral on antigovernment websites.[146] Ryan Payne of the West Mountain Rangers militia offered to help "bring militia units and Patriots from all over the country." Payne got in touch with Stewart Rhodes, head of the Oath Keepers, and Richard Mack, head of the Constitutional Sheriffs and Peace Officers Association (CSPOA). Within days, more than a thousand armed militia members, Oath Keepers, CSPOA members, III Percent Patriots, Tea Partiers, and others arrived at Bundy's ranch.[147]

As usual, the Constitution was understood to be the heart of the dispute. Cliven Bundy asserted that the Constitution gives the United States no authority within a state, and therefore has no power to retain and manage federal lands in Nevada and no power to protect state wildlife like the desert tortoise.[148] That claim conflicts with long-established understanding of federal power. In 1897 the Supreme Court ruled in *Canfield v. United States* that the Property Clause of Article VI gives the federal government authority to retain and manage public lands after admitting new states, and in 1976 it ruled in *Kleppe v. New Mexico* that the government can impose grazing restrictions on public lands to protect wildlife.[149] Bundy and his supporters, however, saw the threatened seizure of his cattle as more than just a dispute over the federal power to regulate grazing. They considered it an attack on the foundational notion of property rights. They considered federal court rulings against Bundy not only to be illegitimate but to be fundamentally un-American. As Bundy put it, he did not need to follow federal court orders that required him to pay the overdue fees because they came from a "foreign court."[150]

Faced with judicial rulings that conflicted with what they consider the fundamental American protection of property rights, Bundy and his supporters did what insurrectionist theory suggests that patriots do: they took up arms to fight the government. Former sheriff Richard Mack said they were "standing up for the God-given principles that made us a country in the first place."[151] Stewart Rhodes defended Bundy as a "principled constitutionalist who refuses to recognize the illegitimate sovereignty of the United States," which he said was devoted to impoverishing the people in the American West.[152]

To Bundy, Mack, and Rhodes, defending Bundy's cattle meant defending what they believed to be the true basis for the nation. "Let's go get those cattle," Bundy told the assembled mob. "We're going to take this country back by force."[153] When the Bureau of Land Management backed down in order to avoid a Waco-like bloodbath, Bundy declared it a victory for "We the People."[154] Appearing at a victory rally, Rhodes agreed that "the People, through their combined arms, had defended the Constitution."[155] "This is how we take back liberty," Mack proclaimed: "This is America, this is the example today."[156]

Leading figures in the conservative movement cheered on the Bundy protests. Fox News commentator Sean Hannity built up the story for weeks, praising Bundy as a hero who was "willing to fight" against the big bad federal government.[157] Andrew Napolitano, billed as the senior judicial analyst at Fox News, called Bundy a "hero for his courageous willingness to stand up" to the tyrannical federal government.[158] Nevada senator Dean Heller called the Bundy militiamen true patriots.[159] Congressman Ron Paul said the armed confrontation was simply a "demonstration against unfairness by our government" and that the federal government needs to give the land back to the people.[160] Bundy's newfound friends scurried away, however, when he revealed that his constitutional philosophy encompassed old-school racism, musing that "the Negro" may have been better off under slavery because now African Americans live on "the government subsidy" and "abort their young children, they put their young men in jail, because they never learned how to pick cotton."[161]

The new insurrectionist movement on display at Bundy's ranch found acceptance among mainstream Republicans and conservatives who had come to embrace the insurrectionist interpretation of the Second Amendment and who, under the influence of the Tea Party movement, had come to believe that the government had been taken over by forces hostile to the Constitution and American values. Although the Tea Party movement did not start out advocating armed resistance as the primary method to defend the Constitution and "take back" the country, it embraced insurrectionist principles and declared that force might one day be needed if patriots couldn't take back the country through the political system.[162]

With the failure to defeat President Obama in his 2012 reelection, a growing chorus within right-wing circles concluded that the time for armed resistance had arrived. The number of private militias more than tripled, and militias and like-minded groups became a significant conservative constituency.[163] Oath Keepers was among the most prominent new militia groups. It claimed to have thirty thousand members who are active duty and reserved military and law enforcement personnel. Members swear an oath to disobey any orders they regard as unconstitutional, including most especially any order "to disarm the American people": "We will never disarm. We will never surrender our military pattern, semi-automatic rifles and the full capacity magazines, parts, and ammunition that go with them. The fundamental purpose of the Second Amendment is to preserve the military power of We the People so we will have effective means to resist tyranny. Regardless of what unholy, unconstitutional filth issues from the mouths of oath breakers in 'Mordor on the Potomac' our answer is MOLON LABE. ['Come and take it.']"[164]

Like other insurrectionists, Oath Keepers asserted that they stand in the shoes of the Founding Fathers, who did not flinch from using force to take on tyranny and fight for the people's rights. Oath Keepers founder Stewart Rhodes declared that federal tyranny today is indistinguishable from the actions of the British in 1775, and the same response may be needed: "What did we do to the Redcoats in April 19, 1775? Did we petition them? Did we invite them to respect our rights? Did we file a court case? What did we do that day? We shot the hell out of them. And that's what we're going to be forced to do again, unless all of you stand up right now. We have a very narrow opportunity to settle this by peaceful means."[165] In October 2013, Oath Keepers announced that its members would begin organizing and training local militia groups to resist plans "by our enemies to scrap the Constitution." Organizing armed resistance is necessary, Oath Keepers explained, because the federal government is "preparing to control and contain us, and to shoot us."[166]

As with other insurrectionary groups that have sought to enforce their constitutional visions through arms, Oath Keepers did not acknowledge that it advocated its own constitutional interpretation or that anyone might disagree with it. They saw the unconstitutionality of the orders they have sworn to resist as simply obvious, self-evident applications of the Founders' vision: "All we're really doing is saying yes, we're reaffirming the principles that are in the Bill of Rights."[167] In the Oath Keepers' worldview, anyone who does not subscribe to their constitutional vision is an oath breaker and a traitor, and such traitors include anyone who votes for political candidates out of step with the Oath Keepers' constitutional ideology.[168] Rhodes described the organization's mission as "Gandhi-like civil disobedience."[169] Gandhi-like, only with high-powered rifles.

Strongly linked to the Oath Keepers is the Constitutional Sheriffs and Peace Officers Association, which also advocates armed resistance to perceived federal abuses.[170] The CSPOA was founded by Richard Mack, who also served on the board of Oath Keepers.[171] CSPOA advanced the Posse Comitatus belief that county sheriffs are the nation's only legitimate law enforcement officers and that they have a constitutional duty to protect citizens from federal abuse.[172] Whereas the Posse movement primarily sought to organize armed citizen cadres to resist federal taxes and other laws it deemed unconstitutional, the CSPOA seeks to persuade local sheriffs to do the same. As its website declares: "The county sheriff is the line in the sand. The county sheriff is the one who can say to the feds, 'Beyond these bounds you shall not pass.' This is not only within the scope of the sheriff's authority; it's the sheriff's sworn duty."[173] The CSPOA encourages local sheriffs and police officers to protect citizens from gun registration laws, tax laws, and Obamacare, and to prohibit federal officials from enforcing any federal laws within the county unless the sheriff gives his consent.[174] As Mack explained: "If our counties, cities, and states and all local officers keep their oaths to protect us from tyranny, we can win this battle to take our country back."[175]

Perhaps the most radical of the new insurrectionary group is the III Percent Patriots, so named because supposedly 3 percent of the colonists refused orders by the British to surrender their firearms.[176] With an estimated 85,000 followers, it may be the largest of the new militia-style groups. Like the others, the III Percent Patriots have expressed support for violence in the name of the Constitution: "We intend to maintain our God-given natural rights to liberty and property, and that means most especially the right to keep and bear arms. Thus, we are committed to the restoration of the Founders' Republic, and are willing to fight, die and, if forced by any would-be oppressor, to kill in the defense of ourselves and the Constitution that we all took an oath to uphold against enemies foreign and domestic."[177] Like the militia groups of the 1990s, the new crop of insurrectionists puts the right to own guns at the center of their vision of the Constitution.

The connections between these new insurrectionist groups and the earlier Posse Comitatus and militia movements are not just ideological.[178] CSPOA founder Richard Mack, a former sheriff of Graham County, Arizona, was a frequent speaker at militia events in the 1990s and strongly supported armed resistance to federal law: "People get all upset when they hear about militias," Mack exclaimed, "but what's wrong with it? I wouldn't hesitate for a minute to call out my posse against the federal government if it gets out of hand."[179] His views have long aligned with the core commitments of the Posse Comitatus movement.[180] In a 2009 interview, Mack said, "I pray for the day that a sheriff in this country will arrest an IRS agent."[181] He continued to espouse New World Order conspiracy theories typical of the 1990s militia movement and declared: "There is one person who I believe can stop this New World Order. His name is your county sheriff. . . . There is no question your sheriff has the responsibility to protect you from tyranny and international bankers."[182] Mack's public speaking career waned with the demise of the militia movement, but the new militia movement has given him a much broader audience speaking to Tea Party, NRA, and Republican groups, and as a frequent guest on Fox News.[183]

The new militia movement was emboldened by its apparent victory at Cliven Bundy's ranch.[184] Mike Vanderboegh, a leader of the III Percent Patriots, saw the events at the ranch as the beginning of the war for liberty: "The feds were routed—routed. There is no other word that applies. Courage is contagious, defiance is contagious, victory is contagious. Yet the war is not over."[185] Within a month after the Bundy ranch standoff, the new insurgents launched new challenges to federal authority. In San Juan County, Utah, commissioner Phil Lyman led a protest against a ban on the use of motorized vehicles. Lyman and several dozen ATV riders—including members of Bundy's family—rode into the canyon to defy BLM authority.[186] The new militia groups, including Oath Keepers and the III Percent Patriots, went to the United States–Mexico border to try to stop illegal immigrants from entering the country and to force the federal government not to relocate undocumented children.[187]

The threats of violence from the new insurrectionists have increased. Phil Lyman said at the Utah protests: "If things don't change, it's not long before shots will be fired."[188] He was right. In June 2014, less than two months after the Bundy revolt, Jerad and Amanda Miller, two of the protesters at the Bundy ranch, shot and killed two Las Vegas police officers and a bystander.[189] "We're freedom fighters," they shouted. "Let the revolution begin!"[190] Before Jerad Miller was shot by police and Amanda Miller took her own life, the Millers draped Gadsden flags ("Don't Tread on Me") over the victims, using the long-standing emblem for liberty adopted by the Tea Party movement.[191]

In January 2016, Ammon and Ryan Bundy led a group of armed protestors to occupy the Malheur National Wildlife Refuge in Harney County, Oregon. Predictably, the group called themselves Citizens for Constitutional Freedom.[192] The occupation nominally arose out of a protest against the imprisonment of Dwight and Steven Hammond, who had been found guilty in 2012 of committing arson on federal land. The Hammonds had a long-standing dispute with federal officials because fences on the refuge prevented them from using public land for grazing. After making numerous death threats against refuge managers, the Hammonds set fire to the refuge land. According to the government's evidence at the arson trial, Steven Hammond told friends that in lighting and dropping matches on the ground they were trying to assault federal power; "they were going to 'light up the whole country on fire.'" The fire burned 139 acres. Found guilty, the Hammonds were each sentenced to five years' imprisonment.

The Bundys declared that they were occupying the refuge to stop the United States from taking the Hammonds into custody. More broadly, they argued that the United States has no right to own a wildlife refuge or to deprive ranchers of their ability to use public lands for grazing.[193] They said that the armed occupation was necessary to stand up for the Constitution and against a tyrannical government: "This is more than about them [the Hammonds]. . . . That if we do not stand and put these things to an end, that what has happened to them will happen to more and more people, and it is that simple, that the violations of the constitution, the blatant violations, will become the normal."[194] The Bundys asserted a constitutional right and a patriotic duty to take up arms against the government. As Ryan Bundy declared, "We the People, being free, need to defend our freedom from time to time against those who would violate our rights as defined by our Creator." He said that state leaders had a duty to protect the people from federal tyranny, but if they refused to do so "then We the People will have to do it ourselves."[195]

The occupation lasted for forty days. In the end, federal officials arrested the Bundys and their supporters. LaVoy Finicum, one of the occupiers and the group's unofficial spokesman, became the latest martyr for the Constitution when he was fatally shot by federal officials as he reached for his gun rather than surrender.[196] Twenty-seven people including the two Bundys were charged with conspiracy to impede officers of the United States from discharging their official duties through the use of force, intimidation, or threats. Twelve pled guilty, and charges were dropped against several others. Ammon and Ryan Bundy went to trial, where they argued that the federal government lacks authority over the wildlife refuge. Ryan Bundy also claimed that he was a "sovereign citizen" and therefore was not subject to federal authority. A jury found them not guilty. When the verdict was announced, Bundy's supporters cheered. Their fellow defendant Shawna Cox said the verdict sent a message to the nation: "Wake up, America, and help us restore the Constitution. Don't sleep with your head in the sand."[197]

Trump's Support for Insurrectionists and the January 6 Insurrection

The election of Donald Trump in November 2016 brought to power a group of officials who agreed with the insurrectionist reading of the Second Amendment and actively supported insurrectionist organizations. The President's 1776 Advisory Commission revealed that support for a constitutional right to insurrection had now reached the White House: "The right to keep and bear arms is required by the fundamental natural right to life: no man may justly be denied the means of his own defense. The political significance of this right is hardly less important. An armed people is a people capable of defending their liberty no less than their lives and is the last, desperate check against the worst tyranny."[198]

The administration's support for insurrectionist groups adhered to this philosophy. Ryan Zinke, secretary of the Interior, the department that oversees federal lands, never criticized the takeover of the Malheur refuge and did not pursue action against the Bundys. Instead, he charged that many Interior staff who enforce federal laws are not patriotic Americans, declaring in a speech before oil executives, "I got 30 percent of the crew that's not loyal to the flag."[199] Zinke's department indicated its general agreement with the Bundys when it reduced the size of federal monuments and initiated broad efforts to return federal lands to local control.[200]

In July 2018, President Trump showed support for the Bundys by issuing pardons for the Hammonds, whose conviction for committing arson on the Malheur refuge sparked the occupation. A White House statement accompanying the pardons said that the Obama administration had been "overzealous" in its prosecution and that the arsonists are "devoted family men, respected contributors to their local community, and have widespread support from their neighbors, local law enforcement, and farmers and ranchers across the West."[201] Hearing the news of the pardons, Ryan Bundy responded, "Awesome, awesome, awesome."[202]

With an ally in the White House, militia groups shifted focus to challenging state governments. In 2020, when many state governments imposed restrictions on businesses and personal travel to address the COVID-19 pandemic, militia groups declared the restrictions tyrannical, un-American, and unconstitutional, and rose in armed protest. In Michigan, armed protesters entered the statehouse carrying Confederate flags and a noose. They vowed to die rather than let the government tell them what to do. Members of the CSPOA declared that they would refuse to carry out state COVID-related restrictions, which they said conflicted with the nation's founding principles of individual freedom. In a tweet, President Trump voiced his support for the insurrectionists: "LIBERATE MICHIGAN."[203] Ammon Bundy was among the leaders of the armed groups protesting pandemic restrictions and declared that being required to wear a mask was tantamount to slavery.[204] He vowed to resist mask restrictions by violence if necessary: "We are prepared to politically, legally, and physically protect the people's rights."[205]

The new insurrectionists also turned their focus toward groups fighting for racial justice. In the summer of 2020, in the wake of the murder of George Floyd, when the Black Lives Matter movement mobilized millions of Americans to protest racist police violence, many armed white militias came to counterprotest. Violent confrontation was inevitable. In August 2020, Kyle Rittenhouse, a seventeen-year-old militia member with the Kenosha Guard, shot and killed two Black Lives Matter protesters. Rittenhouse's lawyer declared that his client had been acting to protect law and order and exercising his Second Amendment rights.[206] State and local governments have failed, the lawyer continued, and private citizens now had no choice but to exercise their Second Amendment rights to restore law and order.[207]

With President Trump's support for insurrectionists, it was no surprise that thousands of Americans, including hundreds of members of militias and other insurrectionist groups, responded to Trump's call to come to Washington on January 6, 2021, when Congress was scheduled to certify the results of the 2020 presidential election. For three months, Trump had declared without support that the election results were fraudulent and that the inauguration of Joseph Biden would be illegitimate. For weeks, Trump had called on supporters to come to Washington for a "Save America" rally scheduled for January 6: "Big protest in D.C. on January 6th," Mr. Trump tweeted on December 19. "Be there, will be wild!"[208]

With all legal challenges to the election exhausted, insurrectionists concluded that the time for violence had arrived. Oath Keepers sent out a message to all members: "All Patriots who can get to DC need to be in DC." The invitation called on members to be prepared to employ violence: "Patriots must prepare to do whatever must be done to honor our oaths to defend the Constitution against all enemies, foreign and domestic. Whatever happens on Jan. 6, you must prepare for standing tall, with courage, in the days ahead. Again, stand now, or kneel forever."[209]

At the January 6 rally, Trump told the crowd it was time for his supporters to take matters into their hands to protect the Constitution: "We're supposed to protect our country, support our country, support our constitution, and protect our constitution."[210] He asserted that the alleged election fraud justified extra-legal action: "When you catch somebody in a fraud, you're allowed to go by very different rules." The time for weakness was over, he told the crowd, because "you will never take back our country with weakness." He called on the crowd to march to the Capitol and said that the time had come to "fight like hell" because "if you don't fight like Hell, you're not going to have a country anymore." The crowd answered by chanting "Fight for Trump! Fight for Trump! Fight for Trump!"[211]

And fight they did. After marching down Constitution Avenue, the crowd pushed past police barricades and surrounded the Capitol. They announced their mission: "To protect the Constitution of the United States."[212] After battling the Capitol police and breaking doors and windows, the mob marched inside, chanting, "Defend your liberty, defend the Constitution."[213] Once inside, the insurrectionists tried to locate members of Congress and Vice President Mike Pence, who they'd threaten to execute. They looted furniture, vandalized House offices, and occupied the Senate Chamber. By the end of the day, one of the rioters had been shot and killed and at least 140 people had been injured, including more than a hundred police officers and many members of the media.[214]

The insurrectionists relied on the same justifications for antigovernment violence used by the Posse Comitatus, Tim McVeigh, and the Bundys: the federal government was controlled by alien forces dedicated to destroying the Constitution and American freedoms. As the Oath Keepers declared:

> What is now being installed is not a constitutional government. It's an illegitimate regime that has unjustly taken power through massive vote fraud, to install a ChiCom [Chinese Communist] puppet who will do the bidding of a mortal enemy of this nation, as well as the bidding of international elites who are in allegiance and alliance with the CCP [Chinese Communist Party] as they pursue a common goal of destroying our Republic and enslaving the American people.[215]

Like the Oath Keepers, members of Three Percent Patriots groups came to DC on January 6 prepared to exercise their Second Amendment rights against a government they considered tyrannical. As one Three Percent Patriots member declared:

> Some people at the highest levels need to be made an example of with an execution or two or three. Because when you commit treason against this country and you disenfranchise the voters of this country and you take away their ability to make decisions for themselves, you strip them of their Constitution rights. That's not hyperbole when we call it tyranny, that's fucking tyranny. And tyrants and traitors need to be executed as an example.[216]

Facing a government they believed was coming under the direct control of foreign Communists and dedicated to the enslavement of the American people, the new insurrectionists called on American patriots to defend their beloved Constitution through violence. Thousands heeded the call.

Conclusion

Movements like the Posse Comitatus, the militias, and new insurrectionists like the Bundys, Oath Keepers, and Three Percent Patriots reveal how readily constitutional nationalism can lead to violence and murder. Members of these movements have declared that devotion to the Constitution is at the heart of what it means to be American, but the nation has lost touch with the true meaning of the Constitution, political elites are destroying the Constitution, and violence is the only viable method to take back America and restore constitutional rule.

Although these movements have used the language of constitutional nationalism to justify violence, one might wonder whether it is fair to say that constitutional nationalism *causes* violence. The movements that have advocated violence discussed in this chapter *say* that they act to defend the Constitution, but maybe this is just talk to conceal their true motives. Maybe there are psychological explanations for the antigovernment violence of political radicals. Maybe killers like Gordon Kahl and Tim McVeigh were plain old psychopaths, who said that they killed for the Constitution just as Charles Manson pointed to the Beatles' song "Helter Skelter" to justify his murderous spree.[217]

It might be reassuring to believe that these acts are simply the results of mental illness, rather than a national constitutional culture. Repeated examinations revealed no basis for concluding that McVeigh, at least, suffered from mental illness. By all accounts, he sincerely believed that killing as many federal employees as he could was necessary to protect the Constitution.[218] And even if McVeigh was deranged, is it possible to dismiss as crazy the thousands or even millions of Americans who have joined the Posse Comitatus, militias, Oath Keepers, and other groups that have used or threatened antigovernment violence, and to deny that our constitutional culture has anything to do with them?

It may be possible to dismiss the constitutional rhetoric used by advocates of violence as what Marxists might call part of the "superstructure" of cultural conceptions that hide the actors' true motives. All the movements discussed in this chapter were overwhelmingly white and male, and it may be that defending the status and power of their race and sex, and not the Constitution, better explains the violence they employed. Yet even if these movements are best explained as acting to defend white male rule, it is significant that they justified their actions in the language of constitutionalism. Like the Klan and the New Christian Right, supporters of the Posse, the militias, and the Oath Keepers perceived a threat to their power, which they understood as a threat to the nation, and they described that threat in constitutional terms.

As earlier chapters showed, constitutional nationalism turns conflicts over national identity, such as whether the United States is a white nation or a Christian nation, into conflicts over the Constitution—conflicts that are framed as asking whether the Constitution protects white rule or Christian rule. At the same time, it turns constitutional disputes into disputes over national identity. Disputes over the validity of federal taxes or federal wildlife refuges can give rise to violence when the dispute speaks to what some consider to be foundational American values. Those who advocate antigovernment violence draw on the prevailing ideology of constitutional nationalism, expressing their grievances in constitutional terms by declaring that those who disagree with them are not merely wrong; they are un-American and must be defeated to protect the nation, by force if necessary. And armed Americans who share their grievances have joined them by the thousands, declaring that they too are willing to kill and die for the Constitution.

Conclusion
Nationalism without the Constitution

My central point in this book has been to challenge the prevailing conception of the role of the Constitution in American nationalism. In that conception, being American means being devoted to a set of principles found in the Constitution. While it is true that Americans frequently express devotion to the Constitution, those expressions have served to convey many competing and widely varying nationalist visions. Rather than expressing a single conception of American identity, constitutional nationalism has provided a neutral and patriotic language for conveying a broad spectrum of nationalist visions. Some of these visions are inclusive and emphasize that anyone who embraces constitutional values has an equal claim to be American, while others have emphasized exclusion and hierarchy.

A funny thing happened while I was writing this book. On November 8, 2016, Donald Trump was elected president after a campaign that focused largely on nationalist themes that emphasized exclusion. He argued that the United States must build a wall to stop an influx of illegal Mexican immigrants who were bringing in crime and destroying the nation's culture. "A nation without borders is not a nation," Trump declared.[1] He railed against immigrants who do not speak English or who refuse to assimilate into what he considered American culture. He promised to ban immigration by Muslims, who Trump said could not become good Americans because they "hate us."[2] His campaign called his domestic agenda "economic nationalism" and his foreign policy "America First."

Trump's rise follows much the same pattern as many movements discussed in this book. As many surveys showed, Trump supporters considered themselves prototypical Americans who feared that they were losing power and status, while the country was becoming transformed into something unrecognizably foreign. Trump spoke to the anxieties and resentments felt by this group of Americans about the nation's growing racial, ethnic, and cultural diversity.[3] They frequently characterized the threat to their status in nationalist terms, as an attack on the nation as they conceived it. As Fox News commentator Laura Ingraham declared, "Massive demographic

changes have been foisted upon the American people, and in some parts of
the country it does seem like the America we know and love doesn't exist
anymore."[4] Like other nationalists, Trump conveyed his agenda as the restoration of the nation's lost glory, expressed by a legion of supporters wearing
red baseball caps that declared "Make America Great Again."

Just one thing was missing from Trump's 2016 campaign: the Constitution. Unlike other nationalist movements examined in this book, Trump
rarely mentioned it. To be sure, Trump gained the attention of conservatives in 2011 because of his support for birtherism, which used constitutional language to declare President Obama a constitutional outsider. Yet
in 2016, constitutional rhetoric was almost entirely absent from the Trump
campaign. It marked a major rhetorical shift from 2012, when Republican
candidate Mitt Romney declared that "the big issues in this campaign turn
on our understanding of the Constitution and how it was meant to guide
the life of our nation," and the Republican Party declared itself "the party
of the Constitution."[5]

Donald Trump didn't talk like this. Strength, not the Constitution, was
his constant theme. Trump diagnosed the country's problem as weakness,
not betrayal of its constitutional ideals. He warned that "our enemies are
getting stronger and we are getting weaker."[6] Trump said that President
Obama was "so weak, and so politically correct, that terror groups are forming and getting stronger! Shame."[7] Hillary Clinton's flaw wasn't her betrayal
of the Constitution but her weakness. "She's got no strength," Trump said,
"She's got no stamina."[8] Trump proclaimed himself the strong leader the
nation needed and promised that he was going to make the nation "stronger than ever before." "We are going to make our country so strong and so
powerful," Trump told a rally in Michigan, "and we are going to make our
country great again. And it's going to be a beautiful, beautiful thing."[9]

On rare occasions Trump did talk about the Constitution, but it was only
to reinforce the theme of strength. Not surprisingly, his favorite constitutional topic was guns. President Obama was "releasing thousands of violent
criminals," Trump told the National Rifle Association, "and many of them
are also illegal immigrants." Real Americans need guns to protect them
from the "thugs" and "terrorists" the Democrats were coddling, Trump
said. Hillary Clinton wanted to keep America weak and would "abolish the
Second Amendment" and "disarm vulnerable Americans in high-crime
neighborhoods."[10] Trump promised not to let that happen. He said that
Americans wouldn't be left defenseless like those French weaklings who sat
helplessly while terrorists killed 130 people in Paris in November 2015.[11]

"If I'd been there with a gun," Trump told an NRA audience, pantomiming holding an assault rifle, "I would have—BOOM!"[12]

The absence of constitutional rhetoric did not stop Trump from campaigning on the same nationalist themes used by nativists, the Tea Party, and others. Instead, the rhetoric of strength allowed Trump to employ these themes in a blunt and direct way.[13] In 2012 Republicans warned that the Democrats supported alien ideologies that did metaphoric violence to American constitutional culture, but in 2016 Trump addressed fears about physical violence by Muslims and undocumented immigrants and their "gangs, drug traffickers and cartels [who] have freely exploited our open borders and committed vast numbers of crimes inside the United States."[14]

Trump was not alone among the 2016 Republican candidates in ignoring the Constitution. Talk of the Constitution had dominated the 2012 Republican campaign, but it practically disappeared among Republicans in 2016. Like Trump, Jeb Bush, Marco Rubio, and Chris Christie didn't mention the Constitution in their speeches announcing their candidacies.[15] The only candidate who talked like it was 2012 was Ted Cruz, who declared, "It is time to reclaim the Constitution," time "to get back to the principles that have made this country great."[16]

Nor was Trump the only Republican candidate in 2016 who made strength rather than the Constitution his central campaign trope. In his announcement speech, Ben Carson declared that his campaign is focused on "one goal" and that is to "strengthen this great nation."[17] Trump wasn't even the strongest candidate, at least measured by the number of times he talked about strength. That title went to John Kasich, who mentioned strength ten times in his announcement speech in declaring that he too considered restoring the nation's strength his top priority.[18]

A statistical examination of Republican campaign rhetoric in 2012 and 2016 confirms that the decline of constitutional rhetoric and the rise of "strength" as a campaign buzzword were independent of Trump. In 2012 the ten Republican presidential candidates mentioned the Constitution an average of four times in their announcement speeches, while in 2016 the seventeen candidates mentioned it on average only once. At the same time, Republican references to "strength" doubled from 2012 to 2016.[19] The same rhetorical shift can be seen in the Republican debates, during which the 2016 candidates referred to the Constitution one-quarter as often as had the 2012 candidates, while strength was mentioned twice as often.[20]

Noticing that Trump didn't talk the constitutional talk, some of his fellow Republicans worried that he lacked the constitutional devotion demanded of a president. After dropping out of the race, Jeb Bush said that he could not support Trump because he "has not displayed a respect for the Constitution."[21] Speaker of the House Paul Ryan wondered if Trump shared conservatives' passion for "adherence to the Constitution."[22] And Ben Sasse, who had been elected to the Senate as a Tea Party Republican, articulated his concerns over Trump in constitutional terms, declaring that "America is first and fundamentally about a shared Constitutional creed," and the president's primary duty is to "defend the Constitution," not "just mindlessly shouting the word 'strong.'"[23]

What accounts for the shift in Republican rhetoric from 2012 to 2016, in which promises to "restore the nation's strength" replaced promises to "restore the Constitution"? And what if anything does the shift away from constitutional rhetoric say about the continuing role of the Constitution in American nationalism?

There are several possible explanations for the apparent decline in constitutional rhetoric. In 2012 Republican candidates spoke often of the Constitution to gain Tea Party credibility, but by 2016 Tea Party power had waned within the GOP, and the Tea Party movement itself had shifted its rhetoric, increasingly emphasizing anti-immigrant themes rather than the fear of big government.[24] Constitutional rhetoric may also have disappeared from the 2016 campaign because the Republicans' opponent was Hillary Clinton and not Barack Obama. Perhaps Republican strategists had believed it was effective when running against a Black candidate to call him un-American, but when the opponent was a woman it was better to call her weak. Trump made the attack personal: "I think that my words represent toughness and strength. Hillary's not strong. Hillary's weak, frankly. She's got no stamina; she's got nothing."[25]

Perhaps the clearest explanation is that by 2016 a majority of white voters no longer needed their candidates to express their resentments and fears in the coded rhetoric of constitutional nationalism. In 2012, expressions of constitutional devotion provided a neutral and patriotic way for those who think of themselves as authentic Americans to talk about what it meant to lose status and power. In 2016 it became apparent that these Americans would listen to a candidate who addressed these fears more directly. To them, it was not enough anymore to talk about how the election of Obama and the nation's increasing pluralism threatened the Constitution. It was time to ban Muslims from entering the country and build a wall to keep Mexicans out. These Americans were ready to buy a nationalism that was explicitly devoted to excluding unwanted foreigners that was sold straight up, undiluted by constitutional tonic.

To his supporters, Trump's unvarnished appeals to the nation's exclusionary impulses made him more, not less, appealing. As polls showed, many Americans found his message straightforward and refreshing. As one pollster put it, "He's tapped into a lot of sentiment about the anger and frustration that people have, which is not new. But he's seen as a straight shooter, and he doesn't hold his punches. That seems to resonate with a lot of people."[26]

Trump's election demonstrated that an American politician could create a successful coalition built on nationalist themes of exclusion without hiding behind the constitutional nationalist rhetoric that had prevailed for decades. Nationalists of all sorts flocked to support Trump because of, and not in spite of, his blunt, uncoded appeals to exclusionary nationalism. White supremacists were some of his first and most enthusiastic supporters. David Duke instructed white Americans that voting for anyone but Trump would be "treason to your heritage."[27] Nativists, fearing that legal and illegal immigration was destroying the nation as they knew it, quickly joined the campaign. Tea Party supporters found in Trump a leader who shared their vision of American exceptionalism, their hostility to the press, and their belief that compromise is weakness.[28] Christian nationalists too joined the Trump campaign, drawn to Trump's frequent invocations of the nation's religious devotion.[29]

The election of a president who campaigned through blunt appeals to exclusionary nationalism has led many to challenge the conventional view of American nationalism. That view, articulated by Franklin Roosevelt in 1943 and accepted as conventional since World War II, has declared that American identity is now and always has been defined by devotion "to our creed of liberty and democracy" and "is not, and never was, a matter of race or ancestry."[30] Since Trump's election, it has become increasingly common to acknowledge the nation's ethnonationalist traditions and to declare that white supremacy and xenophobia are as American as apple pie.[31]

Trump's election should not suggest, however, that constitutional nationalism is declining. While Trump himself did not typically articulate his "America First" brand of nationalism in constitutional terms, many of his appointees and supporters articulated his agenda in the familiar language of constitutional nationalism. When Trump banned immigration from seven predominately Muslim countries, the executive order drawn up by his staff declared that the ban excluded those who "bear hostile attitudes" toward the United States "and its founding principles" and who "do not support the Constitution."[32]

Jeff Sessions, Trump's first attorney general, declared that Islam "fundamentally conflicts with our magnificent constitutional order."[33] Trump's advisor Steve Bannon said that the United States should not accept Syrian refugees because they were not suited for life in a constitutional republic: "These are not Jeffersonian democrats. These are not people with thousands of years of understanding democracy in their DNA."[34] For many Trump supporters, the language of constitutional devotion remained the *lingua franca* even though it was not spoken by their leader.

The Trump administration's embrace of a nationalist vision grounded in the Constitution and devoted to ethnic and religious hierarchy can be seen most clearly in *The 1776 Report*, issued by a presidential advisory commission overseen by the secretaries of the departments of state, defense, and the interior, among others. *The 1776 Report* was plainly intended as a response to the *New York Times*'s 1619 Project, which examined American history through an African American lens. Whereas the 1619 Project saw the African American experience as central to American history, *The 1776 Report* celebrates the nation's English and Protestant traditions. It quotes John Jay's declaration in *Federalist*, no. 2 that Americans were a "people descended from the same ancestors, speaking the same language, professing the same religion, attached to the same principles of government." Acknowledging that the American people "were not quite as homogenous" as Jay suggested, the report professes that American national identity is also informed by dedication to "principles of justice and political legitimacy" as well as "manners, customs, language, and dedication to the common good." The Trump administration thus embraced a form of nationalism in which dedication to principles found in the Constitution formed a central part of American identity, but this identity also includes other cultural elements such as the use of the English language, and celebration of the nation's Protestant and English heritage. Further evidencing a narrow conception of American nationalism, the report declares that progressivism, affirmative action, the administrative state, and identity politics are incompatible with the nation's founding commitments.[35]

Unsurprisingly, Trump's presidency helped make the language of constitutional devotion a dominant framework among his opponents, who accused him of betraying the Constitution and thereby betraying the nation. Describing Trump as a "one man constitutional crisis," ACLU president Anthony Romero said that Trump's policies were "as un-American as it gets."[36] Trump opponents frequently paired the claim that Trump disregarded the Constitution with the claim that he was un-American. "The term that applies best to Donald J. Trump is 'Un-American,'" wrote one critic, because "he has repudiated the oath of office and the documents at the core of our national identity: the Constitution and the Declaration of Independence."[37]

Opposition to Trump follows a similar pattern as many movements discussed in this book. Trump's opponents saw his presidency and the marginalization of many groups of Americans as a threat to their place in American life. Like others, they saw this threat in nationalist terms, as an attack on the nation as they envisioned it, and they sought to mobilize opposition by rallying around the Constitution as the embodiment of their national vision. As in previous episodes of constitutional nationalism, Trump's opponents put constitutional rhetoric to new uses, to express new understandings of what the nation is or should be. Trump's election prompted a need to reconcile a multicultural, inclusive national vision with a new recognition that the United States has long-standing traditions of exclusion and hierarchy based on race, religion, sex, and ethnicity. The eulogy for civil rights giant John Lewis given by former President Obama shows the felt need to try to come to terms with the nation's long-standing exclusionary impulses that Trump exploited. In that eulogy, Obama relied on familiar constitutional nationalist rhetoric and characterized the Constitution as the nation's instruction manual. Unlike past speeches, however, in which Obama, like Roosevelt before him, identified the nation's foundational principles as its commitment to liberty and equality, in his eulogy for Lewis the former president identified a somewhat different core constitutional principle: "We were born with instructions: to form a more perfect union. Explicit in those words is the idea that we are imperfect; that what gives each new generation purpose is to take up the unfinished work of the last and carry it further than anyone might have thought possible."[38]

In this revised constitutional nationalist vision, the nation has not always been committed to liberty and equality. Instead, Obama recognized that the nation's traditions have always embraced exclusion and hierarchy. Yet the nation's core foundational principles, Obama declared—embodied in the Constitution itself—includes the need to overcome these competing traditions of intolerance and inequality and to create a more perfect union.

A few weeks after his eulogy for John Lewis, Obama gave a speech at the 2020 Democratic National Convention, which continued to emphasize that the nation's exclusionary and hateful impulses had been present from the beginning and were embedded in the Constitution. Delivering the speech from the Museum of the American Revolution in Philadelphia in front of a museum display entitled "Writing the Constitution," Obama restated the point he'd made in his eulogy for John Lewis: "I'm in Philadelphia, where our Constitution was drafted and signed. It wasn't a perfect document. It allowed for the inhumanity of slavery and failed to guarantee women—and even men who didn't own property—the right to participate in the political process." Despite these flaws in our founding document, Obama explained, the Constitution gave Americans the means to overcome their traditions of inequality.

A week after Obama spoke at the Democratic National Convention, Trump's oldest son, Donald Trump Jr., spoke before the Republican National Convention and accused Democrats of betraying the nation's constitutional values: "In the past, both parties believed in the goodness of America. . . . This time the other party is attacking the very principles on which our Nation was founded. . . . Our Founders believed there was nothing more important than protecting our God-given right to think for ourselves. Now the Left's trying to 'cancel' all of those Founders." As Obama and Trump Jr.'s speeches should make clear, constitutional nationalism did not die with Donald Trump's election. Expressions of constitutional devotion and accusations of constitutional betrayal continue to be a central way that Americans conceive of and express competing national visions.

In a curious twist, Trump, who did not articulate his national vision in constitutional terms when he campaigned for office in 2016 and 2020, turned to constitutional rhetoric at the very end of his term when he tried to overturn the 2020 election results. When the Supreme Court denied his final legal challenges to the election, he declared that "the justices are bent on destroying our constitution and overthrowing America's founding."[39] In his speech at the "Save America" rally on January 6, 2021, when Trump sought to inspire his supporters to "fight like Hell" to prevent Congress from certifying the election, he told the crowd that what they were fighting was not his personal grip on power; they were fighting to save the Constitution and the nation: "We're supposed to protect our country, support our country, support our constitution, and protect our constitution." Although he acknowledged that election law did not provide a mechanism to prevent the certification, he argued that extra-legal action was justified because, in breaking the law, "you're protecting our country and protecting the constitution."[40] In his desperation to maintain power and to incite his supporters to act, Trump discovered what countless others had learned: devotion to the Constitution can inspire Americans to fight and fight like hell.

Notes

Introduction

1. See, e.g., Press Release, Rep. Hakeem Jeffries, Chairman Jeffries: "Every Second, Every Minute, Every Hour That Donald Trump Remains in Office Presents a Danger to the American People," January 10, 2021, https://www .dems.gov/newsroom/press-releases/chairman-jeffries-every-second-every -minute-every-hour-that-donald-trump-remains-in-office-presents-a-danger -to-the-american-people ("It was an attack on the Congress, an attack on the country and an attack on the Constitution.").

2. Transcript, House Impeachment Managers Present Case to Convict Trump, CNN, February 11, 2021, http://transcripts.cnn.com/TRANSCRIPTS /2102/11/se.09.html.

3. "Call to Action: Time for Diligence," Oath Keepers, January 3, 2021, https://oathkeepers.org/current-posts/ (on file with author).

4. *New Yorker*, "A Reporter's Footage from Inside the Capitol Siege," YouTube, posted January 17, 2021, https://www.youtube.com/watch?v=270F8s5TEKY&t =192s&ab_channel=TheNewYorker (at 1:19).

5. *New Yorker*, "A Reporter's Footage from Inside the Capitol Siege," at 3:20.

6. Michael Kammen, *A Machine That Would Go of Itself: The Constitution in American Culture* (New York: Alfred A. Knopf, 1986), 91.

7. Jeffrey Toobin, "Our Broken Constitution," *New Yorker*, December 2, 2013, 64.

8. Barack Obama, "Inaugural Address by President Barack Obama," Washington, DC, January 21, 2013, https://obamawhitehouse.archives.gov /the-press-office/2013/01/21/inaugural-address-president-barack-obama.

9. Barack Obama, "President Obama's Farewell Address," Chicago, January 10, 2017, https://obamawhitehouse.archives.gov/farewell; Maya Rhodan, "Transcript: Read Full Text of President Barack Obama's Speech in Selma," *Time*, March 7, 2015, http://time.com/3736357/barack-obama-selma-speech -transcript/.

10. Gunnar Myrdal, *An American Dilemma: The Negro Problem and Modern Democracy* (New York: Harper, 1944).

11. Myrdal, *An American Dilemma*, lxx, lxxii, 1021.

12. Hans Kohn, *American Nationalism: An Interpretive Essay* (New York: Collier Books, 1961), 8, 20.

13. Laurence H. Tribe, "America's Constitutional Narrative," *Daedalus* 141, no. 1 (Winter 2012): 18, 23; Steven G. Calabresi, "'A Shining City on a Hill': American Exceptionalism and the Supreme Court's Practice of Relying on Foreign Law," *Boston University Law Review* 86 (Fall 2006): 1414.

14. See, e.g., Michael Billig, *Banal Nationalism* (Thousand Oaks, CA: Sage Publications, 1995), 37; Elie Kedourie, *Nationalism*, 4th ed. (Hoboken, NJ: Wiley-Blackwell, 1993), 1; Anthony D. Smith, *Theories of Nationalism*, 2nd ed. (New York: Holmes & Meier, 1983) 20-21.

15. Elizabeth Theiss-Morse, *Who Counts as an American? The Boundaries of National Identity* (New York: Cambridge University Press, 2009), 4.

16. Michael Ignatieff, *Blood and Belonging* (London: BBC Consumer Publishing, 1993) 5-9; Brian Barry, *Culture and Equality* (Cambridge: Polity, 2000) 79-109; Andrew Mason, *Community, Solidarity, and Belonging* (Cambridge: Cambridge University Press, 2000), 115-147.

17. Jürgen Habermas, "Citizenship and National Identity," in *Between Facts and Norms: Contributions to a Discourse Theory of Law and Democracy*, Jürgen Habermas, trans. William Rehg (Cambridge, MA: MIT Press, 1998).

18. Samuel P. Huntington, *American Politics: The Promise of Disharmony* (Cambridge, MA: Belknap Press, 1981), 30.

19. Anatol Lieven, *America Right or Wrong: An Anatomy of American Nationalism* (New York: Oxford University Press, 2004), 49; Lloyd Kramer, *Nationalism in Europe and America: Politics, Cultures, and Identities since 1775* (Chapel Hill: University of North Carolina Press, 2011) 90.

20. "Praises Army Plan for Japanese Unit," *New York Times*, February 5, 1943, 6.

21. George W. Bush, "Inaugural Address," Washington, DC, January 20, 2001, American Presidency Project, https://www.presidency.ucsb.edu/docu ments/inaugural-address-52.

22. Obama, "Inaugural Address."

23. Bush, "Inaugural Address."

24. Rogers M. Smith, *Civic Ideals: Conflicting Visions of Citizenship in US History* (New Haven, CT: Yale University Press, 1997), 14.

25. Smith, *Civic Ideals*, 23.

26. Smith, 28.

27. Bart Bonikowski and Paul DiMaggio, "Varieties of American Popular Nationalism," *American Sociological Review* 81, no. 5 (September 2016): 949-980; Deborah J. Schildkraut, "Defining American Identity in the Twenty-First Century: How Much "There" Is There?," *Journal of Politics* 69, no. 3 (August 2007): 597-615; Associated Press-NORC Center for Public Affairs Research, "The American Identity: Points of Pride, Conflicting Views, and a Distinct Culture," NORC at the University of Chicago, last modified March 2017, https://apnorc.org/wp-content/uploads/2020/02/APNORC_American

_Identity_2017.pdf; Bruce Stokes, "What It Takes to Truly Be 'One of Us': In US, Canada, Europe, Australia, and Japan, Publics Say Language Matters More to National Identity Than Birthplace," Pew Research Center, last modified February 1, 2017, https://assets.pewresearch.org/wp-content/uploads/sites/2 /2017/04/14094140/Pew-Research-Center-National-Identity-Report-FINAL -February-1-2017.pdf.

28. Kermit Roosevelt III, "America Revisited: The Constitution and Declaration of Independence (A Contrary View)," One Day University, accessed October 9, 2020, https://www.onedayu.com/events/america-revisited-the-con stitution-and-declaration-of-independence-a-contrary-view-nyc/.

29. Randy Barnett, "Is the Constitution Libertarian?," *Cato Supreme Court Review* (2009): 9, 32.

30. Edward A. Purcell Jr., *Brandeis and the Progressive Constitution: Erie, the Judicial Power, and the Politics of the Federal Courts in Twentieth-Century America* (New Haven, CT: Yale University Press, 2000); Bruce Ackerman, *We the People: Foundations* (Cambridge, MA: Harvard University Press, 1991), 3–33; Benjamin N. Cardozo, *The Nature of the Judicial Process* (New Haven, CT: Yale University Press, 1921), 66–67, 71–72, 88–90, 98–102, 135–137; Ronald Dworkin, *Freedom's Law: The Moral Reading of the American Constitution* (Oxford: Oxford University Press, 1996), 1–38; Alexander M. Bickel, "The Original Understanding and the Segregation Decision," *Harvard Law Review* 69, no. 1 (November 1955): 59–65; William J. Brennan Jr., "Speech at the Georgetown University Text and Teaching Symposium" (October 12, 1985), in Paul G. Cassell, ed., *The Great Debate: Interpreting Our Written Constitution* (Washington, DC: Federalist Society, 1986), 11, 17. Of course, there are numerous dissenting voices who view the Constitution as embodying America's history of racism, sexism, and numerous other vices.

31. David Pozen, Eric L. Talley, and Julian Nyarko, "A Computational Analysis of Constitutional Polarization," *Cornell Law Review* 105, no. 1 (2019): 1–84; Mark A. Graber, "Judicial Supremacy and the Structure of Partisan Conflict," *Indiana Law Review* 50, no. 1 (2016): 141, 168.

32. Joseph Story, "Joseph Story to Simon Greenleaf," in William S. Story, ed., *Life and Letters of Joseph Story*, vol. 2, (Boston: Charles C. Little & James Brown, 1851), 514.

33. Ku Klux Klan, "Prescript of the Order" (1868), in *American History Magazine* 5, no. 1 (January 1900): 3, 5; William Joseph Simmons, *The Klan Unmasked* (Atlanta: Wm. E. Thompson Publishing, 1923), 46.

34. Joint Select Committee on the Condition of Affairs in the Late Insurrectionary States, Report to Inquire into the Condition of Affairs in the Late Insurrectionary States, 42nd Cong., February 19, 1872, 39, 48, 75, http:// onlinebooks.library.upenn.edu/webbin/metabook?id=insurrection1872. (hereinafter "Joint Select Committee Report")

35. Jerry Falwell, *Listen, America!* (New York: Bantam Books, 1981), 29.

36. Lochner v. New York, 198 U.S. 45, 48 (1905).

37. Seymour Martin Lipset, *American Exceptionalism: A Double-Edged Sword* (New York: W. W. Norton, 1997), 31.

38. Samuel Huntington, *Who Are We? The Challenges to America's National Identity* (London: Free Press, 2004), xv–xvii, 46.

39. Rich Lowry, *The Case for Nationalism: How It Made Us Powerful, United, and Free* (New York: Broadside Books, 2019), 19.

40. H.R. Rep. No. 350 at 13 (1924).

41. 13 Cong. Rec. 1742 (1882) (statement of Sen. Jones); see also Gabriel J. Chin, "Segregation's Last Stronghold: Race Discrimination and the Constitutional Law of Immigration," *UCLA Law Review* 46, no. 1 (1998): 22–36.

42. See generally "Shariah: The Threat to America," Center for Security Policy, 2010, https://www.centerforsecuritypolicy.org/upload/wysiwyg/article%20pdfs/Shariah%20-%20The%20Threat%20to%20America%20(Team%20B%20Report)%20Web%2009292010.pdf.

43. Knights of the Ku Klux Klan, *Kloran* (Atlanta, GA: W. J. Simmons, 1916).

44. See Theiss-Morse, *Who Counts as an American?*

45. Theiss-Morse, 73, 75, 92–93.

46. Ernest Renan, *"Qu'est-ce que c'est une nation?"* ("What Is a Nation?"), 7–8 (Conférence faite en Sorbonne le 11 mars 1882), in E. J. Hobsbawm, *Nations and Nationalism since 1780: Programme, Myth, Reality*, 2nd ed. (Cambridge: Cambridge University Press, 1992), 12.

47. See Dred Scott v. Sanford, 60 U.S. 393 (1857); First Congress, Sess. II., at 108, An Act to Establish an Uniform Rule of Naturalization, ch. 3 § 1 (March 26, 1790); *Federalist*, no. 2 (John Jay), in Clinton Rossiter, ed., *The Federalist Papers* (New York: Penguin, 1961), 38.

48. Roderick Anscombe, "The Myth of the True Self," *Psychiatry* 52, no. 2 (May 1989): 209–217; Nina Strohminger, Joshua Knobe, and George Newman, "The True Self: A Psychological Concept Distinct from the Self," *Perspectives on Psychological Science* 12, no. 4 (July 2017): 551–560.

49. Jack M. Balkin, *Constitutional Redemption: Political Faith in an Unjust World* (Cambridge, MA: Harvard University Press, 2011), 26.

50. Renan, *"Qu'est-ce que c'est une nation?,"* 12.

51. See Matthew Levinger and Paula Franklin Lytle, "Myth and Mobilization: The Triadic Structure of Nationalist Rhetoric," *Nations and Nationalism* 7, no. 2 (2001): 178; Anthony D. Smith, *Nation in History: Historiographical Debates about Ethnicity and Nationalism* (Hanover, NH: University Press of New England, 2000), 67–68; Kohn, *American Nationalism*, 29.

52. Myrdal, *American Dilemma*, 1003; see also Smith, *Civic Ideals*, 19.

53. Antonin Scalia, "What Makes an American," in Christopher J. Scalia and Edward Whelan, eds., *Scalia Speaks: Reflections on Law, Faith, and Life Well Lived* (New York: Crown Forum, 2017).

54. US Senate, Immigration Commission, 61st Cong., *Dictionary of Races or Peoples*, Senate Doc. No. 662 (Washington, DC: Government Printing Office, 1911), 1.

55. US Senate, Immigration Commission, 61st Cong., *Dictionary of Races or Peoples*, 15, 23, 47.

56. Robert R. McCrae and Antonio Terracciano, "National Character and Personality," *Current Directions in Psychological Science* 15, no. 4 (August 2006): 156–161.

57. McCrae and Terracciano, "National Character and Personality," 156–161.

58. David E. Stannard, "American Historians and the Idea of National Character: Some Problems and Prospects," *American Quarterly* 23, no. 2 (May 1971): 202–220; Michael McGiffert, "Selected Writings on American National Character," *American Quarterly* 15, no. 2, pt. 2: supplement (Summer 1963): 271–288.

59. Eric Hobsbawm and Terence Ranger, eds., *The Invention of Tradition* (Cambridge: Cambridge University Press, 1983).

60. J. Hector St. John de Crevecoeur, *Letters from an American Farmer* (London: Davies & Davis, 1782), 49.

61. Lipset, *American Exceptionalism*; Godfrey Hodgson, *The Myth of American Exceptionalism* (New Haven, CT: Yale University Press, 2009).

62. See John Higham, *Strangers in the Land: Patterns of American Nativism, 1860–1925* (New Brunswick, NJ: Rutgers University Press, 2002), 137. As Rogers Smith has similarly written, the leaders of the American Revolution believed that their "Anglo-Saxon heritage . . . bestow[ed] a special awareness of men's natural liberties and also unique capacities for self-government." Smith, *Civic Ideals*, 86.

63. Thomas Jefferson, *A Summary View of the Rights of British America* (Williamsburg, VA: printed by the author, 1774); Nell Irvin Painter, *The History of White People* (New York: W. W. Norton, 2010), 111.

64. *Federalist*, no. 2 (John Jay).

65. See Sanford Levinson, "What One Can Learn from Foreign-Language Translations of the US Constitution," *Constitutional Commentary* 31 (2016): 64 (arguing that John Jay must have been aware that languages other than English were spoken, given the prevalence of Dutch speakers in New York).

66. De Crevecoeur, *Letters from an American Farmer*, 47.

67. First Cong., Sess. II, at 108, An Act to Establish an Uniform Rule of Naturalization, ch. 3 § 1 (March 26, 1790).

68. Thomas Jefferson, *Notes on the State of Virginia* (Boston: Lilly & Wait, 1832), 144–151.

69. See, e.g., Carol Rose, "The Ancient Constitution vs. the Federalist Empire: Anti-Federalism from the Attack on 'Monarchism' to Modern Localism,"

Northwestern University Law Review 84 (1989): 74; Paul Finkelman, "Antifederalists: The Loyal Opposition and the American Constitution," *Cornell Law Review* 70, (1984): 182; Merrill Jensen, John P. Kaminski, and Gaspare J. Saladino, eds., eds., *The Documentary History of the Ratification of the Constitution* (Madison: Wisconsin Historical Society Press, 1976), 52–56 ("An Old Whig," Letter VIII), 5 ("The Federalist's Political Creed").

70. Joseph S. Moore, Founding Sins: How a Group of Antislavery Radicals Fought to Put Christ into the Constitution (Oxford: Oxford University Press, 2016), 119–151.

71. Phillip S. Paludan, *A Covenant with Death: The Constitution, Law, and Equity in the Civil War Era* (Urbana: University of Illinois Press, 1975); William Lloyd Garrison, *William Lloyd Garrison and the Fight against Slavery: Selections from The Liberator*, ed. William E. Cain (Boston: Bedford Books, 1995), 36.

72. Aziz Rana, "Colonialism and Constitutional Memory," *UC Irvine Law Review* 5 (2015): 263.

73. James Madison, "First Inaugural Address" (March 4, 1809), in *Inaugural Addresses of the Presidents of the United States* (Washington, DC: Government Printing Office, 1989), 27.

74. Joseph Epstein, introduction to *Alexis de Tocqueville, Democracy in America: The Complete and Unabridged Volumes I and II* (New York: Bantam Classics, 2000); see also A. D. Mayo, *Theology in America: A Sermon Delivered on Sunday Evening, March 15, 1857, in the Division Street Church, Albany* (Albany, NY: Weed, Parsons & Co., 1857), 7 ("There is no confirmed American character by which we can at once be distinguished among modern nationalities. We are too young, and have grown too fast, to have a character. . . . [The American people,] separated by barriers of language, culture and distance, cannot at the present stage of our national growth, be one in any vital sense. We are yet many nations, living peaceably together.").

75. Abraham Lincoln, "Address to the Young Men's Lyceum of Springfield, Illinois" (January 27, 1838), in Roy Basler and Don E. Fehrenbacher, eds., *Selected Speeches and Writings* (New York: Vintage, 1992), 13.

76. Lincoln, "Address to the Young Men's Lyceum of Springfield," 13.

77. Lincoln, 13.

78. John Quincy Adams, *The Jubilee of the Constitution: A Discourse Delivered at the Request of the New York Historical Society in the City of New York* (New York: Samuel Colman VIII and Astor House, 1839).

79. Adams, *The Jubilee of the Constitution*.

80. Abraham Lincoln, "First Inaugural Address," March 4, 1861, available at https://www.bartleby.com/124/pres31.html.

81. "Declaration of the Causes of Secession of Georgia" (January 29, 1861), Avalon Project at Yale Law School, http://avalon.law.yale.edu/19th _century/csa_geosec.asp (hereinafter "Georgia Declaration"); see Alfred L.

Brophy, "Slavery, Property, and Constitutionalism in the Secession Debates," in *University, Court, and Slave: Pro-Slavery Thought in Southern Colleges and Courts and the Coming of Civil War* (New York: Oxford University Press, 2016); Order of the Convention, "A Declaration of the Immediate Causes which Induce and Justify the Secession of the State of Mississippi from the Federal Union" (January 9, 1861), in *Journal of the State Convention* (Jackson, MS: E. Barksdale, 1861), 86–88.

82. Randall M. Miller, Harry S. Stout, and Charles Reagan Wilson, eds., *Religion and the American Civil War* (., New York: Oxford University Press, 1998).

83. Gerhard Peters and John T. Woolley, "Democratic Party Platform" (July 4, 1868), American Presidency Project, https://www.presidency.ucsb.edu/documents/1868-democratic-party-platform.

84. *The Constitution and the Ritual of the Knights of the White Camelia* 26 (adopted June 4, 1868), reprinted in Walter Fleming, ed., *The Constitution and the Ritual of the Knights of the White Camelia* (N.p.: Morgantown, WV, 1904).

85. Address of Franklin Lane, in *Proceedings, Americanization Conference*, held under the auspices of the Americanization Division, Bureau of Education, Department of the Interior, Washington, DC, May 12–15, 1919, 295 (Washington, DC: Government Printing Office, 1919); see also Address of Louis Post, in Proceedings of First Citizenship Conference 14 (July 1916) (Asst. Sec. of Labor Louis Post); Edward George Hartmann, *The Movement to Americanize the Immigrant* (New York: Columbia University Press, 1948), 269–270.

86. Calvin Coolidge, *Foundations of the Republic: Speeches and Addresses* (Honolulu: University Press of the Pacific, 2004), 108.

87. Coolidge, *Foundations of the Republic*, 31.

88. Coolidge, 31.

89. Eric Foner, *Who Owns History? Rethinking the Past in a Changing World* (New York: Hill & Wang, 2003), 165.

90. Gunnar Myrdal, *An American Dilemma: The Negro Problem and Modern Democracy* (New York: Harper, 1944), lxx, lxxii, 1021, 1003.

91. Aziz Rana, "Colonialism and Constitutional Memory," *UC Irvine Law Review* 5 (2015): 277.

92. Martin Luther King Jr., "I Have a Dream" Speech (August 28, 1963), in Clayborne Carson and Kris Shepard, eds., *A Call to Conscience: The Landmark Speeches of Dr. Martin Luther King Jr.* (New York: Grand Central Publishing, 2001).

93. Langston Hughes, "Let America Be America Again," in Arnold Rampersad, ed., *The Collected Poems of Langston Hughes* (New York: Vintage, 1995), 189.

94. Aziz Rana, "Constitutionalism and the Foundations of the Security State," *California Law Review* 103, no. 2 (2015).

95. Rana, "Constitutionalism"; Aziz Rana, "Race and the American Creed: Recovering Black Radicalism," n+1 (magazine) 24 (2016), accessed October

22, 2018, https://nplusonemag.com/issue-24/politics/race-and-the-american
-creed/.

96. See generally John Higham, "Changing Paradigms: The Collapse of Consensus History," *Journal of American History* 76, no. 2 (1989): 460–466; Richard Hofstadter, *The American Political Tradition and the Men Who Made It*, 25th anniversary ed. (New York: Vintage, 1973), xxxii; Aziz Rana, review of *The Many American Constitutions: America's Forgotten Constitutions*, by Robert L. Tsai, *Texas Law Review* 93 (2015): 1170–1171; Eric Foner, introduction to *Social Darwinism in American Thought*, by Richard Hofstadter (Boston: Beacon Press, 1992), xxi.

97. Richard Hofstadter, *The American Political Tradition and the Men Who Made It* (New York: Knopf, 1948), xxxvii.

98. Kohn, *American Nationalism*, 20.

99. "Rotunda FAQs," Founding Documents, National Archives Museum, accessed November 10, 2018, https://museum.archives.gov/founding-docu ments.

100. "The National Archives Museum," TripAdvisor, accessed November 10, 2018, https://www.tripadvisor.com/Attraction_Review-g28970-d104857 -Reviews-The_National_Archives_Museum-Washington_DC_District_of _Columbia.html.

101. "About the Constitution Center," Constitution Center, accessed November 10, 2018, http://constitutioncenter.org/about; "Signers Hall," National Constitution Center, accessed November 10, 2018, https://constitu tioncenter.org/experience/exhibitions/main-exhibition/signers-hall.

102. In the latest edition of *Constitutional Faith*, Sanford Levinson discusses why he could not sign the Constitution. Sanford Levinson, "Afterword," *Constitutional Faith*, rev. ed. (Princeton, NJ: Princeton University Press, 2011), 245.

103. Ronald Reagan, "Labor Day Speech," Liberty State Park, Jersey City, NJ, September 1, 1980, Reagan Library, https://reaganlibrary.archives.gov /archives/reference/9.1.80.html.

104. William Jefferson Clinton, "Remarks by the President in Address to the Liz Sutherland Carpenter Distinguished Lectureship in the Humanities and Sciences," Austin, Texas, October 16, 1995, National Archives and Records Administration, https://clintonwhitehouse1.archives.gov/White_House/EOP /OP/html/ut.html.

105. Constitution Day and Citizenship Day, US Code 36 (2014) § 106 et seq.

106. 150 Cong. Rec. 18, 677 (September 20, 2004).

107. See, e.g., David Catrow, *We the Kids: The Preamble to the Constitution of the United States* (New York: Puffin Books, 2005); Jean Fritz, *Shh! We're Writing the Constitution* (New York: Puffin Books, 1997); Lynne Cheney, *We the People: The Story of Our Constitution* (New York: Simon & Schuster, 2012).

108. Baby Professor, *C Is for Constitution* (Washington, DC: US Government Books for Kids, 2017).

109. See Pledge of Allegiance to the Flag, 4 U.S.C. § 4 (2012). The Supreme Court has described the Pledge of Allegiance as an expression of "the ideals that our flag symbolizes," and "its recitation is a patriotic exercise designed to foster national unity and pride in those principles." Elk Grove Unified School District v. Newdow, 541 U.S. 1, 6 (2004).

110. See Rachel Hutchins-Viroux, *Teaching the Nation: Renegotiation of National Identity in United States History Books through the Prism of the Theories of Anthony Smith, in Nationalism in the English-Speaking World* (Newcastle, UK: Cambridge Scholars, 2009), 16; Bruce VanSledright, "Narratives of Nation-State, Historical Knowledge, and School Education," *Review of Research in Education* 32 (2008): 109, 113–117.

111. Florida Statutes § 1003.42(2)(f).

112. Remarks of Senator Lamar Alexander on the American History and Civics Education Act of 2003, June 19, 2003, https://www.alexander.senate .gov/public/index.cfm/speechesfloorstatements?ID=7A6E583F-8955-4A0C -AB10-0FCABF773185.

113. Eric T. Kasper and Quentin D. Vieregge, *The United States Constitution in Film: Part of Our National Culture* (Lanham, MD: Lexington Books, 2018).

114. Lucas Reilly, "When Superman Fought Xenophobia in a 1949 Comic," June 20, 2018, http://mentalfloss.com/article/89914/whats-story-behind -superman-comic.

115. "The Omega Glory," *Star Trek*, Season 2, Episode 23, original air date March 1, 1968, clip available at https://www.constitutionfacts.com/founders -library/founding-documents-in-pop-culture/.

116. "I'm Just a Bill," *Schoolhouse Rock*, YouTube, https://www.youtube .com/watch?v=FFroMQlKiag.

117. "The Preamble," *Schoolhouse Rock*, YouTube, https://www.youtube .com/watch?v=yHp7sMqPLog.

118. Billig, *Banal Nationalism*, 5.

119. Billig, 55.

120. See, e.g., Michael Dorf, "The Undead Constitution," *Harvard Law Review* 125 (2012): 2011, 2016 (reviewing Jack M. Balkin, *Living Originalism* [2011], and David A. Strauss, *The Living Constitution* [2010]).

121. Billig, *Banal Nationalism*, 8.

122. Lincoln, Address to the Young Men's Lyceum of Springfield, 13.

123. US Commission on Immigration Reform, *Report to Congress 1997: Becoming an American: Immigration and Immigrant Policy* (Washington, DC: Government Printing Office, 1997), 25.

124. Mary Douglas, *Purity and Danger: An Analysis of the Concepts of Pollution and Taboo* (London: Routledge, 1966), ch. 1.

125. See, e.g., Kevin Drum, "Recycled: The Tea Party Is a Revolutionary Force. Just not in the Way You've Been Led to Believe," *Mother Jones*, September 1, 2010.

126. See, e.g., Joseph Farah, "Keynote Address to National Tea Party Convention," Nashville, Tennessee, February 5, 2010), C-SPAN, http://www .c-spanvideo.org/program/291955-1; Judson Phillips, "The Eligibility Issue," Tea Party Nation, last modified February 20, 2011, http://www.teapartynation .com/forum/topics/the-eligibility-issue (requires email address and free membership to view content).

127. See, e.g., Alex Altman, "Racism Rift Highlights Dilemma: Who Speaks for the Tea Party?," *Time*, posted July 22, 2010, http://www.time.com/time /politics/article/0,8599,2005371,00.html.

128. Devin Burghart and Leonard Zeskind, *Tea Party Nationalism: A Critical Examination of the Tea Party Movement and the Size, Scope, and Focus of Its National Factions Tea Party Nationalism* (Kansas City, MO: Institute for Research and Education on Human Rights, 2010), 57–67.

129. Belief that Obama is foreign is widespread among conservatives. See, e.g., Steven G. Calabresi, "The Teleprompter Presidency? Justice DeLayed or Denied?," *Politico*, August 17, 2010, http://www.politico.com/arena/perm /Steven_G__Calabresi_A5D4F886-1279-48D4-96B9-D176A986A416.html (asserting that "at some level [Obama] does not really know America very well nor does he thoroughly identify with it"); Dinesh D'Souza, *The Roots of Obama's Rage* (Washington, DC: Regnery Publishing, 2010), 1–15 (claiming that Obama is attempting to carry out the socialist, anticolonial dreams of his Kenyan father).

130. Amy Chua and Jed Rubenfeld, "The Threat of Tribalism," *Atlantic*, October 2018, https://www.theatlantic.com/magazine/archive/2018/10/the -threat-of-tribalism/568342.

131. See, e.g., Joint Select Committee on the Condition of Affairs in the Late Insurrectionary States, Report to Inquire into the Condition of Affairs in the Late Insurrectionary States, 42nd Cong., February 19, 1872, 7, 39, 48, 75, http:// onlinebooks.library.upenn.edu/webbin/metabook?id=insurrection1872. See also Joint Select Committee Report, vol. 2, North Carolina, 422.

132. See Kim E. Nielsen, *Un-American Womanhood: Antiradicalism, Antifeminism, and the First Red Scare* (Columbus: Ohio State University Press, 2001); Susan Goodier, *No Votes for Women: The New York State Anti-Suffrage Movement* (Champaign: University of Illinois Press, 2013), 130.

133. Mary Anne Franks, introduction, *The Cult of the Constitution* (Palo Alto, CA: Stanford University Press, 2019).

134. Writing in 1882, Ernest Renan explained: "A nation is therefore a great solidarity constituted by the feeling of sacrifices made and those that one is still disposed to make." Renan, "*Qu'est-ce que c'est une nation?*," in Geoff Eley and Ronald Grigor Suny, eds., *Becoming National: A Reader* (Oxford:

Oxford University Press, 1996), 42, 53; see also Benedict Anderson, *Imagined Communities: Reflections in the Origin and Spread of Nationalism*, rev. ed. (New York: Verso, 2006), 145 ("Nations inspire love, and often profoundly self-sacrificing love"). For a general discussion of the role of self-sacrifice in fostering patriotism and nationalism in ancient and modern societies, see Anthony D. Smith, *Chosen Peoples: Sacred Sources of National Identity* (London: Oxford University Press, 2004), 218–253.

135. Lou Michel and Dan Herbeck, *American Terrorist: Timothy McVeigh and the Oklahoma City Bombing* (New York: Regan Books, 2001), 231–233.

Chapter 1. The White Constitution

1. Ku Klux Klan, "Prescript of the Order" (1868), in *American History Magazine* 5, no. 1 (January 1900): 3, 5 (hereinafter "Prescript of the Order"); William Joseph Simmons, *The Klan Unmasked* (Atlanta, GA: Wm. E. Thompson Publishing, 1923), 46.

2. "Prescript of the Order," 3, 5.

3. Simmons, *The Klan Unmasked*, 46.

4. See, e.g., "Here Are Twenty Reasons WHY You Should, If Qualified, Join, Aid and Support the White Knights of the Ku Klux Klan of Mississippi," *Activities of the Ku Klux Klan in the U.S.A.*, House Un-American Activities Committee, Part 3, 89th Cong., 2nd Sess., January 13, 1966, 2747, exhibit no. 1 (testimony of Thomas A. Gunter).

5. "Frequently Asked Questions," The Knight's Party, accessed November 18, 2018, https://kkk.bz/frequently-asked-questions/.

6. For a discussion of the second Klan using social movement theory, see Rory McVeigh, *The Rise of the Ku Klux Klan: Right-Wing Movements and National Politics* (Minneapolis: University of Minnesota Press, 2009); for a discussion of the religious orientation of the Klan, see Kelly J. Baker, *Gospel According to the Klan: The KKK's Appeal to Protestant America, 1915–1930* (Lawrence: University Press of Kansas, 2011); for a discussion of the Klan in South Carolina, see Jerry L. West, *The Reconstruction Ku Klux Klan in York County, South Carolina, 1865–1877* (Jefferson, NC: McFarland, 2002); for a discussion of the Klan in Alabama, see Glenn Feldman, *Politics, Society, and the Klan in Alabama, 1915–1949* (Tuscaloosa: University of Alabama Press, 1999); for a discussion of the current Klan, see Patsy Sims, *The Klan* (Lexington: University Press of Kentucky, 1996); for a discussion of women in the Klan, see Kathleen M. Blee, *Women of the Klan: Racism and Gender in the 1920s* (Berkeley: University of California Press, 1991); for a discussion of the role of movies in the Klan, see Tom Rice, *White Robes, Silver Screens: Movies and the Making of the Ku Klux Klan* (Bloomington: Indiana University Press, 2015).

7. Allen W. Trelease, *White Terror: The Ku Klux Klan Conspiracy and Southern Reconstruction* (Baton Rouge: Louisiana State University Press, 1971), 17.

8. Trelease, *White Terror*, 17.

9. Joint Select Committee on the Condition of Affairs in the Late Insurrectionary States, Report to Inquire into the Condition of Affairs in the Late Insurrectionary States, 42nd Cong., February 19, 1872, 39, 48, 75, http://onlinebooks.library.upenn.edu/webbin/metabook?id=insurrection1872 (hereinafter Joint Select Committee Report, various volumes).

10. Richard M. Brown, *Strain of Violence* (Oxford: Oxford University Press, 1975), 95-96, 132; Lisa Cardyn, "Sexualized Racism/Gendered Violence," *University of Michigan Law Review* 100 (2001-2002): 794.

11. See Joshua Rothman, "When Bigotry Paraded through the Streets," *Atlantic*, December 4, 2016, https://www.theatlantic.com/politics/archive/2016/12/second-klan/509468/.

12. Joint Select Committee Report, North Carolina, 422.

13. "Americans, Take Heed! Scum o' the Melting Pot," reprinted in Ku Klux Klan: Hearings Before the Committee on Rules, 67th Cong. 126 (1921).

14. John Powell, "The Klan Un-Klandestine," *Nation*, September 29, 1951, 255.

15. See James O. Eastland, "We've Reached Era of Judicial Tyranny: An Address before the State-Wide Convention of the Association of Citizen's Councils of Jackson, Mississippi," December 1, 1955, Greenwood, Mississippi, https://egrove.olemiss.edu/citizens_pamph/84/.

16. John Drabble, "From White Supremacy to White Power: The FBI, Cointel Pro-White Hate, and the Nazification of the Ku Klux Klan in the 1970s," *American Studies* 48, no. 3 (2007), 50.

17. As John Higham has written, Americans "had always proclaimed orderly self-government as the chief glory of Anglo-Saxons—an inherited capacity so unique that the future of human freedom surely rested in their hands." John Higham, *Strangers in the Land: Patterns of American Nativism 1860-1925*, 2nd ed. (New Brunswick, NJ: Rutgers University Press, 1977), 137; Rogers M. Smith, *Civic Ideals* (New Haven, CT: Yale University Press, 1997), 86.

18. Dred Scott v. Sandford, 60 U.S. 393, 403 (1857).

19. The history of the Klan illustrates group threat theory, which posits that members of culturally and politically dominant groups develop hostility to subordinate groups in response to perceived threats posed to the dominant group's interests. Group threat theory has its origin in Herbert G. Blumer, "Race Prejudice as a Sense of Group Position," *Pacific Sociological Review* 1, no. 1 (Spring 1958): 3, and has been developed by Lawrence Bobo and others. For a review of the literature on group threat theory, see Lincoln Quillian, "Prejudice as a Response to Perceived Group Threat: Population Composition and Anti-

Immigrant and Racial Prejudice in Europe," *American Sociological Review* 60, no. 4 (August 1995): 586.

20. Empirical work by Elizabeth Theiss-Morse has shown that Americans who consider themselves prototypical Americans are more likely to identify their characteristics and values to be national values and perceive criticisms of those values as attacks on the nation. See Elizabeth Theiss-Morse, *Who Counts as an American?* (Cambridge: Cambridge University Press, 2009), 73, 77, 92–93.

21. See Hans Kohn, *American Nationalism: An Interpretive Essay* (New York: Collier Books, 1961), 8; Thomas C. Grey, "The Constitution as Scripture," *Stanford Law Review* 37, no. 1 (November 1984): 3; see generally Sanford Levinson, *Constitutional Faith*, rev. ed. (Princeton, NJ: Princeton University Press, 2011), 11.

22. A discussion of the scale of changes brought about by the war and the history of scholarly attempts to describe them can be found in Eric Foner, *Reconstruction: America's Unfinished Revolution, 1863–1877* (New York: HarperCollins, 1988), xvii–xxv.

23. U.S. Const. Amend. XIII, XIV, XV; E. Nathaniel Gates, "Bondage, Freedom and the Constitution: The New Slavery Scholarship and Its Impact on Law and Legal Historiography," *Cardozo Law Review* 17 (1996): 2116–2117; Robert J. Kaczorowski, "Emancipation and the New Conception of Freedom: Comment on Nieman: Reflections on "From Slaves to Citizens," *Cardozo Law Review* 17 (1996): 2141, 2144.

24. Elections and Votes under the Reconstruction Acts, Act of March 11, 1868, Pub. L. No. 25, U.S. Statutes at Large 15 (1868): 41; 39th Cong., Sess. II, at 428, An Act to Provide for the More Efficient Government of the Rebel States, ch. 153, March 2, 1867, https://www.loc.gov/law/help/statutes-at-large/39th-congress/session-2/c39s2ch153.pdf; An Act Making Appropriations for the Departments of State and Justice and for the Judiciary and or the Departments of Commerce and Labor, for the Fiscal Year Ending June 30, 1926, and for Other Purposes, Pub. L. No. 502, U.S. Statutes at Large 43 (1925): 1023–1024. Act of 40th Cong., Sess. I, at 2, An Act Supplementary to an Act Entitled "An Act to Provide for the More Efficient Government of the Rebel States," Passed March 2, 1867, and to Facilitate Restoration, ch. 6, March 23, 1867, https://www.loc.gov/law/help/statutes-at-large/40th-congress/session-1/c40s1ch6.pdf; Act of 40th Cong., Sess. I, at 14, An Act Supplementary to an Act Entitled "An Act to Provide for the More Efficient Government of the Rebel States," Passed March 2, 1867, and the Act Supplementary Thereto, Passed on the Twenty-Third Day of March, 1867, ch. 30, July. 19, 1867, https://www.loc.gov/law/help/statutes-at-large/40th-congress/session-1/c40s1ch30.pdf. For a discussion of the Black Codes, see Paul Finkelman, "Let Justice Be Done, though the Heavens May Fall: The Law of Freedom," *Chicago-Kent Law Review* 70, no. 2

(1994): 325; Gary Stewart, "Black Codes and Broken Windows: The Legacy of Racial Hegemony in Anti-Gang Civil Injunctions," *Yale Law Journal* 107, no. 7 (May 1998): 2249.

25. 40th Cong., Sess. I, at 28, A Resolution for the Relief of the Destitute in the Southern and Southwestern States, March 30, 1867, http://legisworks .org/sal/15/stats/STATUTE-15-Pg28c.pdf; see Foner, *Reconstruction*, 32; Otis A. Singletary, "The African American Militia During Radical Reconstruction," in Bruce A. Glasrud, ed., *Brothers to the Buffalo Soldiers: Perspectives on the African American Militia and Volunteers 1865–1917*(Columbia: University of Missouri Press, 2011), 19–33.

26. 39th Cong., Sess. I, at 174, An Act to Continue in Force and to Amend "An Act to Establish a Bureau for the Relief of Freedmen and Refugees" and for Other Purposes, ch. 200, July 16, 1866.

27. Foner, *Reconstruction*, 324; Eric Foner, "Rooted in Reconstruction: The First Wave of Black Congressmen," *Nation*, October 15, 2008, https://www .thenation.com/article/rooted-reconstruction-first-wave-black-congressmen/.

28. Statement of General Garnett Andrews, "Alarm among the Whites," in Walter L. Fleming, ed., *Documentary History of Reconstruction: Political, Military, Social, Religious, Educational & Industrial 1865 to the Present Time,* vol. 2 (Cleveland, OH: Arthur H. Clark, 1907), 271.

29. Andrews, "Alarm among the Whites," 338, 339, 351, 358.

30. Trelease, *White Terror*, 3–4. As the founders of the group later explained, "Ku Klux" came from the Greek word *kuklos*, meaning circle or band, and "Klan" added an alliterative touch.

31. Trelease, 4, 10–11.

32. Foner, *Reconstruction*, 425. Although these groups were not all called the Ku Klux Klan, they have long been grouped together as part of the "Klan" movement because of their common mission and methods. See Andrews, "Alarm among the Whites," 327.

33. See "General Forrest's Explanations," in Fleming, *Documentary History of Reconstruction*, 342; "Influence in the Elections," in Fleming, 370; Trelease, *White Terror*, xlvii.

34. Trelease, xlvii, 28, 29, 30, 90, 102, 116, 175.

35. See "The Ku-Klux Laws," *New National Era*, August 8, 1872, 1; "Startling Facts," *Evening Express*, August 22, 1872, 1; for another contemporaneous assessment, see Job E. Stevenson, "Let Us Protect the People in the Enjoyment of Life, Liberty, and Property, and Impartial Suffrage in Peace," Speech, House of Representatives, Washington, DC, April 4, 1871 (n.p.: F. & J. Rives & Geo. A. Bailey, 1871), 32 (estimating 15,000 victims of Klan violence).

36. John Edward Bruce, *The Blood Red Record: A Review of the Horrible Lynchings and Burning of Negroes by Civilized White Men in the United States, As Taken from the Records* (Albany, NY: Argus, 1901), 20.

37. See Ashraf H. A. Rushdy, "The Race of Lynching,"in *American Lynching* (New Haven, CT: Yale University Press, 2012), 61.

38. Trelease, *White Terror*, 399–418.

39. Ku Klux Klan Act of 1871, Pub. L. 42–22, 17 Stat. 13 (April 20, 1871).

40. Trelease, *White Terror*, 399–418.

41. Trelease, 418. In 1875 the Supreme Court ruled that the act was unconstitutional in criminalizing private acts of violence committed because of the victim's race, where there was no evidence that such violence was specifically directed at restricting voting rights. United States v. Harris, 106 U.S. 629, 643–644 (1883).

42. See "Rifle Clubs and Artillery Companies," in Fleming, *Documentary History of Reconstruction*, 407–409.

43. Foner, *Reconstruction*, 558.

44. Foner, 559–562, 419–420.

45. See generally C. Vann Woodward, *Reunion and Reaction: The Compromise of 1877 and the End of Reconstruction* (New York: Cambridge University Press, 1966); see also Foner, 564–601.

46. See James A. Morone, *The Democratic Wish: Popular Participation and the Limit of American Government* (New Haven, CT: Yale University Press, 1998), 189; J. Morgan Kousser, *The Shaping of Southern Politics: Suffrage Restriction and the Establishment of the One-Party South, 1880–1910* (New Haven, CT: Yale University Press, 1974); Smith, *Civic Ideals*, 383.

47. Trelease, *White Terror*, 420.

48. "Organization and Principles of the Ku Klux Klan," in Fleming, *Documentary History of Reconstruction*, 347, 348–349.

49. 5 Joint Select Committee Report, South Carolina, at 1686 (reprinting Klan Constitution for South Carolina).

50. The oath of the Invisible Empire required members to swear: "I promise and swear that I will uphold and defend the Constitution of the United States as it was handed down by our forefathers in its original purity." 2 Joint Select Committee Report, North Carolina, 422; see also "The '76 Association," in Fleming, *Documentary History of Reconstruction*, 355. The Knights of the White Camelia, for instance, declared its goal to be the "preservation of those grand principles" of "the Government of the United States, as originally adopted" and required members to declare support for "the maintenance of the Laws and Constitution as established by the Patriots of 1776." *The Constitution and the Ritual of the Knights of the White Camelia*, edited by Walter Fleming, 1868, 8, 21 (hereinafter *Constitution of the White Camelia*).

51. *Constitution of the White Camelia*, 21, 22.

52. See, e.g., *Oath of the Invisible Empire*, in 2 Joint Select Committee Report, North Carolina, 422.

53. "Prescript of the Order," 68; *Oath of the Invisible Empire*, 422. Another

organization in the Klan orbit, the '76 Association, a Louisiana group that sought to enforce white supremacy through violence and intimidation, declared its dedication to the old Constitution, stating that it was established "to uphold the principles of the United States Constitution *as established and interpreted by its framers*" (my emphasis). "The '76 Association,*"* in Fleming, *Documentary History of Reconstruction*, 355.

54. 2 Joint Select Committee Report, North Carolina, 384.

55. Stevenson, "Let Us Protect the People in the Enjoyment of Life, Liberty, and Property."

56. "Special Correspondence, Cincinnati Commercial (August. 28, 1868)," in Testimony Taken by the Joint Select Committee to Inquire into the Condition of Affairs in the Late Insurrectionary States: Miscellaneous and Florida 13 (1871): 32, 33.

57. "Special Correspondence," 33. Although Forrest later claimed that certain aspects of the interview misrepresented his views, he did not challenge the portion quoted here. "Special Correspondence," 35.

58. In doing so, the Klan engaged in what has recently been described as "popular originalism"—the use of constitutional argument by political movements that claim to be based on the original meaning of the Constitution. See generally Rebecca E. Zietlow, "Popular Originalism? The Tea Party Movement and Constitutional Theory," *Florida Law Review* 64, no. 2 (2012): 483.

59. *Constitution of the White Camelia*, 26.

60. *Constitution of the White Camelia*, 26; see also 2 Joint Select Committee Report, North Carolina, 422.

61. *Constitution of the White Camelia*, 26.

62. See "Charge to Initiates, the Knights of the White Camelia," in Fleming, *Documentary History of Reconstruction*, 349, 351.

63. "Charge to Initiates," 352.

64. See Proceedings in the Ku Klux Trials in Columbia, SC, United States Circuit Court, November Term 1871 (1872), 431–433; see also Trelease, *White Terror*, 399–415; Kermit L. Hall, "Political Power and Constitutional Legitimacy: The South Carolina Ku Klux Klan Trials, 1871–1872," *Emory Law Journal* 33 (1984): 921, 924.

65. Proceedings in the Ku Klux Trials, 431–433 (statement of US District Attorney Daniel T. Corbin).

66. See Trelease, *White Terror*, xlvi; "Constitution of the Union League of America,*"* in Fleming, *Documentary History of Reconstruction*, 7.

67. Trelease, xlvi.

68. "Constitution of the National Council of the Union League of American, Art. II," in Fleming, *Documentary History of Reconstruction*, 6.

69. See 4 Joint Select Committee Report, South Carolina, 951. By 1867

most Black voters belonged to the league and associated groups, which sought to carry out its commitment to racial equality by promoting Black suffrage and constructing Black schools and churches. Foner, *Reconstruction*, 283, 285.

70. Foner, 285.

71. See, e.g., US Const., Art. I, § 2 (the Three-Fifths Clause); Art. I, § 9 (the Slave Trade Clause);and Art. IV, § 2 (the Fugitive Slave Clause); see generally George William Van Cleve, *A Slaveholders' Union: Slavery, Politics, and the Constitution in the Early American Republic* (Chicago: University of Chicago Press, 2010); Paul Finkelman, *Slavery and the Founders*, 2nd ed. (New York: Routledge, 2001); "The Centrality of Slavery in American Legal Development," in Paul Finkelman, ed., *Slavery and the Law* (Madison, WI: Madison House, 1997), 3.

72. Higham, *Strangers in the Land*, 137; see also Smith, *Civic Ideals*, 86.

73. Thomas Jefferson, *A Summary View of the Rights of British America* (Williamsburg, VA: Clementina Rind, 1774).

74. John Jay, *Federalist*, no. 2, in Clinton Rossiter, ed., *The Federalist Papers* (New York: New American Library, 1961), 38.

75. See Sanford Levinson, "What One Can Learn from Foreign-Language Translations of the US Constitution," *Constitutional Comment* 31 (2016): 64.

76. An Act to Establish an Uniform Rule of Naturalization; and to Repeal the Act Heretofore Passed on That Subject, 1 Stat. 414 (1795). The 1795 act replaced a 1790 naturalization law that similarly limited naturalization to "free white person[s]" who swore an oath to "support the Constitution of the United States." 1st Cong., Sess. II, at 108, An Act to Establish an Uniform Rule of Naturalization, ch. 3 § 1 (March 26, 1790). The dual requirements for naturalized citizenship established by Congress in 1795—commitment to constitutional principles and membership in the white race—persisted, with relatively few changes, until 1952, when Congress finally repealed any racial criteria for citizenship. Immigration and Nationality Act, Pub. L. No. 82-414, 66 Stat. 163 (1952).

77. See Dred Scott v. Sandford, 60 U.S. 393, 420 (1857).

78. Annals of Congress, 16th Cong., Sess. 2, 1134 (speech by Charles Pinckney).

79. Daniel A. Farber, "A Fatal Loss of Balance: Dred Scott Revisited," *Pepperdine Law Review* 39 (2011): 13, 28.

80. James H. Kettner, *The Development of American Citizenship, 1608–1870* (Chapel Hill: University of North Carolina Press, 1978), 251–253.

81. Mark A. Graber, "Desperately Ducking Slavery: Dred Scott and Contemporary Constitutional Theory," *Constitutional Commentary* 14 (1997): 296.

82. See, e.g., *South Carolina, Declaration of the Immediate Causes which Induce and Justify the Secession of South Carolina from the Federal Union* (Charleston, SC:

Evans & Cogswell, 1860), 10, http://www.atlantahistorycenter.com/assets/documents/SCarolina-Secession-p1-13.pdf (hereinafter *South Carolina Declaration*); Thomas R. R. Cobb, "Secessionist Speech" (November 12, 1860), in William W. Freehling and Craig M. Simpson, eds., *Secession Debated: Georgia's Showdown* (New York: Oxford University Press, 1992), 8.

83. *Dred Scott*, 60 U.S. at 403.

84. *Dred Scott*, 60 U.S. at 403, 409, 407, 426–427.

85. Graber, "Desperately Ducking Slavery," 280–285.

86. Stephen Douglas, "Speech at First Joint Debate at Ottawa, Illinois" (August 21, 1858), in John G. Nicolay and John Hay, eds., *Complete Works of Abraham Lincoln*, vol. 3 (Gettysburg, PA: Francis D. Tandy, 1894), 237, 255–256; Stephen A. Douglas, "Speech at Jonesboro, Illinois" (September 15, 1858), in Nicolay and Hay, *Complete Works of Abraham Lincoln*, vol. 4, 1, 22–23.

87. Abraham Lincoln, "Speech at Seventh and Last Debate with Stephen Douglas at Alton, Illinois" (October 15, 1858), in Roy P. Basler, ed., *The Collected Works of Abraham Lincoln*, vol. 3 (New Brunswick, NJ: Rutgers University Press, 1953), 283, 289–299; Abraham Lincoln, "Speech, Fourth Debate with Stephen A. Douglas at Charleston, Illinois," in Basler, *Collected Works of Abraham Lincoln*, 145, 179; Abraham Lincoln, "Speech of Abraham Lincoln at Charleston, Illinois" (September 18, 1858), in Edwin E. Sparks, ed., *Lincoln Series, Vol. 1: The Lincoln-Douglas Debates of 1858* (Springfield: Trustees of the Illinois State Historical Library, 1908), 267, 303.

88. "Declaration of the Causes of Secession of Georgia (January 29, 1861)," Avalon Project at Yale Law School, http://avalon.law.yale.edu/19th_century/csa_geosec.asp (hereinafter "Georgia Declaration"); see Alfred L. Brophy, "Slavery, Property, and Constitutionalism in the Secession Debates," in *University, Court, and Slave: Pro-Slavery Thought in Southern Colleges and Courts and the Coming of Civil War* (New York: Oxford University Press, 2016); Order of the Convention, "A Declaration of the Immediate Causes which Induce and Justify the Secession of the State of Mississippi from the Federal Union" (January 9, 1861), in *Journal of the State Convention* (Jackson, MS: E. Barksdale, 1861), 86–88 (hereinafter "Mississippi Declaration").

89. Order of the Convention, "A Declaration of the Immediate Causes."

90. G. Edward White, "Recovering the Legal History of the Confederacy," *Washington and Lee Law Review* 68, no. 2 (2011): 483.

91. "Georgia Declaration"; "South Carolina Declaration"; "Ordinance of Secession, Adopted by the Alabama Constitutional Convention of 1861" (January 8, 1861), Alabama Department of Archives and History, http://digital.archives.alabama.gov/cdm/ref/collection/voices/id/3764; "Missouri Ordinance of Secession" (October 31, 1861), Constitution Society, http://www.constitution.org/csa/ordinances_secession.htm#Missouri.

92. "A Declaration of the Causes which Impel the State of Texas to Secede

from the Federal Union" (February 2, 1861), in E. W. Winkler, ed., *Journal of the Secession Convention of Texas* (Austin: Texas Library and Historical Commission, 1912), 61–66 (hereinafter "Texas Declaration").

93. "South Carolina Declaration."

94. "Texas Declaration."

95. Cobb, "Secessionist Speech," 8; Lucian Lamar Knight, *A Standard History of Georgia and Georgians* (Chicago: Lewis Publishing, 1917), 3.

96. *Constitution of the White Camelia*, 26–27.

97. *The Joint Select Committee to Inquire into the Condition of Affairs the Late Insurrectionary States*, 42 Cong. (1871) (testimony of David Schenck, Esq.), 384.

98. Gerhard Peters and John T. Woolley, "Democratic Party Platform," July 4, 1868, American Presidency Project, https://www.presidency.ucsb.edu/documents/1868-democratic-party-platform.

99. "'Our Ticket, Our Motto: This Is a White Man's Country; Let White Men Rule.' Campaign Badge Supporting Horatio Seymour and Francis Blair, Democratic Candidates for president and vice president of the United States, 1868," Schomburg Center for Research in Black Culture, Photographs and Prints Division, New York Public Library Digital Collections, New York Public Library, December 12, 2018, http://digitalcollections.nypl.org/items/62a9d0e6–4fc9-dbce-e040-e00a18064a66.

100. "Seymour and Blair Democratic Candidate Coin," Coinworld, August 2016, http://www.coinworld.com/content/dam/cw/news/2016/August/08 0816/political-medals-record-presidential-also-rans-alexander/seymour-blair-merged.jpg.

101. A. E. Blackmar and H. Wehrmann, *The White Man's Banner . . . Seymour and Blair's Campaign Song* (New Orleans: A. E. Blackmar, 1868). Photograph: https://www.loc.gov/item/2008661704/.

102. *For Seymour, Blair and Liberty* (Chicago: Lyon & Healy, 1868) Photograph: https://www.loc.gov/item/2008661702/.

103. Peters and Woolley, "Democratic Party Platform."

104. Stewart Mitchell, *Horatio Seymour of New York* (Cambridge, MA: Harvard University Press, 1938), 446.

105. David M. Chalmers, *Hooded Americanism: The History of the Ku Klux Klan* (New York: Quadrangle Books, 1965), 424.

106. 2 Joint Select Committee Report, North Carolina, 414.

107. 3 Joint Select Committee Report, South Carolina, 23.

108. 5 Joint Select Committee Report, 1700 (testimony of Charles W. Foster).

109. 5 Joint Select Committee Report, 1701.

110. 5 Joint Select Committee Report, 1803 (testimony of Osmond Gunthorp).

111. See, e.g., 1 Joint Select Committee Report, 7, 39, 48, 75.

112. 1 Joint Select Committee Report, 23.

113. 2 Joint Select Committee Report, North Carolina, 119 (testimony of James M. Justice).

114. 2 Joint Select Committee Report, 121.

115. See Trelease, *White Terror*, 18.

116. "Prescript of the Order," 22. Other Klan groups employed similar rhetoric. The Knights of the White Camelia, for example, explained that it would "resort to no forcible means, except for purposes of legitimate and necessary defense." "Constitution and Ritual of the Knights of the White Camellia," in Scott J. Hammond and Kevin R. Hardwick, eds., *Classics of American Political and Constitutional Thought: Origins through the Civil War*, vol. 1 (Indianapolis, IN: Hackett, 2007), 1177, 1179.

117. 4 Joint Select Committee Report, South Carolina, 1003.

118. Walter L. Fleming, "A Scalawag's Opinion of the Causes, Ku Klux Report Alabama Testimony," 1871, in *Documentary History of Reconstruction*, 339. The Klan was far from alone in seeing federal occupation and Reconstruction-era governments as illegal and invalid. Marek D. Steedman, "Resistance, Rebirth, and Redemption: The Rhetoric of White Supremacy in Post–Civil War Louisiana," *Historical Reflections* 35, no. 1 (March 2009): 97, 102. Many Southerners believed that laws supporting racial equality were not merely wrong but were invalid, having been enacted through illegitimate means and enforced through illegitimate governments. The *New Orleans Times* declared in July 1868 that laws enacted for the purpose of racial equality "will be disregarded and declared null and void as soon as the inalienable rights of the people are again recognized." Trelease, *White Terror*, xxxvii–xxxviii (quoting *New Orleans Times*, July 28, 1868).

119. "Constitution and Ritual of the Knights of the White Camellia," 1179.

120. "Constitution and Ritual of the Knights of the White Camellia," 800.

121. William Peirce Randel, *The Ku Klux Klan: A Century of Infamy* (Philadelphia: Chilton Books, 1969), 15.

122. David Cunningham, *Klansville, U.S.A.: The Rise and Fall of the Civil Rights–Era Ku Klux Klan* (New York: Oxford University Press, 2012), 21–22.

123. Walter L. Fleming, "Introduction," in John C. Lester and Daniel Love Wilson, *Ku Klux Klan: Its Origin, Growth, and Disbandment* (New York: Neale, 1905), 16–17.

124. Lester and Wilson, *Ku Klux Klan*, 78, 80, 155.

125. In 1896, writing in the *American Historical Magazine*, R. L. McDonald described the Klan as a patriotic organization that sought "to protect life and property and to restore order." R. L. McDonald, "The Reconstruction Period in Tennessee," *The American Historical Magazine* (1896): 307, 321. McDonald asserted that the Klan succeeded in its goals and "proved of vast usefulness, restoring order, preventing crime, and filling the negroes with wholesome awe."

McDonald, "The Reconstruction Period in Tennessee," 322. For additional examples of the early depictions of the Klan in heroic terms, see Joseph G. de Roulhac Hamilton, *Reconstruction in North Carolina* (New York: Columbia University Press, 1914), 452-454; see generally Otto H. Olsen, "The Ku Klux Klan: A Study in Reconstruction Politics and Propaganda," *North Carolina Historical Review* 39, no. 3 (July 1962): 340.

126. For a discussion of the role of Dixon's novels in the creating the mythology of the Klan, see Trelease, *White Terror*, 421; Chalmers, *Hooded Americanism*, 23-25.

127. Thomas Dixon Jr., "The Story of the Ku Klux Klan," in *The Clansman: An American Drama* (New York: American News, 1905), 40, 42.

128. Thomas Dixon Jr., *The Leopard's Spots* (New York: Doubleday, Page & Co., 1902), 439.

129. Dixon, *The Clansman*, 43.

130. John Hope Franklin, "Birth of a Nation: Propaganda as History," *Massachusetts Review* 20, no. 3 (Fall 1979): 417, 420.

131. Franklin, "Birth of a Nation," 423, 432.

132. *The Birth of a Nation*, directed by D. W. Griffith (New York: Kino Lorber, 1915), on YouTube, https://www.youtube.com/watch?v=I3kmVgQHIEY, at 2:05:23.

133. Melvyn Stokes, *D. W. Griffith's* The Birth of a Nation: *A History of the Most Controversial Picture of All Time* (New York: Oxford University Press, 2008), 3.

134. Mark E. Benbow, "Birth of a Quotation: Woodrow Wilson and 'Like Writing History with Lightning,'" *Journal of the Gilded Age and Progressive Era* 9, no. 4 (October 2010): 510, 509-533.

135. Franklin, "Birth of a Nation," 426.

136. See McVeigh, *The Rise of the Ku Klux Klan*, 19.

137. Knights of the Ku Klux Klan, *Constitution and Laws of the Knights of the Ku Klux Klan* (Atlanta, GA: Knights of the Ku Klux Clan, 1921), 3-4.

138. Simmons also made the new Klan look like the one in the film, adopting the white robes and hoods used in the film version. Thomas R. Pegram, *One Hundred Percent American: The Rebirth and Decline of the Ku Klux Klan in the 1920s* (Plymouth, UK: Rowman & Littlefield, 2011), 7. Simmons also used the success of *The Birth of a Nation* to promote the Klan, placing newspaper ads to join the new Klan—described as "The World's Greatest Secret, Patriotic, Fraternal, Beneficiary Order"—next to ads for the film. McVeigh, *The Rise of the Ku Klux Klan*, 20; Franklin, "Birth of a Nation," 430; Baker, *Gospel According to the Klan*, 5.

139. Roger Daniels, *Guarding the Golden Door: American Immigration Policy and Immigrants since 1882* (New York: Hill & Wang, 2004), 5, table 1.2.

140. Helen F. Eckerson, "Immigration and National Origins," *Annals of the American Academy of Political and Social Science* 367, no. 1 (September 1966):

4-14, 6, table 1; David Goldfield, *Encyclopedia of American Urban History*, vol. 1 (Thousand Oaks, CA: Sage Publications, 2007), 122.

141. Jonathan Rees, *Industrialization and the Transformation of American Life: A Brief Introduction* (New York: Taylor & Francis, 2013), 44.

142. "Abolition, Women's Rights, and Temperance Movements," National Park Service, last updated September 20, 2016, https://www.nps.gov/wori /learn/historyculture/abolition-womens-rights-and-temperance-movements .htm.

143. Higham, *Strangers in the Land*, 159-175; see also James S. Pula, "The Progressives, the Immigrant, and the Workplace: Defining Public Perceptions, 1900-1914," *Polish American Studies* 52, no. 2 (Autumn 1995): 57-69.

144. Pegram, *One Hundred Percent American*, 72.

145. Pegram, 11; Chalmers, *Hooded Americanism*, 311.

146. Blee, *Women of the Klan*, 50.

147. Some of the Klan's opponents recognized that the Klan was borne of status anxieties. W. E. B. DuBois called the Klan the "Shape of Fear," a mob that arose to act out of white men's fears "of losing their jobs, of being declassed, degraded or actually disgraced; of losing their hopes, their savings, their plans for their children; of the actual pangs of hunger; of dirt, of crime." W. E. Burghardt Du Bois, "The Shape of Fear," *North American Review* 223, no. 831 (June-August 1926): 291, 295. Contemporary historians have similarly concluded that the second Klan appealed to white Protestants who feared losing social and political power. See McVeigh, *The Rise of the Ku Klux Klan*, 7; Pegram, *One Hundred Percent American*, 11.

148. Hiram Wesley Evans, "The Klan's Fight for Americanism," *North American Review* 223, no. 830 (March-May 1926): 49.

149. Evans, 39.

150. Evans, 34.

151. Evans, 38, 49; H. W. Evans, "Speech at Dallas, Texas" (October 24, 1923) in *The Menace of Modern Immigration* (n.p.: Knights of the Ku Klux Klan, 1924): 19; Women of the Ku Klux Clan, *America for Americans: Creed of Klanswomen* (n.d. [1920s]): 5.

152. Evans, "The Klan's Fight for Americanism," 38. The second Klan can be understood as a prototypical example of Middle American Radicals, a term coined in the 1970s by Donald Warren to describe the cohort of white Americans who resent both the elite establishment that governs the country and the poor and working class, who they see as undeserving beneficiaries of government programs. See Donald Warren, *The Radical Center: Middle Americans and the Politics of Alienation* (Notre Dame, IN: University of Notre Dame Press, 1976); Samuel T. Francis, "Message from MARs: The Social Politics of the New Right," reprinted in *Beautiful Losers: Essays on the Failure of American Conservatism* (Columbia: University of Missouri Press, 1994); Leonard Zeskind, *Blood and*

Politics: The History of the White Nationalist Movement from the Margins to the Mainstream (New York: Farrar, Strauss, Giroux, 2009), 282.

153. McVeigh, *The Rise of the Ku Klux Klan*, 7, 9, 27.

154. McVeigh, 25–26.

155. Chalmers, *Hooded Americanism*, 202.

156. Nancy Maclean, *Behind the Mask of Chivalry: The Making of the Second Ku Klux Klan* (New York: Oxford University Press, 1994), 149–173.

157. McVeigh, *The Rise of the Ku Klux Klan*, 149–156.

158. Maclean, *Behind the Mask of Chivalry*, 164.

159. Maclean, 165.

160. Maclean, 168.

161. W. J. Simmons, "The Ku Klux Kreed," in *Kloran: Knights of the Ku Klux Klan* (Atlanta, GA: Ku Klux Press, 1916): 2, 5; see Pegram, *One Hundred Percent American*, 11.

162. Pegram, 11–12.

163. "Letter from William J. Simmons," reprinted in Ku Klux Klan: Hearings Before the Committee on Rules 67th Cong. (1921): 126, 128; see also Simmons, *The Klan Unmasked*, 46.

164. Danny O. Crew, *Ku Klux Klan Sheet Music: An Illustrated Catalogue of Published Music, 1867–2002* (Jefferson, NC: McFarland, 2003), 53.

165. See Simmons, *The Klan Unmasked*, 54.

166. Simmons, 54; see also H. W. Evans, "Our Mission of Protestant Solidarity," *Kourier Magazine* 2 (July 1926); Women of the Ku Klux Klan, "Ideals of the Women of the Ku Klux Klan" (n.p.: n.d. [1920s]): 3; see also Evans, *The Menace of Modern Immigration*, 4.

167. H. W. Evans, "Our Mission of Protestant Solidarity"; "Ideals of the Women of the Ku Klux Klan," 7. As Imperial Wizard Simmons put it, "Our patriotic principles and Christianity are inseparable and indivisible," and therefore Klan members "hold steadfastly to the Constitution and the Sermon on the Mount." Simmons, *The Klan Unmasked*, 54; see also "Ideals of the Women of the Ku Klux Klan," 3; Evans, *The Menace of Modern Immigration*, 4.

168. See Simmons, *The Klan Unmasked*, 16, 47, 96, 142, 199–200.

169. D. C. Stephenson, "Speech, 'Back to the Constitution,' Kokomo, IN" (July 4, 1923), *Fiery Cross* 2, no. 34 (July 6, 1923).

170. Evans, "The Klan's Fight for Americanism," 53.

171. Writing almost a century after the second Klan, Samuel Huntington identified a core set of American values that is strikingly similar to those identified by Evans: "Americans, it is often said, are a people defined by and united by their commitment to the political principles of liberty, equality, democracy, individualism, human rights, the rule of law, and private property." Samuel Huntington, *Who Are We? The Challenges to America's National Identity* (London: Free Press, 2004), 46.

172. "Americans, Take Heed! Scum o' the Melting Pot," reprinted in Ku Klux Klan: Hearings Before the Committee on Rules, 67th Cong. (1921): 126; see also Stephenson, "Back to the Constitution," 4.

173. Simmons, *The Klan Unmasked,* 47; see also Evans, *The Menace of Modern Immigration,* 21.

174. David Suzuki, *Letters to My Grandchildren* (Vancouver: Greystone Books, 2015), 19.

175. Madison Grant, *The Passing of the Great Race, or the Racial Basis of European History* (New York: Charles Scriber's Sons, 1918), 227. It has been referred to as the "bible of scientific racism," and Adolf Hitler is said to have called the German edition "my bible." Jonathan Peter Spiro, *Defending the Master Race: Conservation, Eugenics, and the Legacy of Madison Grant* (Burlington: University of Vermont Press, 2009), xi, 140; see also Higham, *Strangers in the Land,* 271.

176. Grant, *The Passing of the Great Race,* 228.

177. Clinton Stoddard Burr, *America's Race Heritage* (New York: National Historical Society, 1922), 208.

178. Simmons, *Kloran,* 7; Evans, *The Menace of Modern Immigration,* 21.

179. Simmons, *The Klan Unmasked,* 47; see also Evans, "Our Mission of Protestant Solidarity."

180. vans, *The Menace of Modern Immigration,* 22-23.

181. Evans, 24.

182. Simmons, *The Klan Unmasked,* 240.

183. H. W. Evans, "The Catholic Question as Viewed by the Ku Klux Klan," *Current History* 26 (July 1927): 563.

184. Simmons, *The Klan Unmasked,* 66-78.

185. Edward Price, *Is the Ku Klux Klan Constructive or Destructive? A Debate between Imperial Wizard Evans, Israel Zangwill and Others,* Chicago: Chicago Daily News Company, 1924), 13, 6-7.

186. Alma White, *Klansmen: Guardians of Liberty,* illustrated by Rev. Brandford Clarke (Zarephath, NJ: Pillar of Fire Church, 1926).

187. Joseph Silverman, "The Ku Klux Klan: A Paradox," *North American Review* 223, no. 831 (June-August 1926): 282, 287; see also Lynn Dumenil, "The Tribal Twenties: 'Assimilated' Catholics' Response to Anti-Catholicism in the 1920s," *Journal of American Ethnic History* 11, no. 1 (Fall 1991): 28.

188. Silverman, "The Ku Klux Klan," 283-284. Father Martin Scott also disputed the Klan's claim that only white Protestants could embrace constitutional values, asserting that unlike the Klan, "Catholics stand by and for the Constitution and its Amendments." Martin J. Scott, "Catholics and the Ku Klux Klan," *North American Review* 223, no. 831 (June-August 1926): 283. In Scott's view, it was the Klan, not immigrants, that had undermined the Constitution because Klan members had "done their best to make null and void

the Constitutional Amendments granting the electoral franchise to our colored citizens." Scott, "Catholics and the Ku Klux Klan," 274.

189. James Weldon Johnson, "Is the Negro a Danger to White Culture?," in Sondra Kathryn Wilson, ed., *In Search of Democracy: The NAACP Writings of James Weldon Johnson, Walter White, and Roy Wilkins (1920-1927)* (New York: Oxford University Press, 1999), 105-106.

190. Dumenil, "The Tribal Twenties," 31-32.

191. "Brief of Appellant, the Governor of the State of Oregon, Pierce v. Society of Sisters, 268 U.S. 510 (1925)," reprinted in *Oregon School Cases, Complete Record* (Baltimore: Belvedere Press, 1925), 102-103.

192. "Official Pamphlet, Argument (Affirmative)," reprinted in *Oregon School Cases, Complete Record*, 732; Paula Abrams, "The Little Red Schoolhouse: *Pierce*, State Monopoly of Education and the Politics of Intolerance," *Constitutional Commentary* 20, no. 61 (2003).

193. Pierce v. Society of Sisters, 268 U.S. 510 (1925).

194. See, e.g., Cong. Rec. 11744 (June 24, 1924) (Rep. Johnson).

195. Restriction of Immigration, House of Reps., 68th Cong., 1st Sess., Report no. 350 (March 24, 1924), 13.

196. Imperial Night-Hawk, Ku Klux Klan, September 17, 1924.

197. Simmons, *The Klan Unmasked*, 16, 23, 93.

198. Simmons, 4.

199. Another statement in this document makes the same point perhaps more clearly, declaring that African Americans who get out of line may need to be "reminded" of their proper place in the nation's hierarchy: "We would not rob the colored population of their rights, but we demand that they respect the rights of the White Race in whose country they are permitted to reside. When it comes to the point that they cannot and will not recognize those rights they must be reminded that this is a White Peoples' country, so that they will seek for themselves a country more agreeable to their tastes and aspirations." Women of the Ku Klux Klan, "Ideals of the Women of the Ku Klux Klan," 4-5. Although the Klan women did not specify what precisely should be done to "remind" Black people of their place in the Klan's America, it is apparent that they had violence in mind: violence sufficient to encourage Black people to leave the country if they insisted on demanding equal rights.

200. 1921 Congressional Hearings, 125.

201. As Michael Ignatieff has written, "As a moral ideal, nationalism is an ethic of heroic sacrifice, justifying the use of violence in the defense of one's nation against enemies, internal or external." Michael Ignatieff, *Blood and Belonging: Journeys into the New Nationalism* (New York: Farrar, Straus& Giroux, 1993), 5; see also Ernest Renan, "What Is a Nation?," in Geoff Eley and Ronald Grigor, eds., *Becoming National: A Reader* (New York: Oxford University Press, 1996), 42, 53; Benedict Anderson, *Imagined Communities: Reflections in the Origin*

and Spread of Nationalism, rev. ed. (New York: Verso,2006), 7; Anthony D. Smith, *Chosen Peoples: Sacred Sources of National Identity* (New York: Oxford University Press, 2003), 218-253; Anthony D. Smith, *Nationalism and Modernism* (New York: Routledge, 1998), 97.

202. Simmons, *The Klan Unmasked*, 41-42.

203. Paul Ortiz, *Emancipation Betrayed: The Hidden History of Black Organizing and White Violence in Florida from Reconstruction to the Bloody Election of 1920* (Berkeley: University of California Press, 2005), 171-204.

204. Ortiz, *Emancipation Betrayed*, 205, 214-215.

205. Ortiz, 217-229.

206. See James Weldon Johnson, "Is the Negro a Danger to White Culture?," 18.

207. Ortiz, *Emancipation Betrayed*, 223.

208. Simmons, *The Klan Unmasked*, 41.

209. Simmons, 42.

210. Pegram, *One Hundred Percent American*, 185-216; see McVeigh, *The Rise of the Ku Klux Klan*, 181.

211. Chalmers, *Hooded Americanism*, 323-324.

212. See Chalmers, 289.

213. Chalmers, 191-192.

214. Evans, "New Era Dawns for America," *Fiery Cross* 4, no. 8 (January 9, 1925): 2, https://newspapers.library.in.gov/cgi-bin/indiana?a=d&d=FC19250109.1.2.

215. McVeigh, *The Rise of the Ku Klux Klan*, 189.

216. "Here Are Twenty Reasons WHY You Should, If Qualified, Join, Aid and Support the White Knights of the Ku Klux Klan of Mississippi," *Activities of the Ku Klux Klan in the U.S.A.*, House Un-American Activities Committee, Part 3, 89th Cong., 2nd Sess., January 13, 1966, 2747, exhibit no. 1 (testimony of Thomas A. Gunter); "Fifty Reasons Why You Should Be a Member of the United Klans of America, Inc.," *Activities of the Ku Klux Klan in the USA*, House Un-American Activities Committee, Part 3, 89th Cong., 2nd Sess., January 4, 1966, 2389, exhibit no. 14 (testimony of Murray Martin); see also "The Ku Klux Klan and Its Story," *Fiery Cross* 2, no. 9. (1967): 18.

217. For instance, in December 1949 a group calling itself the Original Southern Klans was formed and proclaimed that it was "launching a crusade for the return of this country back to the principles and ideals and faiths of our forefathers." "National Klan Group Formed," *Montgomery Advertiser*, December 18, 1949.

218. The number of Klan members during the 1940s is subject to widely varying estimates, from as few as 10,000 members to as many as 500,000. Chalmers, *Hooded Americanism*, 333; Stetson Kennedy, "Status of the KKK in the USA" (October 19, 1949), quoted in Evelyn Rich, *Ku Klux Klan Ideology, 1954-1988* (PhD diss., Boston University, 1988), 16.

219. "New Era Dawns for America," *Fiery Cross* 4, no. 8 (January 9, 1925).

220. John Powell, "The Klan Un-Klandestine," *Nation*, September 29, 1951, 255.

221. 102 Cong. Rec. 4460 (1956) ("Southern Manifesto").

222. See George Lewis, *Massive Resistance: The White Response to the Civil Rights Movement* (London: Bloomsbury, 2006).

223. Lewis, *Massive Resistance*, 11.

224. Neil R. McMillen, *The Citizens' Council: Organized Resistance to the Second Reconstruction, 1954–64* (Chicago: University of Illinois Press, 1971), 16.

225. McMillen, *The Citizens' Council*, 153. It is possible, however, that the actual membership in the councils was only half that number.

226. Robert Webb, "Citizen Council No Place for Klan," *Citizens Council* 1, no. 6 (March 1956): 1; Thomas R. Waring, "Mississippi Citizens' Councils Are Protecting Both Races," *Citizens Council* 1, no. 1 (October 1955): 1; Rich, *Ku Klux Klan Ideology*, 27–28.

227. Chalmers, *Hooded Americanism*, 343.

228. Michael Newton, *The FBI and the KKK: A Critical History* (Jefferson, NC: McFarland, 2009), 101.

229. Flyer, United Klans of America, 1965.

230. Arnold Forster and Benjamin R. Epstein, *Report on the Ku Klux Klan* (New York: Anti-Defamation League of B'nai B'rith, 1965), 21.

231. Chalmers, *Hooded Americanism*, 349–350.

232. Chalmers, 370–371, 7.

233. Cunningham, *Klansville, USA*, 55–56; Seth Cagin and Philip Dray, *We Are Not Afraid: The Story of Goodman, Schwerner, and Chaney and the Civil Rights Campaign for Mississippi* (New York: Scribner, 1988).

234. Cunningham, *Klansville, USA*, 69.

235. See, e.g., Lewis, *Massive Resistance*, 44–60.

236. The Southern Manifesto, 102 Cong. Rec. 4460.

237. Lewis, *Massive Resistance*, 44–59.

238. McMillen, *The Citizens' Council*, 74, 109, 189–190.

239. See Walter J. Suthon, "The Dubious Origin of the 14th Amendment," *US News & World Report*, July 20, 1956; David Lawrence, "There Is No 14th Amendment," *US News & World Report*, September 27, 1957, 140.

240. S.J. Res. 39, General Assembly, Georgia, 1957.

241. James O. Eastland, *We've Reached Era of Judicial Tyranny: An Address before the State-Wide Convention of the Association of Citizens' Councils of Mississippi, Jackson, December 1, 1955* (Greenwood: Association of Citizens Councils of Mississippi, 1956): 14–15; see also "Council Actions in Louisiana," *Citizens' Council,* (June 1957, 4. Medford Evans, the editor of the Citizens' Councils newspaper, similarly expounded on the national implications of the fight for segregation: "Since the Southern Way has become the American Way, an attack on the

Southern Way is an attack on the American Way." Joseph Crespino, *In Search of Another Country: Mississippi and the Conservative Counterrevolution* (Princeton, NJ: Princeton University Press, 2007), 26.

242. Cunningham, *Klansville, USA*, 61.

243. Art. II, § 2, Constitution and Law of the United Klans of America, 1965, RL.10135, Box 3, Ku Klux Klan General File, Southern Poverty Law Center Collection, Duke University, Chapel Hill, North Carolina.

244. Dixon, "Ideals of the Ku Klux Klan," 3; see also "White Knights of the Ku Klux Klan," *Klan Ledger*, November 14, 1966, 2.

245. Kloran, Confederate Knights of the KKK, circa 1960s.

246. See, e.g., "White Knights of the KKK of Mississippi," *Klan Ledger* (Early Autumn 1964): 3; "Ideals of the Ku Klux Klan," *Clansman* 2, no. 1 (1967): 3; Ku Klux Klan, "Principles and Purposes of the Knights of the Ku Klux Klan" (n.d.).

247. United Klans of America, "White Christians of the South: The Most Persecuted Minority in the Nation!," *Fiery Cross*, February 1968, 25.

248. See, e.g., McMillen, *The Citizens' Council*, 195; *The Principles of the United Klans of America, Inc.* (Tuscaloosa, AL: Knights of the Ku Klux Klan, 1965).

249. Senator Max Eastland of Mississippi asserted in 1955 that in *Brown v. Board of Education*, "the Court has responded to a radical, pro-Communist political movement in this country." Eastland, "We've Reached Era of Judicial Tyranny," 5. This movement, Eastland asserted, is "bent upon the destruction of the American system of government, and the mongrelization of the white race" (Eastland, 5). White Citizens' Councils also frequently described the civil rights movement as a Communist front and declared that segregation must be maintained because it was "only a short step from integration to communization." "Deadly Parallel: Only a Short Step from Integration to Communization," *Citizens' Council* 2, no. 11 (August 1957): 1; see Medford Evans, "Forced Integration Is Communism in Action," *Citizen* (September 1962): 6, 11; see also Tom Ethridge, "Mississippi Notebook" (Citizens Council), *Clarion Ledger*, October 1955), 8; *Forty Reasons for Segregation* (pamphlet) (MD: Klan, n.d.). According to a 1965 Gallup poll, almost half of all American adults believed that Communists had been very involved in civil protests. See "Public Opinions Polls on Civil Rights Movement, 1961–1969," Civil Rights Movement Veterans, uploaded March 17, 2016, http://www.crmvet.org/docs/60s_crm_public-opinion.pdf. As Eldon Lee Edwards, founder of US Klans, Knights of the Ku Klux Klans, declared: "The good [niggers] don't want this integration any more than we do. It is the NAACP that is trying to jam it down our throats, and it is backed by Jew money. . . . [It is] Russia's intention to Mongrelize the world, to mix the white race with the black so as to bring it under Communist control." Rich, *Ku Klux Klan Ideology*, 34–35.

250. See, e.g., "Why the Ku Klux Klan," *Weekly Report*, Invisible Empire,

United Florida Ku Klux Klan (n.d.), https://archive.org/details/AryanBook StoreHansDiebelHQ97108/page/n1/mode/2up.

251. See, e.g., Oren F. Potito, "Stand Your Ground—Segregate or Integrate," The *Clansman*, Vol. 2, no. 1, at 6 (1967); *Wake Up* (undated flyer).

252. See *Wake Up*; see also White Knights of the Ku Klux Klan of Mississippi, "Special Presidential Edition," *Klan Ledger*, April 1965, http://www.lib.usm .edu/legacy/spcol/exhibitions/anti-comm/civil_rights-10.html.

253. See Eastland, "We've Reached Era of Judicial Tyranny," 2.

254. "Ideals of the Ku Klux Klan," *Clansman* 2, no. 1 (1967), 3.

255. White Knights of the Ku Klux Klan of Mississippi, "Special Greenwood, LeFlore County Edition," *Klan Ledger*, Summer 1966, 1; *The Principles of the United Klans of America, Inc.*, (Tuscaloosa, AL: Knights of the Ku Klux Klan, 1965); Robert M. Shelton, *Introduction to the Knights of the Ku Klux Klan* (Tuscaloosa, AL: United Klans of America, circa 1960s), 2; *Some Questions that Need Straight Answer,* (Natchez, MS: United Klans of America, Knights of the Ku Klux Klan, circa 1966). The Klan believed that Klansmen had been crucial to American history long before the Klan was created in 1866. Knights of the Ku Klux Klan, *Back Off Heathens* (Columbus, MS: United Klans of America, n.d.). Indeed, the Klan traced itself back to time immemorial: "The Invisible Empire, in a very loose and generalized sense, may be said to have existed since the dawn of civilization whenever men banded themselves together to fight for liberty and freedom." United Klans of America, "The Ku Klux Klan and Its Story," *Fiery Cross*, 2, no. 9 (1967), 2.

256. See, e.g., White Knights of the Ku Klux Klan of Mississippi, "Special Greenwood, LeFlore County Edition," *Klan Ledger*, Summer 1966.

257. See Cunningham, *Klansville, USA*, 102. The Klan's open support for violence also distinguished the civil rights–era Klan from the Klan of the 1920s, which had sought mainstream respectability and publicly denied any involvement in violence.

258. See Southern Manifesto, 102 Cong. Rec. 4460.

259. See McMillen, *The Citizens' Council*, 360-361.

260. White Knights of the Ku Klux Klan of Mississippi, "Special Greenwood, LeFlore County Edition," *Klan Ledger*, Summer 1966.

261. White Knights of the Ku Klux Klan of Mississippi, 2.

262. White Knights of the Ku Klux Klan of Mississippi, "My Fellow American: Here Are Twenty Reasons WHY You Should If Qualified, Join, Aid and Support the White Knights of the Ku Klux Klan of Mississippi" (n.d.).

263. *Activities of the Ku Klux Klan in the USA*, House Un-American Activities Committee, Part 3, 89th Cong., 2nd Sess., January 13, 1966, 2759 (testimony of Thomas A. Gunter).

264. United Klans of America, "Robert M. Shelton's Homecoming Address," *Fiery Cross*, January 1970, 11; see also White Knights of the Ku Klux

Klan of Mississippi, "Special Greenwood, LeFlore County Edition," *Klan Ledger*, Summer 1966, 1.

265. See, e.g., Knights of the Green Forest, "A Message from the Knights of the Green Forest, Inc.," Tupelo, MS, circa 1960s; see also, e.g., White Knights of the Ku Klux Klan of Mississippi, "Special Greenwood, LeFlore County Edition," *Klan Ledger*, Summer 1966, 2.

266. White Knights of the Ku Klux Klan of Mississippi, "Special Greenwood, LeFlore County Edition," *Klan Ledger*, Summer 1966, 2; see also Rich, *Ku Klux Klan Ideology*, 120.

267. See, e.g., White Knights of the Ku Klux Klan of Mississippi, "Special Neshoba County Fair Edition," *Klan Ledger*, August 1964.

268. See, e.g., Thomas A. Tarrants III, *The Conversion of a Klansman: The Story of a Former Ku Klux Klan Terrorist* (Garden City, NJ: Doubleday, 1979), 73; *The Principles of the United Klans of America, Inc.* (Tuscaloosa, AL: Knights of the Ku Klux Klan, 1965); Shelton, *Introduction to the Knights of the Ku Klux Klan*, 2.

269. See White Knights of the Ku Klux Klan of Mississippi, "Thomas Gunter Exhibit No. 3," *Klan Ledger*, July 4, 1964.

270. As discussed in chapter 6, in recent decades, gun rights advocates have claimed that the Second Amendment protects a right to bear arms for the purpose of giving individuals the ability to resist government tyranny. See, e.g., Joshua Horwitz and Casey Anderson, *Guns, Democracy, and the Insurrectionist Idea* (Ann Arbor: University of Michigan Press, 2009); Carl Bogus, "The Hidden History of the Second Amendment," *University of California Davis Law Review* 31, no. 2 (Winter 1998): 309, 390–404; Charles J. Dunlap, "Revolt of the Masses: Armed Citizens and the Insurrectionary Theory of the 2nd Amendment," *Tennessee Law Review* 62 (1995): 643; Dennis Henigan, "Arms, Anarchy and the Second Amendment," *Valparaiso Law Review* 26, no. 1 (1991): 107; David B. Kopel, "It Isn't About Duck Hunting: The British Origins of the Right to Arms," *Michigan Law Review* 93, no. 6 (1995): 1333; Thomas M. Moncure Jr., "The Second Amendment Ain't About Hunting," *Howard Law Journal* 34 (1991): 589.

271. *Activities of the Ku Klux Klan in the USA*, House Un-American Activities Committee, Part 4, 89th Cong., 2nd Sess., February 1, 1966, 2924 (testimony of Sam Holloway Bowers Jr.).

272. Adam Nossiter, *Of Long Memory: Mississippi and the Murder of Medgar Evers* (Boston: Addison-Wesley, 1994), 90.

273. "Local Councils throughout South Have Busy Month of Meetings; Big Membership Drives Planned," *Citizens' Council*, April 1960, 3 (quoting Farley Smith, executive director of the South Carolina White Citizens' Council).

274. Thomas R. Waring, "Private Citizens Formed Citizens Councils," *Citizens Council*, November 1955, 1 (quoting Robert Patterson).

275. In fact, council members sometimes were explicit in declaring that

violence would be justified after the failure of lawful resistance. As one council member said, if the council failed in its fight to prevent integration of a local swimming pool and African Americans were to swim in the pool, "I figure any time one of them gets near the pool, we can let some redneck take care of him for us." Crespino, *In Search of Another Country*, 26.

276. Cagin and Dray, *We Are Not Afraid*, 206.

277. See Cagin and Dray, 109–111.

278. As James Venable, leader of the National Knights of the Ku Klux Klan, told a Klan rally: Klan violence to defend segregation was not really unlawful because "you'll never be able to convict a white man that killed a nigger what encroaches on the white race in the South." "Political Power Claimed," *New York Times*, September 6, 1964, 34; see also Rich, *Ku Klux Klan Ideology*, 88.

279. As Mark Tushnet has explained, interposition theory posits that "if a state disagreed on constitutional grounds with the national government, it could 'interpose' its sovereign power between the national government and its people, thereby effectively nullifying the national action." Mark V. Tushnet, *Making Civil Rights Law: Thurgood Marshall and the Supreme Court 1936–1961* (New York: Oxford University Press, 1994), 240.

280. Davison M. Douglas, "The Rhetoric of Moderation: Desegregating the South during the Decade after *Brown*," *Northwestern University Law Review* 89 (1994): 93 n5 (collecting citations).

281. Lucas A. Powe Jr., *The Warren Court and American Politics* (Cambridge, MA: Belknap Press, 2000), 60 (quoting S.J. Res. 3, 1956 General Assembly, Reg. Sess., 1956 VA Acts 1213, 1215).

282. Michael J. Klarman, *From Jim Crow to Civil Rights: The Supreme Court and the Struggle for Racial Equality* (New York: Oxford University Press, 2004), 385–442.

283. Civil Rights Act of 1964, Pub. L. No. 88–352, 78 Stat. 241 (1964); Voting Rights Act of 1965, Pub. L. No. 89–110, 79 Stat. 437 (1965); Civil Rights Act of 1968, Pub. L. No. 90–284, 82 Stat. 73 (1968).

284. Charles W. Eagles, "White Citizens' Councils," in Donald T. Critchlow and Philip R. VanderMeer, eds., *Oxford Encyclopedia of American Political and Legal History* (New York: Oxford University Press, 2012), 383, 384.

285. John Drabble, "From White Supremacy to White Power: The FBI, COINTELPRO-WHITE HATE, and the Nazification of the Ku Klux Klan in the 1970s," in *American Studies* 48, no. 3 (Fall 2007): 49, 50.

286. See Charles E. Case and Andrew M. Greeley, "Attitudes toward Racial Equality," *Humboldt Journal of Social Relations* 16, no. 1 (1990): 67, 69 fig. 1.

287. See Cunningham, *Klansville, USA*, 184–213.

288. Drabble, "From White Supremacy to White Power," 56.

289. See Rich, "Ku Klux Klan Ideology," 124.

290. David Mark Chalmers, *Backfire: How the Ku Klux Klan Helped the Civil*

Rights Movement (Lanham, MD: Rowman & Littlefield, 2003), 151; see also Rich, *Ku Klux Klan Ideology*, 148–150.

291. Drabble, "From White Supremacy to White Power," 49.

292. Tyler Bridges, *The Rise of David Duke* (Jackson: University Press of Mississippi, 1994), 35–36; Zeskind, *Blood and Politics*, 34–45.

293. Tom Snyder of the *Tomorrow Show* said Duke was "intelligent, articulate, charming," and Barbara Walters called him "a very effective spokesman for his cause." Bridges, *The Rise of David Duke*, 45–47.

294. Bridges, 16, 43; Zeskind, *Blood and Politics*, 36, 41.

295. William Luther Pierce, "Mightier than an Army," *National Vanguard* 94 (April 1983): 2–4, https://nationalvanguard.org/2016/05/mightier-than-an -army/.

296. Zeskind, *Blood and Politics*, 40.

297. Zeskind, 40.

298. Rich, *Ku Klux Klan Ideology*, 171.

299. Rich, 262 (quoting David Duke, *Duke Speaks Out*, 39, Crusader 6).

300. Zeskind, *Blood and Politics*, 40.

301. Bridges, *The Rise of David Duke*, 22.

302. Wilmot Robertson, *The Dispossessed Majority* (Cape Canaveral, FL: Howard Allen, 1972), 195.

303. Robertson, *The Dispossessed Majority*, 100.

304. Drabble, "From White Supremacy to White Power," 61.

305. Rich, *Ku Klux Klan Ideology*, 210–211, 219.

306. Rich, 308–311.

307. For instance, in 1980 former Nazi party member Frazier Glenn Miller formed a new Klan group, the Carolina Knights, which changed its name to the Confederate Knights of the Ku Klux Klan and later became the White Patriot Party. Rich, 300.

308. William Luther Pierce [Andrew MacDonald], *The Turner Diaries* (Larchmont, NY: Barricade Press, 1978), 2, 29.

309. Zeskind, *Blood and Politics*, 97. Timothy McVeigh was also inspired by *The Turner Diaries*. In the chapter McVeigh found most significant, the novel's hero blows up the FBI building using a truck filled with fertilizer and fuel. Zeskind, 399. McVeigh gave away copies of *The Turner Diaries* to any friend who would take it, sold the book at gun shows, and left a quote from the book in his getaway car on April 19, 1995, after he used a fertilizer bomb to blow up the Murrah Building in Oklahoma City, Oklahoma, killing 168 people. Zeskind, 456.

310. Kerry Noble, *Tabernacle of Hate: Seduction into Right-Wing Extremism*, 2nd ed. (Syracuse, NY: Syracuse University Press, 2010), 188; see also Robert J. Mathews, "Call to Aryan Warriors," speech, the National Alliance, Arlington, Virginia, September 4, 1983, YouTube, https://www.youtube.com/watch?v =xDQdKBaFibw.

311. Robert J. Mathews, "Robert Mathews' Last Letter," 1984, http://www.vanguardnewsnetwork.com/wolzek/1984_BobMathewsLastLetter.html.

312. Robert J. Mathews, "Robert Jay Mathews' Declaration of War," 1984, http://www.mourningtheancient.com/mathews2.htm.

313. Zeskind, *Blood and Politics*, 97–99.

314. See Brent L. Smith, *Terrorism in America: Pipe Bombs and Pipe Dreams* (Albany: State University of New York Press, 1994), 85.

315. Betty A. Dobratz and Stephanie L. Shanks-Meile, *The White Separatist Movement in the United States: White Power, White Pride!* (New York: Twayne Publishers, 1997), 193–194; Zeskind, *Blood and Politics*, 99.

316. Drabble, "From White Supremacy to White Power," 57.

317. Sims, *The Klan*, 102.

318. Rich, *Ku Klux Klan Ideology*, 315.

319. Rich, 303–304.

320. Bridges, *The Rise of David Duke*, 85.

321. Dobratz and Shanks-Meile, *The White Separatist Movement in the United States*, 50.

322. In September 2015, Miller was convicted of murdering three people at a Jewish Community Center and Jewish retirement center in Kansas City. Diana Reese, "Jury Recommends Death Penalty for White Supremacist Frazier Glenn Miller," *Washington Post*, September 8, 2015, https://www.washingtonpost.com/news/post-nation/wp/2015/09/08/white-supremacist-frazier-glenn-miller-sentenced-to-die/?noredirect=on&utm_term=.04413ccda612.

323. Rich, *Ku Klux Klan Ideology*, 345–346.

324. Anti-Defamation League, *Tattered Robes: The State of the Ku Klux Klan in the United States*, 2016, https://www.adl.org/sites/default/files/documents/assets/pdf/combating-hate/tattered-robes-state-of-kkk-2016.pdf.

325. Dobratz and Shanks-Meile, *The White Separatist Movement in the United States* (quoting Dennis Mahon, *What's All this C.R.A.P.?* WAR, (June 1994, 6), 83.

326. Dobratz and Shanks-Meile, 150–151.

327. See, e.g., David Lane, "The 88 Precepts," David Lane 1488, 41, accessed on December 17, 2018, http://www.davidlane1488.com/88precepts.pdf.

328. Lane, "The 88 Precepts," 28.

329. Louis R. Beam Jr., *Essays of A Klansman* (Hayden Lake, ID: Louis Beam, 1983), viii, 48.

330. Beam, vii, 23, 17, 18.

331. Doreen Carvajal, "Group Tries to Halt Selling of Racist Novel," *New York Times*, April 20, 1996.

332. Pierce, *The Turner Diaries*, 173.

333. Pierce, 173–174.

334. Aryan Nations, *Platform for the Aryan National State*, n.d., 5–6, https://archive.org/stream/AryanNationsInfoPack/AN#page/n5/mode/2up.

335. See, e.g., Dobratz and Shanks-Meile, *The White Separatist Movement in the United States*, 102 (quoting Donald V. Clerkin, *Essay—The Coming Aryan Republic, Euro-American Quarterly X* [1989], 1-6); see generally Dobratz and Shanks-Meile, 97-109; Lane, "The 88 Precepts," 50.

336. "Northwest American Republic Constitution," Northwest Front, http://northwestfront.org/about/nar-constitution/1-nationhood-and-citizenship/; see also Robert L. Tsai, *America's Forgotten Constitutions: Defiant Visions of Power and Community* (Cambridge, MA: Harvard University Press, 2014), 253-291.

337. The Nationalist Front is an umbrella group of white separatist organizations that includes the National Socialist Movement, a neo-Nazi group; League of the South, a Southern secessionist group; and White Lives Matter. "Membership," Nationalist Front, https://www.nfunity.org/membership/.

338. "Fourteen Points," Nationalist Front, https://www.nfunity.org/14-points/.

339. "Unity Statement," Nationalist Front, https://www.nfunity.org/unity/.

340. "Fourteen Points," Nationalist Front.

341. League of the South, a Southern secessionist group, voices much the same position that nations can only survive if organized around blood and soil, rather than on universalistic principles. "Kith and Kin or a Proposition Nation," League of the South, http://leagueofthesouth.com/kith-and-kin/.

342. "Fellow Patriots," Knights Party, https://kkk.bz/fellow-patriots/.

343. "Platform," Knights Party, https://kkk.bz/platform-2/.

344. "Frequently Asked Questions," Knights Party, https://kkk.bz/frequently-asked-questions/.

345. Thomas Robb, the leader of the Knights, has been a leading voice describing federal policies as "white genocide," and the Knights have identified ending white genocide as its top priority. "Frequently Asked Questions," Knights Party.

346. While members of the Nationalist Front express this position explicitly, traditionalist groups like the Knights frequently make slightly more subtle references to "internationalists," "globalists," and "bankers." Compare "Unity Statement," Nationalist Front, with "The KKK and the Federal Government," Knights Party, http://kkk.bz/the-kkk-and-the-federal-government/.

347. See Dara Lind, "Unite the Right: The Violent White Supremacist Rally in Charlottesville," *Vox*, August 14, 2017, https://www.vox.com/2017/8/12/16138246/charlottesville-nazi-rally-right-uva.

348. Sheryl Gay Stolberg and Brian M. Rosenthal, "Man Charged after White Nationalist Rally in Charlottesville Ends in Deadly Violence," *New York Times*, August 12, 201.

349. "Deconstructing the Symbols and Slogans Spotted in Charlottesville," *Washington Post*, August 18, 2017; Emma Green, "Why the Charlottesville Marchers Were Obsessed with Jews," *Atlantic*, August 15, 2017.

350. See Theiss-Morse, *Who Counts As an American?*, 73, 77, 92-93.

Chapter 2. The Christian Constitution

1. To be sure, the Constitution contains a number of oblique references to religion that contemporary Christian nationalists occasionally identify as proof that the Constitution is Christian. Article I, Section 7 provides that the president has ten days, not including Sundays, to sign a bill into law, a provision that acknowledges the Sunday Sabbath.

2. See Akhil Reed Amar, *America's Unwritten Constitution: The Precedents and Principles We Live By* (New York: Basic Books, 2012), 71–73.

3. Thomas Jefferson et al., Declaration of Independence, paras. 1, 2, 5 (1776).

4. Articles of Confederation, Art. XIII.

5. See Amar, *America's Unwritten Constitution*, 74–75.

6. Joseph S. Moore, *Founding Sins: How a Group of Antislavery Radicals Fought to Put Christ into the Constitution* (New York: Oxford University Press, 2016), 55–57.

7. Luther Martin, *The Genuine Information Delivered to the Legislature of the State of Maryland Relative to the Proceedings of the General Convention Lately Held at Philadelphia, XII*, February 8, 1788.

8. Moore, *Founding Sins*, 56.

9. Morton Borden, *Jews, Turks, and Infidels* (Chapel Hill, NC: University of North Carolina Press, 1984), 59.

10. Chauncey Lee, *The Government of God: The True Source and Standard of Human Government* (Hartford, CT: Hudson & Goodwin, 1813); Borden, *Jews, Turks, and Infidels*, 59 (emphasis in original).

11. Borden, 60.

12. *Journal of the House of Reps.*, 28th Cong. (1844), 418.

13. Moore, *Founding Sins*, 2.

14. Moore, 3, 57.

15. Moore, 65.

16. Borden, *Jews, Turks, and Infidels*; see also Moore, 123.

17. See Mark A. Noll, *The Civil War as a Theological Crisis* (Chapel Hill: University of North Carolina Press, 2006); Robert J. Miller and James M. McPherson, *Both Prayed to the Same God: Religion and Faith in the American Civil War* (Lanham, MD: Lexington Books, 2007).

18. See Randall Miller, Harry S. Stout, and Charles Reagan Wilson, eds., *Religion and the American Civil War* (New York: Oxford University Press, 1998), 6, 21–40.

19. In 1863 the Senate unanimously adopted a resolution urging the president to set apart a day of "prayer and humiliation" over "the national offenses which have provoked his righteous judgment." Borden, *Jews, Turks, and Infidels*, 66. Adhering to the request, Lincoln issued a proclamation declaring

a day of thanksgiving, in which he expressed the view "the Most High God" was "dealing with us in anger for our sins," and called upon the American people to undertake "humble penitence for our national perverseness and disobedience." Abraham Lincoln, "Thanksgiving Proclamation," Washington, DC, October 3, 1863, https://www.gilderlehrman.org/content/thanksgiving -proclamation-1863. In his second inaugural address, Lincoln expanded on the conception of the Civil War as divine punishment for the sin of slavery. Abraham Lincoln, "Second Inaugural *Address at Washington, DC*" (1865), in Roy P. Basler, ed., *Collected Works of Abraham Lincoln*, vol. 8 (New Brunswick, NJ: Rutgers University Press, 1953), 332, 333 ("If we shall suppose that American Slavery is one of those offences which, in the providence of God, must needs come, but which, having continued through His appointed time, He now wills to remove, and that He gives to both North and South, this terrible war, as the woe due to those by whom the offence came, shall we discern therein any departure from those divine attributes which the believers in a Living God always ascribe to Him?").

20. Gaines M. Foster, *Moral Reconstruction, Christian Lobbyists and the Federal Legislation of Morality, 1865–1920* (Chapel Hill: University of North Carolina Press, 2002), 19-20.

21. The preamble to the Confederate Constitution declared: "We, the people of the Confederate States, each State acting in its sovereign and independent character, in order to form a permanent federal government, establish justice, insure domestic tranquility, and secure the blessings of liberty to ourselves and our posterity *invoking the favor and guidance of Almighty God* do ordain and establish this Constitution for the Confederate States of America." Preamble, Constitution for the Confederate States of America (emphasis added).

22. Moore, *Founding Sins*, 124.

23. National Reform Association, *Proceedings of the National Convention to Secure the Religious Amendment of the Constitution of the United States*, Cincinnati, Ohio, January 31–February 1, 1872 (Philadelphia: Jas. B. Rodgers, 1872), iv–v (hereinafter *Proceedings of the 1872 National Reform Association Convention*).

24. *Proceedings of the 1872 National Reform Association Convention*, vii–viii (emphasis added).

25. Steven K. Green, *The Bible, the School, and the Constitution: The Clash That Shaped Modern Church-State Doctrine* (New York: Oxford University Press, 2012), 141.

26. *Proceedings of the 1872 National Reform Association Convention*.

27. *Proceedings*, ix–x. Later, the association embellished the story of its meeting with Lincoln and frequently claimed that Lincoln was committed to their cause but that his assassination the following year prevented him from fulfilling that commitment. Green, *The Bible, the School, and the Constitution*, 141.

28. Green, 142.

29. Cong. Globe, 38th Cong., 2nd Sess. (March 2, 1865): 1272.

30. *Proceedings of the 1872 National Reform Association Convention*, 15; Foster, *Moral Reconstruction*, 83.

31. Foster, 83.

32. Green, *The Bible, the School, and the Constitution*, 161.

33. See National Reform Association, *Proceedings of the Fifth National Reform Convention to Aid in Maintaining the Christian Features of the American Government and Securing a Religious Amendment to the Constitution of the United States*, Pittsburg, Pennsylvania, February 4–5, 1874 (Philadelphia: Christian Statesman Association, 1874) (hereinafter *Proceedings of the 1874 National Reform Association Convention*).

34. Well into the nineteenth century, many states required an oath of devotion to Christ to hold public office. See Edwin S. Gaustad and Leigh Eric Schmidt, *The Religious History of America: The Heart of the American Story from Colonial Times to Today* (New York: HarperCollins, 2002), 232. For a history of laws regarding Sabbath observance, see Andrew J. King, "Sunday Law in the Nineteenth Century," *Albany Law Review* 64, no. 2 (Winter 2000): 675, 677.

35. Green, *The Bible, the School, and the Constitution*, 13–20; Noah Feldman, "Non-Sectarianism Reconsidered," *Journal of Law and Politics* 18, no. 1 (Winter 2003): 65, 66.

36. Green, *The Bible, the School, and the Constitution*, 30–33.

37. Feldman, "Non-Sectarianism Reconsidered," 66.

38. Green, *The Bible, the School, and the Constitution*, 120, 126.

39. Green, 8.

40. The theory has its origin in Herbert G. Blumer, "Race Prejudice as a Sense of Group Position," *Pacific Sociological Review* 1 (1958): 3–7, and has been developed by Lawrence Bobo and others. For a review of the literature on group threat theory, see Lincoln Quillian, "Prejudice as a Response to Perceived Group Threat: Population Composition and Anti-Immigrant and Racial Prejudice in Europe," *American Sociological Review* 60, no. 4 (August 1995): 586–611.

41. See, e.g., Mark A. Fosset and K. Jill Kiecolt, "The Relative Size of Minority Populations and White Racial Attitudes," *Social Science Quarterly*, 70, no. 4 (1989): 825–835; Lincoln Quillian, "Group Threat and Regional Change in Attitudes toward African-Americans," *American Journal of Sociology* 102, no. 3 (November 1996): 816–860.

42. Thomas C. Wilson, "Americans' Views on Immigration Policy: Testing the Role of Threatened Group Interests," *Sociological Perspectives* 44, no. 1 (2001): 485–501.

43. John Higham, *Strangers in the Land: Patterns of American Nativism 1860–1925*, 2nd ed. (New Brunswick, NJ: Rutgers University Press, 1977), 29.

44. *Proceedings of the 1872 National Reform Association Convention*, 17, 44.

45. Rev. David McAllister, "The Aims and Methods of the Movement," in *Proceedings of the 1872 National Reform Association Convention*, 4, 41.

46. McAllister, 4.

47. J. R. W. Sloane, "The Moral Character and Accountability of the Nation", in *Proceedings of the 1872 National Reform Association Convention.*

48. *Proceedings of the 1872 National Reform Association Convention,* 5.

49. *Proceedings of the 1872 National Reform Association Convention,* 17–18 (A. D. Mayo).

50. *Proceedings of the 1874 National Reform Association Convention,* iv, xi–xii.

51. *Proceedings of the 1874 National Reform Association Convention,* 61 (address of Rev. Edwards).

52. T. P. Stevenson, "The Legal and Practical Effect of the Proposed Amendment," in *Proceedings of the 1874 National Reform Association Convention,* 56; see also *Proceedings,* 38 (Rev. David McAllister); *Proceedings,* 84 (Rev. A. A. Hodge).

53. See Elizabeth Theiss-Morse, *Who Counts as an American? The Boundaries of National Identity* (New York: Cambridge University Press, 2009).

54. Theiss-Morse, *Who Counts as an American?,* 73, 75, 92–93.

55. Theiss-Morse, 159.

56. See Moore, *Founding Sins,* 126.

57. *Proceedings of the 1872 National Reform Association Convention,* 17.

58. *Proceedings,* 18; As Wilbur F. Crafts, who lobbied for decades to create a Sabbath observance law, declared, "With the Sabbath our Christianity and our country stand or fall." Foster, *Moral Reconstruction,* 93.

59. *Proceedings of the 1872 National Reform Association Convention,* 23, 35, 70 (A. D. Mayo).

60. *Proceedings,* 61 (address of Rev. Edwards).

61. *Christian Statesman,* May 21, 1885.

62. Steven K. Green, *Inventing a Christian America: The Myth of the Religious Founding* (New York: Oxford University Press, 2015); see also Stephen M. Stookey, "In God We Trust?: Evangelical Historiography and the Quest for a Christian America," *Southwest Journal of Theology* 41 (1999): 42.

63. *Proceedings of the 1872 National Reform Association Convention,* xi.

64. *Proceedings of the 1874 National Reform Association Convention,* xi, 15.

65. *Proceedings of the 1872 National Reform Association Convention,* iv, xi–xii.

66. *Proceedings,* xi–xii (quoting Updegraph v. Commonwealth, 11 Serg. & Rawle 394, 399 [Pa. 1824]).

67. *Proceedings,* xii.

68. See, e.g., *Proceedings of the 1874 National Reform Association Convention,* 61–64.

69. The structure of the appeal developed in support of the Christian amendment followed what Andrew Murphy has described as a typical American jeremiad, "a form of political rhetoric that explicitly invokes the past as a corrective to the problems of the present." American jeremiads typically involve

the following claims: (1) "Jeremiads identify problems that signal decline vis a vis the past"; (2) "jeremiads identify a point in the past in which the harmful idea or practice responsible for decline first made its appearance, and trace out the injurious consequences from its earliest inception to the present day"; and (3) "jeremiads call for reform, repentance, or renewal—a specific course of action to reverse contemporary decline and to reclaim the original promise of communal life." Andrew Murphy, "Longing, Nostalgia, and Golden Age Politics: The American Jeremiad and the Power of the Past," *Perspectives on Politics* 7, no. 1 (March 2009): 125.

70. *Proceedings of the 1872 National Reform Association Convention*, 59, 7.

71. See *Proceedings*, 37.

72. *Proceedings*, 6 (apparently referring to John A. Jameson, "A Treatise on Constitutional Conventions" § 63 [1867]). As another speaker put it, "The design of a written Constitution is simply to exhibit and declare the exact features of the unwritten Constitution, or the actual character of the nation." Rev. T. P. Stephenson, "The Legal and Practical Value of the Proposed Amendment," in *Proceedings*, 56, 58. Yet another speaker put it similarly: "We must then seek the character of the State in the official principles it adopts. And where shall we look for these principles unless in the Constitution which proclaims to the world the truths from which the State is to draw its life; which defines its rights and powers; which establishes its various departments, and organizes them into one symmetrical whole? The laws and usages which spring from this constitution, as their parent, are but the exponents of its character." O. N. Stoddard, "The Relation of the Written Constitution to the True Character and Welfare of the Nation," in *Proceedings*, 50, 53.

73. *Proceedings*, 6.

74. Rev. T. P. Stephenson, "The Legal and Practical Value of the Proposed Amendment," in *Proceedings*, 58.

75. Rev. J. Edwards, "The Proposed Amendment and the Conscience Question," in, 67, 68; see also "Resolution of 1872 Convention," in *Proceedings*, 50 (emphasis in the original).

76. *Proceedings*, 6 (McAllister).

77. *Proceedings*, 50; see also "The State and the Church," *American Sentinel*, 1, no. 2 (February 1886): 10, http://documents.adventistarchives.org/Periodicals /AmSn/AmSn18860201-V01-02.pdf.

78. *Proceedings*, 7.

79. The leading opponents were Seventh-Day Adventists, who had long been persecuted for observing Saturday as the Sabbath, in violation of Sunday closing laws. Foster, *Moral Reconstruction*, 108; Green, *The Bible, the School, and the Constitution*, 149. In 1886 the Seventh-Day Adventists launched the *American Sentinel*, a newspaper devoted principally to opposing the NRA. See "The American Sentinel," *American Sentinel* 1, no. 1 (January 1886): 1, http://documents

.adventistarchives.org/Periodicals/AmSn/AmSn18860101-Vo1–01.pdf. Jewish organizations also petitioned Congress to oppose the amendment. "Hebrews to Petition Congress," *New York Times*, March 16, 1896, 5. Liberal religionists and freethinkers also organized to oppose the Christian amendment, creating in 1867 the Free Religious Association that became the leading voice of secularism.

80. "What Is the Harm?," *American Sentinel* 1, no. 2 (February 1886): 13, http://documents.adventistarchives.org/Periodicals/AmSn/AmSn18860201-Vo1–02.pdf.

81. "What Is the Harm?," 10.

82. "Secularized Christianity," *American Sentinel* 1, no. 2 (February 1886): 1, http://documents.adventistarchives.org/Periodicals/AmSn/AmSn18860201-Vo1–02.pdf; John W. Chadwick, "Liberty and the Church in America," in Committee of the Free Religious Association, ed., *Freedom and Fellowship in Religion* (Boston: Free Religious Association, 1875), 299, 308.

83. The *American Sentinel* declared, "There are many different churches and religions, or forms of religion, in the land, and no constitutional provision or judicial decision can declare that *all* these are conformable to the Christian faith and practice." "Secularized Christianity," 2; see also Chadwick, "Liberty and the Church in America," 310. In 1894 Jewish organizations declared that the amendment conflicted with principles of equality among faiths and would raise up one doctrine over all others. "Hebrews to Petition Congress," *New York Times*, March 16, 1896, 5. Opponents pointed not only to diversity between Christians and other religions but the substantial religious diversity among Christians. See "A 'Non-Sequitur,'" *American Sentinel* 1, no. 1 (January 1886): 8, http://documents.adventistarchives.org/Periodicals/AmSn/AmSn18860101-Vo1–01.pdf. Another writer argued that if the amendment were adopted, "the court shall decide what is and what is not a Christian law or institution, and how Christian laws and institutions shall or shall not be observed, and what is and what is not a violation of the laws of Christianity." "Secularized Christianity," *American Sentinel* 1, no. 2 (February 1886): 1.

84. Chadwick, "Liberty and the Church in America," 309. See also "Christianity by Legislation," *New York Times*, March 15, 1896, 4.

85. The amendment, one writer asserted, "will disfranchise every one who will not acknowledge, and submit to, the provisions which they choose to embody in their Religious Amendment to the Constitution." "National Reform and the Rights of Conscience," *American Sentinel* 1, no. 2 (February 1886): 11, http://documents.adventistarchives.org/Periodicals/AmSn/AmSn18860201-Vo1–02.pdf.

86. "A Christian Nation," *American Sentinel* 1, no. 1 (January 1886): 7, 14, http://documents.adventistarchives.org/Periodicals/AmSn/AmSn18860101-Vo1–01.pdf; see also "Not a Christian Nation," *American Sentinel* 1, no. 2 (February

1886): 14, http://documents.adventistarchives.org/Periodicals/AmSn/AmSn 18860201-Vo1-02.pdf.

87. In fact, in 1874 the Free Religious Association countered the NRA by proposing its own constitutional amendment, the Free Religious Amendment, which would have extended the First Amendment's prohibition on establishment of religion to the states. Green, *The Bible, the School, and the Constitution,* 162–163.

88. Hearings on H. Res. 28 Joint Resolution Proposing Amendment to the Constitution of the United States, Before the Committee on the Judiciary, House of Representatives, 54th Cong. 3–4, March 11, 1896 (statement of Rev. H. H. George, Field Secretary, National Reform Association).

89. See, e.g., Cong. Globe, 38th Cong., 2nd Sess., (March 2, 1865): 1272.

90. Rector of Holy Trinity Church v. United States, 143 U.S. 457-471 (1892).

91. "The Supreme Court Decision: The Greatest Occasion for Thanksgiving," *Christian Statesman,* November 19, 1892.

92. *Christian Statesman,* June 25, 1892. Compare Moore, *Founding Sins,* 134; and Jay Alan Sekulow, *Witnessing Their Faith: Religious Influences on Supreme Court Justices and Their Opinions* (Lanham, MD: Rowman & Littlefield, 2008), 152; with Steven K. Green, "Justice David Josiah Brewer and the 'Christian Nation' Maxim," *Albany Law Review* 63, no. 2 (Winter 1999): 458.

93. C. B. Waite, "In a Great Crisis," *American Sentinel* 8, no. 6 (February 8, 1893): 43, http://documents.adventistarchives.org/Periodicals/AmSn/AmSn 18930209-Vo8-06.pdf.

94. W. H. M., "The Supreme Court and a National Religion," *American Sentinel* 7, no. 15 (April 14, 1892): 114, http://documents.adventistarchives. org/Periodicals/AmSn/AmSn18920414-Vo7-15.pdf.

95. See, e.g., *American Sentinel* 7, no. 20 (May 19, 1892): 155, http:// documents.adventistarchives.org/Periodicals/AmSn/AmSn18920519-Vo7-20 .pdf; See also United States v. Virginia, 518 U.S. 515, 533 (1996). This is not the only time that proponents of a constitutional amendment arguably got what they wanted in litigation without securing a constitutional amendment. One example is the child labor amendment, which would have authorized Congress to prohibit child labor, which failed to win passage by state legislatures, but in 1941 the Supreme Court ruled that Congress already had such power under the Commerce Clause. United States v. Darby, 312 U.S. 100 (1941). As David Strauss commented, "It was as if the Child Labor Amendment not only had been adopted but also had been given an especially expansive reading." David A. Strauss, "The Irrelevance of Constitutional Amendments," *Harvard Law Review* 114, no. 5 (2001): 1476; see Reva Siegel, "Constitutional Culture, Social Movement Conflict and Constitutional Change: The Case of the De Facto ERA," *California Law Review* 94, no. 5 (October 2006): 1332–1334, 1351–1366.

96. Green, *The Bible, the School, and the Constitution*, 176.

97. Wilbur Fisk Crafts, *Practical Christian Sociology* (New York: Funk & Wagnall, 1895), 197.

98. "Is This a Christian Nation?," *Sentinel of Liberty* 15, no. 27 (July 12, 1900): 419.

99. See Borden, *Jews, Turks, and Infidels*, 74.

100. *The Christian Amendment Movement: What It Is, What You Can Do to Help* (Pittsburgh, PA: Christian Amendment Movement, circa 1960): 3, http://digitalcollections.baylor.edu/cdm/ref/collection/cs-vert/id/8125.

101. *The Christian Amendment Movement*, 12.

102. See *American Christians, Awake!* (Pittsburgh, PA: Christian Amendment Movement, circa 1960): 1, http://digitalcollections.baylor.edu/cdm/compoundobject/collection/cs-vert/id/8116/rec/4.

103. Ronald J. Sider and Diane Knippers, eds., *Toward an Evangelical Public Policy: Political Strategies for the Health of the Nation* (Grand Rapids, MI: Baker Books, 2005), 42.

104. Hearings on S.J. Res. 87, Before a Subcommittee of the Committee on the Judiciary, U.S. Senate, 83rd Cong. 29–30, 35, 45, 52 (1954).

105. Hearings on S.J. Res. 87, 8 (testimony of Mrs. P. de Shishmareff), 21 (testimony of Remo Robb), 28–29 (testimony of R. E. Robb), 43 (testimony of J. Renwick Patterson).

106. See, e.g., Hearings on S.J. Res. 87, 28–29 (testimony of R. E. Robb).

107. Hearings on S.J. Res. 87, 8 (testimony of Mrs. P. de Shishmareff), 21 (testimony of Remo Robb), 28–29 (testimony of R. E. Robb), 43 (testimony of J. Renwick Patterson).

108. See Hearings on S.J. Res. 87, 69–74 (testimony of Rabbi Isidor Breslau, Synagogues Council of America), 86–92 (testimony of David Brody, Anti-Defamation League), 74–82 (testimony of Leo Pfeffer, Synagogue Council of America), 82 (statement of Protestants and Other Americans United for Separation of Church and State), 85 (letter of ACLU).

109. The NRA was so obscure in 1954 that one writer on its history believed it had folded long before. See Borden, *Jews, Turks, and Infidels*, 74.

110. See Mary E. Stuckey, *Defining Americans: The Presidency and National Identity* (Lawrence: University Press of Kansas, 2004), 167–170.

111. Mark Silk, "Notes on the Judeo-Christian Tradition in America," *American Quarterly* 36, no. 1 (1984): 66.

112. Silk, "Notes on the Judeo-Christian Tradition in America," 65.

113. See generally Will Herberg, *Protestant, Catholic, Jew: An Essay in American Religious Sociology* (New York: Doubleday, 1955).

114. Kevin Kruse, *One Nation Under God: How Corporate America Invented Christian America* (New York: Basic Books, 2015), ix.

115. Silk, "Notes on the Judeo-Christian Tradition in America," 69.

116. Kruse, *One Nation Under God*, xi.

117. Kruse, 104.

118. Rev. George Macpherson Docherty, "Under God," sermon, New York Avenue Presbyterian Church, New York City, February 7, 1954, http://www .christianheritagemins.org/articles/UNDER%20GOD.pdf. All quotes from next four paragraphs are from this source.

119. Kruse, *One Nation Under God*, 107–108.

120. Kruse, 109.

121. 100 Cong. Rec. 1700 (1954); emphasis added.

122. Miscellaneous Hearings on H.R. 619, Before the Committee on Banking and Currency, 84th Cong., 1st Sess., 49 (1956); see also 100 Cong. Rec. 7332 (June 7, 1954) (Rep. Bolton).

123. Dwight D. Eisenhower, "Statement by the President Upon Signing Bill to Include the Words 'Under God' in the Pledge to the Flag," June 14, 1954, *American Presidency Project*, https://www.presidency.ucsb.edu/node/232153.

124. Kruse, *One Nation Under God*, 110.

125. 100 Cong. Rec. 8617 (1954).

126. 31 U.S.C.A. § 5114(b); Kruse, *One Nation Under God*, 119.

127. Kruse, 119.

128. National Motto Act of 1955, Pub. L. No. 84-140, 69 Stat. 290 (1956); National Motto, 36 U.S.C. § 302 (2002); Kruse, 123–125.

129. Engel v. Vitale, 176 N.E.2d 579, 581 (N.Y. Ct. of App. 1961).

130. State Board of Regents, "The Regents Statement on Moral and Spiritual Training in the Schools (n.p., 1951).

131. Engel v. Vitale, 176 N.E.2d 579, 581 (N.Y. Ct. of App. 1961).

132. Engel v. Vitale, 370 U.S. 421, 425 (1962).

133. Engel v. Vitale, 370 U.S. at 434-435.

134. School Dist. of Abington Tp. v. Schempp, 374 U.S. 203 (1963).

135. See Kruse, *One Nation Under God*, 185.

136. Kruse, 188.

137. Kruse, 185.

138. "Congress Fails to Act on School Prayer Amendments," in *CQ Almanac 1964*, 20th ed. (Washington, DC: Congressional Quarterly, 1965): 398-404, http://library.cqpress.com/cqalmanac/cqa164-1304697.

139. Kruse, *One Nation Under God*, 205; see also, e.g., Hearing on the Proposed Amendments to the Constitution Relating to Prayers and Bible Readings in the Public Schools, Before the Committee on the Judiciary, House, 88th Cong., 2nd Sess., 311 (1964) (hereinafter 1964 School Prayer Amendment Hearings).

140. See, e.g., 1964 School Prayer Amendment Hearings, 307, 318, 638, 1405.

141. Kruse, *One Nation Under God*, 205.

142. "Congress Fails to Act on School Prayer Amendments," 398–404.

143. Linda Lyons, "The Gallup Brain: Prayer in Public Schools," Gallup, posted on December 10, 2002, http://www.gallup.com/poll/7393/gallup -brain-prayer-public-schools.aspx.

144. Kruse, *One Nation Under God*, 211.

145. Kruse, 212; Republican National Committee, "We Believe in America: 2012 Republican Platform," August 27, 2012, American Presidency Project, 12, https://www.presidency.ucsb.edu/documents/2012-republican-party-plat form.

146. See, e.g., 1964 School Prayer Amendment Hearings, 218, 329, 740, 780; Kruse, 189.

147. Some members of Congress believed that adoption of the Christian amendment, rather than the school prayer amendment, was the proper response to *Engel* and *Schempp*. See Prayers in Public Schools and Other Matters, Hearings on S.J. Res. 205, Before the Committee on the Judiciary, 87th Cong., 2nd Sess., 43–44 (July 26 and August 2, 1962) (testimony of Rep. Eugene Siler), 81 (testimony of Rep. John Anderson), 82–83 (testimony of Rep. J. Floyd Breeding).

148. Hearings on S.J. Res. 205, 1077 (statement by Rev. Creighton), 1087 (statement by Rev. Mosley), 1290 (statement by Protestants and other Americans United for Separation of Church and State), 1345 (statement by Prof. Kenealy), 1370 (statement by Prof. Littell).

149. "Congress Fails to Act on School Prayer Amendments," 398–404.

150. The Republican Party has continued to endorse the prayer amendment, in various formulations, ever since. President Reagan submitted a new version of the proposal in 1982. "Reagan Proposes School Prayer Amendment," *New York Times*, May 18, 1982, A24, http://www.nytimes.com/1982/05/18/us/reagan -proposes-school-prayer-amendment.html; Ronald Reagan, "Radio Address to the Nation on Prayer in Schools," February 25, 1984, American Presidency Project, http://www.presidency.ucsb.edu/ws/?pid=39565.

151. See Robert C. Liebman and Robert Wuthnow, eds., *The New Christian Right: Mobilization and Legitimation* (New York: Aldine, 1983); Michael Lienesch, *Redeeming America: Piety and Politics in the New Christian Right* (Chapel Hill: University of North Carolina Press, 1993).

152. Liebman and Wuthnow, *The New Christian Right*, 1–3.

153. See, e.g., Liebman and Wuthnow, *The New Christian Right*; Steve Bruce, The Rise and Fall of the *New Christian Right: Conservative Protestant Politics in America, 1978–1988* (London: Oxford University Press, 1988), 1–24.

154. See Lienesch, *Redeeming America*, 147.

155. "Religion," in Depth Topics, Gallup, accessed on September 21, 2018, http://www.gallup.com/poll/1690/religion.aspx.

156. See Liebman and Wuthnow, *The New Christian Right*, 16; Axel R. Schäfer,

Countercultural Conservatives: American Evangelicalism from the Postwar Revival to the New Christian Right (Studies in American Thought and Culture) (Madison: University of Wisconsin Press, 2011), 131.

157. Jerry Falwell, *Listen, America!* (New York: Bantam Books, 1981).

158. Clyde Wilcox, "The Christian Right in Twentieth-Century America: Continuity and Change," *Review of Politics* 50, no. 4 (Autumn 1988): 664–665.

159. Macel Falwell and Melanie Hemry, *Jerry Falwell: His Life and Legacy* (New York: Howard Books, 2008), 96.

160. Falwell, *Listen, America!*, 255–266.

161. Falwell, 222, 121; Seth Dowland, "'Family Values' and the Formation of a Christian Right Agenda," *Church History* 78, no. 3 (September 2009): 606–631.

162. Falwell, *Listen, America!*, 124, 150.

163. Falwell, 208–213, 165–240.

164. Falwell, 222; see Nathaniel Klemp and Stephen Macedo, "The Christian Right, Public Reason, and American Democracy," in Steven G. Brint and Jean Reith Schroedel, eds., *Evangelicals and Democracy in America, Vol. II: Religion and Politics* (New York: Russell Sage Foundation, 2009), 209.

165. Rhys H. Williams, "Politicized Evangelicalism and Secular Elites: Creating a Moral Other," in Brint and Schroedel, *Evangelicals and Democracy in America*, 163.

166. Klemp and Macedo, "The Christian Right, Public Reason, and American Democracy," 221.

167. Dowland, "'Family Values' and the Formation of a Christian Right Agenda," 606–631 (quoting Moral Majority pamphlet); see also Falwell, *Listen, America!*, 121–137; Christopher P. Toumey, "Evolution and Secular Humanism," *Journal of the American Academy of Religion* 61, no. 2 (Summer 1993): 275–301.

168. Tim LaHaye, *The Battle for the Mind: A Subtle Warfare* (Grand Rapids, MI: Fleming H. Revell, 1980), 57, 27; see also Jeffrey K. Hadden and Charles E. Swann, *Prime Time Preachers: The Rising Power of Televangelism* (Boston: Addison-Wesley, 1983), 86.

169. LaHaye, *The Battle for the Mind*, 26.

170. See Don Melichar, "A Leap of Faith: The New Right and Secular Humanism," *English Journal* 72, no. 6 (October 1983): 55–58, 56.

171. Falwell, *Listen, America!*, 65; see also Pat Robertson, *The New World Order* (Nashville, TN: W Publishing, 1991), 170; John Whitehead and John Conlan, "The Establishment of the Religion of Secular Humanism," *Texas Tech Law Review* 66 (1978): 30–31.

172. Falwell, *Listen, America!*, 66.

173. As Ed Rowe, president of Christian Mandate for America, put it, secular humanism is based on "the idea that man doesn't need God" and "out of that corrupt fountain have come the various movements which have disturbed

Planet Earth in this century—Socialism, Communism, Fascism, Nazism, and now a movement which I choose to call New Age Globalism." Ed Rowe, *New Age Globalism: Humanist Agenda for Building a New World without God* (Berkeley, CA: Growth Publishing, 1985), 1.

174. See, e.g., Falwell, *Listen, America!*, 17–23; Francis A. Schaeffer, *A Christian Manifesto* (Wheaton, IL: Crossway Books, 1981), 42, 49, 112; John W. Whitehead, *The Second American Revolution* (Elgin, IL: David C. Cook Publishing, 1982), 33–42; Robertson, *The New World Order*, 143.

175. See, e.g., Falwell, *Listen, America!*, 222; M. G. "Pat" Robertson, "Religion in the Classroom," *William and Mary Bill Rights Journal* 4, no. 2 (1995): 595; John W. Whitehead, *The Separation Illusion: A Lawyer Examines the First Amendment* (Fenton, MI: Mott Media, 1977), 111–124.

176. Falwell, 65, 87–232.

177. Schaeffer, *A Christian Manifesto*, 53.

178. See Jeremy Brooke Straughn and Scott L. Feld, "America as a 'Christian Nation'? Understanding Religious Boundaries of National Identity in the United States," *Sociology of Religion* 71, no. 3 (2010): 280–306.

179. See Theiss-Morse, *Who Counts as an American?*

180. See, e.g., Edward B. Jenkinson, "The Search for Alien Religions in School Textbooks," *Educational Horizons* 70, no. 4 (Summer 1992): 181–188.

181. LaHaye, *The Battle for the Mind*, 26.

182. Falwell, *Listen, America!*, 57.

183. Falwell, 22–23.

184. Whitehead, *The Separation Illusion*, 62.

185. Whitehead, 62–63, 35.

186. Justin Watson, *The Christian Coalition: Dreams of Restoration, Demands for Recognition* (New York: St. Martin's Press, 1997), 93.

187. Alan M. Dershowitz, *The Vanishing American Jew: In Search of Jewish Identity for the Next Century* (New York: Touchstone, 1997), 149.

188. Wayne King, "The Record of Pat Robertson on Religion and Government," *New York Times*, December 27, 1987, 1.

189. Pat Robertson, *The New World Order*, 218.

190. Falwell, *Listen, America!*, 53, 29, 16, 29–50, 47; see also Rector of Holy Trinity Church, 143 U.S. at 457.

191. Rev. Pat Robertson, "The 700 Club," broadcast December 20, 1981; see also Whitehead, *The Separation Illusion*, 114.

192. Pat Robertson, *Courting Disaster: How the Supreme Court Is Usurping the Power of Congress and the People* (Brentwood, TN: Integrity Publishers, 2004), 113–114 (quoting 1963 letter).

193. Robertson, "Religion in the Classroom," 595–596; see also Engel, 370 U.S. at 421.

194. Robertson, 595–596; see also David Barton, *The Myth of Separation:*

What Is the Correct Relationship between Church and State (Aledo, TX: WallBuilder Press, 1992), 209–216.

195. See Bruce J. Dierenfield, *The Battle over School Prayer: How* Engel v. Vitale *Changed America* (Lawrence: University Press of Kansas, 2007), 187–212.

196. See, e.g., Falwell, *Listen, America!*, 222; Robertson, "Religion in the Classroom."

197. Barton, *The Myth of Separation*, 47–82, 83–136.

198. Barton, 39, 33.

199. See, e.g., Erik Eckholm, "Using History to Mold Ideas on the Right," *New York Times*, March 4, 2001, A1; Stephen M. Stookey, "In God We Trust? Evangelical Historiography and the Quest for a Christian America," *Southwest Journal of Theology* 41, no. 2 (Spring 1999): 47–48 (reviewing Barton's work); Garrett Epps, "Genuine Christian Scholars Smack down an Unruly Colleague," *Atlantic Monthly*, August 10, 2012, https://www.theatlantic.com/national/archive/2012/08/genuine-christian-scholars-smack-down-an-unruly-colleague/260994/.

200. Chris Vaughn, "Fort Worth Star-Telegram—A Man with a Message; Self-Taught Historian's Work on Church-State Issues Rouses GOP," *Baylor in the News*, May 22, 2005, http://web.archive.org/web/20060920013836/http://www.baylor.edu/pr/bitn/news.php?action=story&story=34559; see also Robertson, *Religion in the Classroom* (citing Barton ten times in as many pages).

201. Right Wing Watch and People for the American Way, *Barton, Inc.: Hack "Historian" Hits the Big Time in Tea Party America*, 2011, 3, http://files.rightwingwatch.org/uploads/rww-in-focus-david-barton-5-3-11.pdf. In addition, Barton has been a frequent guest on Glenn Beck's radio and television shows, and Beck has called him "the most important man in America."

202. For discussion of the different tactics for accomplishing constitutional change, see Bruce Ackerman, *We The People, Volume 2: Transformations* (Cambridge, MA: Belknap Press, 1998), 15–27; Donald S. Lutz, *Principles of Constitutional Design* (New York: Cambridge University Press, 2006), 178–179; Heather K. Gerken, "The Hydraulics of Constitutional Reform: A Skeptical Response to Our Undemocratic Constitution," *Drake Law Review* 55, no. 4 (2007), 926–927; Stephen M. Griffin, "Constitutionalism in the United States: From Theory to Politics," in Sanford Levinson, ed., *Responding to Imperfection: The Theory and Practice of Constitutional Amendment* (Princeton, NJ: Princeton University Press, 1995), 37, 54; Adam M. Samaha, "Dead Hand Arguments and Constitutional Interpretation," *Columbia Law Review* 108, no. 3 (January 2008): 616–618.

Chapter 3. The Nativist Constitution

1. See, e.g., Rogers M. Smith, "The 'American Creed' and American Identity: The Limits of Liberal Citizenship in the United States," *Western Political Quarterly* 41, no. 2 (June 1988): 228.
2. John Higham, *Strangers in the Land: Patterns of American Nativism 1860–1925*, 2nd ed. (New Brunswick, NJ: Rutgers University Press, 1977), 4; see also Brian N. Fry, *Nativism and Immigration: Regulating the American Dream* (New York: LFB Scholarly Publishing, 2007), 1–8.
3. Higham, *Strangers in the Land*, 4.
4. Benjamin Franklin, "Observations Concerning the Increase of Mankind," in Leonard W. Labaree and Whitfield J. Bell Jr., eds., *The Papers of Benjamin Franklin*, vol. 4, 1745–1750 (New Haven, CT: Yale University Press, 1961), 234.
5. Franklin, "Observations Concerning the Increase of Mankind," 234. For a discussion of how the same metaphors are often used to describe unwanted immigration and unwanted insects, see generally Jared A. Goldstein, "Aliens in the Garden," *University of Colorado Law Review* 80, no. 3 (2009): 685.
6. Naturalization Act of 1790, ch. 3, 1 Stat. 103, 1st Cong. (1790). In 1795 Congress amended the act in several ways but maintained the limitations that naturalization was only available to "free white persons" who could show they were "attached to the principles of the constitution of the United States." Act of January 29, 1795, ch. 20, 1 Stat. 414, 3rd Cong. (1795).
7. Dred Scott v. Sandford, 60 U.S. 393, 407 (1856).
8. See Kevin Phillips, *The Cousins' Wars* (New York: Basic Books, 1999), 483; see also Roger Daniels, *Guarding the Golden Door: American Immigration Policy and Immigrants since 1882* (New York: Hill & Wang, 2004), 10–11.
9. See *American Platform of Principles* (February 21, 1856), par. 2, accessed on January 18, 2019, https://glc.yale.edu/american-platform-principles.
10. Peter Schrag, *Not Fit for Our Society: Nativism and Immigration in America* (Berkeley: University of California Press, 2010), 31–32 (quoting "Rome and America Eternal Opposites," *The True American's Almanac and Politician's Manual for 1857*).
11. *American Platform of Principles*, par. 3.
12. "1876 Democratic Party Platform," June 22, 1876, American Presidency Project, https://www.presidency.ucsb.edu/documents/1876-democratic-party-platform.
13. "1880 Republican Party Platform," June 2, 1880, par. 5, American Presidency Project, https://www.presidency.ucsb.edu/documents/republican-party-platform-1880.
14. See generally Act of May 6, 1882, ch. 126, 22 Stat. 58, 47th Cong. (1882).
15. 13 Cong. Rec. 1583 (statement of Sen. Maxey).
16. 13 Cong. Rec. 1742 (1882) (statement of Sen. Jones); see also

Gabriel J. Chin, "Segregation's Last Stronghold: Race Discrimination and the Constitutional Law of Immigration," *UCLA Law Review* 46, no. 1 (1998): 22-36.

17. 13 Cong Rec. 2223 (statement of Rep. Cannon); 13 Cong Rec. 1978 (statement of Rep. Cassidy).

18. In the 1850s, 2.6 million immigrants came to the United States, and in the 1880s that number increased to 5.2 million. In the first decade of the twentieth century 8.8 million people immigrated to the United States. Daniels, *Guarding the Golden Door*, 5, table 1.2.

19. Daniels, table 1.1.

20. Helen F. Eckerson, "Immigration and National Origins," *Annals of the American Academy of Political and Social Science* 367, no. 1 (September 1966): 6.

21. David Goldfield, *Encyclopedia of American Urban History*, vol. 1 (Thousand Oaks, CA: Sage Publications, 2007), 122.

22. Higham, *Strangers in the Land*, 159-175; see also James S. Pula, "The Progressives, the Immigrant, and the Workplace: Defining Public Perceptions, 1900-1914," *Polish American Studies* 52, no. 2 (Autumn 1995): 57-69.

23. Robert De C. Ward, "Fallacies of the Melting-Pot Idea and America's Traditional Immigration Policy," in Madison Grant and Chas. Stewart Davison, eds., *The Alien in Our Midst* (New York: Galton Publishing, 1930), 231.

24. Israel Zangwill, *The Melting Pot: Drama in Four-Acts* (New York: Macmillan, 1909).

25. J. Hector St. John De Crevecoeur, *Letters from an American Farmer and Sketches of Eighteenth-Century America* (New York: Penguin American Library, 1981), 69-70.

26. Higham, *Strangers in the Land*, 235.

27. Steven K. Green, *The Bible, the School, and the Constitution: The Clash That Shaped Modern Church-State Doctrine* (New York: Oxford University Press, 2012), 11.

28. Green, *The Bible, the School, and the Constitution*, 11-12.

29. Higham, *Strangers in the Land*, 237.

30. Higham, 238.

31. Higham, 238-239.

32. See "Melting Pot Ceremony at Ford English School, July 4, 1917," The Henry Ford Archive, accessed November 6, 2017, https://www.thehenryford .org/collections-and-research/digital-collections/artifact/254569.

33. Clinton C. DeWitt, "Industrial Teachers, Address of Mr Clinton C. DeWitt, director of Americanization, Ford Motor Co.," in *Proceedings, Americanization Conference, Held under the Auspices of the Americanization Division, Bureau of Education, Department of the Interior, Washington, DC, 1919* (Washington, DC: Government Printing Office, 1919), 114, 119 (hereinafter *Proceedings, Americanization Conference*).

34. A photograph and description of the ceremony can be found at the

website of the Henry Ford Archive, https://www.thehenryford.org/collections
-and-research/digital-collections/artifact/254569.

35. *Proceedings, Americanization Conference,* 119.

36. Edward George Hartmann, *The Movement to Americanize the Immigrant* (New York: Columbia University Press, 1948), 24.

37. Christina A. Ziegler-McPherson, *Americanization in the States: Immigrant Social Welfare Policy, Citizenship, and National Identity in the United States, 1908–1929* (Gainesville: University of Florida Press, 2009), 20, 25.

38. Higham, *Strangers in the Land,* 237.

39. Higham, 238; see also Ziegler-McPherson, *Americanization in the States,* 10.

40. Higham, 237; Hartmann, *The Movement to Americanize the Immigrant,* 218, 220.

41. Higham, 255; see also Fred H. Ringe Jr., "Promotion of Work for Foreigners and Illiterates in the Lumber Camps," in *Proceedings, Americanization Conference, 1919,* 165, 166.

42. Higham, 195. See also Address of Mr. S. E. Weber, in *Proceedings, Americanization Conference,* 150.

43. See Higham, 198.

44. Higham, 199; Theodore Roosevelt, "America for Americans," speech, St. Louis, Missouri May 31, 1916, http://www.theodore-roosevelt.com/images/research/txtspeeches/672.pdf.

45. Fred C. Butler, "Purposes of the Conference and Plans of the Americanization Division," in *Proceedings Americanization Conference,* 24; see, e.g., "Origins of the Federal Naturalization Service," Official Website of the Department of Homeland Security, updated December 4, 2019, https://www.uscis.gov/history-and-genealogy/our-history/agency-history/origins-federal-naturalization-service.

46. In its coursebook for citizenship, the Bureau of Naturalization declared: "The matter most intimately concerning the naturalization of aliens is such an understanding of the principles of the Constitution as to make credible the declaration that he is 'attached' to those principles." US Department of Labor, Bureau of Naturalization, *An Outline Course in Citizenship to Be Used in the Public Schools for the Instruction of the Foreign and Native Born Candidate for Adult-Citizenship Responsibilities* (Washington, DC: Government Printing Office, 1916), 3; see also Hartmann, *The Movement to Americanize the Immigrant,* 220 (quoting National Security League pamphlet).

47. Bureau of Naturalization, *An Outline Course in Citizenship,* 3; Desmond King, *Making Americans: Immigration, Race, and the Origins of the Diverse Democracy* (Cambridge, MA: Harvard University Press, 2000), 88.

48. See "Address of Felix J. Streyckmans, Securing Interest of and Cooperation with National and Local Racial Organizations, in *Proceedings, Americanization Conference,* 204; see also Grover C. Huebner, "The Americanization of the

Immigrant," *Annals of the American Academy of Political and Social Science* 27 (May 1906): 191–213 (defining Americanization as "the process by which immigrants are transformed into Americans. . . . An immigrant has been Americanized only when his mind and will have been united, with the mind and will of the American so that the two act and think together."); see also "Address of John J. Mahoney," *Proceedings, Americanization Conference*, 126; "Address of S. E. Weber," in *Proceedings*, 151.

49. Commission of Immigration & Housing of California, Annual Report, *Journals of the Legislature of the State of California* (1919): 5, 11; Hartmann, *The Movement to Americanize the Immigrant*, 124–126.

50. William Lamkie, "Americanizing the Immigrant through Industrial Employment," in *Proceedings, Americanization Conference*, 179.

51. Address of Franklin Lane, in *Proceedings, Americanization Conference*, 18.

52. See generally *Proceedings, Americanization Conference*.

53. See P. P. Claxton, "Commissioner of Education, Education in Americanization," *Proceedings, Americanization Conference*, 27.

54. See Address of H. D. Rickard, in *Proceedings, Americanization Conference*, 60–61.

55. Address of Franklin Lane, in *Proceedings, Americanization Conference*, 295; see also Address of Louis Post, in *Proceedings of First Citizenship Conference* 14 (July 1916); see also Hartmann, *The Movement to Americanize the Immigrant*, 269–270.

56. Elswood Griscom Jr., *Americanization: A School Reader and Speaker* (1920). To be sure, another less widely distributed Americanization handbook presented more varied and contemporary materials, including excerpts from John Dewey, W. E. B. DuBois, and Walt Whitman. Winthrop Talbot and Julia E. Johnsen, eds., *Americanization: Principals of Americanism, Essentials of Americanization, Technic of Race-Assimilation*, 2nd ed. (New York: H. W. Wilson, 1920).

57. Address of William McAndrew, in *Proceedings, Americanization Conference*, 242.

58. See, e.g., Address of Mrs. J. E. Owen Phillips, in *Proceedings, Americanization Conference*, 102.

59. Benjamin Schwarz, "Exporting the Myth of a Liberal America," *World Policy Journal* 15, no. 3 (Autumn 1998): 72; see also Hearings on Immigration, Before the House Immigration Committee, U.S. House, 67th Cong., 3d Sess., November 21, 1923 (testimony, "Analysis of the Metal and Dross in America's Melting Pot," Harry H. Laughlin).

60. Michael R. Olneck, "Americanization and the Education of Immigrants, 1900–1925: An Analysis of Symbolic Action," *American Journal of Education* 97, no. 4 (August 1989): 400.

61. Constitution of the Immigration Restriction League , art. II. Although other groups joined with the IRL in urging immigration restriction, I focus on the IRL because it has been well-recognized as the leading anti-immigrant

group of the era, whose advocacy led directly to the enactment of the 1924 Immigration Act. See Daniels, *Guarding the Golden Door*, 31.

62. See, e.g., Immigration Restriction League, *Study These Figures and Draw Your Own Conclusions: Recent Changes in the Nationality of Immigrants*, no. 2, 2nd ed. (Boston: Immigration Restriction League, 1894); see Immigration Restriction League, *The Present Aspect of the Immigration Problem*, no. 1, 2nd ed. (Boston: Immigration Restriction League, 1894), 4 ("Our immigration has, until lately, been chiefly made up of the most intelligent and of the most desirable races of Europe, but recently the numbers have greatly increased of those who are without question the most illiterate and the most depraved people of that continent.").

63. See, e.g., Immigration Restriction League, *The Present Aspect*, 6; see also Immigration Restriction League, *Twenty Reasons Why Immigration Should Be Further Restricted Now*, no. 4 (Boston: Immigration Restriction League, 1894), 6–8.

64. See Immigration Restriction League, *Twenty Reasons*, 2.

65. See Robert De C. Ward, *The Restriction of Immigration* (New York: North American Review Publishing, 1904), 230; see also Immigration Restriction League, *Twenty Reasons*, 8.

66. See Prescott F. Hall, "The Future of American Ideals," *North American Mandate* 195, no. 674 (January 1912): 95.

67. Immigration Restriction League, *Twenty Reasons*, 19.

68. See Hall, "The Future of American Ideals," 100, 102.

69. Eugenicists dreamed of improving the human race through the social control of breeding. As Francis Galton, founder of the eugenics movement, pronounced, "If talented men were mated with talented women . . . generation after generation, we might produce a highly-bred human race." Jonathan Peter Spiro, *Defending the Master Race: Conservation, Eugenics, and the Legacy of Madison Grant* (Burlington: University of Vermont Press, 2009), 120–121 (quoting Francis Galton, "Hereditary Talent and Character, Second Paper," *Macmillan's Magazine* 12, no. 70 [August 1865]: 319). See also Hall, "The Future of American Ideals," 101.

70. Hall, 94. See also Prescott F. Hall, "The Present and Future of Immigration," *North American Review* 213, no. 786 (1921): 606.

71. Hall, "The Future of American Ideals," 95; see also Hall, "The Present and Future of Immigration," 605.

72. Hall, "The Future of American Ideals," 97–98, 101.

73. It has been referred to as the "bible of scientific racism," and Adolf Hitler is said to have called the German edition "my bible." Spiro, *Defending the Master Race*, xi, 140. See also Higham, *Strangers in the Land*, 271

74. Madison Grant, *The Passing of the Great Race or the Racial Basis of European History* (New York: Charles Scriber's Sons, 1918), 227; see also Henry Fairfield Osborn, "Preface," in Grant, *The Passing of the Great Race*, vii.

75. Grant, 227, 229, 228.

76. Grant, 167, 214–215.

77. Grant, 228.

78. Clinton Stoddard Burr, *America's Race Heritage* (New York: National Historical Society, 1922).

79. Grant, *The Passing of the Great Race*, 83–84, 88, 218, 89–90.

80. Grant, 12.

81. See Grant, 17–18 ("What the Melting Pot actually does in practice can be seen in Mexico, where the absorption of the blood of the original Spanish conquerors by the native Indian population has produced the racial mixture which we call Mexican and which is now engaged in demonstrating its incapacity for self-government. . . . Whether we like to admit it or not, the result of the mixture of two races, in the long run, gives us a race reverting to the more ancient, generalized and lower type.").

82. Ward, *The Restriction of Immigration*, 230–231.

83. See Hall, "The Future of American Ideals," 97–98.

84. See Hall, "The Present and Future of Immigration," 607.

85. Higham, *Strangers in the Land*, 103.

86. See Immigration Restriction League, *The Case for the Literacy Test* (New York: Henry Holt, 1915), 12–14, 17, previously published as "The Case for the Literacy Test," in *Unpopular Review* (January-March 1916); Immigration Restriction League, *The Present Italian Influx: Its Striking Illiteracy*, no. 14 (Boston: Immigration Restriction League, 1896).

87. Higham, *Strangers in the Land*, 103.

88. 28 Cong. Rec., 54th Cong., 1st Sess., 2817 (1896) (statement of Sen. Lodge).

89. 28 Cong. Rec., 54th Cong., 1st Sess., 2817–2818.

90. See 28 Cong. Rec., 54th Cong., 1st Sess., 819–820 (raising the concern that the immigrants of "other races of totally different race origin" will bring down the "higher [race]," resulting in a population more susceptible to socialism that would threaten the stability of the United States). The bill's supporters in the House agreed. See, e.g., 28 Cong. Rec., 54th Cong., 1st Sess., 5475 (1896) (statement of Rep. Mahany) (declaring that from the Germanic race "we draw . . . those democratic ideas which are the historic foundation of this very House now deliberating on this question"); 28 Cong. Rec., 54th Cong., 1st Sess., 5474.

91. Grover Cleveland, "Veto Message," in James D. Richardson, ed., *A Compilation of the Messages and Papers of the Presidents*, vol. 13 (New York: Bureau of National Literature, 1897), 6189, 6191 ("I can not believe that we would be protected against these evils by limiting immigration to those who can read and write in any language twenty-five words of our Constitution.").

92. Cleveland, "Veto Message," 6190.

93. John M. Lund, "Boundaries of Restriction: The Dillingham Commission,"

History Review 6 (December 1994), http://www.uvm.edu/~hag/histreview/vo16 /lund.html.

94. See James S. Pula, "American Immigration Policy and the Dillingham Commission," *Polish American Studies* 37, no. 1 (Spring 1980): 5, 8, 14.

95. US Senate, Immigration Commission, 61st Cong., *Dictionary of Races or Peoples*, Senate Doc. No. 662 (Washington, DC: Government Printing Office, 1911), 1 ,15, 47.

96. US Senate, Immigration Commission, 61st Cong., *Abstracts of Reports of the Immigration Commission, Brief Statement of the Investigations of the Immigration Commission, with Conclusions and Recommendations and Views of the Minority*, Senate Doc. No. 747, vol. 1 (Washington, DC: Government Printing Office, 1911), 13 (hereinafter, *Brief Statement of the Investigations of the Immigration Commission*); see also *Dictionary of Races or Peoples*, 32.

97. *Brief Statement of the Investigations of the Immigration Commission*, 13–14.

98. US Senate, Immigration Commission, 61st Cong., *Brief Statement of the Conclusions and Recommendations of the Immigration Commission, with Views of the Minority* (Washington, DC: Government Printing Office, 1910), 40.

99. See US Senate, Immigration Commission, 61st Cong., *Emigration Conditions in Europe: Reports of the Immigration Commission*, vol. 2 (Washington, DC: Government Printing Office, 1911), 27–28.

100. US Senate, Immigration Commission, 61st Cong., *Emigration Conditions in Europe, Reports of the Immigration Commission* (Washington, DC: Government Printing Office, 1911), 31.

101. See George M. Stephenson, *A History of American Immigration: 1820–1924* (Boston: Ginn, 1926), 166.

102. H.R. 10384, 64th Cong., 2nd Sess. (1917).

103. Higham, *Strangers in the Land*, 308.

104. Higham, 313.

105. See Emergency Immigration Legislation, Hearings Before the Committee on Immigration and Naturalization, House of Reps., 67th Cong., 1st Sess. (April 15 and 26, 1921), 23.

106. Hartmann, *The Movement to Americanize the Immigrant*, 269, 225, 236, 237–253.

107. See Constantine Panunzio, *Immigration Crossroads* (New York: Macmillan, 1927), 254.

108. Hartmann, *The Movement to Americanize the Immigrant*, 259. As one Italian-language newspaper declared, "Americanization is an ugly word. Today it means to proselytize by making the foreign-born forget his mother country and mother tongue." Hartmann, 257 (quoting *L'Aurora*, Reading, Pennsylvania, June 12, 1920).

109. Hartmann, 257–258.

110. Henry Pratt Fairchild, *Immigration: A World Movement and Its American Significance* (New York: Macmillan, 1925), 431 (emphasis in original).

111. See Higham, *Strangers in the Land*, 263.

112. Higham, 307, 313–314; Spiro, *Defending the Master Race*, 203.

113. Higham, 313–314.

114. See H.R. 4075, 67th Cong., 1st Sess. (1921); see also Higham, 308–311.

115. See the Immigration Act of 1924, Pub L. No. 68-139, 43 Stat. 153 (1924).

116. Immigration Act of 1924 § 11(a).

117. Eckerson, *Immigration and National Origins*, 9, table 2.

118. Immigration Act of 1924 § 2(a), 5. The Naturalization Act of 1870 had opened the naturalization process to "aliens of African nativity and to persons of African descent" and thus, as a theoretical matter at least, the 1924 National Origins Act did not foreclose immigration by persons of African descent. However, no immigration quotas were allotted to any African countries under the act because immigrant visas were allocated solely based on the nation's white population.

119. See, e.g., Cong. Rec. 11744 (June 24, 1924) ("Mr. Speaker, with this new immigration act the United States is undertaking to regulate and control the great problem of the commingling of races. Our hope is in a homogeneous Nation.") (statement of Rep. Johnson).

120. See 1921 Hearings at 23. Organized labor, which had supported immigration restriction to avoid economic competition, began to argue, as the president of the American Federation of Labor declared, that immigration restriction was also necessary to protect "American character and national unity." Higham, *Strangers in the Land*, 305–306.

121. See 68 Cong. Rec. 5847 (statement of Rep. Stengle) ("We should thoroughly realize that one of the greatest menaces to the proper development of our cherished ideals lies in the invasion of our country by that class of foreign Immigrants who have no conception of nor Interest In those ideals and principles for which we stand but have been taught and trained in antagonistic principles for many generations in the countries of their nativity."); 68 Cong. Rec. 5852 (Rep. Reynolds) (declaring that foreigners were flooding into the country who "have never drawn the breath of freedom; they have never lived under a republic" and they are "spreading their doctrines in this country and undertaking to force the same upon us.").

122. See 65 Cong. Rec. 5848 (1924): 5852 (statement of Rep. McReynolds).

123. Restriction of Immigration, House of Reps. 68th Cong., 1st Sess., Report no. 350 (March 24, 1924), 13; John Trevor, a prominent eugenicist and advisor to the House Immigration Committee, put it even more bluntly: from the time of the founding, Trevor wrote, "citizenship in the United States

is limited, with one exception, arising from the suppression of slavery within the States, to those races of mankind who by tradition, ideals and habits of life would tend to support and perpetuate the principles of Republican Government in this nation." John B. Trevor, "An Analysis of the American Immigration Act of 1924," *International Conciliation*, no. 202 (New York: Carnegie Endowment for International Peace, Division of Intercourse and Education, 1924), 375, 376–377.https://iiif.lib.harvard.edu/manifests/view/drs:4907177$1i

124. Calvin Coolidge, "Whose Country Is This?," *Good Housekeeping* 72, no. 2 (February 1921): 14.

125. Calvin Coolidge, "First Annual Message," speech, Washington DC, December 6, 1923, American Presidency Project, https://www.presidency.ucsb.edu/node/206712http://www.presidency.ucsb.edu/ws/?pid=29564.

126. Bureau of Foreign and Domestic Commerce, US Department of Commerce, *Statistical Abstract of the United States: Fifty First Number* (Washington, DC: Government Printing Office, 1929), 100, chart 111.

127. See Mae M. Ngai, "The Architecture of Race in American Immigration Law: A Reexamination of the Immigration Act of 1924," *Journal of American History* 86, no. 1 (June 1999): 67, 74, table 1.

128. See An Act to Limit the Immigration of Aliens into the United States, and for Other Purposes, US Statutes at Large, 68th Cong., Sess. 1 (1924), 153–169; see § 11(d) (excluding "aliens ineligible to citizenship or their descendants" from allocation of immigration quotas).

129. National Origins Act §§ 11, 11(d).

130. See National Origins Act, §§ 4, 11(d).

131. National Origins Act §§ 4, 11(d); Letti Volpp, review of Mae Ngai, *Impossible Subjects: Illegal Aliens and the Making of Modern America, Michigan Law Review* 103, no. 6 (2005): 1599.

132. National Origins Act § 11(a).

133. Aziz Rana traces the now-conventional universalistic conception of America's civic identity to the closing of the frontier and the Spanish-American War. See Aziz Rana, "Colonialism and Constitutional Memory," *UC Irvine Law Review* 5 (2015): 268.

134. "Praises Army Plan for Japanese Unit," *New York Times*, February 5, 1943, 6.

135. McCarran-Walter Act, Pub. L. No. 82-414, §211(c), 66 Stat. 163 (1952), 181.

136. Harry S. Truman, "Veto of Bill to Revise the Laws Relating to Immigration, Naturalization, and Nationality," speech, Washington, DC, June 25, 1952, American Presidency Project, https://www.presidency.ucsb.edu/node/231060.

137. 99 Cong. Rec. 1517 (March 2, 1953).

138. 99 Cong. Rec. 1518 ("I believe that this nation is the last hope of

Western civilization and if this oasis of the world shall be overrun, perverted, contaminated or destroyed, then the last flickering light of humanity will be extinguished."). McCarran believed that even with restrictive immigration laws, dangerous aliens had already infiltrated the nation. ("We have in the United States today hard-core, indigestible blocs which have not become integrated into the American way of life, but which, on the contrary are its deadly enemies.").

139. The President's Commission on Immigration and Naturalization, *Whom We Shall Welcome: Report of the President's Commission on Immigration and Naturalization* (Washington, DC: Government Printing Office, 1953), xii (hereinafter *Whom We Shall Welcome*); see also Edward M. Kennedy, "The Immigration Act of 1965," *Annals of the American Academy of Political and Social Science* 367, no.1 (1966): 138.

140. *Whom We Shall Welcome*, 92–93 (quoting Ralph L. Beals, former president of the American Anthropological Association); see also xiv, 15.

141. See *Whom We Shall Welcome*, 53 (reporting that a "large number of witnesses in the Commission's hearings stressed the continuing harm to our foreign relations caused by discriminations of the national origins law against the nonwhite people of the world," and that "the U.S.S.R. is skillfully and continuously making the most of our ethnic and racist doctrines"); *Whom We Shall Welcome*, 55 (noting that in Africa, "with one hand we spend time and money to fight" anti-American racial propaganda, but "with the other hand we feed the propaganda mill with our discriminatory policies"). For an additional history of the propaganda problems resulting from the national origins system, see Gabriel J. Chin, "The Civil Rights Revolution Comes to Immigration Law: A New Look at the Immigration and Nationality Act of 1965," *North Carolina Law Review* 75, no. 1 (Fall 1996): 288–297.

142. Walter A. Jackson, *Gunnar Myrdal and America's Conscience: Social Engineering and Racial Liberalism, 1938–1987* (Chapel Hill: University of North Carolina Press, 1990), xi.

143. Martin Luther King Jr., "The American Dream," commencement address, Lincoln University, Jefferson City, Missouri, June 6, 1961, Lincoln University, https://www.lincoln.edu/news-and-events/news/celebrating-life-and-legacy-martin-luther-king-jr; see also Aziz Rana, "Race and the American Creed: Recovering Black Radicalism," *n+1* 24 (Winter 2016), https://nplusonemag.com/issue-24/politics/race-and-the-american-creed/.

144. See Rana, "Colonialism and Constitutional Memory," 278. During the Cold War, the fight for civil rights and a race-neutral understanding of American identity was also recognized to serve important foreign policy goals by countering Communist propaganda that focused on racism in the United States. Defining American nationalism solely by commitment to creed served to cleanse the nation's character from the stains of racism. See generally Mary L. Dudziak, "Desegregation as a Cold War Imperative," *Stanford Law Review* 41

(1988): 69–70; Rana, "Constitutionalism and the Foundations of the Security State," 335.

145. "Republican Party Platform of 1960," July 25, 1960, American Presidency Project, https://www.presidency.ucsb.edu/node/273401; see also Daniels, *Guarding the Golden Door*, 129.

146. "1960 Democratic Party Platform," July 11, 1960, American Presidency Project, https://www.presidency.ucsb.edu/node/273234; see also Daniels, 129.

147. Special Message to the Congress on Immigration, 1 Pub. Papers 37 (January 13, 1965).

148. 111 Cong. Rec. 24 (1965), 225 (statement of Sen. Kennedy), 21, 778 (statement of Rep. Krebs).

149. 111 Cong. Rec. 21, 783 (statement of Rep. Burton); see also Chin, "The Civil Rights Revolution," 302 n120 (listing similar remarks).

150. 111 Cong. Rec. 23 (1965): 793 (statement of Sen. Byrd).

151. 111 Cong. Rec. 23, 794.

152. For instance, Marion Moncure Duncan, president general of the Daughters of the American Revolution, testified that the national origins system represents "a first line of defense in perpetuating and maintaining our institutions of freedom and the American way of life." "Statement of Marion Moncure Duncan, National Origins Quotas Should Be Retained" (1964), in Nicolas Capaldi, ed., *Immigration: Debating the Issues* (New York: Prometheus Books, 1997) 117, 118.

153. Immigration and Nationality Act of 1965, Pub L. No. 89–236, 79 Stat. 911 (1965).

154. 8 U.S.C. § 1152(a)(1)(A) (2012).

155. Remarks at the Signing of the Immigration Bill, Liberty Island, New York, 2 Pub. Papers 1037 (October 3, 1965), 1038.

156. Immigration: Hearing on S. 500 Before the Subcommittee on Immigration and Naturalization of the S. Comm. of the Judiciary, 89th Cong., Sess. 2 (1965) (statement of Edward M. Kennedy, senator of Massachusetts). For a discussion of the context of Kennedy's remarks, see Chin, "The Civil Rights Revolution," 334–335.

157. "Press Release," US Census Bureau, released on March 13, 2018, https://www.census.gov/newsroom/press-releases/2018/cb18-41-population-projections.html.

158. See Devin Burghart and Leonard Zeskind, "Special Report: Beyond FAIR: The Decline of the Established Anti-Immigrant Organizations and the Rise of Tea Party Nativism," *Institute for Research and Education on Human Rights* (2012): 3, https://www.irehr.org/2012/11/20/beyond-fair-report-pdf/. At its peak, FAIR and associated organizations had as many as 1.2 million members and over 400 local groups.

159. Burghart and Zeskind, "Special Report: Beyond FAIR," 3; see also "Federation for American Immigration Reform," Southern Poverty Law Center, https://www.youtube.com/watch?v=cY6t2ckpb5g.

160. "Federation for American Immigration Reform," Southern Poverty Law Center, https://www.splcenter.org/fighting-hate/extremist-files/group /federation-american-immigration-reform; "Race Science and the Pioneer Fund," *Searchlight* 277 (July 7, 1998), http://faculty.ferris.edu/ISAR/Institut /pioneer/search.htm.

161. John H. Tanton, "End of the Migration Epoch? Time for a New Paradigm," in John H. Tanton, Denis McCormack, and Joseph Wayne Smith, eds., *Immigration and the Social Contract: The Implosion of Western Societies* (Brookfield, VT: Avebury, 1996), 3, 17.

162. Heidi Beirich, "The Nativist Lobby: Three Faces of Intolerance," in Mark Potok, ed. *Report from the Southern Poverty Law Center*, February 2009, 5.

163. Beirich, "The Nativist Lobby," 10.

164. Examining the Practices and Policies of the Immigration and Naturalization Service as It Relates to the Naturalization Process, Before the Subcommittee on Immigration of the Senate Committee on the Judiciary, 104th Cong. 291 (1996) (statement of Dan Stein, Executive Director, Federation for American Immigration Reform). In a video program produced by FAIR, Stein spoke more bluntly, asking: "How can we preserve America if it becomes 50 percent Latin American?" "Federation for American Immigration Reform," Southern Poverty Law Center, https://www.splcenter.org/fighting-hate/extremist-files /group/federation-american-immigration-reform.

165. Brimelow appeared on a television show produced by FAIR and was interviewed by FAIR's president; see "Federation for American Immigration Reform," Southern Poverty Law Center, https://www.splcenter.org/fighting -hate/extremist-files/group/federation-american-immigration-reform.

166. In *Alien Nation*, Brimelow expanded his essay "Time to Rethink Immigration," which appeared in the *National Review* in June 1992 and has been called "a sort of ur-text for today's alt-right." Robert Draper, "National Revolt," *New York Times Sunday Magazine*, October 2, 2016, MM36; "VDARE," Southern Poverty Law Center, https://www.splcenter.org/fighting-hate/extremist-files /group/vdare.

167. Peter Brimelow, *Alien Nation: Common Sense about America's Immigration Disaster* (New York: Random House, 1995), 10 ("The American nation has always had a specific ethnic core. And that core has been white.").

168. Brimelow, *Alien Nation*, 59. In depicting the authentic America to be white, Brimelow embraces ethnonationalism, defining a nation as an "ethnocultural community" (Brimelow, 203). See also Brimelow, 57.

169. Brimelow, 100–101, 105–107; "Federation for American Immigration

Reform," Southern Poverty Law Center, https://www.splcenter.org/fighting -hate/extremist-files/group/federation-american-immigration-reform.

170. Brimelow, 13.

171. See Brimelow, 56n (citing Richard J. Herrnstein and Charles Murray, *The Bell Curve: Intelligence and Class Structure in American Life* [1994], 359); see also Brimelow, 184.

172. Brimelow, xix, 56.

173. Brimelow, 209–210 (alterations in original; emphasis omitted) (quoting US Constitution Preamble). He argues that the Founders themselves shared his conception that the American people are defined by their common ancestry and the Constitution speaks only to those within the ethnic fold. Brimelow, 210 (quoting *Federalist*, no. 2, 16.

174. "About Us," *American Renaissance*, https://www.amren.com/about/.

175. Jared Taylor, *White Identity: Racial Consciousness in the 21st Century* (n.p.: New Century Books, 2011), 223. Taylor has explained that the name "American Renaissance" refers to the goal of making America great again by making it white again. Jared Taylor, "Twelve Years of American Renaissance," *American Renaissance*, November 2002, 1, 2, http:// www.amren.com/ar/pdfs /2002/200211ar.pdf.

176. Jared Taylor, "What the Founders Really Thought about Race," National Policy Institute, January 17, 2012, http://www.npiamerica.org /research/category/what-the-founders-really-thought-about-race#fn:59.

177. Leonard Zeskind, *Blood and Politics: The History of the White Nationalist Movement from the Margins to the Mainstream* (New York: Farrar, Strauss, Giroux, 2009), 288. Francis had worked for the Heritage Foundation in the 1970s and 1980s and became a columnist for the conservative *Washington Times* in the 1990s until he was fired when his calls for white nationalism became too explicit. Zeskind, 288, 424–425. Afterward, Francis published frequently in Jared Taylor's *American Renaissance* and on Peter Brimelow's VDare.com. Francis worked with FAIR on numerous projects and also served as chairman of the American Immigration Control Foundation, a virulently anti-immigrant group, which like FAIR was funded by the eugenicist Pioneer Foundation. Southern Poverty Law Center, "Anti-Immigration Groups," *Intelligence Report*, March 21, 2001, 1–3, https://www.splcenter.org/fighting-hate/intelligence -report/2001/anti-immigration-groups.

178. Samuel Francis, "Race and the American Prospect: An Introduction," VDare.com, September 5, 2006, http://www.vdare.com/articles/race-and-the -american-prospect-an-introduction.

179. Samuel Francis, "Prospects for Racial and Cultural Survival," *American Renaissance*, March 1995), https://www.amren.com/news/2011/06/prospects _for_r/.

180. Samuel Francis, ed., *Race and the American Prospect: Essays on the Racial Realities of Our Nation and Our Time* (Mt. Airy, MD: Occidental Press, 2006).

181. Zeskind, *Blood and Politics*, 236, 237, 279.

182. Steven A. Holmes, "The 1992 Campaign: Candidates Records; White House Hopes to Trip Buchanan on His Paper Trail," *New York Times*, March 1, 1992, http://www.nytimes.com/1992/03/01/us/1992-campaign-candidates-records-white-house-hopes-trip-buchanan-his-paper-trail.html?pagewanted=all.

183. *This Week with David Brinkley*, December 8, 1991.

184. See Patrick J. Buchanan, "Mexico: Who Was Right?," *New York Times*, August 25, 1995, A27. At the 1992 Republican National Convention, Buchanan gave a vitriolic address that described the presidential election as part of a "religious war going on in our country for the soul of America. It is a cultural war, as critical to the kind of nation we will one day be as was the Cold War itself." Patrick Buchanan, "1992 Republican National Convention Speech," Houston, August 17, 1992, http://buchanan.org/blog/1992-republican-national-convention-speech-148. On one side in this war for America's soul, Buchanan said, stood the Clintons and the rioters in Los Angeles. On the other side were traditional Americans, who he said were fighting to "take back our cities, and take back our culture, and take back our country."

185. See "Is Pat Buchanan Anti-Semitic?," *Newsweek*, December 22, 1991, http://www.newsweek.com/pat-buchanan-anti-semitic-201176.

186. George F. Will, "Protest! What the Buchanan Candidacy Is All About," *Baltimore Sun*, December 12, 1991, http://articles.baltimoresun.com/1991-12-12/news/1991346117_1_president-buchanan-david-duke-confetti.

187. For instance, Buchanan was endorsed by former Klansman David Duke, and the *Spotlight*, published by Willis Carto's Liberty Lobby, recognized Buchanan as the new voice of white nationalism. See Zeskind, *Blood and Politics*, 281.

188. In his book *State of Emergency: Third World Invasion and Conquest of America*, Buchanan refers to both Francis and Brimelow as his friends and cites their work repeatedly. See generally Patrick J. Buchanan, *State of Emergency: Third World Invasion and Conquest of America* (New York: Thomas Dunne Books, 2006), vii.

189. Buchanan, *State of Emergency*, 239, 428. Buchanan finds support for his view in the work of Samuel Huntington, who argued that the American Creed can only be understood as an expression of "Anglo-Protestant culture" and that "Anglo-Protestant culture has been central to American identity for three centuries." Samuel Huntington, *Who Are We? The Challenges to America's National Identity* (London: Free Press, 2004), xv–xvii.

190. Huntington, *Who Are We?*, 151.

191. Higham, *Strangers in the Land*, 102–103; see generally Bluford Adams,

"World Conquerors or a Dying People? Racial Theory, Regional Anxiety, and the Brahmin Anglo-Saxonists," *Journal of the Gilded Age and Progressive Era* 8, no. 2 (April 2009): 189; Barbara Miller Solomon, "The Intellectual Background of the Immigration Restriction Movement in New England," *New England Quarterly* 25, no. 1 (March 1952): 47.

192. Zeskind, *Blood and Politics*, 279–284.

193. Samuel Francis, *Beautiful Losers: Essays on the American Conservatism* (Columbia: University of Missouri Press, 1993), 62.

194. In fact, empirical studies confirmed that many middle-class whites felt alienated from American institutions and considered themselves a victimized minority, with a distinct racial consciousness. See Zeskind, *Blood and Politics*, 290.

195. E.g., Bonnie K. Goodman, "Overviews and Chronologies: 1992," Presidential Campaign and Elections Reference, https://presidentialcampaignse lectionsreference.wordpress.com/overviews/20th-century/1992-overview/.

196. E.g., David Leip, "1996 Presidential Republican Primary Election Results," Atlas of US Presidential Elections, last updated in 2016, https:// uselectionatlas.org/RESULTS/national.php?year=1996&f=0&off=0&elect=2.

197. See Aziz Rana, "Decolonizing Obama: What Happened to the Third-World Left?," *n+1* 27 (Winter 2017), https://nplusonemag.com/issue-27 /politics/decolonizing-obama/.

198. Barack Obama, "Inaugural Address by President Barack Obama." speech, Washington, DC, January 21, 2013, White House, http://www.white house.gov/the-pressoffice/2013/01/21/inaugural-address-president-barack -obama.

199. Maya Rhodan, "Transcript: Read Full Text of President Barack Obama's Speech in Selma," *Time*, March 7, 2015, http://time.com/3736357/barack -obama-selma-speech-transcript/.

200. Ashley Parker and Steve Eder, "Inside the Six Weeks Donald Trump Was a Nonstop 'Birther,'" *New York Times*, Jul. 2, 2016, https://www.nytimes .com/2016/07/03/us/politics/donald-trump-birther-obama.html?_r=0.

201. *See* Josh Voorhees, "All of Donald Trump's Birther Tweets," *Slate*, September 16, 2016, http://www.slate.com/blogs/the_slatest/2016/09/16 /donald_trump_s_birther_tweets_in_order.html.

202. "Immigration Reform That Will Make America Great Again," Donald J. Trump for President, https://assets.donaldjtrump.com/Immigration-Reform - Trump.pdf.

203. "Here's Donald Trump's Presidential Announcement Speech," *Time*, June 16, 2015, http://time.com/3923128/donald-trump-announcemen -speech/.

204. Matt Flegenheimer, "Habla Español? Tim Kaine Is Latest Candidate to Use Spanish," *New York Times*, July 28, 2016 ("This is a country where we speak English . . . not Spanish.") (quoting Donald Trump).

205. Eric Bradner, "Ben Carson Again Explains Concerns with a Muslim President," CNN, September 27, 2015, http://www.cnn.com/2015/09/27/politics/ben-carson-muslim-president-sharia-law/.

206. Jacob Gardenswartz, "Transcript: President Donald Trump's Rally in Melbourne, Florida," *Vox*, February 18, 2017, http://www.vox.com/2017/2/18/14659952/trump-transcript-rally-melbourne-florida.

207. Susan B. Glasser, "Michael Anton: The Full Transcript," *Politico*, April 17, 2017, http://www.politico.com/magazine/story/2017/04/michael-anton-the-full-transcript-215029.

208. Publius Decius Mus, "The Flight 93 Election," *Claremont Review of Books*, September 5, 2016, http://www.claremont.org/crb/basicpage/the-flight-93-election/.

209. See "White Genocide in the USA," White Genocide Project, accessed October 25, 2017, http://whitegenocideproject.com/white-genocide-in-usa/; Christian Miller, "The White Genocide Evidence Project: Immigration," Majori tyrights.com, March 9, 2011, https://majorityrights.com/weblog/comments/the_white_genocide_evidence_project_immigration (identifying the 1965 Im-migration Act as a "treasonous and traitorous piece of legislation").

210. Chris Cillizza, "Pat Buchanan Says Donald Trump Is the Future of the Republican Party," *Washington Post*, January 12, 2016, https://www.washingtonpost.com/news/the-fix/wp/2016/01/12/pat-buchanan-believes-donald-trump-is-the-future-of-the-republican-party/?utm_term=.6492ca57436c; see also Jeff Greenfield, "Trump Is Pat Buchanan with Better Timing," *Politico*, September–October 2016, http://www.politico.com/magazine/story/2016/09/donald-trump-pat-buchanan-republican-america-first-nativist-214221.

211. Michael Wolff, "Ringside with Steve Bannon at Trump Tower as the President-Elect's Strategist Plots 'An Entirely New Political Movement,'" *Hollywood Reporter*, November 18, 2016, http://www.hollywoodreporter.com/news/steve-bannon-trump-tower-interview-trumps-strategist-plots-new-political-movement-948747.

212. John Judis, "The Return of the Middle American Radical: An Intellectual History of Trump Supporters," *National Journal*, October 2, 2015, https://www.nationaljournal.com/s/74221/return-middle-american-radical.

213. Ann Coulter, *In Trump We Trust: How He Outsmarted the Politicians, the Elites and the Media* (New York: Sentinel, 2016), 10.

214. "Executive Order: Protecting the Nation from Foreign Terrorist Entry into the United States," White House, January 27, 2017, https://www.whitehouse.gov/the-press-office/2017/01/27/executive-order-protecting-nation-foreign-terrorist-entry-united-states.

215. Amy B. Wang, "Trump Asked for a 'Muslim Ban,' Giuliani Says—and Ordered a Commission to Do It 'Legally,'" *Washington Post*, January 29, 2017,

https://www.washingtonpost.com/news/the-fix/wp/2017/01/29/trump -asked-for-a-muslim-ban-giuliani-says-and-ordered-a-commission-to-do-it -legally/?utm_term=.4e7a865c9743; Reply in Support of Emergency Motion Pending Appeal at 6, Washington v. Trump, No. 17–35105 (9th Cir., February 6, 2017) (arguing the order is "neutral with respect to religion.").

216. "Executive Order: Protecting the Nation from Foreign Terrorist Entry into the United States."

217. George W. Bush, "'Islam Is Peace' Says President," speech, Islamic Center of Washington, DC, September 17, 2001), White House Archives, https:// georgewbush-whitehouse.archives.gov/news/releases/2001/09/20010917 -11.html).

218. See generally Wajahat Ali et al., *Fear, Inc.: The Roots of the Islamophobia Network in America*, Center for American Progress, August 2011, https:// cdn.americanprogress.org/wp-content/uploads/issues/2011/08/pdf /islamophobia.pdf (detailing positions of the anti-Muslim activists and experts).

219. Robert Spencer, *Arab Winter Comes to America: The Truth about the War We're In* (Washington, DC: Regnery Publishing, 2014).

220. See generally Center for Security Policy, "Shariah: The Threat to America," *Center for Security Policy* (2010), https://www.centerforsecuritypolicy.org /upload/wysiwyg/article%20pdfs/Shariah%20-%20The%20Threat%20 to%20America%20(Team%20B%20Report)%20Web%2009292010.pdf.

221. Center for Security Policy, 7; see also William Wagner, "Islam, Shariah Law, and the American Constitution," Family Research Council (May 2011), 5, http://www.frc.org/issueanalysis/islam-shariah-law-and-the-american-constitu tion.

222. Center for Security Policy, "Shariah," 6–7.

223. Ali et al., *Fear, Inc.*, 28.

224. New Jersey Tea Party Coalition, "Sharia Law vs. the Constitution," YouTube, January 17, 2011, https://www.youtube.com/watch?v=02f5m-mI8Io.

225. "Here Are the 10 Ways Islam Is Incompatible with the Constitution," Teaparty.org, January 10, 2016, http://www.teaparty.org/10-ways-islam -incompatible-constitution-140410/.

226. Wagner, "Islam, Shariah Law, and the American Constitution," 3.

227. R. James Woolsey, Andrew C. McCarthy, and Harry E. Soyster, "Second Opinion Needed on Shariah," *Washington Times*, September 14, 2010, http:// www.washingtontimes.com/news/2010/sep/14/needed-a-second-opinion-on -shariah/.

228. Newt Gingrich, "America at Risk: Camus, National Security and Afghanistan," speech, American Enterprise Institute, Washington, DC, July 29, 2010, YouTube, https://www.youtube.com/watch?time_continue=7&v =ht98odLCg4M; see also Carol Kuruvilla, "5 Things You Need to Know about Sharia Law: Asking American Muslims to Swear off Sharia Law Is a

Violation of Religious Liberty," *Huffington Post*, January 31, 2017, http://www.huffingtonpost.com/entry/5-facts-you-need-to-know-about-sharia-law _us_5788f567e4b03fc3ee507c01 (quoting Newt Gingrich).

229. The campaign succeeded in enacting an anti-sharia law in Oklahoma, which was later struck down as unconstitutional. See, e.g., Awad v. Ziriax, 670 F.3d 1111 (10th Cir. 2012).

230. Brandon Moseley, "Sessions Says that West Needs a Long-term Strategy to Deal with Islamist Ideology," *Alabama Political Reporter*, September 16, 2015, http://www.alreporter.com/2015/09/17/sessions-says-that-west-needs-a-long -term-strategy-to-deal-with-islamist-ideology/.

231. "Here Are The 10 Ways Islam Is Incompatible with the Constitution"1; Sept. 20, 2015," *Meet the Press*, NBC, September 20, 2015, http://www.nbcnews .com/meet-the-press/meet-press-transcript-september-20–2015-n430581.

232. Uri Friedman, "The Coming War on 'Radical Islam,'" *Atlantic*, November 29, 2016, https://www.theatlantic.com/international/archive/2016/11/trump -radical-islam/508331/.

233. "Dr. Thomas D. Williams," *Breitbart News Daily*, April 7, 2016, https:// soundcloud.com/breitbart/breitbart-news-daily-dr-thomas-d-williams-april -7-2016.

234. Neil Munro, "Left Protests while Trump Junks Obama's Global Immigration Plan," *Breitbart News*, January 30, 2017, http://www.breitbart.com /big-government/2017/01/30/trump-changes-immigration-favor-american -values/.

235. See, e.g., Anatol Lieven, *America Right or Wrong: An Anatomy of American Nationalism*, 2nd ed. (New York: Oxford University Press, 2012), 7 (contrasting nativism and civic nationalism); Jeffrey Mirel, *Patriotic Pluralism: Americanization Education and European Immigrants* (Cambridge, MA: Harvard University Press, 2010), 11 (same); James M. McPherson, *Is Blood Thicker Than Water?: Crises of Nationalism in the Modern World* (New York: Vintage Books, 1999), 37 (same).

Chapter 4. The Businessman's Constitution

1. See generally George Wolfskill, *The Revolt of the Conservatives: A History of the American Liberty League 1934–1940* (New York: Houghton Mifflin, 1962); Frederick Rudolph, "The American Liberty League, 1934–1940," *American Historical Review* 56, no. 1 (October 1950): 19.

2. See, e.g., Carl W. Ackerman, "The Test of Citizenship," July 16, 1935, *American Liberty League Document No. 61*, 4; Raoul E. Desvernine, "The Principles of Constitutional Democracy and the New Deal," July 11, 1935, *American Liberty League Document No. 52*, 19. The pamphlets published by the American Liberty League can be found in the Special Collections at the University

of Kentucky Libraries and are available at http://kdl.kyvl.org/catalog/xt7ww
p9t2q46/guide.

3. See James A. Farley, *Behind the Ballots: The Personal History of a Politician*,
2nd ed. (Westport, CT: Greenwood Press, 1972), 294.

4. Farley, *Behind the Ballots*, 295.

5. See Wolfskill, *The Revolt of the Conservatives*, 210.

6. See Rudolph, "The American Liberty League," 21–22.

7. See Rudolph, 26.

8. See Rudolph, 22, 30–31.

9. Eric F. Goldman, "All against That Man," *New York Times*, February 11,
1962, 6.

10. See Kim Phillips-Fein, *Invisible Hands: The Making of the Conservative
Movement from the New Deal to Reagan* (New York: W. W. Norton, 2009), xi–xii;
Goldman, "All against That Man," 6.

11. Rudolph, "The American Liberty League," 21–22.

12. Rudolph, 21.

13. Jeff Shesol, *Supreme Power: Franklin Roosevelt vs. The Supreme Court* (New
York: W. W. Norton, 2010), 109–110; Rudolph, "The American Liberty
League," 22.

14. See, e.g., J. Howard Pew, "Which Road to Take?," July 12, 1935, *American
Liberty League Document No. 53*, 3; Walter E. Spahr, "The People's Money," July
10, 1935, *American Liberty League Document No. 51*, 7; Demarest Lloyd, "Fabian
Socialism in the New Deal," July 9, 1935, *American Liberty League Document No.
50*, 16; "Raskob to Expand Liberty League," *New York Times*, February 1, 1936, 2.

15. See Wolfskill, *The Revolt of the Conservatives*, 37–55.

16. Wolfskill, 50.

17. See *Prohibition and the Bill of Rights: How the Constitutional Guarantees
Disappear under the Dry Regime*, Minute Man, March 22, 1923, available at http://
libraries.uky.edu/libpage.php?lweb_id=474&llib_id=13&ltab_id=898.

18. Jouett Shouse, the president of the AAPA, explained that the organization was founded "primarily and wholly for a constitutional principle," to take a
"police statute" from the federal power. Wolfskill, *The Revolt of the Conservatives*,
46. In addition to their constitutional concerns, leaders of the AAPA may have
been motivated by their personal interests, in that they believed that corporate
and personal income taxes could be eliminated if Prohibition were repealed
and beer and liquor were taxed instead. See, e.g., Association Against the Prohibition Amendment, *Cost of Prohibition and Your Income Tax* (1929): 11; David E.
Kyvig, *Repealing National Prohibition*, 2nd ed. (Kent: Kent State University Press,
2000), 50; Wolfskill, *The Revolt of the Conservatives*, 48.

19. Wolfskill, 54, 55.

20. See Jouett Shouse, "The Constitution Still Stands," February 12, 1935,
American Liberty League Document No. 16, 13–14.

21. See, e.g., Fitzgerald Hall, "The Imperilment of Democracy," July 18, 1935, *American Liberty League Document No. 58*, 3.

22. See, e.g., Frederick H. Stinchfield, "The American Constitution—Whose Heritage? The Self-Reliant or Those Who Would Be Wards of the Government?," January 18, 1936, *American Liberty League Document No. 90*, 6.

23. See "The Carpenter and Raskob Letters," *New York Times*, December 21, 1934, 2.

24. "The Carpenter and Raskob Letters," 2.

25. See Robert F. Burk, *The Corporate State and the Broker State: The Du Ponts and American National Politics, 1925–1940* (Cambridge, MA: Harvard University Press, 1990), 134–138, 141–142.

26. Wolfskill, *The Revolt of the Conservatives*, 26.

27. Burk, *The Corporate State and the Broker State*, 138.

28. See Arthur M. Schlesinger Jr., *The Age of Roosevelt: The Politics of Upheaval* (New York: Houghton Mifflin, 1960), 7; Shesol, *Supreme Power*, 158.

29. Shesol, *Supreme Power*, 158.

30. See Wolfskill, *The Revolt of the Conservatives*, 10–11.

31. Wolfskill, 20–21; "League Is Formed to Scan New Deal, 'Protect Rights,'" *New York Times*, August 23, 1934, 1.

32. See Shesol, *Supreme Power*, 110–111; "Shouse Elected by Liberty League," *New York Times*, September 7, 1934, 5.

33. Jouett Shouse, President, American Liberty League, "Statement Made at Time of the Announcement of the Formation of the American Liberty League," August 23, 1934, https://exploreuk.uky.edu/fa/findingaid/?id=xt7w wp9t2q46.

34. See Wolfskill, *The Revolt of the Conservatives*, 29, 56.

35. "League Is Formed to Scan New Deal, 'Protect Rights,'" *New York Times*, August 23, 1934, 1.

36. "Topics in Wall Street," *New York Times*, August 24, 1934, 23.

37. "Finance Welcomes Liberty League," *New York Times*, August 24, 1934, 2.

38. "Unexceptionable Aims," *New York Times*, August 23, 1934, 16.

39. "Roosevelt Twits Liberty League as Lover of Property," *New York Times*, August 25, 1934, 2.

40. "Roosevelt Twits Liberty League as Lover of Property," 1.

41. As Roosevelt put it, the league "paid little attention to the commitment of government to help the unemployed, to make work, to aid people in keeping their homes, to provide facilities for education and those other factors summed up in the commandment 'Thou shalt love thy neighbor as thyself.'" "Roosevelt Twits Liberty League as Lover of Property," 2.

42. "Capital Expects Smith Move Next in Liberty League," *New York Times*, August 27, 1934, 1.

43. "Pledges Pour in at Liberty League," *New York Times*, August 29, 1934, 2.

290 I NOTES TO PAGES 146-147

44. Wolfskill, *The Revolt of the Conservatives*, 62–63.

45. See "Liberty League Income Equals Major Parties," *Washington Post,* January 3, 1936, 9.

46. Wolfskill, *The Revolt of the Conservatives*, 57.

47. See "Liberty League Pays Shouse Top Salary," *New York Times,* March 17, 1936, 7.

48. See, e.g., Arthur M. Schlesinger Jr., *The Age of Roosevelt: The Coming of the New Deal* (New York: Houghton Mifflin, 1959), 484; Shesol, *Supreme Power*, 161.

49. See, e.g., Rudolph, *The American Liberty League*, 21.

50. See Wolfskill, *The Revolt of the Conservatives*, 56, 62, 63.

51. See Wolfskill, 56; Arthur Krock, "Liberty League Is Distinctly Pro-Landon," *New York Times,* August 7, 1936, 18.

52. See, e.g., "Assert President Betrayed Oath," *New York Times,* January 26, 1936, L37.

53. See Wolfskill, *The Revolt of the Conservatives*, 65.

54. Wolfskill, 65–66.

55. "The AAA Amendments," April 1935, *American Liberty League Document No. 30*; "The Bituminous Coal Bill," April 1935, *American Liberty League Document No. 32.*

56. William H. Stayton, "Is the Constitution for Sale?," May 30, 1935, *American Liberty League Document No. 40*; Raoul E. Desvernine, "Americanism at the Crossroads," January 15, 1936), *American Liberty League Document No. 88*; James M. Beck, "What Is the Constitution between Friends?," March 27, 1935), *American Liberty League Document No. 22.*

57. Shesol, *Supreme Power*, 161–162. Examples of news coverage generated by Liberty League pamphlets can be seen in various national newspapers. "Assails New Deal Record," *New York Times,* May 28, 1936, L2; "Guffey Predicts Roosevelt Sweep," *New York Times,* August 24, 1936, L6; "New AAA Law Hit by Liberty League," *New York Times,* March 9, 1936, L8; "New Taxes Assailed as Dictatorship Step," *New York Times,* July 20, 1936, L5; "Plans to Share Wealth Called Quack Schemes," *Washington Post,* February 10, 1936, 2; "'Socialization' Held Goal of Power Drive," *New York Times,* June 15, 1936, L3.

58. Search of ProQuest Historical Newspapers database.

59. See S. J. Woolf, "It Won't Happen Here, Lewis Believes," *New York Times,* October. 4, 1936, SM3.

60. See John Dewey, "A Liberal Speaks Out for Liberalism," *New York Times,* February 23, 1936, SM3. Historian Charles Beard also chided the league for misunderstanding constitutional history. "Dr. Beard Asks Broader View of Constitution," *Washington Post,* January 14, 1936, 5.

61. See "Social Weal Held Guiding Public Aim," *New York Times,* May 10, 1936, L39.

62. Wolfskill, *The Revolt of the Conservatives*, 56.

63. Only historian George Wolfskill gave the Liberty League's ideology any serious consideration, declaring that the league's pamphlets "represented perhaps the most concise and thorough summary of conservative political thought written in the United States since *The Federalist* papers." Wolfskill, 65.

64. Max Lerner, "Constitution and Court as Symbols," *Yale Law Journal* 46 (1937): 1305.

65. Rudolph, "The American Liberty League," 22. This rhetoric, Rudolph explained, "was made of respectable generalities, partial self-delusion, intense sincerity, and frequently embarrassing hypocrisy."

66. Schlesinger, *The Age of Roosevelt*, 488.

67. Shesol, *Supreme Power*, 108.

68. Wolfskill, *The Revolt of the* Conservatives, 111.

69. Several other groups—the Southern Committee to Uphold the Constitution, the Sentinels of the Republic, the Farmers' Independence Council of America—made broadly similar claims. See J. Richard Piper, *Ideologies and Institutions: American Conservative and Liberal Governance Prescriptions since 1933* (Lanham, MD: Rowman & Littlefield, 1997), 70 (stating that the American Liberty League "occupied the central role in the conservative propaganda campaign" in the period leading up to the 1936 election); Wolfskill, 231, 239, 241–242.

70. Herbert Hoover, *The Challenge to Liberty* (New York: C. Scribner's Sons, 1934), 85; see also Edward S. Corwin, "Book Reviews," *Yale Law Journal* 44 (1935): 547.

71. Hoover, *The Challenge to Liberty*, 85.

72. See Hoover, 1; Schlesinger, *The Age of Roosevelt*, 475–476. Moreover, during the 1934 midterm election campaign, the Republican Party likewise made the claim that the New Deal amounted to an attack on American individualism, declaring that "in place of individual initiative [Roosevelt and his advisors] seek to substitute government control of all agricultural production, of all business activity." Schlesinger, 481.

73. Hoover, 5. See also Schlesinger, 475. Hoover himself declined the invitation to join the Liberty League, declaring that he had "no more confidence in the Wall Street model of human liberty, which this group so well represents, than I have in the Pennsylvania Avenue model upon which the country now rides." Herbert Hoover, *The Memoirs of Herbert Hoover: The Great Depression 1929–1941*, vol. 3 (New York: Macmillan, 1952), 454–455.

74. See Rudolph, "The American Liberty League," 20.

75. Desvernine, "Americanism at the Crossroads," 4–5, 18–19; William H. Ellis, "The Spirit of Americanism," April 26, 1935, *American Liberty League Document No. 59*, 4–5.

76. Hall, "The Imperilment of Democracy," 4. See also Shouse, "Democracy or Bureaucracy," 20. As another pamphlet declared, "This nation was

established for the specific purpose, above all others, of enabling our people, in the stimulating atmosphere of such freedom, to climb by their individual and ingenious efforts to any heights to which human beings might reason-ably aspire." Spahr, "The People's Money," 7. Americanism means "respect for the sacredness of an individual's personality and of his right to develop it to the limit of his capacity."

77. See, e.g., Ackerman, "The Test of Citizenship," 10; Desvernine, "Americanism at the Crossroads," 7.

78. As John Davis, the 1924 Democratic presidential candidate, declared, "Regulation is a term behind which every form of tyranny, great and small, can hide itself." John W. Davis, "The Redistribution of Power," January 24, 1936, *American Liberty League Document No. 93*, 15; See also Albert C. Ritchie, "The American Form of Government—Let Us Preserve It," January 18, 1936, *American Liberty League Document No. 92*, 6-7.

79. R. E. Desvernine, Letter to the Editor, "Position Defined," *New York Times*, October 11, 1936, E9.

80. See, e.g., Ritchie, "The American Form of Government," 9 (claiming that the measures and policies under the New Deal will destroy the American form of government); James W. Wadsworth, "The Blessings of Stability," July 12, 1935, *American Liberty League Document No. 54*, 10; "Shouse Upholds Revolt in Party," *New York Times*, June 21, 1936, L27.

81. See Stinchfield, "The American Constitution," 5-6 (discussing how New Deal legislation like the Social Security bill and the Labor Relations statute take the country away from the principle of self-reliance and toward paternalism).

82. Stinchfield, 14 (quoting Alexis Carrel, *Man, the Unknown* [New York: Harper & Brothers, 1935], 298-299).

83. G. W. Dyer, "Regimenting the Farmers," May 5, 1935, *American Liberty League Document No. 33*, 5; See also Desvernine, "The Principles of Constitutional Democracy and the New Deal," 19; Lloyd, "Fabian Socialism in the New Deal," 7. Al Smith thus charged that the New Deal was spending tax money "to train young men to go out and preach communism, to preach the gospel of 'down with property, down with capital, down with government, down with church, yes, down with God.'" F. Raymond Daniell, "Smith Links Reds with Roosevelt," *New York Times*, November 1, 1936, 42.

84. Wolfskill, *The Revolt of the Conservatives*, 112.

85. See, e.g., "The AAA and Our Form of Government," December 1935, *American Liberty League Document. No. 80*, 2. Al Smith—a former governor of New York and 1928 Democratic presidential candidate—broke with Roosevelt and supported the Liberty League, asserting that Roosevelt had chosen Karl Marx over Thomas Jefferson. See Alfred E. Smith, "The Facts in the Case," January 25, 1936, *American Liberty League Document No. 97*, 14. Smith said that Roosevelt merely pretended to follow the founders of the Democratic Party: "It is all right

with me if they want to disguise themselves as Norman Thomas or Karl Marx, or Lenin, or any of the rest of that bunch, but what I won't stand for is allowing them to march under the banner of Jefferson, Jackson or Cleveland."

86. Hall, "The Imperilment of Democracy," 5; "Shouse Upholds Revolt in Party," *New York Times*, June 21, 1936, L27.

87. Desvernine, "Americanism at the Crossroads," 13.

88. See, e.g., Desvernine, 12 (declaring that "our individuality, our independence is being merged into and subordinated to a superstate"); Stinchfield, "The American Constitution," 6.

89. Albert C. Ritchie, "The American Bar—the Trustee of American Institutions," June 29, 1935), *American Liberty League Document No. 48*, 4. In another league pamphlet, Nicholas Roosevelt—the president's cousin—warned that the New Deal "means substituting an economic dictatorship for a political democracy. I, for one, regard this as a threat to the very foundations of our civilization." Nicholas Roosevelt, "Two Amazing Years," July 8, 1935, *American Liberty League Document No. 49*, 14.

90. Roosevelt, "Two Amazing Years," 6. By providing federal relief, the New Deal coddled the weak and lazy at the expense of the strong and hardworking, who had lawfully earned the money that the government then took from them and redistributed. See Roosevelt, 14.

91. Stinchfield, "The American Constitution," 6-7.

92. Stinchfield, 4-5. For instance, the Agricultural Adjustment Act—held unconstitutional in *United States v. Butler*, 297 U.S. 1 (1936)—"told every man what, where, and how much to sow, and when and how much to reap." Stinchfield, 5. Jouett Shouse agreed that the AAA "embodie[d] the very basis" of the "New Deal philosophy": "Under the guise of benefits to the farmers the effort is being made to regiment and to regulate the whole life of the American people." Jouett Shouse, "Arousing Class Prejudices," December 23, 1935, *American Liberty League Document No. 84*, 5.

93. See, e.g., Hall, "The Imperilment of Democracy," 7.

94. See, e.g., Desvernine, "The Principles of Constitutional Democracy and the New Deal," 3.

95. Desvernine, "Americanism at the Crossroads," 8.

96. Charles I. Dawson, "The President Has Made the Issue," January 25, 1936, *American Liberty League Document No. 95*, 14.

97. Lloyd, "Fabian Socialism in the New Deal," 16.

98. See Carter v. Carter Coal Co., 298 U.S. 238, 311, 316-317 (1936) (holding unconstitutional the Bituminous Coal Conservation Act of 1935); United States v. Butler, 297 U.S. 1, 78 (1936) (holding unconstitutional the Agricultural Adjustment Act of 1933); Louisville Joint Stock Land Bank v. Radford, 295 U.S. 555, 601-602 (1935) (striking down the Frazier-Lemke Act); A. L. A. Schechter Poultry Corp. v. United States, 295 U.S. 495, 551 (1935)

(holding much of the National Industrial Recovery Act unconstitutional); R. R. Ret. Bd. v. Alton R. R. Co., 295 U.S. 330, 374 (1935) (invalidating the Railroad Retirement Act of 1934); Panama Ref. Co. v. Ryan, 293 U.S. 388, 433 (1935) (invalidating a section of the National Industrial Recovery Act).

99. See Basil Rauch, *The History of the New Deal 1933–1938* (New York: Creative Age Press, 1944), 233.

100. See, e.g., Bruce Ackerman, *We the People, Volume 2: Transformations* (Cambridge, MA: Belknap Press, 1998), 295; Michael J. Gerhardt, "The Constitution outside the Courts," *Drake Law Review* 51 (2003): 787; John C. Yoo, "In Defense of the Court's Legitimacy," *University of Chicago Law Review* 68 (2001): 780. This view is widely shared outside the academy. For instance, anticipating that the Supreme Court would rule against the Affordable Care Act, Democratic Congressman James Clyburn urged President Obama to run against the Court just like Roosevelt supposedly did. See Sam Stein, "Barack Obama Could Go after Supreme Court on Health Care, James Clyburn Suggests," *Huffington Post*, April 2, 2012, http://www.huffingtonpost.com/2012/04/02/barack-obama -supreme-court-health-care-james-clyburn_n_1396375.html.

101. G. Edward White, *The Constitution and the New Deal* (Cambridge, MA: Harvard University Press, 2002), 13–14.

102. See, e.g., William E. Leuchtenburg, "When the People Spoke, What Did They Say?: The Election of 1936 and the Ackerman Thesis," *Yale Law Journal* 108 (1999): 2084; Michael J. Klarman, "Constitutional Fact/Constitutional Fiction: A Critique of Bruce Ackerman's Theory of Constitutional Moments," *Stanford Law Review* 44 (1992): 771 (book review); See also Barry Cushman, *Rethinking the New Deal Court: The Structure of a Constitutional Revolution* (New York: Oxford University Press, 1998), 27.

103. Cushman, *Rethinking the New Deal Court*, 27; See also Leuchtenburg, "When the People Spoke, What Did They Say?," 2084–2085. Indeed, strong evidence suggests that Roosevelt expressly rejected the suggestion that he take his case against the Court to the American people. See Shesol, *Supreme Power*, 215. Historians have written that Roosevelt followed the advice of Felix Frankfurter that "a general attack on the Court . . . would give opponents a chance to play on vague fears of a leap in the dark and upon the traditionalist loyalties the Court is still able to inspire." Shesol, 145–146 (quoting letter from Felix Frankfurter to Roosevelt, May 29, 1935); Leuchtenburg, 2087–2088. But see Robert H. Jackson, *The Struggle for Judicial Supremacy* (New York: Alfred A. Knopf, 1941), 177.

104. See Harold L. Ickes, *The Secret Diary of Harold L. Ickes. Volume 1: The First Thousand Days 1933–1936* (New York: Simon & Schuster, 1953), 530; Rauch, *The History of the New Deal 1933–1938,* 233.

105. See Shesol, *Supreme Power*, 145–146.

106. Shesol, 216.

107. See Wolfskill, *The Revolt of the Conservatives*, 210.

108. "Democracy Saved, Farley Declares," *New York Times*, February 23, 1936, L33; see also "Farley Blasts G.O.P. Critics of Roosevelt," *Washington Post*, February 23, 1936, 8.

109. See Wolfskill, *The Revolt of the Conservatives*, 210–211.

110. Farley, *Behind the Ballots*, 294; See also William E. Leuchtenburg, *The FDR Years: On Roosevelt and His Legacy* (New York: Columbia University Press, 1995), 103–104.

111. Charles Michelson, "Democratic Strategy Is Told by Michelson," *New York Times*, November 15, 1936, E10.

112. "Farley Back, Unworried over the Liberty League," *New York Times*, April 14, 1936, 1.

113. Franklin D. Roosevelt, "Annual Message to the Congress," January 3, 1936), in *The Public Papers and Addresses of Franklin D. Roosevelt: The People Approve, 1936*, vol. 5 (New York: Random House, 1938), 13–18.

114. "Congress to Hear President in a Night Session Friday; He Seeks a 'Fireside' Chat," *New York Times*, January 1, 1936, 1.

115. Roosevelt, "Annual Message to the Congress," 13–18.

116. See, e.g., "F. D. Roosevelt, Jr., Weds Ethel du Pont in June," *Washington Post*, November 15, 1936, M1; "Roosevelt and du Pont Banns Await Election," *Chicago Tribune*, October 1, 1936, 3; "Roosevelt Condemns All Warlike Countries; Defies His Critics to Repeal New Deal Laws; Demonstration Greets Belligerent Message," *Washington Post*, January 4, 1936, 1; "'Stump Talk,' Say Some Papers; 'Imperishable,' Others Declare," *Washington Post*, January 5, 1936, 8.

117. Roosevelt, "Annual Message to the Congress," 13–14.

118. Roosevelt, 15–16.

119. See, e.g., Ralph M. Shaw, "The New Deal: Its Unsound Theories and Irreconcilable Policies," May 31, 1935, *American Liberty League Document No. 39*, 13; Jouett Shouse, "Recovery, Relief and the Constitution," December 8, 1934, *American Liberty League Document No. 7*, 12–14; Roosevelt, 15.

120. See, e.g., "New Work-Relief Funds," April 1936, *American Liberty League Document No. 117*, 3; "Work Relief: A Record of the Tragic Failure of the Most Costly Governmental Experiment in All World History," November 1935, *American Liberty League Document No. 78*, 13.

121. Roosevelt, "Annual Message to the Congress," 15.

122. See National Lawyers Committee of the American Liberty League, *Report on the Constitutionality of the National Labor Relations Act* (1935), iii; "The National Labor Relations Act," September 1935, *American Liberty League Document No. 66*, 4; Roosevelt, 15.

123. See Walter E. Spahr, "The Fallacies and Dangers of the Townsend Plan,"

January 3, 1936, *American Liberty League Document No. 85*, 8–18; "Townsend Plan 'Absurd,' Avers Yale Professor," *Washington Post*, February 16, 1936, M13; Roosevelt, 16.

124. As William Forbath has argued, the New Deal constitutional philosophy did not consist solely of the assertion of broad federal power to enact programs for economic protection; it also consisted of the assertion that Congress had a moral and constitutional duty to do so. William E. Forbath, "The New Deal Constitution in Exile," *Duke Law Journal* 51 (2001): 176–178.

125. Roosevelt, "Annual Message to the Congress," 15–16.

126. At the Democratic National Convention, Roosevelt again declared that strong government action was necessary to protect the people from the tyranny of the "economic royalists": "For too many of us the political equality we once had won was meaningless in the face of economic inequality. A small group had concentrated into their own hands an almost complete control over other people's property, other people's money, other people's labor—other people's lives. . . . Against economic tyranny such as this the citizen could only appeal to the organized power of government." "Text of Roosevelt Address," *New York Times*, June 28, 1936, 25. Roosevelt's convention speech likewise took up the argument that his opponents hid behind lofty constitutional rhetoric: "In vain they seek to hide behind the flag and the Constitution. In their blindness they forget what the flag and the Constitution stand for." At the convention, James Farley likewise charged that the Liberty League used patriotic and constitutional rhetoric to instill fear in voters: "I am forced to conclude that . . . they hope to create a bugaboo to frighten the American voters." "Critics' 'Bugaboo' Derided by Farley," *New York Times*, June 14, 1936, L33.

127. "Roosevelt Fiscal Plans Go to Congress at Noon; Active Week Is Forecast," *New York Times*, January 6, 1936, 1.

128. "Guilty," bulletin of American Liberty League, January 15, 1936, 1; see also "Dispute Rages on President's Night Message," *Washington Post*, January 6, 1936, 2.

129. Neil Carothers, "Time to Stop," January 25, 1936, *American Liberty League Document No. 94*, 5.

130. George Barton Cutten, "Entrenched Greed," February 8, 1936, *American Liberty League Document No. 109*, 1, 4.

131. "Washington Dinner," bulletin of American Liberty League, January 15, 1936, 2.

132. Shesol, *Supreme Power*, 201. For instance, in October 1934 Father Charles Coughlin, the radio priest who launched his own Fascist-leaning movement against the New Deal, had criticized the American Liberty League as the mere "mouthpiece of bankers," whose sole aim was to protect the value of their bonds. "Coughlin Assails Liberty League: Priest Calls Organization 'The Mouth-

piece of Bankers' in Fight to Protect Bonds," *New York Times*, October 29, 1934, L11.

133. See "New-Deal Attack Prepared by Smith," *New York Times*, January 24, 1936, L6; Ray Tucker, "New Role Is Taken by Liberty League," *New York Times*, January 26, 1936, E12.

134. Tucker, "New Role Is Taken by Liberty League," E12.

135. Sidney Olson, "Al Smith Opens War on His Political Pupil, Franklin D. Roosevelt," *Washington Post*, February 2, 1936, B3.

136. See Schlesinger, *The Age of Roosevelt*, 482–484.

137. Wolfskill, *The Revolt of the Conservatives*, 143; "Smith to Decline White House Bid; New Attack Seen," *New York Times*, December 29, 1935, 1.

138. See "G.O.P. Primes Heavy Artillery for Campaign," *Washington Post*, January 23, 1936, 9.

139. See "Scheme to Split Party Charged by Democrats," *Washington Post*, January 2, 1936, 1.

140. See Ickes, *The Secret Diary of Harold L. Ickes*, 516–517 ("I am worried about the political situation. . . . Here is the situation. Al Smith is to speak in Washington at a big dinner next Saturday night under the auspices of the Liberty League. He has been getting a wonderful build-up for this meeting. . . . Smith is to have up to an hour on a national hookup. . . . Every indication is that he is going after the Administration with a savage attack. The whole country will be listening in and the newspapers will give wide publicity to the speech.").

141. "Text of Address of Alfred E. Smith at Anti-New Deal Dinner in Washington," *New York Times*, January 26, 1936, 36.

142. Wolfskill, *The Revolt of the Conservatives*, 152.

143. "The Fog Dispelled," bulletin of American Liberty League, February 15, 1936, 1.

144. "Liberty Bloc Hints Drive to Enlarge," *Salt Lake Tribune*, February 1, 1936, 1.

145. Congressman Hamilton Fish of New York declared that Smith "takes exactly the same point of view as the Republican Party. . . . There is not a single statement by Gov. Smith which I cannot indorse personally." Felix Bruner, "New Deal Leaders in House Invite Smith to 'Take a Walk,'" *Washington Post*, January 28, 1936, 2. Colonel Frank Knox, running for the Republican presidential nomination (and who was later nominated as the vice presidential candidate), predicted that Smith's speech "unquestionably will have the effect of swinging millions of Democratic votes to the support of the Republican ticket next fall" (Bruner, "New Deal Leaders," 2). Welcoming Smith to the anti–New Deal fold, Governor Eugene Talmadge of Georgia predicted that he would lead Southern Democrats to join Smith and Northern Democrats to block the renomination of Roosevelt as the party's presidential candidate. Franklin Waltman Jr., "Al Smith

'Changed Allegiance' in Face of Foe, Robinson Says; Talmadge Supporters Gather," *Washington Post*, January 29, 1936, 1.

146. See F. Lauriston Bullard, "New England Takes Sides," *New York Times*, February 2, 1936, E4.

147. See, e.g., Arthur Krock, "Smith's 'Walk' May Start New Party Alignment," *New York Times*, January 27, 1936, 16.

148. As the *New York Times* reported, "the popular reaction was strong among members of the Democratic political community against the former Governor's new association with du Ponts and other millionaires." Arthur Krock, "President Works on Amid Verbal Barrage," *New York Times*, February 2, 1936, E3.

149. Franklyn Waltman, "Al Smith Puts on Good Political Show; Effect on Coming Election Problematic," *Washington Post*, January 27, 1936, 2.

150. Bruner, "New Deal Leaders in House Invite Smith to 'Take a Walk,'" 2.

151. "Notes Smith's Company," *New York Times*, January 27, 1936, 2.

152. "Text of Senator Robinson's Reply to Ex-Gov. Smith's Speech," *New York Times*, January 29, 1936, 12. See also Meyer Berger, "The High Hat Turns the Corner, Too: Its Devoted Cult Knows that Prosperity Is Here," *New York Times*, December 27, 1936, SM8.

153. See "Lewis Hits Smith, Backs Roosevelt," *New York Times*, January 29, 1936, 1.

154. "Lewis Hits Smith, Backs Roosevelt," 14. See also "Smith Is Booed by 1,700 Mine Delegates Here," *Washington Post*, January 29, 1936, 1.

155. Louis Stark, "Miners Warned on Guffey Act," *New York Times*, February 6, 1936, 5. See also "Liberty League Held 'Inimical' at Mine Parley," *Washington Post*, February 6, 1936, 2.

156. For instance, the head of the Amalgamated Clothing Workers called on labor to help defeat the Liberty League and related forces, which "resent every attempt to give the workers either a new deal, a square deal or any other kind of a deal, except a raw deal." "Hillman Demands Vote for President," *New York Times*, April 10, 1936, 14. Roosevelt supporters also sought to rally African American voters to their side by pointing to the Liberty League, saying that the league and its lawyers "are principally engaged in preserving the liberty of a few men to wring their bread from the sweat of other men's faces." "26 Negro Rallies Back Roosevelt," *New York Times*, September 22, 1936, 4.

157. Louis Stark, "Labor Chiefs Give Roosevelt Pledge," *New York Times*, May 12, 1936, 2.

158. See William V. Nessly, "Senate to Study U.S. Fund Use for Campaigns," *Washington Post*, April 2, 1936, 1; Stark, "Labor Chiefs Give Roosevelt Pledge."

159. See Stark, "Labor Chiefs Give Roosevelt Pledge."

160. Louis Stark, "Asks Union Labor to Support Roosevelt," *New York Times*, May 26, 1936, 14. At the Republican National Convention, the president of the Amalgamated Clothing Workers likewise described the Republican Party as the

"political agents of the Liberty League." "Labor Executives Criticize Speech," *New York Times*, July 24, 1936, 12. John L. Lewis said that Republican candidate Alf Landon was a puppet of the Liberty League and big business. "Lewis Declares Landon Is 'Puppet,'" *New York Times*, September 20, 1936, 27.

161. James Farley described the league as the "center and soul of the predatory powers." "Farley Scores Liberty League as Anti-Social," *Washington Post*, February 6, 1936, 2. Secretary Ickes declared that the league was simply "an alias for big business." "Ickes Says Hoover Aims to Stir Fear," *New York Times*, February 27, 1936, 8. Mayor Fiorella LaGuardia of New York declared, "God help this country when the unemployed will be at the mercy of the Liberty League who would continue to feed the hungry on ticker tape, epigrams, wisecracks and slogans." "Mayor Backs WPA and Warns Moses," *New York Times*, March 15, 1936, 31. One Democratic senator called the league the "American 'Lobby' League" and said it was "composed in large part of a group of griping and disgruntled politicians. . . . masquerading as patriots but in reality apostles of greed." "Harrison Hits Plan of Liberty League," *New York Times*, December 27, 1935, 4; See also "House in Uproar on Liberty League," *New York Times*, February 1, 1936, 2; "Text of Senator Robinson's Reply to Ex-Gov. Smith's Speech," *New York Times*, January 29, 1936, 12. Democrats frequently referred to the league as the "du Pont Liberty League." See, e.g., "M'nutt Says Others May Control Landon," *New York Times*, July 22, 1936, 13; "'Nonpartisan' Fight on Roosevelt Is Opened by the Liberty League," *New York Times*, July 1, 1936, 17.

162. Eunice Barnard, "Dr. Counts Assails 'Liberty's Enemies,'" *New York Times*, February 24, 1936, 5.

163. "Connally Defends New Deal," *Washington Post*, March 29, 1936, 6 (quoting Senator Connally of Texas in his critique of the American Liberty League).

164. James D. Secrest, "House Blocks Rep. Blanton in Red Fight," *Washington Post*, February 1, 1936, 13.

165. Franklyn Waltman, "Administration's Strategy Believed Aimed to Keep AAA Substitute Apart from Taxes," *Washington Post*, February 19, 1936, 2.

166. "Political Battleground Shifts East Again to New York State," *Washington Post*, April 12, 1936, B1.

167. "The Part of Wisdom," *Washington Post*, August 7, 1936, X6.

168. See, e.g., Arthur Krock, "Political Tide Turns Again to Roosevelt," *New York Times*, March 22, 1936, E3.

169. Arthur Krock, "Black Committee Exposes the Political Promoter," *New York Times*, April 17, 1936, 20.

170. "Liberty League Is Target," *New York Times*, January 26, 1936, 37.

171. See, e.g., Gerald T. Dunne, *Hugo Black and the Judicial Revolution* (New York: Simon & Schuster, 1977), 48; Shesol, *Supreme Power*, 216.

172. See, e.g., Shesol, 216.

173. Wolfskill, *The Revolt of the Conservatives*, 225.

174. Wolfskill, 227.

175. Black's biographers have agreed with the assessment that the investigation of the Liberty League was driven by politics, probably at the suggestion of the White House. See Dunne, *Hugo Black and the Judicial Revolution*, 158; Wolfskill, *The Revolt of the Conservatives*, 227.

176. "Liberty League Is Target," *New York Times*, January 26, 1936, 37.

177. See Roger K. Newman, *Hugo Black: A Biography* (New York: Pantheon Books, 1994), 185.

178. "Saints and Sinners," *New York Times*, March 11, 1936, 18. Catching the drift of Senator Black's investigation, the *Times* asked, "What was the connection between these organizations whose business it was to attack the New Deal?" Wolfskill, *The Revolt of the Conservatives*, 228.

179. See, e.g., "House, 153 to 137, Rebukes Senate Lobby Committee; Bars Higher Counsel Fee," *New York Times*, April 16, 1936, 1-2; "Say New Deal Foes Have Same Donors," *New York Times*, March 22, 1936, 13. Liberty League president Jouett Shouse strongly denied that, even though the same backers funded them all, each of these other organizations was merely "one of the interlocking branches of the Liberty League." Wolfskill, *The Revolt of the Conservatives*, 233.

180. "New Deal Foes Help Sentinels, Inquiry Is Told," *Washington Post*, April 18, 1936, 5. Wolfskill, *The Revolt of the Conservatives*, 231, 233; see also "Say New Deal Foes Have Same Donors," *New York Times*, March 22, 1936, 13; "Says Smith Spoke for Liberty League to Remove 'Taint,'" *New York Times*, April 18, 1936, 1, 4.

181. See "Five Big Guns," *New York Times*, February 2, 1936, E1.

182. Wolfskill, *The Revolt of the Conservatives*, 177; see also "'Grassroots' Open War on New Deal; Boom Talmadge," *New York Times*, January 30, 1936, 1, 8.

183. Wolfskill, 242. The committee discovered that one anti–New Deal group, the Farmers' Independence Council, was run directly out of the Liberty League offices and was funded by the league. Wolfskill, 239-240. In rhetoric almost identical to the Liberty League, the group called on farmers "who wish to preserve their liberty and our present form of government" to rise up to preserve the "principles of Americanism" against the radical, tyrannical policies of the New Deal. See James C. Carey, "The Farmers' Independence Council of America, 1935-1938," *Agricultural History* 35, no. 2 (1961): 72; "Anti–New Dealers Backed Farm Group," *New York Times*, April 15, 1936, 1, 11. Black asked derisively: "Does Mr. Jouett Shouse devote much time to farming?" "Shouse Denies League Backs Farm Council," *Washington Post*, April 11, 1936, X4.

184. See Shesol, *Supreme Power*, 216-217.

185. See Shesol, 217.

186. See Franklyn Waltman Jr., "Foreign Affairs Stand Overshadows

Domestic Issues as President Calls for Neutrality Law," *Washington Post*, January 4, 1936, 1.

187. The Democrats alleged that the Republicans had chosen Alf Landon because "the DuPont Liberty League crowd is less afraid of him" than other Republicans, so he was acceptable to the Liberty League. "Governor Is Recognized as Likely Opponent for First Time," *Washington Post*, May 21, 1936, 6. In his keynote address to the Democratic National Convention, Senator Alben Barkley called the American Liberty League the Republican Party's "illegitimate brother." "The Keynote Speech," *New York Times*, June 24, 1936, 16. At the convention, the Democrats portrayed the election as a choice between Roosevelt and the Liberty League. As Pennsylvania governor George Earle put it, "The more the people realize and the more they keep in mind that the issue is the liberalism of Roosevelt versus the big business fascism of the Liberty League the better it will be." "Leading Democrats Minimize Effect of the Conservative Group Bolt," *New York Times*, June 23, 1936, 12. Throughout the campaign, the Democrats continued the assault on Landon as the puppet of the Liberty League. See, e.g., "Farley Deplores Campaign of Fear," *New York Times*, August 20, 1936, 11; "M'nutt Says Others May Control Landon," *New York Times*, July 22, 1936, 13; "Robinson Derides Landon Tax Ideas," *New York Times*, August 29, 1936, 4.

188. "Farley Asserts Administration Rescued Trade," *Washington Post*, February 22, 1936, 1–2; see also "Farley Blasts G.O.P. Critics of Roosevelt," *Washington Post*, February 23, 1936, 1, 3.

189. "Farley's Address on National Issues before Democrats at Albany," *New York Times*, April 16, 1936, 18. Speaking at the Democratic National Convention in June 1936, Farley likewise charged that "behind the Republican ticket is the crew of the du Pont Liberty League and their allies." "Farley's Address to the Delegates," *New York Times*, June 24, 1936, 14; *see also* "Farley Scores Liberty League as Anti-Social," *Washington Post*, February 6, 1936, 2.

190. See "Du Ponts' $144,430 Tops Landon Gifts," *New York Times*, December 2, 1936, 10; "Hamilton Asks Senate to Rush WPA Inquiry," *Washington Post*, October 17, 1936, X7; "$2,524,950 Spent by Republicans," *New York Times*, September 11, 1936, 10.

191. "Du Pont Funds Aid Landon in Maine," *New York Times*, September 10, 1936, 1, 4.

192. See "Comment Acrid on Bolt Threat of Smith Bloc," *Washington Post*, June 22, 1936, 2 (noting Al Smith's support of Landon); "Hamilton Asks Senate to Rush WPA Inquiry," *Washington Post*, October 17, 1936, X7 (noting the du Ponts' endorsements of Landon); "'Remedy for All Our Ills,'" *New York Times*, October 2, 1936, 1, 5 (highlighting Al Smith's support of Landon).

193. "Liberty League Tends Republican," *New York Times*, January 26, 1936, 37.

194. "Republican Party Platform of 1936," June 9, 1936, American Presidency Project, https://www.presidency.ucsb.edu/documents/republican -party-platform-1936. The Republicans' focus on the Constitution was a new development. The 1932 platform had not presented the party's agenda in constitutional terms and had mentioned the Constitution only in relation to the campaign to repeal the Prohibition Amendment. "Republican Party Platform of 1932," June 14, 1932, American Presidency Project, https://www.presidency .ucsb.edu/documents/republican-party-platform-1932.

195. See "Ickes Attacks Landon 'Anti-Dictator' Role, Citing 1933 Plea for Oil Control," *Washington Post*, August 4, 1936, X4.

196. "Baltimore Crowd Cordial to Landon," *New York Times*, October 27, 1936, 20.

197. For instance, before the campaign Landon had supported federal regulation of the oil and gas industries but now argued that such regulation violated states' rights. See "Ickes Attacks Landon 'Anti-Dictator' Role, Citing 1933 Plea for Oil Control"; see also "Text of Secretary Ickes Radio Reply to Governor Landon and Colonel Knox," *New York Times*, August 4, 1936, 12 (reproducing text of speech).

198. See "Says Farley Is 'Scared,'" *New York Times*, May 22, 1936, 3. The Liberty League problem was apparent by the Republican National Convention in June 1936, when one potential vice presidential candidate was eliminated from consideration because of his connection with the Liberty League. Charles R. Michael, "Cleveland Marks Turning Point for Republicans," *New York Times*, June 7, 1936, 61.

199. Arthur Krock, "Liberty League Is Distinctly Pro-Landon," *New York Times*, August 7, 1936, 18.

200. "Landon Packs Rods for Colorado Trip," *New York Times*, June 24, 1936, 13.

201. See, e.g., Krock, "Liberty League Is Distinctly Pro-Landon," 18.

202. See "'Nonpartisan' Fight on Roosevelt Is Opened by the Liberty League," 1; see also "Party Link Denied by Liberty League," *New York Times*, August 6, 1936, 11.

203. See, e.g., "Farley's Address on National Issues before Democrats at Albany"; Arthur Krock, "Liberty League Is Distinctly Pro-Landon at 18; The Part of Wisdom," *Washington Post*, August 7, 1936, X6.

204. "Declares Landon Offers Only Dole," *New York Times*, October 4, 1936, 42 (internal quotation mark omitted).

205. See, e.g., "Money in Elections," *New York Times*, September 12, 1936, 16.

206. Michael Nelson, ed., *Congressional Quarterly's Guide to the Presidency*, vol. 1, 2nd ed. (New York: Routledge, 2015), 375; Yanek Mieczkowski, *The Routledge Historical Atlas of Presidential Elections* (New York: Routledge, 2001), 100; Leuchtenburg, "When the People Spoke, What Did They Say?," 2108.

207. Mieczkowski, *The Routledge Historical Atlas of Presidential Elections,* 100.

208. See, e.g., "Pinchot Urges Party to Shed Rule by Rich," *Washington Post,* November 23, 1936, X22.

209. Speaking in 1938, Chairman Farley declared that the 1936 election definitively repudiated the Liberty League's attempt to "steer our people back to a reactionary system." "Farley Ridicules Speech by Frank," *New York Times,* February 1, 1938, 9; see also Franklyn Waltman, "Second Decisive Defeat in Two Campaigns Has Started Tongues to Wagging Relative to the Future of the Republican Party," *Washington Post,* November 6, 1936, X2; but see "Landslide Vote Is Not Blanket Indorsement of New Deal," *Washington Post,* November 8, 1936, B1.

210. See, e.g., "Pinchot Urges Party to Shed Rule by Rich."

211. See Michael Kent Curtis, "The Bill of Rights and the States: An Overview from One Perspective," *Journal of Contemporary Legal Issues* 18, no. 1 (2009): 6.

212. See "Liberty League to Go On," *New York Times,* November 13, 1936, 14; "Liberty League Won't Disband, Shouse States," *Washington Post,* November 13, 1936, X7.

213. Wolfskill, *The Revolt of the Conservatives,* 247.

214. "The Nation's Passing Show," *New York Times,* December 20, 1936, E9.

215. See Wolfskill, *The Revolt of the Conservatives,* 247–249, 251.

216. Barry Cushman, "Mr. Dooley and Mr. Gallup: Public Opinion and Constitutional Change in the 1930s," *Buffalo Law Review* 50, no. 1 (2002): 10.

217. See National Labor Relations Board v. Jones & Laughlin Steel Corp., 301 U.S. 1 (1937) (upholding constitutionality of the National Labor Relations Act); West Coast Hotel Co. v. Parrish, 300 U.S. 379 (1937) (upholding state minimum wage law); United States v. Darby, 312 U.S. 100 (1941) (upholding Fair Labor Standards Act); Wickard v. Filburn, 317 U.S. 111 (1942) (upholding Agricultural Adjustment Act).

218. See, e.g., Bruce Ackerman, *We the People, Volume 1: Foundations* (Cambridge, MA: Belknap Press, 1991), 58; Ackerman, *We the People: Transformations,* 25; Cushman, *Rethinking the New Deal Court,* 5–6; Laura Kalman, *The Strange Career of Legal Liberalism* (New Haven, CT: Yale University Press, 1996), 19; William E. Leuchtenburg, *The Supreme Court Reborn: The Constitutional Revolution in the Age of Roosevelt* (New York: Oxford University Press, 1995), 233.

219. Ackerman, *We the People: Transformations,* 343.

220. Ackerman, 268–269.

221. See, e.g., Ackerman, 295, 306–311; Michael J. Gerhardt, "The Constitution outside the Courts," *Drake Law Review* 51 (2003): 787; John C. Yoo, "In Defense of the Court's Legitimacy," *University of Chicago Law Review* 68 (2001): 780. This view is widely shared outside the academy. For instance, anticipating that the Supreme Court would rule against the Affordable Care Act, Congressman Clyburn urged President Obama to run against the Court

just like Roosevelt supposedly did. See Sam Stein, "Barack Obama Could Go After Supreme Court on Health Care, James Clyburn Suggests," *Huffington Post*, April 2, 2012, http://www.huffingtonpost.com/2012/04/02/barack-obama -supreme-court-health-care-james-clyburn_n_1396375.html.

222. Ackerman, *We the People: Transformations*, 309; Ackerman, *We the People: Foundations*, 58–80.

223. Ackerman, *Transformations*, 280.

224. See, e.g., Leuchtenburg, "When the People Spoke, What Did They Say?," 2077.

225. Terrance Sandalow, "Abstract Democracy: A Review of Ackerman's We the People" (book review), *Constitutional Comment* 9 (1992): 329.

226. See, e.g., Leuchtenburg, "When the People Spoke, What Did They Say?," 2084.

227. Michael J. Klarman, "Constitutional Fact/Constitutional Fiction: A Critique of Bruce Ackerman's Theory of Constitutional Moments" (book review), *Stanford Law Review* 44 (1992): 771 (footnote omitted); see also Cushman, *Rethinking the New Deal Court*, 27; Leuchtenburg, "When the People Spoke, What Did They Say?," 2084.

228. Ackerman, *We the People: Transformations*, 280, 311.

229. Leuchtenburg, "When the People Spoke, What Did They Say?," 2079; see also Cushman, *Rethinking the New Deal Court*, 26–27; Klarman, "Constitutional Fact/Constitutional Fiction," 771.

230. See, e.g., Cushman, 27.

231. See generally Kammen, *A Machine That Would Go of Itself*.

232. See, e.g., Robert J. Delahunty, "Federalism and Polarization," *University of St. Thomas Journal of Law and Public Policy* 1 (2007): 83.

233. See "Text of Roosevelt Address," *New York Times*, June 28, 1936.

234. Roosevelt in turn argued that his opponents hid behind lofty constitutional rhetoric while ignoring the nation's true values: "In vain they seek to hide behind the flag and the Constitution. In their blindness they forget what the flag and the Constitution stand for. Now, as always, the flag and the Constitution stand for democracy, not tyranny; for freedom, not subjection, and against a dictatorship by mob rule and the overprivileged alike" ("Text of Roosevelt Address").

Chapter 5. The Partisan Constitution

1. Larry D. Kramer, "Undercover Anti-Populism," *Fordham Law Review* 73 (2005): 1344.

2. Larry D. Kramer, *The People Themselves: Popular Constitutionalism and Judicial Review* (New York: Oxford University Press, 2004), 247; Mark Tushnet, *Taking*

the Constitution Away from the Courts (Princeton, NJ: Princeton University Press, 1999), 52; see also Robert Post and Reva Siegel, "Popular Constitutionalism, Departmentalism, and Judicial Supremacy," *California Law Review* 92 (2004): 1042–1043.

3. See, e.g., Kramer, *The People Themselves*, 217–218; Robert C. Post, "Foreword: Fashioning the Legal Constitution: Culture, Courts, and Law," *Harvard Law Review* 117 (2003): 36; William E. Forbath, "The New Deal Constitution in Exile," *Duke Law Journal* 51 (2001): 181.

4. Franklin D. Roosevelt, "President of the United States, Address on Constitution Day, Washington, DC: The Constitution of the United States Was a Layman's Document, Not a Lawyer's Contract," September 17, 1937, in Samuel I. Rosenman, ed., *The Public Papers and Addresses of Franklin D. Roosevelt*, vol. 1 (New York: Macmillan, 1941), 359, 361.

5. See, e.g., Bruce Ackerman, *We the People, Volume 2: Transformations* (Cambridge, MA: Belknap Press, 1998), 295.

6. See, e.g., Kate Zernike, *Boiling Mad: Inside Tea Party America* (New York: Times Books, 2010), 44; John M. O'Hara, *A New American Tea Party: The Counterrevolution against Bailouts, Handouts, Reckless Spending, and More Taxes* (Hoboken, NJ: John Wiley & Sons, 2010), 4; Tea Party Declaration of Independence, February 24, 2010, 5, http://www.csa1776.org/docs/Dec-of-Tea-Party-Independencev.pdf.

7. See, e.g., Dick Armey and Matt Kibbe, *Give Us Liberty: A Tea Party Manifesto* (New York: Harper Collins, 2010), 19–20; O'Hara, *A New American Tea Party*, 1; see also Zernike, *Boiling Mad*, 13.

8. "Rick Santelli's Shout Heard 'Round the World," CNBC.com, February 22, 2009, http://www.cnbc.com/id/29283701.

9. See Armey and Kibbe, *Give Us Liberty*, 19.

10. Armey and Kibbe, 34.

11. Zernike, *Boiling Mad*, 21–25; Devin Burghart and Leonard Zeskind, *Tea Party Nationalism: A Critical Examination of the Tea Party Movement and the Size, Scope, and Focus of Its National Factions Tea Party Nationalism* (Kansas City, MO: Institute for Research and Education on Human Rights, 2010): 16–17.

12. Zernike, 22.

13. Christopher S. Parker and Matt A. Barreto, *Change They Can't Believe In: The Tea Party and Reactionary Politics in America* (Princeton, NJ: Princeton University Press, 2013), 2.

14. Leigh A. Bradberry and Gary C. Jacobson, "Does the Tea Party Still Matter? Tea Party Influence in the 2012 Elections," paper presented at American Political Science Association 2013 Annual Meeting, 14, table 4, https://papers.ssrn.com/so13/papers.cfm?abstract_id=2301066.

15. Jeffrey M. Jones, "Debt, Gov't. Power among Tea Party Supporters' Top Concerns," *USA Today*/Gallup Poll, July 5, 2010, http://www.gallup

.com/poll/141119/debt-gov-power-among-tea-party-supporters-top-concerns.aspx.

16. "National Survey of Tea Party Supporters," *New York Times* and CBS News, April 5–12, 2010, 33, http://s3.amazonaws.com/nytdocs/docs/312/312.pdf at 40–41; Gary Langer, "2010 Elections Exit Poll Analysis: The Political Price of Economic Pain," ABC News, November 3, 2010, http://abcnews.go.com/Politics/2010-midterms-political-price-economic-pain/story?id=12041739.

17. "National Survey of Tea Party Supporters," 41.

18. "National Survey of Tea Party Supporters," 14–15, 26, 30–31.

19. Joseph Farah, *The Tea Party Manifesto: A Vision for an American Rebirth* (Washington, DC: WNDBooks, 2010), 115.

20. Robb Willer, Matthew Feinberg, and Rachel Wetts, "Threats to Racial Status Promote Tea Party Support among White Americans," Working Paper No. 3422, *Stanford Business*, https://www.gsb.stanford.edu/faculty-research/working-papers/threats-racial-status-promote-tea-party-support-among-white; "National Survey of Tea Party Supporters," 14, 33; Farah, 85.

21. Vanessa Williamson, Theda Skocpol, and John Coggin, "The Tea Party and the Remaking of Republican Conservatism," *Perspectives on Politics* 9, no. 1 (March 2011): 25.

22. "National Survey of Tea Party Supporters," 14; Zernicke, *Boiling Mad*, 7.

23. Theda Skocpol and Vanessa Williamson, *The Tea Party and the Remaking of Republican Conservatism* (New York: Oxford University Press, 2016), 68.

24. Donald Warren, *The Radical Center: Middle Americans and the Politics of Alienation* (Notre Dame, IN: University of Notre Dame Press, 1976); Samuel Francis, *Beautiful Losers: Essays on the Failure of American Conservatism* (Columbia: University of Missouri Press, 1993), 62; Leonard Zeskind, *Blood and Politics: The History of the White Nationalist Movement from the Margins to the Mainstream* (New York: Farrar, Strauss, Giroux, 2009), 290.

25. Willer, "Threats to Racial Status Promote Tea Party Support among White Americans"; Eric D. Knowles et al., "Race, Ideology, and the Tea Party: A Longitudinal Study," *PLos ONE*, June 25, 2013, https://www.researchgate.net/publication/245029949_Race_Ideology_and_the_Tea_Party_A_Longitudinal_Study.

26. See, e.g., Zernike, *Boiling Mad*, 44; O'Hara, *A New American Tea Party*, 4; "Declaration of Tea Party Independence," 5, http://www.csa1776.org/docs/Dec-of-Tea-Party-Independencev.pdf.

27. Farah, *The Tea Party Manifesto*, 85.

28. Zernike, *Boiling Mad*, 44.

29. O'Hara, *A New American Tea Party*, 4.

30. Parker and Barreto, *Change They Can't Believe In*, 3.

31. See, e.g., Charly Gullett, *Official Tea Party Handbook: A Tactical Playbook for Tea Party Patriots* (Prescott, AZ: Warfield Press, 2009), 12.

32. Parker and Barreto, *Change They Can't Believe In*, 288, table A1.1.

33. Sometimes the rhetoric of invasion is literal. See, e.g., Farah, *The Tea Party Manifesto*, 69 (asserting that the "political and cultural elite" have sought to prevent American sovereignty by "conspiring to bring into American millions and millions more sheep—illegally").

34. Farah, 85.

35. Farah, 91; Zernike, *Boiling Mad*, 70–71.

36. See, e.g., Jillian Rayfield, "Tea Party Nation Founder: Obama Wants China to Fund His Campaign Like Hamas," TPM, January 19, 2011, https://talkingpointsmemo.com/muckraker/tea-party-nation-founder-obama-wants-china-to-fund-his-campaign-like-hamas-did-in-08; Joe Garofoli, "Extreme Words No Longer Left to Fringe," *San Francisco Chronicle*, November 19, 2013, A1.

37. Brian Tashman Phillips, "Obama and His Regime Are Not Real Americans," RightWingWatch, May 4, 2011, http://www.rightwingwatch.org/post/phillips-obama-and-his-regime-are-not-real-americans/.

38. Joseph Farah, "Address at the National Tea Party Convention," February 5, 2010, C-SPAN, http://www.c-spanvideo.org/program/291955-1.

39. See, e.g., Farah, *The Tea Party Manifesto*, 84, 88; Bill O'Reilly, "Sarah Palin on National Day of Prayer Controversy," Fox News, May 7, 2010, http://www.foxnews.com/story/0,2933,592422,00.html#ixzz1EqH8bfmI.

40. See, e.g., Kevin Drum, "Recycled: The Tea Party Is a Revolutionary Force. Just not in the Way You've Been Led to Believe," *Mother Jones*, September 1, 2010, http://findarticles.com/p/articles/mi_m1329/is_5_35/ai_n56345646/ ("'Obama isn't a US socialist,' thundered Fox News commentator Steven Milloy at a tea party convention earlier this year, 'he's an international socialist!'").

41. See, e.g., Joseph Farah, "Keynote Address to National Tea Party Convention," Nashville, Tennessee, February 5, 2010, C-SPAN, http://www.c-spanvideo.org/program/291955-1; Judson Phillips, "The Eligibility Issue," Tea Party Nation, last modified February 20, 2011, http://www.teapartynation.com/forum/topics/the-eligibility-issue (requires email address and free membership to view content). On April 27, 2011, President Obama released a copy of his long-form birth certificate; see Dan Pfeiffer, "President Obama's Long Form Birth Certificate," *White House Blog*, posted April 27, 2011, http://www.whitehouse.gov/blog/2011/04/27/president-obamas-long-form-birth-certificate. Many Tea Partiers rejected this evidence as a forgery. See, e.g., Alan Caruba, "Pageantry, History and Change," Tea Party Nation, posted May 1, 2011; "Is Obama's Birth Certificate a Fake?," *Patriot Update*, posted April 27, 2011, http://patriotupdate.com/6137/is-obama%E2%80%99s-birth-certificate-a-fake.

42. See, e.g., Alex Altman, "Racism Rift Highlights Dilemma: Who Speaks for the Tea Party?," *Time*, posted July 22, 2010, http://www.time.com/time/politics/article/0,8599,2005371,00.html.

43. See Burghart and Zeskind, *Tea Party Nationalism*, 57–67.

44. Belief that Obama is foreign is widespread among conservatives. See, e.g., Steven G. Calabresi, "The Teleprompter Presidency? Justice DeLayed or Denied?," *Politico*, posted August 17, 2010, http://www.politico.com/arena /perm/Steven_G__Calabresi_A5D4F886-1279-48D4-96B9-D176A986A416 .html (asserting that "at some level [Obama] does not really know America very well nor does he thoroughly identify with it"); Dinesh D'Souza, *The Roots of Obama's Rage* (Washington, DC: Regnery Publishing, 2010), 1–15 (claiming that Obama is attempting to carry out the Socialist, anticolonial dreams of his Kenyan father).

45. Kate Zernicke and Megan Thee-Brenan, "Poll Finds Tea Party Backers Wealthier and More Educated," *New York Times*, April 14, 2010, https://www .nytimes.com/2010/04/15/us/politics/15poll.html.

46. See, e.g., Burghart and Zeskind, *Tea Party Nationalism*, 68–69.

47. See Tea Party Declaration of Independence, 4 ("We reject the idea that the Tea Party Movement is 'led' by anyone other than the millions of average citizens who make it up. The Tea Party Movement understands that as a Free People, we need to SAVE OURSELVES, BY OURSELVES, FOR OURSELVES. The Tea Party Movement is not 'led.' The Tea Party Movement LEADS.").

48. The Tea Party literature I rely upon includes the mission statements of the six national Tea Party umbrella organizations—FreedomWorks Tea Party, 1776 Tea Party, Tea Party Nation, Tea Party Patriots, ResistNet, and Tea Party Express; books written by recognized Tea Party leaders and insiders, including Farah, *The Tea Party Manifesto*; Armey and Kibbe, *Give Us Liberty*; Gullett, *Official Tea Party Handbook*; and O'Hara, *A New American Tea Party*; as well as speeches given at Tea Party events. I also rely on two books on the Constitution that predate the Tea Party movement, W. Cleon Skousen, *The Five Thousand Year Leap: 28 Great Ideas that Changed the World*, 30-Year Anniversary ed. (Franklin, TN: American Documents Publishing, 2009); and W. Cleon Skousen, *The Making of America: The Substance and Meaning of the Constitution*, 2nd ed. (Malta, ID: National Center for Constitutional Studies, 1985), which are considered by many to be the most influential books on the Tea Party's constitutional vision, and which have been used by hundreds of Tea Party groups to educate their members and the public about the meaning of the Constitution. See Jeffery Rosen, "Radical Constitutionalism," *New York Times Magazine*, November 28, 2010, MM34 (characterizing Skousen as "the constitutional guru of the Tea Party movement"). In addition, I have found useful several books and other materials describing the movement from the outside, including Jill Lepore, *The Whites of Their Eyes: The Tea Party's Revolution and the Battle over American History* (Princeton, NJ: Princeton University Press, 2011); Zernike, *Boiling Mad*; and Burghart and Zeskind, *Tea Party Nationalism*.

49. See Carl Andrews, "Tea Party Nation Drafts Declaration of Indepen-

dence," *American Conservative Daily*, February 25, 2010, http://www.ameri canconservativedaily.com/2010/02/tea-party-nation-drafts-declaration-of -independence/.

50. See, e.g., "Tea Party Patriots Mission Statement and Core Values," Tea Party Patriots, http://www.teapartypatriots.org/Mission.aspx; "What Is Tea Party Nation?," Frequently Asked Questions, Tea Party Nation, http://www .teapartynation.com/page/frequentlyasked-questions.

51. Tea Party Declaration of Independence, 4.

52. For discussion of American exceptionalism see, e.g., Seymour Martin Lipset, *American Exceptionalism: A Double-Edged Sword* (New York: W. W. Norton, 1997); Godfrey Hodgson, *The Myth of American Exceptionalism* (New Haven, CT: Yale University Press, 2010); Deborah L. Madsen, *American Exceptionalism* (Jackson: University of Mississippi Press, 1998); Steven G. Calabresi, "'A Shining City on a Hill': American Exceptionalism and the Supreme Court's Practice of Relying on Foreign Law," *Boston University Law Review* 86 (2006): 1335–1416.

53. Judson Phillips, "I Am Tired of Pat Buchanan," Tea Party Nation, December 14, 2010, http://www.teapartynation.com/forum/topics/i-am -tired-of-pat-buchanan; see also Tea Party Declaration of Independence, 4; "Excerpt from Sarah Palin's Address to the Tea Party Express Rally," *Las Vegas Sun*, March 28, 2010, http://www.lasvegassun.com/news/2010/mar/28 /excerpt-sarah-palins-address/.

54. Sarah Palin, *America by Heart: Reflections on Family, Faith, and Flag* (New York: Harper Collins, 2010), 262. Rush Limbaugh also called President Obama the first "anti-American President." See Limbaugh, "'Imam Hussein Obama' Is Probably the 'Best Anti-American President the Country's Ever Had,'" Media Matters for America, August 18, 2010, http://mediamatters.org/mmtv /201008180035.

55. Palin, 63; see also "Excerpt from Sarah Palin's Address to the Tea Party Express Rally," *Las Vegas Sun*, March 28, 2010, http://www.lasvegassun.com /news/2010/mar/28/excerpt-sarah-palins-address/.

56. See Tea Party Declaration of Independence, 4.

57. Tea Party Patriots Mission Statement.

58. See, e.g., Chicago Tea Party, "The Meaning of Limited Government," http://teapartychicago.netboots.net/node/175.

59. Tea Party Declaration of Independence, 4; see also Richmond Tea Party, "Why Limited Government?," http://www.richmondteaparty.com/2010/09 /why-limited-government/ ("A small, limited government, therefore, is the only possible government for a free people. All else, to one degree or another, is slavery."); Zernike, *Boiling Mad*, 42.

60. See, e.g., William F. Buckley Jr., "Our Mission Statement," *National Review*, November 19, 1955; Barry M. Goldwater, *The Conscience of a Conservative* (Shepardsville, KY: Victor Publishing, 1960); George H. Nash, *The Conservative*

Intellectual Movement in America since 1945, 30th Anniversary ed. (Wilmington, DE: Intercollegiate Studies Institute, 2006).

61. See, e.g., Michelle Malkin, Foreword, in O'Hara, *A New American Tea Party*, xxi; Tea Party Declaration of Independence, 2.

62. Farah, *The Tea Party Manifesto*, 91.

63. Farah, 102; see also O'Reilly, "Sarah Palin on National Day of Prayer Controversy" ("[The founding documents] are quite clear that we would create law based on the God of the Bible and the Ten Commandments. It's pretty simple."); Zernike, *Boiling Mad*, 67 ("If you don't understand the Constitution, I'll buy you a dictionary.") (quoting Dick Armey).

64. Farah, 103; see also Farah, 98. See also Armey and Kibbe, *Give Us Liberty*, 65–67 (noting that the Constitution is only four pages long because, like the Tea Party, it expresses a simple idea: the need to leave citizens alone).

65. See Molly K. Hooper, "Constitution Is This Year's Big Best-Seller," *The Hill*, May 21, 2010, http://thehill.com/homenews/administration/99099-constitution-is-this-years-big-best-seller.

66. See Lepore, *The Whites of Their Eyes*.

67. Larry Schweikart and Michael Allen, *A Patriot's History of the United States* (New York: Sentinel, 2007), inside dust jacket; Lepore, 16.

68. Glenn Beck, "Restoring History," Fox News, July 9, 2010, http://video.foxnews.com/v/4278075/beck-restoring-history/; see also Sean Wilentz, "Confounding Fathers: The Tea Party's Cold War Roots," *New Yorker*, October 18, 2010, 32.

69. Beck, "Restoring History."

70. See, e.g., Jay A. Parry, *The Real George Washington* (Malta, ID: National Center for Constitutional Studies, 1991); Andrew M. Allison, *The Real Thomas Jefferson* (Malta, ID: National Center for Constitutional Studies, 1983); Andrew M. Allison, *The Real Benjamin Franklin* (Malta, ID: National Center for Constitutional Studies, 1982).

71. Skousen, *The Five Thousand Year Leap*; Skousen, *The Making of America*.

72. See Rosen, "Radical Constitutionalism"; Jeffrey Rosen, "Economic Freedoms and the Constitution," *Harvard Journal of Law and Public Policy* 35 (2012): 16.

73. Krissah Thompson, "Conservative Class on Founding Fathers' Answers to Current Woes Gains Popularity," *Washington Post*, June 5, 2010, A4; Stephanie Mencimer, "One Nation under Beck: In Which Our Reporter Learns about the Divine Origins of the Constitution at a Tea Party Seminar," *Mother Jones*, May 1, 2010, http://motherjones.com/politics/2010/03/glenn-beck-constitution-tea-party.

74. Wayne Slater, "Perry Uses Glenn Beck Favorite as Election Ally," *Dallas Morning News*, October 1, 2009, 3A; Marc Hansen, "Best Part of Romney Interview Was Off Air," *Des Moines Register*, August 9, 2007, B1; Mark Hemingway,

"Romney's Radical Roots," *National Review Online*, August 6, 2007, http://article.nationalreview.com/323634/romneys-radical-roots/mark-hemingway. Senator Hatch spoke at Skousen's funeral and read a poem he had written in honor of Skousen. "Funeral Program for Willard Cleon Skousen," Skousen 2000, January 14, 2006, http://www.skousen2000.com/funeral.htm; David Corn, "Ben Carson's Love Affair with a 'Nutjob' Conspiracy Theorist," *Mother Jones*, September 29, 2015, https://www.motherjones.com/politics/2015/09/ben-carson-conspiracy-theory-cleon-skousen/; Rosen, "Radical Constitutionalism"; "Iron Will Drives Pearce, Agenda," *Arizona Republic*, June 6, 2010, A1.

75. Skousen, *The Five Thousand Year Leap*; Skousen, *The Making of America*; Rosen, "Radical Constitutionalism."

76. In 2009 Glenn Beck began touting *The Five Thousand Year Leap* as offering "answers to [the] questions plaguing America." Glenn Beck, dust jacket, in Skousen, *The Five Thousand Year Leap*. After its 2009 reissuance with a new introduction by Beck, the book became the nation's best-selling book on law and, for a few months, the best-selling book, period, according to sales on Amazon.com. Sharon Haddock, "Beck's Backing Bumps Skousen Book to Top," *Deseret Morning News*, March 9, 2010, http://www.desertnews.com/article/705292222/Becks-backing-bumps-Skousen-book-to-top.html?pg=1; David Weigel, "Glenn Beck's Book Club: What the Far Right Is Reading," *Washington Monthly*, November 1, 2009, http://www.washintonmonthly.com/features/2009/0911.tms.html.

77. Sean Wilentz, "Confounding Fathers," *New Yorker*, October 18, 2010.

78. Jill Lepore, "Tea and Sympathy: Who Owns the American Revolution?," *New Yorker*, May 3, 2010, 26.

79. Lepore, *The Whites of Their Eyes*, 16; Linford D. Fisher, "Of Tea Parties, Historical Fundamentalism, and Antihistory, Religion in American History: A Group Blog on American Religious History and Culture," *U.S. Religion*, October 27, 2010, http://usreligion.blogspot.com/2010/10/of-tea-parties-historical.html; Rosen, "Radical Constitutionalism."

80. See Matthew Levinger and Paula Franklin Lytle, "Myth and Mobilization: The Triadic Structure of Nationalist Rhetoric," *Nations and Nationalism* 7, no. 2 (2001): 178 ("Numerous scholars have remarked on a curious dimension of nationalist rhetoric: namely, that all nations possess glorious pasts."); see Anthony D. Smith, *Nation in History: Historiographical Debates about Ethnicity and Nationalism* (Hanover, NH: University Press of New England, 2000), 67–68 ("Similarly, memories of political, religious, economic, and artistic 'golden ages' may continue to inspire later generations of that *ethnie* and become the canon of authenticity and creativity for latter day nationalists."); Hans Kohn, *American Nationalism: An Interpretive Essay* (New York: Collier Books, 1961), 29 ("Nationalist historiography desires not only to describe a people's life but to help form it and to make its history appear as the fulfillment of a supposed national destiny.").

81. Levinger and Lytle, "Myth and Mobilization," 188.

82. Jack M. Balkin, "Original Meaning and Constitutional Redemption," *Constitutional Commentary* 24 (2007): 509.

83. Skousen, *The Five Thousand Year Leap*, 118; see also W. Cleon Skousen, *The Naked Communist* (Salt Lake City, UT: Ensign Publishing, 1958), 259-262.

84. Skousen, *The Five Thousand Year Leap*, iii, 135; Skousen, *The Making of America*, 217.

85. Levinger and Lytle, "Myth and Mobilization," 178.

86. Skousen, *The Five Thousand Year Leap*, 17, 15, 225.

87. Skousen, 76; see also Farah, *The Tea Party Manifesto*, 74 (asserting that the Founders "got their inspiration from another radical document—the Bible" and, in fact, "many of the founders were biblical scholars").

88. Skousen, 63, 80, 11-18, 86, 88-89, 118.

89. Skousen, 33-40; Skousen, *The Making of America*, 195.

90. Skousen, *The Five Thousand Year Leap*, 40, 20, 103-104, 38.

91. Skousen, 87-91.

92. Skousen, *The Making of America*, 218-219, 391-392. The story is widely quoted among conservatives; see, e.g., 149 Cong. Rec. H465-08, H495 (February 13, 2003) (statement of Rep. Ron Paul). But it has no basis in fact. See Jim Boylston, "Crockett and Bunce: A Fable Examined," *Crockett Chronicle*, November 2004.

93. Skousen, *The Five Thousand Year Leap*, 124, 126-129, 87, 341.

94. According to Skousen, the Constitution paved the way for what he refers to as the industrial revolution, the machine revolution, the transportation revolution, the communications revolution, the energy resource revolution, and the computer revolution. Skousen, *The Making of America*, 2-3. See also Tea Party Declaration of Independence, 1 ("For much of its history the United States has been a land of prosperity and liberty, sound policies such as fiscal responsibility, constitutionally limited government and a belief in the free market have safeguarded this condition.").

95. Skousen, *The Five Thousand Year Leap*, 5.

96. See, e.g., O'Hara, *A New American Tea Party*, 21; Farah, *The Tea Party Manifesto*, 82.

97. Lepore, *The Whites of Their Eyes*, 12 (discussing Tea Party view that "liberals had contaminated the teaching of American history").

98. Skousen, *The Five Thousand Year Leap*, 134.

99. Skousen, *The Making of America*, 407 ("Unconstitutional Doctrines Dominate Today").

100. Skousen, 255, 387-392.

101. Skousen, *The Five Thousand Year Leap*, 350.

102. Skousen, *The Making of America*, 351-353; Tea Party Declaration of Independence, 2; Farah, *The Tea Party Manifesto*, 70.

103. Tea Party Declaration of Independence, 2.

104. For instance, Tea Party Nation founder Judson Phillips declared: "McCarthy had one simple idea. If you are going to work in a sensitive position for the government, you should be loyal to America. It is a pity that rule is not in effect today. If it were, Obama and his entire regime would be gone." Judson Phillips, "If They Call It 'McCarthyism' He Must Be on to Something," Tea Party Nation, http://www.teapartynation.com/forum/topics/if-they-call-it -mccarthyism-he.

105. Glenn Beck, Introduction, in Skousen, *The Five Thousand Year Leap*, 6.

106. Video of the funeral is available online. GOPTrust, "Funeral for the Constitution at Virginia Tea Party Convention," YouTube, October 12, 2010, http://www.youtube.com/watch?v=10pw13RZ-SQ.

107. "Funeral for the Constitution at Virginia Tea Party Convention," National Republican Trust Political Action Committee, July 19, 2011, http:// www.goptrust.com/Tea_Party_Convention_Funeral.html.

108. The theme of the Virginia Tea Party Patriots Convention was "The Constitutional Still Matters," and keynote speaker Lou Dobbs bemoaned that it was a sad day in America when the people have to remind the politicians that the Constitution matters, but it is "oh so necessary." Catfishhilton, "Lou Dobbs at VA Tea Party Convention in Richmond, Virginia," YouTube, October 9, 2010, http://www.youtube.com/watch?v=RTD-IJKRoZo.

109. Jim Norman, "In US, Support for Tea Party Drops to New Low," Gallup, October 26, 2015, https://news.gallup.com/poll/186338/support-tea -party-drops-new-low.aspx?g_source=Politics&g_medium=newsfeed&g _campaign=tiles.

110. See Jeff Zeleny, "For Republicans, too, a Broad Power Shift after the Elections," *New York Times*, February 10, 2011, A18; Janie Lorber, "Republicans Form Caucus for Tea Party in the House," *New York Times*, July 21, 2010, A18. See also Skocpol and Williamson, *The Tea Party and the Remaking of Republican Conservatism*, 158–163; Tom Curry, "What Exit Polls Say about Tea Party Movement," MSNBC, November 3, 2010, http://www.msnbc.msn.com/id /39979427/ns /politics-decision_2010/.

111. Bradberry and Jacobson, "Does the Tea Party Still Matter?"

112. Rich Lowry, "The Right's Post-Constitutional Moment," *Politico*, December 23, 2015, https://www.politico.com/magazine/story/2015/12 /donald-trump-constitution-opinion-213458.

113. "Little Compromise on Compromising," Pew Research, September 20, 2010, http://www.pewresearch.org/2010/09/20/little-compromise-on -compromising/. Andy Barr, "The GOP's no-compromise pledge," *Politico*, October 28, 2010, https://www.politico.com/story/2010/10/the-gops-no -compromise-pledge-044311.

114. James H. Fitzgerald, "Our Moment: No Compromise. No Surrender.

Total Victory," *Tea Party Tribune*, August 5, 2011, http://www.teapartytribune .com/2011/08/05/our-moment-no-compromise-no-surrender-total-victory/.

115. "Rick Santorum Announcement Speech," 4President.org, June 6, 2011, http://www.4president.org/speeches/2012/ricksantorum2012announce ment.htm.

116. "Michele Bachmann Officially Announces Her Run for the Presidency of the United States in Waterloo, Iowa," 4President.org, 2012, http://www .4president.org/speeches/2012/michelebachmann2012announcement.htm.

117. "Ron Paul 2012 Presidential Campaign Announcement Speech," 4President.org, May 13, 2011, http://www.4president.org/speeches/2012 /ronpaul2012announcement.htm.

118. Mitt Romney, "Remarks to the National Rifle Association National Convention," St. Louis, Missouri, April 13, 2012), American Presidency Project, http://www.presidency.ucsb.edu/ws/index.php?pid=100578.

119. Devin Dwyer, "Obama Rebuffs Romney on 'American Exceptionalism,'" ABC News, April 2, 2012, https://abcnews.go.com/blogs/politics/2012/04 /obama-rebuffs-romney-on-american-exceptionalism/.

120. Ezra Klein, "Romney's Theory of the 'Taker Class,' and Why It Matters," *Washington Post*, September 17, 2012, https://www.washingtonpost.com/news /wonk/wp/2012/09/17/romneys-theory-of-the-taker-class-and-why-it-matters/.

121. "Republican Party Platform 2012," August 27, 2012, American Presidency Project, https://www.presidency.ucsb.edu/documents/2012-repub lican-party-platform.

122. Matt Kibbe, "The Tea Party Is Officially Dead. It Was Killed by Partisan Politics," *Reason*, February 11, 2018, https://reason.com/archives /2018/02/11/the-tea-party-is-dead-long-live-liberty.

123. Jeffrey M. Berry, "Tea Party Decline," paper delivered at American Political Science Association Annual Meeting, San Francisco, August 2017, https://as.tufts.edu/politicalscience/sites/all/themes/asbase/assets /documents/berry/teaPartyDecline.pdf.

124. Jim Norman, "In US, Support for Tea Party Drops to New Low," Gallup, October 26, 2015, https://news.gallup.com/poll/186338/support -tea-party-drops-new-low.aspx?g_source=Politics&g_medium=newsfeed&g _campaign=tiles.

125. Kibbe, "The Tea Party Is Officially Dead"; Devin Burghart and Leonard Zeskind, "Special Report: Beyond FAIR: The Decline of the Established Anti-Immigrant Organizations and the Rise of Tea Party Nativism," *Institute for Research and Education on Human Rights* (2012): 3, https://www.irehr.org/2012/11/20 /beyond-fair-report-pdf/.

126. Larry D. Kramer, "The People Themselves," 247; Tushnet, *Taking the Constitution Away from the Courts*, 52; see also Post and Siegel, "Popular Constitu-tionalism, Departmentalism, and Judicial Supremacy," 1042–1043.

127. Kramer, "The People Themselves," 242 (quoting Richard Parker, *Here the People Rule: A Constitutional Populist Manifesto* [Cambridge, MA: Harvard University Press, 1994], 58).

128. Tushnet, *Taking the Constitution Away from the Courts*, 185, 190.

129. See, e.g., Tea Party Declaration of Independence, 2.

130. See, e.g., Farah, *The Tea Party Manifesto*, 113.

131. Skousen, *The Five Thousand Year Leap*, 114–118.

132. Senator Rand Paul repeatedly emphasized this trope in his campaign. See, e.g., RemnantMan, "Rand Paul: We Are a Republic, Not a Democracy," *World News*, November 20, 2009, http://wn.com/Rand_Paul__We_are a_Re public__not_a_Democracy. The slogan traces back to the John Birch Society, which used it to challenge "collectivism," "statism," and communism. See Robert G. Natelson, "A Republic, Not a Democracy? Initiative, Referendum and the Constitution's Guarantee Clause," *Texas Law Review* 80 (2002): 809 n7. In 1989 the Arizona Republican Party, led by Arizona governor Evans Mecham, adopted a declaration that the US Constitution created "a republic based upon the absolute laws of the Bible, not a democracy." T. R. Reid, "Republicans Rue Mecham's Return: Arizona's Maneuvers Embarrassing National Party Leaders," *Washington Post*, March 14, 1989, A12; see also Patrick J. Buchanan, "A Republic, Not a Democracy," AntiWar.com, March 2, 2005, http://antiwar .com/pat/?articleid=5015.

133. See, e.g., Farah, *The Tea Party Manifesto*, 113.

134. To be sure, as Ilya Somin has pointed out, the Tea Party movement is hardly the first political movement to accuse its opponents of being un-American for supporting opposing policies that the movement considers to embody fundamental American values. Ilya Somin, "The Tea Party Movement and Popular Constitutionalism," *Northwestern University Law Review Colloquy* 105 (2011): 303–304, http://www.law.northwestern.edu/lawreview/colloquy /2011/12/LRColl2011n12Somin.pdf. Unlike the groups cited by Somin, however, which occasionally employed nationalist rhetoric, nationalist rhetoric dividing "true Americans" from others based on their allegiance to the Founders' Constitution was central the Tea Party movement.

135. Zernike, *Boiling Mad*, 127.

136. Skocpol and Williamson, *The Tea Party and the Remaking of Republican Conservatism*, 200.

Chapter 6. The Violent Constitution

1. See, e.g., Stephen van Evera, "Hypotheses on Nationalism and War," *International Security* 18, no. 4 (Spring 1994): 5–39.

2. See Testimony of Jennifer McVeigh (May 5, 1997), in United States v.

Timothy McVeigh, 964 F. Supp. 313 (1997), http://law2.umkc.edu/faculty/projects/ftrials/mcveigh/jennifertestimony.html.

3. See Lou Michel and Dan Herbeck, *American Terrorist: Timothy McVeigh and the Oklahoma City Bombing* (New York: First Harper Collins, 2001), 180.

4. George W. Bush, "First Inaugural Address at Washington, DC," January 20, 2001), in Selected Speeches of President George W. Bush, 2001–2008, 2, http://georgewbush-whitehouse.archives.gov/infocus/bushrecord/documents/Selected_Speeches_George_W_Bush.pdf.

5. See Barack Obama, "Inaugural Address by President Barack Obama," Washington, DC. January 21, 2013, http://www.whitehouse.gov/the-press office/2013/01/21/inaugural-address-president-barack-obama.

6. Sheriff's Posse Comitatus, 1973 (hereinafter Posse Blue Book), https://www.scribd.com/document/419422786/Posse-Comitatus-BlueBook; Daniel Levitas, *The Terrorist Next Door: The Militia Movement and the Radical Right* (New York: St. Martin's, 2004), 8.

7. For varying accounts of the history of the militia movement, see Levitas, *The Terrorist Next Door*, 301–316; Leonard Zeskind, *Blood and Politics: The History of the White Nationalist Movement from the Margins to the Mainstream* (New York: Farrar, Strauss, Giroux, 2009), 308–319; Lane Crothers, *Rage on the Right: The American Militia Movement from Ruby Ridge to Homeland Security* (Lanham, MD: Rowman & Littlefield, 2003); Robert H. Churchill, *To Shake Their Guns in the Tyrant's Face: Libertarian Political Violence and the Origins of the Militia Movement* (Ann Arbor: University of Michigan Press, 2009); D. J. Mulloy, *American Extremism: History, Politics, and the Militia Movement* (New York: Routledge, 2004).

8. See "Nevada Rancher Renews Fight against Big Gov: 'We're Standing Up for the Constitution,'" Fox News, April 11, 2014, http://foxnewsinsider.com/2014/04/11/nevada-rancher-fights-big-gov-protests-escalate-over-land-dispute; see also Jared A. Goldstein, "Before Bundy Ranch: What Happens When Constitutional Vigilantes Go Mainstream," *Slate*, April 23, 2014, https://slate.com/news-and-politics/2014/04/bundy-ranch-vigilantism-going-mainstream-the-idea-that-the-constitution-is-interpreted-at-the-point-of-a-gun-isnt-new.html.

9. Ryan Lenz and Mark Potok, Southern Poverty Law Center, *War in the West: The Bundy Ranch Standoff and the American Radical Right* 14 (July 2014), http://www.splcenter.org/sites/default/files/downloads/publication/war_in_the_west_report.pdf.

10. "'We the People Have Spoken': Bundy Family Responds to Nevada Standoff over Grazing Fees," Fox News, April 14, 2014, http://foxnewsinsider.com/2014/04/14/%E2%80%98we-people-have-spoken%E2%80%99-bundy-family-responds-nevada-standoff-over-grazing-fees.

11. "Call to Action: Time for Diligence," Oath Keepers, January 3, 2021, https://oathkeepers.org/current-posts/ (on file with author); *New Yorker*,

"A Reporter's Footage from Inside the Capitol Siege," YouTube, January 17, 2021, https://www.youtube.com/watch?v=270F8s5TEKY&t=192s&ab_channel =TheNewYorker (at 1:19); *New Yorker*, "A Reporter's Footage from Inside the Capitol Siege," at 3:20.

12. See, e.g., Silveira v. Lockyer, 328 F.3d 567, 570 (9th Cir. 2003) (Kozinski, J., dissenting from denial of rehearing en banc) (describing the Second Amendment as a "doomsday provision, one designed for those exceptionally rare circumstances where all other rights have failed").

13. Michael Ignatieff, *Blood and Belonging: Journeys into the New Nationalism* (New York: Farrar, Strauss, Giroux, 1993), 5.

14. See Levitas, *The Terrorist Next Door*, 108-112, 61-65; Zeskind, *Blood and Politics*, 72; Leonard Zeskind, *The Christian Identity Movement: A Theological Justification for Racist and Anti-Semitic Violence* (New York: Division of Church and Society of the National Council of the Churches of Christ in the USA, 1986).

15. It was not the first time that Gale sought to create antigovernment guerilla organizations. In the 1950s and 1960s, Gale helped organize the Christian Defense League and the California Rangers, which sought to recruit militant racists and anti-Semites to fight the federal government, but those efforts collapsed when federal agents arrested one member for attempting to sell a 50-caliber machine gun. Levitas, *The Terrorist Next Door*, 66.

16. Gale, *The Faith of Our Fathers*, 28; William P. Gale, *Separation of Church and State*, available at http://greatwhitedesert.org/dir/index.php?title=Separation _of_Church_and_State; Michael Barkun, *Religion and the Racist Right* (Chapel Hill: University of North Carolina Press, 1997), 286.

17. Posse Blue Book; Levitas, *The Terrorist Next Door*, 8.

18. Levitas, 66-73.

19. See William F. Buckley Jr., "Goldwater, the John Birch Society, and Me," *Commentary*, March 2008, http://www.commentarymagazine.com/article/gold water-the-john-birch-society-and-me/; see also Carl Bogus, *Buckley: William F. Buckley Jr. and the Rise of American Conservatism* (New York: Bloomsbury, 2011), 190-198.

20. Levitas, *The Terrorist Next Door*, 72.

21. The Posse's hyper-localist philosophy reflected broader views of the dominance of state and local power over federal authority: "Those who believe that the federal government is above the States which created it have accepted Satan's communistic philosophy that the created is above the Creator." William P. Gale, *The Faith of Our Fathers* (Mariposa, CA: Ministry of Christ Church, 1963), 31, 32-33.

22. *Black's Law Dictionary*, 9th ed. (St. Paul, MN: West, 2009); Posse Blue Book, 1; see also Levitas, *The Terrorist Next Door*, 8. For an attempt to justify this philosophy while distancing himself from Gale and the Posse Comitatus

movement, see David B. Kopel, "The Posse Comitatus and the Office of Sheriff: Armed Citizens Summoned to the Aid of Law Enforcement," *Journal Criminal Law and Criminology* 104 (2014): 761.

23. Posse Blue Book, 1, 2; see also Daniel Lessard Levind and Michael W. Mitchell, "A Law unto Themselves: The Ideology of the Common Law Court Movement," *South Dakota Law Review* 44 (1999), 15; Levitas, *The Terrorist Next Door*, 109.

24. Levitas, 109.

25. Posse Blue Book, 2; Zeskind, *Blood and Politics*, 357–366.

26. Posse Blue Book, 1, 16, 5, 10, 11.

27. Posse Blue Book, 1, 2.

28. Levitas, *The Terrorist Next Door*, 143.

29. Levitas, 144.

30. Posse Blue Book, 3; see also Gale, *The Faith of Our Fathers*, 31, 32.

31. Levitas, *The Terrorist Next Door*, 1 (quoting transcript of National Identity Broadcast, aired July 12, 1982).

32. Levitas, 169, 119, 164, 8, 184–185.

33. Violence was not the Posse's only tool of vigilante resistance. Posse members also engaged in various kinds of paper terrorism, such as filing nuisance liens and lawsuits, which tied up the courts, and tax protests, either by refusing to file income tax returns or refusing to pay what they owed. Levitas, chapters 19, 26, 28.

34. Levitas, 120, 139, 141, 133.

35. See Gordon Kahl, "Letter to Aryan Nations," Outpost of Freedom, http://www.outpost-of-freedom.com/kah101.htm; Zeskind, *Blood and Politics*, 75; Levitas, 5.

36. Levitas, 5; Zeskind, 76.

37. Kahl, "Letter to Aryan Nations."

38. Levitas, *The Terrorist Next Door*, 229–230. In 1988 Posse founder William Potter Gale was convicted in a plot to kill IRS officials and a federal judge in Nevada.

39. Levitas, 9, 209, 256.

40. See Francis X. Sullivan, "The "Usurping Octopus of Jurisdictional/Authority": The Legal Theories of the Sovereign Citizen Movement," *Wisconsin Law Review* (1999): 785 (tracing the origins and influences of the Posse Comitatus movement); Ryan Lenz and Mark Potok, *War in the West: The Bundy Ranch Standoff and the American Radical Right*, Southern Poverty Law Center, July 2014, 19–20, http://www.splcenter.org/sites/default/files/downloads/publication/war_in_the_west_report.pdf (tracing the continuing influence of the Posse movement).

41. American Defamation League, "'Patriot' Movement," https://www.adl.org/resources/glossary-terms/patriot-movement.

42. See Churchill, *To Shake Their Guns in the Tyrant's Face*, 241–244; The Militia Movement in the United States, Hearing Before the Subcommittee on Terrorism, Technology, and Government Information of the Committee on the Judiciary, United States Senate, 104th Cong., 1st Sess., S. Hrg. 104–804 (June 15, 1995), 7 (statement of Sen. Baucus) (hereinafter Senate Militia Hearing).

43. See Churchill, 242–245; Senate Militia Hearing, 118 (testimony of Norm Olson).

44. Mulloy, *American* Extremism, 12–16.

45. Stuart Wright, *Patriots, Politics, and the Oklahoma City Bombing* (New York: Cambridge University Press, 2007), 116 (quoting Violence Policy Center, 1996).

46. Wright, 162.

47. Pratt, *Armed People Victorious*, 71; Wright, *Patriots, Politics, and the Oklahoma City Bombing*, 124.

48. See Mulloy, *American Extremism*, 12–16; Churchill, *To Shake Their Guns in the Tyrant's Face*, 188–195.

49. See Zeskind, *Blood and Politics*, 308–319; Levitas, *The Terrorist Next Door*, 301; Crothers, *Rage on the Right*, 75–97.

50. Zeskind, 303. Weaver apparently refused to cooperate with federal officials because he believed them to be agents of Satan. Zeskind, 302.

51. Levitas, *The Terrorist Next Door*, 303–304.

52. During the siege on Ruby Ridge, a vigil arose near the Weaver home, attended by neighbors, skinheads, Identity believers, and Aryan Nations members. Zeskind, *Blood and Politics*, 304.

53. Churchill, *To Shake Their Guns in the Tyrant's Face*, 105.

54. Jon Roland, "Constitutional Militias Forming across Nation" *Constitutional Society*, August 7, 1994, http://www.constitution.org/mil/pr_4807.htm.

55. Churchill, *To Shake Their Guns in the Tyrant's Face*, 232.

56. Roland, "Constitutional Militias Forming across Nation."

57. Zeskind, *Blood and Politics*, 314.

58. Levitas, *The Terrorist Next Door*, 303. Another speaker agreed: "All of us in our groups could not have done in the next twenty years what the federal government did for our cause in eleven days" in Ruby Ridge. Zeskind, 312.

59. Levitas, 303, 315–316.

60. Wright, *Patriots, Politics, and the Oklahoma City Bombing*, 37.

61. Churchill, *To Shake Their Guns in the Tyrant's Face*, 2, 225.

62. Although the movement has been depicted as a primarily rural phenomenon, recent scholarship suggests that it was concentrated in suburban and suburbanizing locations. Churchill, 226, appendix.

63. Churchill, 200–207. As Churchill acknowledges, racist attitudes were prevalent across the movement, even if many militias did not identify white supremacy as part of the movement's mission. Churchill, 221.

64. See Levitas, *The Terrorist Next Door*, 302.

65. Churchill, *To Shake Their Guns in the Tyrant's Face*, 4.

66. Jon Roland, "Militias against Fascism," *Constitutional Society*, 1994, http://www.constitution.org/mil/milfascm.htm.

67. Senate Militia Hearing, 85. Trochmann made the statement at a Senate hearing on the militia movement. Trochmann's fellow witnesses, representing a range of militia views, agreed. Senate Militia Hearing, 103 (testimony of J. J. Johnson) ("What we stand for here is the Constitution. That is it."). To be sure, some Christian Identity adherents rejected the Constitution as the source of authority for the militia—and rejected the Constitution itself. See Martin Lindstedt, "There Ain't No Such Thing as a Constitutional Militia," *Modern Militiaman: A Journal of the Modern Resistance Movement* 6, July 4, 1997, http://white nationalist.org/lindstedt/mmmisu6.html#mm62.

68. Churchill, *To Shake Their Guns in the Tyrant's Face*, 222. The Ohio Unorganized Militia manual said that violence should never be used against "unarmed nationals," suggesting tolerance for violence against unarmed racial minorities—so-called Fourteenth Amendment citizens. Churchill, 222–223.

69. Jon Roland, "Constitution in Peril," *Constitutional Society*, 1994, http://www.constitution.org/conperil.htm. The Texas Constitutional Militia adopted a comprehensive "Statement of Grievances and Demands for Redress" that accused federal officials of having "made war on the People, violated their natural and constitutional rights, exceeded the limited powers delegated to them under the Constitution, and betrayed their oaths to faithfully fulfill the provisions of the Constitution and to execute just treaties, laws and contracts pursuant thereto." The Statement lists twenty-four grievances against the federal government, including the illegal imposition of income taxes based on the Sixteenth Amendment, which it asserted was never actually ratified; establishment of the Federal Reserve and the use of currency not backed by gold or silver; excessive regulations under the Commerce Clause; and the use of federal officials to perform police functions. Jon Roland, "Statement of Grievances and Demands for Redress," *Constitutional Society*, http://www .constitution.org/grievred.htm.

70. See, e.g., Senate Militia Hearing, 7, 86 (statement of John Trochmann); Jon Roland, "The Shadow Government," *Constitutional Society*, http://www .constitution.org/shad4816.htm (asserting that the major newspapers, television, and radio stations are controlled by a shadow government).

71. Senate Militia Hearing, 25–34 (declaration of John Trochmann).

72. See Roland, "Statement of Grievances."

73. Senate Militia Hearing, 85, 98.

74. As Mulloy put it, militia leaders sought to "cloak the modern militia movement in the heroic respectability offered by the militiamen of the past." Mulloy, *American Extremism*, 34. Historians, however, have portrayed the actual

role of the militias in the Revolutionary War in much less heroic terms. Although the modern militias frequently describe George Washington leading "a rag-tag collection of militia men," in fact Washington commanded a professional army and was highly critical of the citizen militias, telling Congress that they were "worse than useless" and urging "the creation of a European-style, long-service, tightly disciplined force." Mulloy, 58; see also Jon Roland, "Reviving the Ready Militia," *Constitutional Society*, 1994, http://www.constitution.org/mil/rev_read.htm.

75. Senate Militia Hearing, 83. Comparing the militia movement to the patriots who fought for American independence, Trochmann submitted an annotated copy of the Declaration of Independence, adding the militia's complaints about the current US regime to the charges made in the Declaration, charging for instance that the federal government violated American sovereignty by acceding to international treaties like the GATT and NAFTA and "Aligning with Nations into a World Government." Senate Militia Hearing, 87. See also Senate Militia Hearing, 93 (statement of J. J. Johnson); Mulloy, *American Extremism*, 47 (quoting James A. McKinzey, "H.Q. Bunker," *Necessary Force* [January 1997]: 2).

76. Mulloy, 35.

77. Jon Roland, "Memo to 'All Militia Units and Other Patriots,'" *Constitutional Society*, February 20, 1995, http://www.constitution.org/mil/522oraid.htm.

78. Roland, "The Shadow Government."

79. See Mark Tushnet, *Taking the Constitution Away from the Courts* (Princeton, NJ: Princeton University Press, 1999); Larry D. Kramer, *The People Themselves: Popular Constitutionalism and Judicial Review* (New York: Oxford University Press, 2004).

80. See, e.g., Roland, "Statement of Grievances"; Senate Militia Hearing, 120.

81. As one militia newsletter said, the Founding Fathers "were able to articulate . . . things in a way that all could understand." Mulloy, *American Extremism*, 40 (quoting Kay Sheil, "A Document for All Time," *Necessary Force*, June 1997). See David C. Williams, "The Militia Movement and Second Amendment Revolution: Conjuring with the People," *Cornell Law Review* 81, no. 4 (1996): 887.

82. See Jon Roland, "Declaration of Constitutional Principles," *Constitution Society*, 1994, http://www.constitution.org/consprin.htm.

83. See, e.g., David L. Franklin, "Popular Constitutionalism as Presidential Constitutionalism?," *Chicago-Kent Law Review* 81 (2006): 1069.

84. Larry Alexander and Lawrence B. Solum, "Popular? Constitutionalism?," *Harvard Law Review* 118 (2005): 1594, 1635 (book review).

85. Norm Olson, who cofounded the Texas Constitutional Militia with Jon Roland, explained that violence would not be necessary if the United States

returns to its valid constitutional form: "When government is given back to the people at the lowest level, the citizen militia will return to its natural place, resident within the body of the people. Civil war and revolution can be avoiding by re-investing government power to the people." Senate Militia Hearing, 96.

86. Williams, "The Militia Movement and Second Amendment Revolution," 915–916. See also Churchill, *To Shake Their Guns in the Tyrant's Face*, 224; Mulloy, *American Extremism*, 145.

87. Senate Militia Hearing, 119 (testimony of Norm Olson), 128.

88. Mulloy, *American Extremism*, 66 (quoting George Eaton, Patriot Report).

89. Mulloy, 64 (quoting Editorial, "Don't Tread on Me!," *Common Sense* 1 [1994]). To help convince their fellow citizens to recognize the tyranny the nation faced, many militias made educating the public about the true meaning of the Constitution a central part of their mission. The Ohio Unorganized Militia explained that it had been formed in part "to educate ourselves and our fellow countrymen concerning America's history, the United States Constitution, principles of Constitutional government, and responsible citizenship" in order to address "problems which have been created primarily by a departure from the aforementioned principles." Mulloy, 45 (quoting Ohio Unorganized Militia, "Statement of Principle and Mission"). Some militia leaders considered education a more important militia objective than paramilitary training. See Senate Militia Hearing, 107 (testimony of Bob Fletcher, cofounder of the Militia of Montana) (militias "are predominately educational in nature, and by that I mean that is what we do, mostly. You will not find us out in our camouflage and that type of thing very regularly at all.").

90. Williams, "The Militia Movement and Second Amendment Revolution," 895.

91. Churchill, *To Shake Their Guns in the Tyrant's Face*, 251–253.

92. See Williams, "The Militia Movement and Second Amendment Revolution," 894 ("The Second Amendment isn't about hunting or target-shooting. . . . It's about FREEDOM!") (quoting T-shirt).

93. William Clinton, "Remarks at the Michigan State University Commencement Ceremony," East Lansing, Michigan, May 5, 1995, American Presidency Project, http://www.presidency.ucsb.edu/.

94. See Silveira v. Lockyer, 328 F.3d 567, 570 (9th Cir. 2003) (Kozinski, J., dissenting from denial of rehearing en banc) (describing the Second Amendment as a "doomsday provision, one designed for those exceptionally rare circumstances where all other rights have failed"). Carl T. Bogus, "The Hidden History of the Second Amendment," *University of California Davis Law Review* 31 (1998): 387 n386.

95. See Jon Roland, "Militia Q&A," *Constitution Society*, n.d., http://www.constitution.org/.

96. See Roland, "Statement of Grievances"; Senate Militia Hearing, 86–88

("updated" Declaration of Independence submitted by John Trochmann); Senate Militia Hearing, 118 (written testimony of Norman Olson).

97. See Roland, "Statement of Grievances."

98. For instance, Linda Thompson, self-proclaimed acting adjutant general of the Unorganized Militia of the USA, declared that every member of Congress who refused to repeal federal gun laws and other laws deemed tyrannical by the militia movement "will be identified as a Traitor, and you will be brought up on charges for Treason before a Court of the Citizens of this Country." Williams, "The Militia Movement and Second Amendment Revolution," 916; see also Senate Militia Hearing, 118.

99. David Williams characterized this strategy as "conjuring with the People": "militia writers assume that a people exists, that it is angry with the government, and that it will soon take up arms to assert its rights." Williams, "The Militia Movement and Second Amendment Revolution," 882. For examples, see Senate Militia Hearing, 118–119 (statement of Norman Olson); Senate Militia Hearing, 90 (statement of Bob Fletcher of the Militia of Montana).

100. Roland, "Reviving the Ready Militia."

101. Michel and Herbeck, *American Terrorist*, 108, 117–123, 127, 141, 205–220.

102. Testimony of Jennifer McVeigh (May 5, 1997), in United States v. Timothy McVeigh, 964 F. Supp. 313 (1997), http://law2.umkc.edu/faculty/projects/ftrials/mcveigh/jennifertestimony.html.

103. Michel and Herbeck, *American Terrorist*, 88–89.

104. William Luther Pierce [Andrew MacDonald], *The Turner Diaries* (Larchmont, NY: Barricade Press, 1978), 29. For a discussion of McVeigh's fascination with the book, see Michel and Herbeck, 38–39, 304. For a discussion of the significance of the book among white nationalists, see Zeskind, *Blood and Politics*, 29–33.

105. Pierce, *The Turner Diaries*, 38–43.

106. Pierce, 59–60, 88, 124–125, 228.

107. Michel and Herbeck, *American Terrorist*, 205–206. McVeigh's coconspirator Terry Nichols also had strong ties to the white supremacist wing of the militia movement. Nichols had once declared that he was a "sovereign citizen" and therefore was immune from federal jurisdiction. Zeskind, *Blood and Politics*, 457.

108. Michel and Herbeck, *American Terrorist*, 108–109, 118–122.

109. See Testimony of Jennifer McVeigh (May 5, 1997), in United States v. Timothy McVeigh, 964 F. Supp. 313 (1997), http://law2.umkc.edu/faculty/projects/ftrials/mcveigh/jennifertestimony.html.

110. Michel and Herbeck, *American Terrorist*, 108.

111. See "15 Years Later, Hear McVeigh's Confession," NBC News, April 18, 2010, http://www.nbcnews.com/id/36633900/ns/msnbc-documentaries/t

/years-later-hear-mcveighs-confession/#.U-WSLU13u00; Michel and Herbeck, 161.

112. Timothy McVeigh, "Letter from Timothy McVeigh," World Libertarian Revolution, http://wl0418.tripod.com/wr/id18.html.

113. Michel and Herbeck, *American Terrorist,* 329.

114. Michel and Herbeck, 153–154.

115. Timothy McVeigh, "The McVeigh Letters: Why I Bombed Oklahoma," *The Guardian,* May 6, 2001, http://www.theguardian.com/.

116. Michel and Herbeck, *American Terrorist,* 228, 383.

117. See, e.g., James D. Nichols and Robert S. Papovich, *Freedom's End: Conspiracy in Oklahoma* (OK: Freedom's End, 1997); Jon Rappoport, *Oklahoma City Bombing: The Suppressed Truth* (Escondido, CA: Book Tree, 1997); Senate Militia Hearing, 46 (statement of Norm Olson); Jon Roland, "Conversation with Ambrose," *Constitutional Society,* 1996, http://www.constitution.org/okc/6730ae-p.txt; Zeskind, *Blood and Politics,* 402, 404–407.

118. Zeskind, 408, 412, 413; Southern Poverty Law Center, "Thirty Terror Plots Foiled since Oklahoma City Bombing," *Intelligence Report No. 102,* Summer 2001, http://www.splcenter.org/.

119. "Texas Separatists Call for Help," *Chicago Tribune,* April 29, 1997, http://articles.chicagotribune.com/.

120. See Churchill, *To Shake Their Guns in the Tyrant's Face,* 270–272; Zeskind, *Blood and Politics,* 413–416.

121. See Churchill, 274; Anti-Defamation League, "The Quiet Retooling of the Militia Movement," 2004, 1, http://www.adl.org/assets/pdf/combating-hate/Militia_retools.pdf.

122. See Darrell A. H. Miller, "Guns as Smut: Defending the Home-Bound Second Amendment," *Columbia Law Review* 109 (2009): 1312–1313; Casey Anderson, "Taking Gun Rights Seriously: The Insurrectionist Idea and Its Consequences," *Albany Government Law Review* 1 (2008): 498.

123. Standard Examination Form, Activities of Ku Klux Klan Organizations in the United States, Hearings Before the House Committee on Un-American Activities, 89th Cong. 2924 (1966) (Exhibit 9 to testimony of Sam Holloway Bowers Jr.).

124. Posse Blue Book, 1, 2.

125. United States v. Miller, 307 U.S. 174 (1939).

126. Reva Siegel, "Dead or Alive: Originalism as Popular Constitutionalism in Heller," *Harvard Law Review* 122 (2008): 205.

127. Ronald Reagan, "Ronald Reagan Champions Gun Ownership," *Guns & Ammo,* September 1975, 34.

128. Siegel, "Dead or Alive," 210–215.

129. Staff of Subcommittee on the Constitution of the Senate Committee on

the Judiciary, 97th Cong., "The Right to Keep and Bear Arms," viii (Washington, DC: Government Printing Office, 1982).

130. Staff of Subcommittee, viii; see also Staff of Subcommittee, 95 (emphasis added).

131. See Joshua Horwitz and Casey Anderson, *Guns, Democracy, and the Insurrectionist Idea* (Ann Arbor: University of Michigan Press, 2009).

132. Wayne LaPierre, *Guns, Crime and Freedom* (Washington, DC: Regnery Publishing, 1994), 7. With the ascension of LaPierre as its CEO, the NRA has expanded its mission from providing gun-safety education and protecting gun rights to protecting guns in order to preserve core American values. As LaPierre declared: "The NRA, all we believe in and fight for, has become a metaphor for the core American freedoms we all want preserved. Standing with the NRA is a massive declaration of individual rights, an unwavering determination to secure the survival of everything we cherish. Our struggle is noble, as like-minded people coming together to protect and defend what makes us free. We are exactly what our founding fathers were and envisioned us to always be." Wayne LaPierre, "Speech to the Conservative Political Action Committee," National Harbor, Maryland, March 6, 2014), C-SPAN, https://www.c-span.org /video/?318134-8/wayne-lapierre-addresses-cpac.

133. Charlton Heston, "Speech, National Rifle Association Future," National Press Club, September 11, 1997, National Rifle Association, https://www .c-span.org/video/?90857-1/national-rifle-association-future.

134. Horwitz and Anderson, *Guns, Democracy, and the Insurrectionist Idea*, 23.

135. Newt Gingrich, *To Renew America* (New York: Harper Collins, 1996), 202.

136. Sahil Kapur, "Ted Cruz: 2nd Amendment Is 'Ultimate Check against Government Tyranny,'" Talking Points Memo, April 16, 2015, https://talking pointsmemo.com/dc/ted-cruz-second-amendment-government-tyranny.

137. Carl T. Bogus, "Heller and Insurrectionism," *Syracuse Law Review* 59 (2008): 264–265.

138. See District of Columbia v. Heller, 128 S. Ct. 2783, 2798–2799 (2008); see also Miller, "Guns as Smut," 1314; Bogus, "Heller and Insurrectionism," 253.

139. District of Columbia v. Heller, 2798–2799.

140. Miller, "Guns as Smut," 1317–1321, 1321–1336; Horwitz and Anderson, *Guns, Democracy, and the Insurrectionist Idea*, 79–117.

141. Bogus, "The Hidden History of the Second Amendment," 387 n386.

142. See Jared A. Goldstein, "The New Militia Moment," Balkinization (blog), May 2, 2014, http://balkin.blogspot.com/2014/05/the-new-militia -moment.html; Lenz and Potok, *War in the West*; Charles Tanner Jr., "White, Far Right and Armed: Tea Party and Militias Mobilize to Defend Nevada County

Supremacy Activist," *Institute for Research and Education on Human Rights*, April 2014, http://www.irehr.org/issue-areas/tea-party-nationalism/tea-party-news-and-analysis/553-bundy-standoff.

143. See, e.g., Lenz and Potok, 14.

144. See "Statement from Director of the Bureau of Land Management Neil Kornze on the Cattle Gather in Nevada," Bureau of Land Management, April 12, 2014, http://www.blm.gov/nv/st/en/info/newsroom/2014/april/national_office__statement.html.

145. Sarah Childress, "The Battle over Bunkerville: The Bundys, the Federal Government and the New Militia Movement," *Frontline*, May 16, 2017, https://www.pbs.org/wgbh/frontline/article/the-battle-over-bunkerville/.

146. See Lenz and Potok, *War in the West*, 10.

147. Lenz and Potok, 11; Tanner, "White, Far Right and Armed."

148. See Ammon Bundy, "Unnamed Blog Post," Bundy Ranch (blog), April 22, 2014, http://bundyranch.blogspot.com/2014_04_01_archive.html.

149. Canfield v. United States, 167 U.S. 518 (1897); Kleppe v. New Mexico, 426 U.S. 529 (1976).

150. Lenz and Potok, *War in the West*, 13.

151. Sheriff Richard Mack, "VICTORY" (speech), Bunkerville, Nevada, April 10, 2014, http://www.youtube.com/watch?v=SpOuLYtNDqo.

152. "Bundy Ranch Explained—Stewart Rhodes Oath Keepers Update," YouTube, http://www.youtube.com/watch?v=roudaojwmIc. The Oath Keepers have since been banned from YouTube; the video is no longer available.

153. Lenz and Potok, *War in the West*, 14.

154. See "We the People Have Spoken': Bundy Family Responds to Nevada Standoff over Grazing Fees," Fox News, April 14, 2014, http://foxnewsinsider.com/2014/04/14/%E2%80%98we-people-have-spoken%E2%80%99-bundy-family-responds-nevada-standoff-over-grazing-fees.

155. "Stewart Rhodes Speaks at Cliven Bundy Ranch Victory Rally," YouTube, April 12, 2014, http://www.youtube.com/watch?v=CfY3kIqSNvI.

156. Mack, "VICTORY."

157. "Cliven Bundy Takes on the Nevada Ranch Rhetoric," Fox News, April 21, 2014, http://www.foxnews.com/on-air/hannity/transcript/2014/04/22/cliven-bundy-takes-nevada-ranch-rhetoric; Emily Arrowood, "Hannity's Dangerous Game Touting a Rogue Rancher and His Violent Threats," Media Matters, April 11, 2014, http://mediamatters.org/blog/2014/04/11/hannitys-dangerous-game-touting-a-rogue-rancher/198864.

158. "Judge Napolitano: Bundy Ranch Brought Attention to Gov't Overreach," Fox News Radio, April 21, 2014, http://radio.foxnews.com/2014/04/21/judge-napolitano-bundy-ranch-brought-attention-to-govt-overreach/.

159. Niels Lesniewski, "Heller Calls Bundy Ranch Supporters 'Patriots'; Reid Sticks with 'Domestic Terrorists,'" Roll Call, April 18, 2014, http://blogs

.rollcall.com/wgdb/heller-calls-bundy-ranch-supporters-patriots-reid-sticks-with-domestic-terrorists/.

160. Juliet Lapidos, "The Pretend Complexity of the Nevada Cattle-Grazing Dispute," *New York Times*, April 18, 2014, http://takingnote.blogs.nytimes.com/2014/04/18/the-pretend-complexity-of-the-nevada-cattle-grazing-dispute/.

161. Adam Nagourney, "A Defiant Rancher Savors the Audience that Rallied to His Side," *New York Times*, April 23, 2014, http://www.nytimes.com/.

162. Sam Stein, "Sharron Angle Floated '2nd Amendment Remedies' as 'Cure' for 'The Harry Reid Problems," *Huffington Post*, June 16, 2010, http://www.huffingtonpost.com/2010/06/16/sharron-angle-floated-2nd_n_614003.html.

163. Mark Potok, "Rage on the Right: Intelligence Report," Southern Poverty Law Center, Spring 2010, http://www.splcenter.org/get-informed/intelligence-report/browse-all-issues/2010/spring/rage-on-the-right.

164. See "About Oath Keepers," Oath Keepers, http://oathkeepers.org/oath/about/; see also "Oath Keepers Is Going Operational by Forming Special Civilization Preservation Teams," Oath Keepers, October 21, 2013, http://oathkeepers.org/oath/2013/10/21/oath-keepers-is-going-operational-by-forming-special-civilization-preservation-teams/; "Molon Labe Pledge," Oath Keepers, http://oathkeepers.org/oath/pledge/; "Declaration of Orders We Will Not Obey," Oath Keepers, March 3, 2003, http://oathkeepers.org/oath/2009/03/03/declaration-of-orders-we-will-not-obey/.

165. "Stewart Rhodes—Founder of Oath Keepers," YouTube, March 27, 2013, http://www.youtube.com/watch?v=CwSRH18h-co at 7:14.

166. See "Oath Keepers Is Going 'Operational' by Forming Special 'Civilization Preservation' Teams." Originally, Oath Keepers planned to call these units "Civilization Preservation Teams" but later decided to rename them "Community Preparedness" teams because it sounded "a little more 'down home.'"

167. "Oath Keepers: Sworn to Serve Our Country, Not Our Government," YouTube, posted March 1, 2010, https://www.youtube.com/watch?v=1IzGEJvxOOo (at 1:45).

168. "Stewart Rhodes—Founder of Oath Keepers," at 5:00 (calling John McCain an "oath breaker" and a "traitor").

169. "Oath Keepers: Sworn to Serve Our Country, Not Our Government," at 2:28.

170. About CSPOA, https://cspoa.org/about/.

171. See "Oath Keepers Board of Directors," Oath Keepers, http://oathkeepers.org/oath/bios/.

172. About CSPOA, https://cspoa.org/about/.

173. See Statement of Constitutional Sheriff, 2021, https://cspoa.org

/statement-of-constitutional-sheriff/." See also Richard Mack, "The County Sheriff: The Ultimate Check and Balance", Constitutional Law Enforcement Association, January 30, 2008, http://constitutionallawenforcementassoc .blogspot.com/.

174. See "Resolution Drafted by the Constitutional Sheriffs and Peace Officers Association," Constitutional Sheriffs and Peace Officers Association, January 24, 2014, http://cspoa.org/cspoa-jan-2014-resolution/.

175. Joe Wolverton, II, *Constitutional Sheriffs Convention Focus: States' Rights, 2nd Amendment*, Tenth Amendment Center, May 30, 2013, https://blog.tenth amendmentcenter.com/2013/05/constitutional-sheriffs-convention-focus -states-rights-2nd-amendment/.

176. See III Percent Patriots, http://iiipercent.blogspot.com/.

177. See "What Is a 'Three Percenter'?," *Sipsey Street Irregulars* (blog), February 17, 2009, http://sipseystreetirregulars.blogspot.com/2009/02/what -is-three-percenter.html.

178. Oath Keepers founder Stewart Rhodes, a lawyer, has represented militia leaders charged with possessing machine guns in violation of federal law, and Rhodes expressed his personal view that the Second Amendment protects the right of citizen militias to possess machine guns in order to resist federal tyranny. Stewart Rhodes, "US vs. Fincher Appeal" (blog), July 25, 2007, http:// stewart-rhodes.blogspot.com/2007/07/us-vs-fincher.html ("This case goes right to the heart of the purpose of the Second Amendment—which is most emphatically not about duck hunting, and is also not just about self defense against common criminals. . . . The Second Amendment is about the right and the power of we the people, who are the militia, by the way, and in this case were further formed into a state militia, to bear battlefield effective arms, suitable for militia service."); see also United States v. Fincher, 538 F.3d 868 (8th Cir. 2008) (holding that the Second Amendment does not protect possession of machine guns for use by unorganized citizen militias).

179. Jack Anderson, *Inside the NRA: Armed and Dangerous—An Expose* (Beverly Hills, CA: Dove Books, 1996), 84.

180. Richard Mack, *The County Sheriff: America's Last Hope* (Self-published, 2009).

181. "Oath Keeper Sheriff Richard Mack," YouTube, April 19, 2009, http:// www.youtube.com/watch?v=bLJgPuNAh6o.

182. "Richard Mack—Alex Jones Pt ¼," YouTube, February 11, 2009, https://www.youtube.com/watch?v=RV7iIFyR3Ns (at 4:50).

183. "Speaking Engagements," SheriffMac.com, http://sheriffmack.com/.

184. Lenz and Potok, *War in the West*, 7.

185. "Courage Is Contagious, Defiance Is Contagious, Victory Is Contagious: The Huge Win in the Desert at the Bundy Ranch," *Sipsey Street Irregulars* (blog),

April 12, 2014, http://sipseystreetirregulars.blogspot.com/2014/04/courage
-is-contagious-defiance-is.html.

186. Lenz and Potok, *War in the West*, 15.

187. See "Letter from 12 Democratic Lawmakers to Texas Attorney General Greg Abbott," My San Antonio, July 30, 2014, http://www.mysanantonio.com /file/861/861-Letter_to_Atty_Gen_Abbott_73014.pdf; Manny Fernandez, "Towns Fight to Avoid Taking in Migrant Minors," *New York Times*, July 16, 2014, http://www.nytimes.com/2014/07/17/us/towns-fight-to-avoid-taking -in-migrant-minors.html.

188. Lenz and Potok, *War in the West*, 16. The same month, Texas militias protested a BLM survey of more than 90,000 acres along the Red River, fearing the federal government was planning a land grab.

189. "Shooters Identified in Slaying of Metro Police Officers, Bystander," *Las Vegas Sun*, June 9, 2014, http://www.lasvegassun.com/news/2014/jun/09 /neighbors-couple-suspected-las-vegas-killing-spree/.

190. Dylan Scott, "Facebook Posts Reveal Vegas Shooter Thought Bundy Ranch Was 'Start of Revolution,'" Talking Points Memo, June 9, 2014, http:// talkingpointsmemo.com/muckraker/vegas-shooter-bundy-ranch-facebook; Devin Burghart, "Tea Party Followers Kill Police in Las Vegas Killing Spree," *Institute for Research and Education on Human Rights*, June 11, 2014, http://www .irehr.org/issue-areas/tea-party-nationalism/tea-party-news-and-analysis/563 -tea-party-followers-kill-police-in-las-vegas-killing-spree.

191. See "Las Vegas Shooter Jerad Miller Had Numerous Run-ins with Police," *Los Angeles Times*, June 10, 2014, http://www.latimes.com/nation /nationnow/la-na-nn-jerad-miller-timeline-20140609-story.html; "Video Shows Last Moments of Cop-Killers' Lives," *Las Vegas Sun*, August 13, 2014, http:// www.lasvegassun.com/news/2014/jun/11/-metro-confirms-police-fire-took -out-cop-killer/. Jerad Miller called Americans traitors if they "don't agree with and hold dear the second amendment" and said that he might be considered a radical but so were "the founding fathers" because they too believed "that each man has constitutional rights that are God given and cannot be taken away no matter what." See Scott, "Facebook Posts Reveal Vegas Shooter"; Burghart, "Tea Party Followers Kill Police."

192. Wanda Moore, "Militia Leader Explains Takeover, Says Group Has Name,"KTVZ,January4,2016,https://web.archive.org/web/20160104211508 /http://www.ktvz.com/news/refuge-occupiers-settle-in-concerns-mount-in -burns/37249044.

193. Ryan Bundy, "The Constitution of the United States on Federal Land Ownership," Bundy Ranch (blog), December 7, 2015, http://bundyranch.blog spot.com/2015/12/the-constitution-of-united-states-on.html [https://perma .cc/LS25-UXZ9].

194. Ammon Bundy, "Dear Friends," YouTube, January 1, 2016, https:// www.youtube.com/watch?v=M7MomG6HUyk&t=1s [https://perma.cc/U6FM -LXKX].

195. Ryan Bundy, "The Constitution of the United States on Federal Land Ownership."

196. "41 Days: An OPB Documentary on the Oregon Occupation," Oregon Public Broadcasting, February 15, 2016, http://www.opb.org/news /series/burns-oregon-standoff-bundy-militia-news-updates/oregon-standoff -occupation-malheur-41-days-opb-documentary/; Allegra Kirkland, "Oregon Standoff Supporters Quickly Turn Slain Occupier into Martyr for the Cause," Talking Points Memo, January 27, 2016, http://talkingpointsmemo.com/.

197. Fred Barbash, "'Off the Charts Unbelievable': Will Acquittal of Oregon Refuge Occupiers Embolden Extremists, Militias?," Washington Post, October 28, 2016, https://www.washingtonpost.com/news/morning-mix /wp/2016/10/28/off-the-charts-unbelievable-will-acquittal-of-oregon-refuge -occupiers-embolden-extremists-militias/?utm_term=.3369df6b46e5.

198. The President's Advisory 1776 Commission, The 1776 Report, January 2021, 10.

199. Max Greenwood, "Interior Secretary: One-Third of Employees 'Not Loyal to the Flag,'" The Hill, September 26, 2017, http://thehill.com/blogs /blog-briefing-room/news/352411-interior-secretary-estimates-one-third-of -department-employees.

200. Julie Turkewitz and Lisa Friedman, "Interior Secretary Proposes Shrinking Four National Monuments," New York Times, August 25, 2017, https://www.nytimes.com/2017/08/24/us/bears-ears-utah-monument.html; Bartholomew D. Sullivan, "Republicans Making Progress on Longtime Goal for More Local Control of Federal Lands," USA Today, August 11, 2017, https:// www.usatoday.com/story/news/politics/2017/08/10/republicans-making -progress-longtime-goal-more-local-control-federal-lands/548969001/.

201. "Statement from the Press Secretary Regarding Executive Clemency for Dwight and Steven Hammond," White House, July 10, 2018, https://www .whitehouse.gov/briefings-statements/statement-press-secretary-regarding-ex ecutive-clemency-dwight-steven-hammond/.

202. Eileen Sullivan and Julie Turkewitz, "Trump Pardons Oregon Ranchers Whose Case Inspired Wildlife Refuge Takeover," New York Times, July 10, 2018, https://www.nytimes.com/2018/07/10/us/politics/trump-pardon -hammond-oregon.html.

203. Luke Mogelson, "The Militias against Masks," New Yorker, August 17, 2020.

204. "Ammon Bundy Speaks," YouTube, July 19, 2020, https://youtu .be/J11qgCEQy9s; Chuck Tanner, "People's Rights Protest Demonstrates Far Right Roots, Again," Institute for Research and Education on Human Rights,

August. 17, 2020, https://www.irehr.org/2020/08/17/peoples-rights-protest
-demonstrates-far-right-roots-again/#_ednref11.

205. "Your Daily 6: Melania Models a Mask, Ammon Bundy Wants the
Virus and SNL Returns," *St. Louis Post Dispatch*, April 10, 2020, https://www
.stltoday.com/news/national/your-daily-6-melania-models-a-mask-ammon
-bundy-wants-the-virus-and-snl-returns/collection_f6890691–8f8b-5bf0-bb7c
-59fd1b614978.html#1.

206. "Tracking the Suspect in the Fatal Kenosha Shootings," *New York Times*,
August 28, 2020, https://www.nytimes.com/2020/08/27/us/kyle-rittenhouse
-kenosha-shooting-video.html?searchResultPosition=1.

207. "Kyle Rittenhouse Defended Himself, 'Did Nothing Wrong,' Attorney
Says," NBC Chicago, (August 28, 2020, https://www.nbcchicago.com/news
/local/kyle-rittenhouse-defended-himself-did-nothing-wrong-attorney-says
/2330687/.

208. Dan Barry and Sheera Frenkel, "Be There. Will Be Wild!': Trump All
but Circled the Date," *New York Times*, January 7, 2021, A17.

209. "Oath Keepers Deploying to DC to Protect Events, Speakers & Attendees
on Jan. 5-6: Time to Stand!," https://oathkeepers.org/2021/01/oath-keepers
-deploying-to-dc-to-protect-events-speakers-attendees-on-jan-5-6-time-to-stand
/ (last accessed June 6, 2021).

210. "Read: Former President Donald Trump's January 6 Speech," CNN,
https://www.cnn.com/2021/02/08/politics/trump-january-6-speech-tran
script/index.html.

211. Donald Trump Speech "Save America" Rally Transcript, January 6,
2021, https://www.rev.com/blog/transcripts/donald-trump-speech-save-amer
ica-rally-transcript-january-6.

212. *New Yorker*, "A Reporter's Footage from Inside the Capitol Siege," You
Tube, January 17, 2021, https://www.youtube.com/watch?v=270F8s5TEKY&t
=192s&ab_channel=TheNewYorker (at 1:19).

213. *New Yorker*, "A Reporter's Footage from Inside the Capitol Siege," at
3:20.

214. Indictment, par. 11, United States v. Alan Hostetter et al., US
District Court for the District of Columbia (filed June 9, 2021), https://www
.washingtonpost.com/context/u-s-v-alan-hostetter-et-al-indictment/10ab4e7f
-7e44-46de-b61b-85457604a4d6/?itid=lk_interstitial_manual_13.

215. "Red Alert! Oath Keepers Warning Order Part I," https://oathkeepers
.org/2021/01/oath-keepers-warning-order-part-i/ (last accessed June 6, 2021).

216. Indictment, par. 21a, United States v. Alan Hostetter et al., US
District Court for the District of Columbia (filed June 9, 2021), https://www
.washingtonpost.com/context/u-s-v-alan-hostetter-et-al-indictment/10ab4e7f
-7e44-46de-b61b-85457604a4d6/?itid=lk_interstitial_manual_13.

217. In 1969 Charles Manson believed that the Beatles' song "Helter

Skelter" foretold an apocalyptic race war, and he instructed his followers to commit murder to help precipitate the war. One of his followers wrote "Healter Skelter" in blood on the refrigerator of one of the murder victims. Vincent Bugliosi and Curt Gentry, *Helter Skelter: The True Story of the Manson Murders* (New York: W. W. Norton, 1974), 70, 322–329.

218. See Michel and Herbeck, *American Terrorist*, 287–290; see also "Inside McVeigh's Mind," ABC News, March 29, 2001, http://abcnews.go.com/Prime time/story?id=132276.

Conclusion

1. "'A Nation without Borders Is Not a Nation': Trump Moves Forward with US-Mexico Wall," NPR, January 25, 2017, https://www.npr.org/sections /thetwo-way/2017/01/25/511565740/trump-expected-to-order-building-of -u-s-mexico-wall-wednesday.

2. Paul Miller, "Worshipping at the Altar of the Nation," *The American Interest*, May 1, 2017, https://www.the-american-interest.com/2017/05/01/wor shipping-at-the-altar-of-the-nation/.

3. Brenda Major et al., "The Threat of Increasing Diversity: Why Many White Americans Support Trump in the 2016 Presidential Election," *Group Processes and Intergroup Relations* (2016): 1–10.

4. Kate Riga, "Ingraham: The 'America We Know and Love' Is Gone Due to Immigration," Talking Points Memo, August 9, 2018, https://talkingpoints memo.com/livewire/ingraham-the-america-we-know-and-love-is-gone-due-to -immigration.

5. "We Believe in America, 2012 Republican Party Platform," August 27, 2012, American Presidency Project, http://www.presidency.ucsb.edu/papers _pdf/101961.pdf.

6. Donald Trump, "Presidential Announcement Speech," *Time*, June 16, 2015, http://time.com/3923128/donald-trump-announcement-speech/.

7. Donald J. Trump, Twitter post, March 22, 2016, 12:17 p.m., https://twit ter.com/realdonaldtrump/status/712357600621432832.

8. David Denby, "The Plot against America: Donald Trump's Rhetoric," *New Yorker*, December 15, 2015, https://www.newyorker.com/culture/cultural -comment/plot-america-donald-trumps-rhetoric.

9. "FULL Donald Trump Rally—Grand Rapids, Michigan 12-21-15 (FNN)," YouTube, December 21, 2015, https://www.youtube.com/watch?v =hXe FmooecKk; Mark Liberman, "Trump's Rhetorical style," Language Log, December 26, 2015, http://languagelog.ldc.upenn.edu/nll/?p=23057.

10. Donald Trump, "Speech: Donald Trump Speech at the NRA-ILA Forum

in Louisville, KY," Factbase, May 20, 2016, https://factbase/transcript/donald
-trump-speech-louisville-ky-may-20–2016.

11. Jeremy Diamond, "Trump: Paris Massacre Would Have Been 'Much
Different' If People Had Guns," CNN, November 14, 2015, https://www.cnn
.com/2015/11/14/politics/paris-terror-attacks-donald-trump-guns/.

12. Amita Kelly, "'I Will Never Let You Down,' Trump Tells National Rifle Association," CNN, May 20, 2016, https://www.npr.org/2016/05/20
/478864228/i-will-never-let-you-down-trump-tells-national-rifle-association.

13. Ronald Brownstein, "Trump's Rhetoric of White Nostalgia," *Atlantic*,
June 2, 2016, https://www.theatlantic.com/politics/archive/2016/06/trumps
-rhetoric-of-white-nostalgia/485192/.

14. Donald Trump, "Presidential Announcement Speech," *Time*, June 16,
2015, http://time.com/3923128/donald-trump-announcement-speech/.

15. "Full Text of Marco Rubio's 2016 Presidential Campaign Announcement," *Washington Post*, April 13, 2015, https://www.washingtonpost.com/news
/post-politics/wp/2015/04/13/full-text-of-marco-rubios-2016-presidential
-campaign-announcement/?noredirect=on&utm_term=.4dod2fc71259; "Chris
Christie: I'm Running for President," 4President.org, June 23, 2021, http://
www.4president.org/speeches/2016/chrischristie2016announcement.htm.

16. "Transcript: Ted Cruz's Speech at Liberty University," *Washington Post*,
March 23, 2015, https://www.washingtonpost.com/politics/transcript-ted
-cruzs-speech-at-liberty-university/2015/03/23/41c4011a-d168–11e4-a62f
-ee745911a4ff_story.html?utm_term=.3c7d4459e3e1.

17. "Ben Carson Announces Exploratory Committee," 4President.org,
http://www.4president.org/speeches/2016/bencarson2016announcement
.htm.

18. "Transcript of Remarks—Ohio Governor John Kasich's Presidential Campaign Announcement," 4President.org, http://www.4president.org/speeches
/2016/johnkasich2016announcement.htm.

19. Data on the frequency of references in the 2012 and 2016 Republican
presidential campaign announcements were drawn from the set of speeches
found at http://www.4president.org/ocmi2012.htm and http://www.4presi
dent.org/ocmi2016.htm.

20. Data on the frequency of references in the 2012 and 2016 Republican
presidential debates were drawn from the set of debate transcripts found at
"Presidential Debates," American Presidency Project, http://www.presidency
.ucsb.edu/debates.php.

21. Kristin Salaky, "Jeb Bush Won't Vote Trump: He Hasn't Shown 'Respect for the Constitution,'" Talking Points Memo, May 6, 2016, https://talking
pointsmemo.com/livewire/jeb-bush-no-vote-trump-clinton.

22. Katie Reilly, "Read Paul Ryan's Interview about Not Supporting Don-

ald Trump Yet," *Time*, May 6, 2016, http://time.com/4320476/paul-ryan-inter view-transcript-donald-trump-endorsement/.

23. Ben Sasse, "An Open Letter to Trump Supporters," Facebook, February 28, 2016, https://www.facebook.com/sassefornebraska/posts/56107359739 1141.

24. Devin Burghart and Leonard Zeskind, "Special Report: Beyond FAIR: The Decline of the Established Anti-Immigrant Organizations and the Rise of Tea Party Nativism," Institute for Research and Education on Human Rights, 2012, http://www.irehr.org/2012/11/20/beyond-fair-report-pdf/.

25. Anne Gearan and Abby Phillip, "Behind Trump's Strong New Push to Attack Clinton as 'Weak,'" *Washington Post*, January 1, 2016, https:// www.washingtonpost.com/politics/behind-trumps-strong-new-push-to -attack-clinton-as-physically-weak/2016/01/01/96e3196c-ae65-11e5-b820 -eea4d64be2a1_story.html?utm_term=.bc67174c1fbf.

26. See, e.g., Jessica Taylor, "Why Trump Is Here to Stay—At Least for a While," NPR, August 21, 2015, https://www.npr.org/sections/itsallpolitics /2015/08/21/433263471/trump-is-here-to-stay-at-least-for-a-while-heres-why.

27. Glenn Kessler, "Fact Checker: Donald Trump and David Duke: For the Record," *Washington Post*, March 1, 2016, https://www.washingtonpost.com /news/fact-checker/wp/2016/03/01/donald-trump-and-david-duke-for-the- record/?utm_term=.8851e49e6ffb; "Hail Trump: White Nationalists Mark Trump Win with Nazi Salute," BBC News, November 22, 2016, https://www .bbc.com/news/av/world-us-canada-38057104/hail-trump-white-nationalists -mark-trump-win-with-nazi-salute; Robert P. Jones, "Poll: White Evangelical Support for Donald Trump at an All-Time High," Public Religion Research Institute, April 18, 2018, https://www.prri.org/spotlight/white-evangelical -support-for-donald-trump-at-all-time-high/.

28. Vanessa Williamson, "What the Tea Party Tells Us about the Trump Presidency," Brookings, November 9, 2016, https://www.brookings.edu/blog /fixgov/2016/11/09/tea-party-and-trump-presidency/; Jane Coaston, "In 2018, the Tea Party Is All In for Trump," *Vox*, May 16, 2018, https://www.vox .com/2018/5/15/17263774/tea-party-trump-2018.

29. Gene Zubovich, "The Christian Nationalism of Donald Trump," *Religion & Politics*, July 17, 2018, https://religionandpolitics.org/2018/07/17/the -christian-nationalism-of-donald-trump/; Andrew L. Whitehead et al., "Nation- alism and Voting for Donald Trump in the 2016 Presidential Election," *Sociology of Religion* 79, no. 2 (May 2018): 147–171.

30. "Praises Army Plan for Japanese Unit," *New York Times*, February 5, 1943, 6.

31. "White Supremacy Is as American as Apple Pie," Scheer Intelligence, August 30, 2019, https://www.kcrw.com/culture/shows/scheer-intelligence /white-supremacy-is-as-american-as-apple-pie.

32. "Executive Order: Protecting the Nation from Foreign Terrorist Entry into the United States."

33. Brandon Moseley, "Sessions Says that West Needs a Long-term Strategy to Deal with Islamist Ideology," *Alabama Political Reporter*, September 16, 2015, http://www.alreporter.com/2015/09/17/sessions-says-that-west-needs-a-long-term-strategy-to-deal-with-islamist-ideology/.

34. "Dr. Thomas D. Williams," *Breitbart News Daily*, April 7, 2016, https://soundcloud.com/breitbart/breitbart-news-daily-dr-thomas-d-williams-april-7-2016.

35. The President's Advisory 1776 Commission, *The 1776 Report*, January 2021, 10.

36. Anthony D. Romero, "Donald Trump: A One-Man Constitutional Crisis," https://www.aclu.org/issues/civil-liberties/executive-branch/donald-trump-one-man-constitutional-crisis.

37. John J. Pitney Jr., "Donald Trump, Un-American: Again and Again, the President Has Rejected America's Founding Principles," The Bulwark, April 24, 2020, https://thebulwark.com/donald-trump-un-american/; Neal K. Katyal, "It's the Worst Possible Time for Trump to Make False Claims of Authority," *New York Times*, April 14, 2020.

38. "Full Transcript of Obama's Eulogy for John Lewis," *New York Times*, July 30, 2020, https://www.nytimes.com/2020/07/30/us/obama-eulogy-john-lewis-full-transcript.html?searchResultPosition=1.

39. Donald Trump Rally Speech Transcript, Dalton, Georgia: Senate Runoff Election, January 4, 2021, https://www.rev.com/blog/transcripts/donald-trump-rally-speech-transcript-dalton-georgia-senate-runoff-election.

40. Donald Trump Speech "Save America" Rally Transcript, January 6, 2021, https://www.rev.com/blog/transcripts/donald-trump-speech-save-america-rally-transcript-january-6.

Index